China on Film

China on Film

A Century of Exploration, Confrontation, and Controversy

Paul G. Pickowicz

ROWMAN & LITTLEFIELD PUBLISHERS, INC.
Lanham • Boulder • New York • Toronto • Plymouth, UK

Published by Rowman & Littlefield Publishers, Inc.
A wholly owned subsidiary of The Rowman & Littlefield Publishing Group, Inc.
4501 Forbes Boulevard, Suite 200, Lanham, Maryland 20706
www.rowmanlittlefield.com

Estover Road, Plymouth PL6 7PY, United Kingdom

Copyright © 2012 by Rowman & Littlefield Publishers, Inc.
First paperback edition 2013

All rights reserved. No part of this book may be reproduced in any form or by any electronic or mechanical means, including information storage and retrieval systems, without written permission from the publisher, except by a reviewer who may quote passages in a review.

British Library Cataloguing in Publication Information Available

The hardback edition of this book was previously cataloged by the Library of Congress as follows:

Pickowicz, Paul.
  China on film : a century of exploration, confrontation, and controversy / Paul G. Pickowicz.
     p. cm.
  Includes bibliographical references and index.
  1. Motion picture industry—China—History—20th century. 2. Motion pictures—Political aspects—China—History—20th century. 3. Motion pictures—Social aspects—China—History—20th century. 4. China—In motion pictures. I. Title.
  PN1993.5.C4P53 2012
  791.43095109'04—dc23
                                                                    2011041693

ISBN 978-1-4422-1178-0 (cloth : alk. paper)
ISBN 978-1-4422-1179-7 (pbk. : alk. paper)
ISBN 978-1-4422-1180-3 (electronic)

∞™ The paper used in this publication meets the minimum requirements of American National Standard for Information Sciences—Permanence of Paper for Printed Library Materials, ANSI/NISO Z39.48-1992.

Printed in the United States of America

To the UC San Diego Chinese history crew,
a magnificent constellation of bright stars.

Thanks for the memories!

Emily Baum
Julie Broadwin
Jeremy Brown
David Chang
Michael Chang
Jim Cook
Madeleine Dong
Mark Eykholt
Sue Fernsebner
Josh Goldstein
Maggie Greene
Miriam Gross
Brent Haas
Chris Hess
Dahpon Ho
Ellen Huang
Jenny Huangfu
Justin Jacobs
Matt Johnson
Judd Kinzley
Liu Lu
Cecily McCaffrey
Andrew Morris
Jeremy Murray
Charles Musgrove
Amy O'Keefe
Sigrid Schmalzer
Jomo Smith
Elena Songster
Doug Stiffler
Wang Liping
Xiao Zhiwei
Elya Zhang
Zheng Xiaowei

Contents

Acknowledgments — ix

Introduction: The Sorrows and Joys of Chinese Filmmaking: Political and Personal Contexts — 1

1 Shanghai Twenties: Early Chinese Cinematic Explorations of the Modern Marriage — 19

2 The Theme of Spiritual Pollution in Chinese Films of the 1930s — 43

3 Melodramatic Representation and the May Fourth Tradition of Chinese Cinema — 73

4 Never-Ending Controversies: The Case of *Remorse in Shanghai* and Occupation-Era Chinese Filmmaking — 101

5 Victory as Defeat: Postwar Visualizations of China's War of Resistance — 121

6 Acting like Revolutionaries: Shi Hui, the Wenhua Studio, and Private-Sector Filmmaking, 1949–1952 — 157

7 Zheng Junli, Complicity, and the Cultural History of Socialist China, 1949–1976 — 189

8 The Limits of Cultural Thaw: Chinese Cinema in the Early 1960s — 213

9 Popular Cinema and Political Thought in Early Post-Mao China: Reflections on Official Pronouncements, Film, and the Film Audience — 251

10	On the Eve of Tiananmen: Huang Jianxin and the Notion of Postsocialism	271
11	Velvet Prisons and the Political Economy of Chinese Filmmaking in the Late 1980s and Early 1990s	301
12	Social and Political Dynamics of Underground Filmmaking in Early Twenty-First-Century China	325

Additional Work on Chinese Cinema	345
Index	347
About the Author	365

Acknowledgments

First and foremost, I thank Susan McEachern, my editor at Rowman & Littlefield, for working so closely with me on *China on Film* and for her enthusiastic support for several book projects during the last twenty years. I deeply value her sage advice and look forward to working with her yet again on *Restless China*, a new book that is already in the works. I also wish to thank the excellent Rowman & Littlefield staff (especially Grace Baumgartner and Alden Perkins) who labored so hard on this volume, my friend Bruce Tindell who did his usual excellent job on the index, and my fantastic student intern Kristin Shen who solved so many nagging problems.

In my introduction to *China on Film* I mention the names of the many film artists in China—starting with the legendary silent screen actress Wang Renmei—who helped me over the years. Spending countless hours with them discussing the sorrows and joys of their film careers was every bit as interesting as viewing their splendid movies.

My research on the history of Chinese filmmaking has been actively supported over the years by the China Film Archive, the National University of Singapore, East China Normal University, City University of Hong Kong, the University of Oxford, and, above all, my home institution, the University of California, San Diego.

This is the time and place to thank three special friends of Chinese historical studies at UC San Diego for their extraordinary generosity over the years: Martin Gleisch, John Moores, Jr., and Michael Ricks. What would we have done without them?

I have been blessed with many superb China studies colleagues at UC San Diego, including Matthew Chen, Jim Cheng, Dorothy Ko, Lu Weijing, Dick Madsen, Barry Naughton, Sarah Schneewind, Shen Kuiyi, Susan Shirk,

William Tay, and Zhang Yingjin. I have learned a great deal about China from each one of them and I value their friendship more than they will ever know. I love to do group projects and these are the campus colleagues with whom I have collaborated most closely.

As everyone knows, Joe Esherick has been my closest collaborator. For more than twenty years we have worked hard to create one of the most distinctive PhD programs in modern Chinese history. I will be forever grateful that in 1990 Joe accepted an invitation to join us in San Diego.

I thank Michael Bernstein, former History Department chair and former Division of Arts and Humanities dean at UC San Diego, for his remarkable and long-term support for Chinese studies in general and my own research and teaching activities in particular. I have fond memories of showing him around China in 1989 (and again in 1992!) and much more.

Beyond the UC San Diego campus, my work on film has benefited enormously from my many interactions with such outstanding scholars as Chris Berry, Michael Berry, Yomi Braester, Nick Browne, Tina Chen, Chen Xiaomei, Chen Xihe, Cheng Jihua, Robert Chi, Paul Clark, Kirk Denton, Poshek Fu, Ed Gunn, Nicole Huang, Jiang Jin, Andrew Jones, Lee Haiyan, Leo Ou-fan Lee, Song Hwee Lim, Lin Nien-tung, Perry Link, Sheldon Lu, Ma Ning, Scott Meek, Marco Müller, Laikwan Pang, Tony Rayns, Vivian Shen, David Wang, Wang Yiman, Julian Ward, Wei Hongbao, Nico Volland, Yang Lijun, Esther Yau, Xu Lanjun, and Yung Sai Shing.

My closest associations in the broader field of Chinese studies have been with Julia Andrews, Tom Bernstein, Robert Bickers, Cyril Birch, Chen Jian, Cheng Pei-kai, Sherm Cochran, Debbie Davis, Prasenjit Duara, Lee Feigon, Al Feuerwerker, Josh Fogel, Ed Friedman, Howard Goldblatt, Merle Goldman, Chuck Hayford, Christian Henriot, Gail Hershatter, Phil Huang, Joan Judge, Bill Kirby, Dick Kraus, Ching Kwan Lee, Ken Lieberthal, Katie Lynch, Bob Marks, Rod McFarquhar, Mauri Meisner, Rana Mitter, Peter Perdue, Liz Perry, Bill Rowe, Michael Schoenhals, Vera Schwartz, Mark Selden, Shen Zhihua, Vivienne Shue, Dori Solinger, Matt Sommer, Jonathan Spence, Julia Strauss, Fred Wakeman, Andy Walder, Jeff Wasserstrom, Susan Wilf, Sue Williams, Yang Kuisong, Yeh Wen-hsin, Zhang Jixun, and Zhang Longxi.

Outside the China field, my greatest debts are to Dick Atkinson, Frank Carpenter, John Dower, Harry Harootunian, Pat Ledden, Tetsuo Najita, Gene Rich, Ramon Ruiz, Paul Saltman, Harry Scheiber, and Jim Scott.

This book is lovingly dedicated to all the PhD students in modern Chinese history who joined our program at UC San Diego after it was launched in 1988. I have always been dazzled by their creativity and I deeply cherish our ongoing intellectual and personal relationships.

Words cannot express my boundless thanks to Li Huai, a Fifth Generation graduate of the Beijing Film Academy and a member of the UC San Diego Visual Arts faculty, and our daughter Natasha, my shining star and inspiration.

Introduction

The Sorrows and Joys of Chinese Filmmaking: Political and Personal Contexts

When I was reviewing the essays contained in this book, it occurred to me that virtually everything I have written on the history of Chinese filmmaking has been shaped by various personal and political engagements with people in China. Many would say that historical scholarship is not supposed to have overt emotional dimensions. But I have never tried to distance my academic research on China from my personal involvements with a wide range of people in China. In fact, my work has benefited enormously from personal engagements.

I have been traveling back and forth to China for long and short stays since 1971—the middle of the Cultural Revolution. I got interested in Chinese film during my first visit, but learning about the history of Chinese filmmaking has never been easy. I discovered at once that the history of the Chinese film industry is a politically sensitive topic because China has been a highly politicized place in the years since the birth of Chinese cinema. Many of the research taboos of forty years ago are still sensitive today. I have encountered many people who want to cover up and conceal important but controversial aspects of China's film history, as well as many who work openly or behind the scenes to tear down barriers and eliminate taboos. Over the decades I have gotten entangled (willingly and unwillingly) in the sometimes bitter political struggles that pit people who are determined to conceal against people who want to reveal.

I owe a tremendous debt to those who took me into their lives and shared so much with me. They did so at some risk to themselves. In the late 1970s and early 1980s, a time when foreign scholars were supposed to be kept on very short leashes and when all "interviews" with film personalities were supposed to be arranged and strictly monitored by official "minders" from the Ministry of Culture, many film personalities were happy, even eager, to meet with me privately and to form long-term friendships. I still recall the thrilling sensation I had in 1979 when personal friends arranged for me to meet the marvelous 1940s actress Wang Danfeng in her cramped and run-down Cultural Revolution–era residence in Shanghai. Later, during my first official visit to the Shanghai Film Studio, we had to pretend we did not know each other. The sense of danger and intrigue was quite thrilling—for her and for me.

It seemed very human to visit people in their homes and to establish personal relationships with them, but many officials were absolutely opposed to unscripted home visits and personal relationships of affection. That is why I will never forget the people who ignored officialdom and took me into their homes and lives at a time when everyone knew it was risky. I am thinking of the great late-1940s actor Shi Yu, the passionate Eugene O'Neill fan Huang Zongjiang, the legendary silent screen actresses Wang Renmei and Li Lili, the veteran director Ling Zifeng, the embittered screenwriter Wu Zuguang, and many others. In fall 1982 I savored a long, personally arranged visit to the home of Qian Zhongshu, the author of China's great twentieth-century novel *Fortress Besieged*. I arrived by motorcycle, and the impish Qian was waiting by the front steps of his apartment, a broad, approving smile on his face. Halfway through our conversation he said, "You're a dangerous man!" Coming from him, it was a huge compliment. He liked my agenda and research mode.

I spent the entirety of 1982–1983 as a mostly unwelcome guest at the China Film Archive. I was part of a U.S.-China research exchange program and, as such, had been forced on the archive by the U.S. National Academy of Sciences, my funding agency. The video age was just dawning in China, and I decided (without seeking prior Chinese approval) to bring with me a tape deck, a color monitor, and a number of VHS videotapes of Academy Award–winning American movies. After I politely declined to live in a university space set aside for "foreign guests," I moved in with the family of Chinese friends. An American journalist told me later that I was probably the only American citizen in Beijing living with a Chinese family. This lovely human arrangement allowed me to invite Chinese friends, including many recent and soon-to-be-famous Fifth Generation graduates of the Beijing Film Institute (Beijing dianying xueyuan) and veteran members of the Chinese Filmworkers Association (Zhongguo dianyingjia xiehui), into "my home" to socialize and view exciting and critical American films. To me, this was what cultural exchange was all about. It was exhilarating to watch such classics as *Easy Rider* (d. Dennis Hopper, 1969), *Catch-22* (d. Mike Nichols, 1970), *One Flew over the Cuckoo's Nest* (d. Milos Forman, 1975), *Elephant Man* (d. David Lynch, 1980), and *Raging Bull* (d. Martin Scorsese, 1980) with these colleagues.

Introduction 3

The great 1940s performers Shi Yu (*left*) and Shangguan Yunzhu (*right*) appear as unsavory mobsters in *The Rogues* (1948, d. Xu Changlin). Photo courtesy of Shi Yu.

Their honest and frank remarks taught me a great deal about China and America. After viewing *One Flew over the Cuckoo's Nest*, an energetic and irrepressible film critic stunned me when she coldly commented, "That's China." I pondered that remark for many weeks.

But this account dwells on the good and makes everything sound too easy. Nothing could be further from the truth. Behind the scenes an internal factional battle was unfolding. A low-level ministry official (Wang Jiadong) was trying to discredit a rival (Yu Huijun) in order to advance his own career. Both were Party members. Wang told his superiors I was "out of control" and that his irresponsible colleague had aided and abetted me. He also went to the new National Security Ministry (Anchuan bu) and asserted that I was a "cultural spy" (*wenhua tewu*). His colleague was soon relieved of her duties and sent to a Party school to "study." My collection of American videotapes was confiscated by the police, I was forced out of the family I was living with, and a long "investigation" ensued. Interestingly, most of my private friends in the film world (Party and non-Party people alike) stuck with me and even gave me sage advice about how to navigate these swirling political waters. Among those who quietly refused to drop me like a hot potato were Shi Fangyu (head of the Film Bureau of the Ministry of Culture), Cheng Jihua (the leading historian of Chinese film), and Situ Zhaodun (a professor at the Film Institute). All were Party members, and

Cheng and Situ had served long prison terms during the Cultural Revolution. I remember Cheng Jihua telling me at a private meeting, "I want you to see that there are good people in the Party!"

Months later I was cleared, the woman official (who had been secretly communicating with me and providing behind-the-scenes information) was allowed to return to her job, and the security unit responsible for the investigation summoned me to a meticulously rehearsed meeting and apologized without using the word "apology." One young agent complimented me on my motorcycling skills. He had been assigned to tail me and had been frustrated on occasion by the strategies I sometimes used to shake him off. A close friend from the Filmworkers Association later cryptically asked me if the security people had poured tea for me at the meeting. When I responded that they had, she sighed, "That's good."

These anecdotes sum up what it has been like all these years doing research on the history of Chinese cinema—depressing disappointments followed by unexpected breakthroughs and surprises; encounters with those who conceal followed by interaction with whose who are determined to

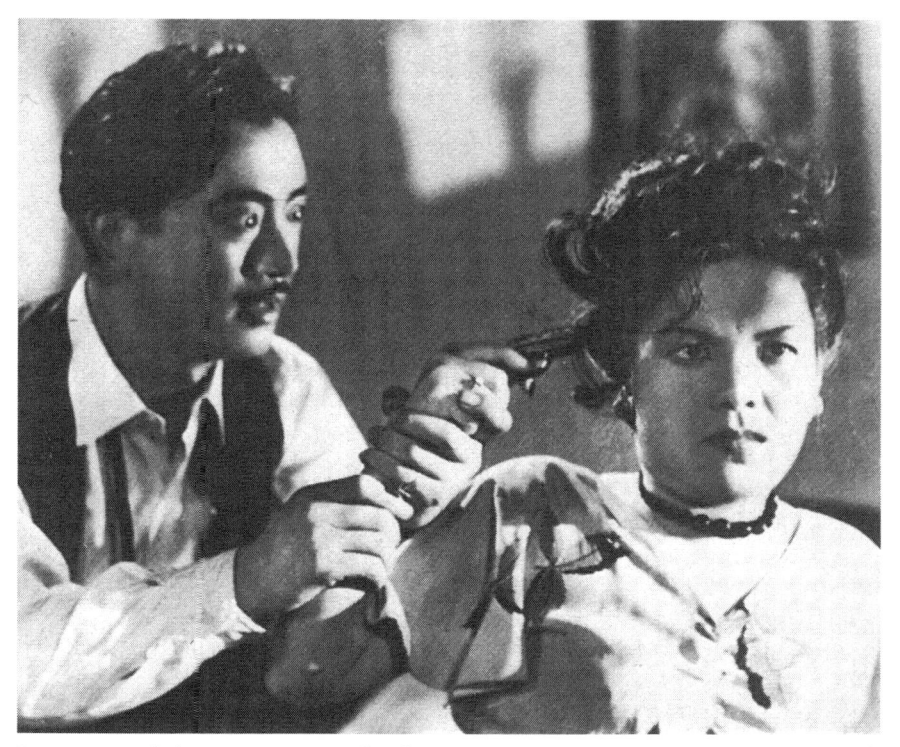

Postwar social disintegration tears families apart in *A Spring River Flows East* (1947, d. Cai Chusheng, Zheng Junli). China Film Archive

reveal. The first chapter in this volume, "Shanghai Twenties: Early Chinese Cinematic Explorations of the Modern Marriage," grew out of a refreshing moment of openness. Although it deals with the 1920s period of silent-era Chinese filmmaking, it was written quite recently in connection with a rare opportunity to teach Chinese film in China. In spring 2010 I was invited by friends at East China Normal University (ECNU), one of the most forward-looking institutions in China, to teach a course in Chinese on 1920s and early-1930s silent-era Chinese filmmaking. I had fantasized about teaching one of my film courses in China and could not resist the temptation after being given assurances that I could teach the course exactly as I teach it at the University of California. Once the class started, I was rather surprised to learn that none of my forty-two Shanghai students had seen a single one of the seventeen silent-era films I brought with me, despite the fact that all of the films had been made in Shanghai itself, the Hollywood of China in the 1920s. The students did not know what to expect, but before long they became mesmerized by the quality and openness of the films. I felt good about being able to help the students fill a conspicuous gap in their knowledge of Shanghai's rich cultural history. One student conceded in a confidential course evaluation I administered at the end that it was a bit odd having an American professor come to Shanghai to teach a course on the glories of Shanghai's old film culture. I think he or she meant, "Why didn't we know this material already?" Another student said that some of the old films were "more open than the ones we have today."

I presented "Explorations of the Modern Marriage" at a large gathering of faculty and graduate students at ECNU. The whole point of the chapter is to question the idea that nothing culturally interesting or substantial was produced by the Shanghai film world in the 1920s, prior to the launching of what was later celebrated as the "leftist" film movement of the early 1930s. The films discussed in this chapter deal explicitly with the fumbling attempts of young people to define modernity. The questions they asked in the 1920s about modernity (How is the modern marriage defined? What constitutes a transgression in such a marriage? How should transgressions be handled?) are being hotly debated once again in present-day China. These ancient films seem very timely.

My Shanghai students were surprised by two of the political thrusts of these early films on the modern marriage. First, the quest for a modern identity did not seem to have a direct connection to nationalism or nation building. In fact, China is nowhere mentioned in the three 1920s films about the modern marriage discussed in this chapter. If the protagonists identified with any spatial unit, it was the decidedly sub-national space called Shanghai. In short, a modern identity did not necessarily require a national or nationalist identity. Second, the desire to be involved in a modern marriage did not necessarily mean a desire or demand for gender equality. Scholars frequently talk about the importance of women's rights issues during the New Culture and May Fourth movements of the late 1910s and 1920s,[1] but the cutting-edge modern marriages that were gaining ground in Shanghai in the 1920s, like their counterparts in post-Victorian London, Paris, New York, and Tokyo, rarely embraced gender equality. The absence of gender equality in these modern marriages did not mean that young urbanites had sold out to tradition, but rather that their relationships were consistent with modern marriage patterns worldwide.

Chapter 2, "The Theme of Spiritual Pollution in Chinese Films of the 1930s," was written long ago and was a direct response to the vicious crackdown (complete with executions) on Western spiritual pollution launched by the Chinese authorities in 1983 when I was living in Beijing. The strategy of hardliners was to blame everything that was wrong in contemporary Chinese society on the "spiritually polluting" aspects of Western bourgeois culture that had allegedly slipped into China when the socialist economy was reformed in the late 1970s and early 1980s. Rather than look internally for the causes of unrest among young people, Party leaders scapegoated Western culture. My response was to argue that there was nothing new or revolutionary about the Party's notion of spiritual pollution (*jingshen wuran*). My posture was noticeably defensive in large part because at that very moment (mid-1983) I was in the throes of trying to get married in China to a citizen of the People's Republic, an extraordinarily rare and difficult undertaking at that time. The law was on our side because freedom of choice in marriage was in theory guaranteed in China, but many conservatives were opposed to "mixed" marriages. For them, I was a living example of spiritual pollution.

My scholarly argument was that politically expedient attacks on the allegedly spiritually polluting thrust of Western culture had been a common occurrence in China throughout the twentieth century. The representations of so-called Western culture in such attacks were crude and essentialistic caricatures that shed little light on the dynamics of Western culture. I argued that the stinging critiques of spiritual pollution produced by the film world in the 1930s were associated with all sorts of political tendencies, including conservative, humanist, and leftist filmmaking. Whether the assault came from the right or the left, the concern was the same: citizens should think less about "self-interest" and more about the "national" and "collective" agenda mapped out by self-styled revolutionary parties. In short, by scapegoating Western culture, the Communist Party was doing in the 1980s exactly what the Nationalist Party and other anticommunists had done in the mid-1930s.

When that article first appeared, an academic friend wrote me a note thanking me for weighing in on the notion of Occidentalism. He was right. Although I did not use the term *Occidentalism* anywhere in the piece, I was in fact saying that crude Chinese caricatures of some imagined Occidental "Other" had little to do with achieving a better understanding of the complexities of Western culture and everything to do with the pursuit of domestic political goals in China. In short, in both the 1930s and the 1980s, heated discussions about Western culture tell us far more about the dynamics of Chinese politics than about the culture of the West. If we agree that there are "Orientalists" in the West, it follows that there must be "Occidentalists" in China.

Chapter 3, "Melodramatic Representation and the May Fourth Tradition of Chinese Cinema," was my first effort to deal with a problem related to genre. This research was first presented at a conference held at Harvard. The goal of the conference was to question the assumption that the "new" and compelling cultural production of the early post-Mao era was in fact strikingly new. I agreed with the conference organizers, David Wang and Ellen Widmer, that much of the most interesting early post-Mao culture, including film production, was connected to and resonated with important developments in pre-Mao, Republican-era tendencies. Scholars were right to be excited about what was different about post-Mao culture, but they tended to jump the gun by calling too much of it new.

Speaking of guns, it is important to point out that the Harvard conference was held in the immediate aftermath of the June 1989 massacres of peaceful protestors in Beijing and elsewhere. The disgust and anger that swept through the China studies field at that time can still be felt today. In 1986, a high point in post–Cultural Revolution film productivity, Xie Jin's powerful new film *Hibiscus Town* was being widely acclaimed. Its blunt criticism of aspects of Communist Party history seemed daring and hopeful. It provided an opportunity for catharsis, but in the immediate aftermath of the 1989 massacres of citizens, it was possible to see the film in a very different light. First, in terms of its structural paradigm and internal logic, it differed in no significant artistic way from such great film melodramas of the 1930s and 1940s as *Small Toys* (1933) and *Heavenly Spring Dream* (1947). Second, although *Hibiscus Town* was talked about as a towering work of realism, it was not really an example of film realism. I argued that critics and scholars were in the habit of mistaking melodramatic representation for realist representation. Borrowing heavily from the film traditions of the 1930s and 1940s, post–Cultural Revolution filmmakers like Xie Jin produced melodramas that successfully masqueraded as realist works. Melodrama dwells on the moral binaries of good and evil. It may have been cathartic for 1986 film audiences to see the Communist Party of the 1950s and 1960s associated with "evil," but the moral categories of good and evil obscured the complexities of life as it was in fact experienced by most people. The state just as easily made use of the melodramatic mode by referring to the patriotic protesters of 1989 as thugs and rioters, and by describing murderous PLA soldiers as patriots, heroes, and martyrs.

Chapter 4, "Never-Ending Controversies," deals with the most politically controversial subject in the history of Chinese filmmaking, the fate of the industry during the 1937–1945 occupation of Shanghai by Japanese forces. Film historian Cheng Jihua was willing to list the pictures of mid-1937 to late 1941 (when Shanghai was partially occupied by Japan) in his comprehensive filmography of Chinese movies, but he refused to list any titles from 1942 to 1945 (when Shanghai was fully occupied). The implication was that these were the works of collaborators and traitors and should not be regarded as Chinese films. After I began doing research in the Film Archive of China in 1982, I had an opportunity to meet privately with the well-known actor Ying Ruocheng (who later served as vice minister of culture). Almost immediately he asked me, "Will they let you watch occupation-era films?" He acknowledged that he had no access to such films, but he was certain that evidence of the influence of German expressionism could be found in them. I had been viewing films of the early 1930s and late 1940s at the archive, but after talking with Ying I made inquiries about films of the 1937–1945 period and learned quickly that the subject was strictly taboo and nearly impossible to research.

I did in fact learn a bit about the topic in a series of informative interviews I conducted in the mid-1980s in New York with the sensational occupation-era actress Li Lihua. But there were almost no films of that era available for viewing. I refrained from writing anything because I have always been disinclined to talk about films I have not seen. But after nearly twenty years of trying, I finally put my hands on *Remorse in Shanghai* (1944), perhaps the most controversial Chinese film ever made—a work of treason, some said. It starred the young Li Lihua.

By coincidence, at about the same time I located a copy of this important film, a gala Chinese film festival and academic conference was scheduled to be held in New York. It was the spring of 2005, and the occasion was the centennial anniversary of Chinese filmmaking. Films were to be shown at the Lincoln Center, and a huge delegation of Chinese celebrities, including director Xie Jin, was to be flown in. I was invited to present a research paper. After I was sent a list of the films to be screened and the topics of the papers to be presented, I noticed that the entire period from 1937 to 1945 had been left out. I volunteered to write a paper on the wartime years and *Remorse in Shanghai* in particular. When I presented the paper I also screened some clips from this rare film. The audience, including many from China, was riveted, as moving images of such famous people as Li Lihua, Wang Danfeng, and Mei Xi flickered across the screen, but the presentation was followed by stony silence and almost no discussion. I concluded that my effort to make a contribution had made people nervous. The topic of filmmaking in occupied Shanghai was still too sensitive.

But in fall 2006 when I was on sabbatical leave at Oxford, I was surprised to receive a message from Chen Xihe, a Shanghai-based Chinese film scholar who had been present at my *Remorse in Shanghai* presentation. He said that he really liked my paper and that there were several younger scholars in China who were eager to break the taboo and work on the wartime period. I was highly skeptical when he said my paper should and could be published in Chinese in China, but Chen was right and the paper came out later in *Wenyi yanjiu*, one of the leading academic periodicals in China. In late summer 2007 Chen invited me to come to China to present a public lecture to graduate students and faculty at Shanghai University on the subject of occupation-era filmmaking. The controversy over *Remorse in Shanghai* is told in chapter 4.

Chapter 5, "Victory as Defeat," originally presented at a conference held at the University of California, Berkeley, takes us into the 1945–1949 postwar period, one of the real highlights of Chinese filmmaking. My thinking about this period has always been shaped by the stark fact that a massive civil war was raging in China during those painful years. Owing to censorship priorities, the civil war between the Nationalists and the Communists could not be mentioned explicitly in any of these films, but it was the key subtext in many great works. Once again, the connection between cinema and politics seemed to be all-important. I was extremely fortunate to have had the opportunity to talk with many of the most influential directors, actresses, and actors of that era, including Sang Hu, Huang Zuolin, Zhang Junxiang, Bai Yang, Ke Ling, Zhang Ruifang, Shi Yu, Han Fei, Huang Zongjiang, Sun Daolin, Wei Wei, and Li Lihua. My debt to them is enormous.

"Victory as Defeat" discusses the many ways in which postwar filmmakers dealt with the widespread phenomenon of postwar alienation and malaise, the sense that somehow the victory in the war against Japan had been converted into a defeat for ordinary Chinese. This chapter emphasizes the determination of filmmakers to craft powerful and popular family melodramas that functioned as national allegories. Audiences could identify with gripping narratives that showed how wartime traumas continued to destabilize family life well after the war ended. Tragic family narratives could be interpreted as disturbing examples of the plight of the entire postwar nation. These explosive and influential melodramas were not meant to be mirror-like reflections of reality but worked more as meaningful fabrications that captured a potent psychological reality.

The films of the civil war era did a great deal to undermine the authority and the legitimacy of the postwar Nationalist government, but it is simply not the case that all of this impressive body of disruptive filmmaking was the work of leftists. The tensions of the civil war period were extremely complicated. Thus it is important for scholars to recognize the extent to which critical filmmaking of the postwar era was produced by nonleftists in Nationalist state-owned film studios as well as in middle-of-the-road privately owned studios.

It is precisely one of those influential, self-centered, nonleftist figures, Shi Hui, whose story is taken up in chapter 6, "Acting like Revolutionaries." When I first began doing research on Chinese cinema in the 1970s, I was struck by three dimensions of Shi Hui's short life. First, he was, in my mind at least, the greatest and most versatile screen actor of the late 1940s; second, he desperately wanted to be accepted by the Communist authorities after they took power in 1949; and third, he decided to commit a ritualistic suicide in 1957. I wondered why so little research had been done on his case and vowed to write a piece as soon as I felt I had something to say. It is always hard to judge the impact of one's own work, so I was taken by surprise when a visiting PhD student from Shanghai mentioned during a meeting of my 2009 graduate seminar that she had read my essay on Shi Hui. I asked innocently what she thought of the essay. I was deeply touched when she said the essay made her cry.

My chapter on Shi Hui seeks to understand the sometimes humorous, sometimes pathetic, and sometimes deadly serious attempts of the various private-sector film celebrities who had dominated Chinese filmmaking for decades to adjust to the introduction of a Stalinist, state socialist system of cultural production. Shi Hui despised the Nationalist government, chose to stay in China at a time when some of his friends decided to flee, and was virtually obsessed by a desire to be accepted by the new government. He certainly "acted like a revolutionary," but the language I use to account for people like Shi Hui is intentionally ambiguous. Was he in fact really behaving like a revolutionary and a sincere convert? Or was it an act? In the end, it is plain to see, he failed to make the transition; there was no place for people like him. But is it the case that all such efforts at transformation are doomed during a time of revolution?

Film studies involve more than the study of individual film artifacts. In the case of China, it has always been important to ask questions about the culture, including the political culture, of filmmaking. Chapter 7, originally presented at a conference in London, is on noted director Zheng Junli and the problem of complicity. It addresses subject matter treated in *The Lives of Others* (d. Florian Henckel von Donnersmarck, 2006), a brilliant German film that deals effectively with the complicated relationship between artists and the state in socialist East Germany. While chapter 6 treats Shi Hui and his failure to work his way into the system, chapter 7 continues the story about political accommodation by discussing the remarkable success of Zheng Junli in making the transition to socialism and "acting like a revolutionary."

Zheng was well known in the 1930s and 1940s, first as an actor and then as a director. He was every bit as bourgeois as Shi Hui. But unlike Shi Hui, Zheng had participated in several right-wing, pro-Nationalist film projects. On the other hand, he had moved to the left sooner than Shi Hui during the civil war period and was better positioned in 1949 than Shi Hui to engage in politically useful social networking.

The German film *The Lives of Others* helps us understand people like Shi Hui and Zheng Junli because it is not the least bit melodramatic and refuses to focus on a moral binary that features Communist monsters and innocent, victimized artists. Instead, it reveals a complicated range of possibilities for artists, including collaboration, complicity, accommodation, and various forms of resistance (active and passive). Most artists cooperated in one way or another, sometimes informing on their colleagues in order to advance their careers or to survive. We should refrain from being too judgmental about such behavior. Are we absolutely certain of what we would do under similar circumstances? Many Chinese film artists were not proud of the survival strategies they adopted.

Like Shi Hui, Zheng Junli ran into serious political trouble in the early years of the People's Republic, but he was much better than Shi Hui at navigating the roiling waters of China's new socialist cultural sphere. By the late 1950s he was at the very summit of the film world and was asked to direct *Lin Zexu* (1959), a highly nationalistic work about the Opium War of 1839 that was the artistic centerpiece of the celebration of the tenth anniversary of the People's Republic. Unlike Shi Hui and most prerevolution film world celebrities, Zheng Junli was finally invited to join the Communist Party. Mao's utopian Great Leap Forward was under way, and Zheng, the quintessential insider by this time, must have thought he was invulnerable. After all, he had been acting like a Maoist. How could he know that arrest and death in prison were on his horizon?

Zheng Junli pretended to be a Maoist, but he was an anti-Maoist at heart. In the aftermath of the Great Leap famine that cost the lives of at least 30 or 40 million people, the most important anti-Maoist in the Chinese film world was undoubtedly Xia Yan, a 1930s-vintage, Europeanized intellectual who had joined the urban Communist movement well before 1949. Xia Yan, Zheng Junli, and people like them were appalled by the ravages of Mao's Great Leap into oblivion. Although the concept of "soft power" was not in use at the time, Xia Yan was one of the main architects of a post-Leap, anti-Maoist cultural initiative that sought to present a softer, less militant, less threatening picture of China and the Chinese revolution.

Chapter 8, "The Limits of Cultural Thaw," presented originally at a conference at Harvard, looks closely at film production in the comparatively liberal period between the demise of the Great Leap in 1960 and the onset of Mao's Cultural Revolution in early 1966. Funds were scarce and output was drastically cut back, but the films of the early 1960s were a high point in the history of state socialist filmmaking in China. These films were condemned during the Cultural Revolution, and very few Western scholars had seen them prior to the 1979 Harvard conference. But by good fortune, I was living in Hong Kong in 1977–1978 when the films of the early 1960s were once again made available for viewing. I was among a handful of delighted Western scholars who rushed to various leftist exhibition venues in Hong Kong to see these formerly banned works. "The Limits of Cultural Thaw," the product of my Hong Kong viewing, examines three types of early 1960s films: movies that treated the late imperial era in respectful and surprisingly nuanced ways, movies that paid homage to the humanistic May Fourth approach to the complex history of the Republican era, and movies about the history of the People's Republic that conveyed not-so-subtle criticisms of the wasteful excesses associated with Maoism.

When the early 1960s thaw ended, Xia Yan was one of the main targets of Mao's vindictive Cultural Revolution, but unlike Zheng Junli, he survived the Cultural Revolution and was "rehabilitated" in the late 1970s. I was finally able to meet him in 1982. I wanted to talk about his leading role in the early 1960s, and I wanted to tell him about my own Film Archive research on the late 1940s. My hopes were high. In the end, however, it was a very disappointing meeting. I had to go through official ministry channels, thus the whole "interview" was stiff, staged, and ice cold. Xia Yan was surrounded throughout by fawning low-level bureaucrats who seemed interested in little more than photo opportunities. Xia Yan had nothing to say about his anti-Maoism of the 1960s and seemed puzzled that I was emphasizing the late 1940s in my archival viewing. Instead, he wanted to talk about the early 1930s and mythologies of the leftist film movement of that time—that is, legends about the leadership role supposedly played by the Communist Party in promoting a politically healthy film world.

Xia Yan's comments were revealing. The early 1960s cultural thaw he led is certainly very interesting, but it must be defined primarily by its limitations. The thaw was welcomed by film professionals, but it raised no questions about the need for monopolistic Communist Party control of the film world. Xia Yan detested the Maoist agitprop agenda and passionately called for more space for "art" and narrative complexity in the early 1960s. But he was incapable of imagining vibrant independent filmmaking that competed with and challenged the socialist state sector. Even the most liberal reformers of the early 1960s had to legitimize their ideas by making it clear that the goal was to strengthen, not weaken, the dominant position of the Communist Party.

The Cultural Revolution of 1966–1976 went very badly for intellectuals and professional filmmakers like Xia Yan. The film experiments of the early

1960s were terminated. Filmmaking was virtually suspended in the early years of the Cultural Revolution. Then, in the early 1970s, the industry devoted itself to the production of a few film versions of the model ballets and operas promoted by Mao's wife, Jiang Qing. Feature film production was renewed to a limited extent in the final years of the Cultural Revolution, but the work consisted mainly of Maoist propaganda about the history of the Chinese Communist revolution.

I visited China for the first time in summer 1971, the middle of the Cultural Revolution. The trip kindled my interest in Chinese cinema, but opportunities to learn were severely limited. I participated in a long meeting that included cultural ideologist Yao Wenyuan (later identified as one of the Gang of Four), a man who had a lot to say about the role of film as a weapon. I was given a 35 mm print of the model film *Red Detachment of Women* (1971). And I visited a factory in Nanjing that produced mobile film projectors for use in the countryside. But the films made during the early years of the People's Republic, not to mention the movies of the 1920s–1940s, were off-limits, along with virtually all of the screenwriters, directors, actresses, and actors who made them. Toward the end of the Cultural Revolution, it became increasingly clear that the film professionals who had managed to survive the Cultural Revolution were anxiously waiting for a chance to make a comeback. But what kind of comeback could they mount?

Chapter 9, "Popular Cinema and Political Thought in Early Post-Mao China," deals with the immediate aftermath of the Cultural Revolution. The remnants of the old film bureaucracy returned to power after Mao's death and the arrest of many of his leading followers, including Yao Wenyuan. But the recovery of the industry was very slow at first, and the behavior of the old elites was exceedingly cautious. The Cultural Revolution line on culture lingered for a time. The bureaucracy was still sensitive to the charge that it was right-wing. To make sure it would no longer be discredited as an insufficiently socialist force, lip service and more was paid in the late 1970s to the need to consolidate the socialist system and carry on socialist revolution. Xia Yan and other veterans sought to stage another early-1960s-style cultural thaw in order to bury Maoism once and for all, but they had to do it gingerly and under the banner of "real" socialism.

This chapter was inspired not by these early and decidedly uneven efforts to revive the film world, but by exhilarating expressions of dissent and opposition that were visible on the streets of Beijing and other major cities, expressions that frightened people like Xia Yan. Events on the street were running far ahead of developments in the stodgy Ministry of Culture. I was fortunate to have a chance to visit Democracy Wall in Beijing and interact with people there before the movement was crushed in 1979.

"Popular Cinema and Political Thought in Early Post-Mao China" deals with three enormously successful film melodramas that were released in the immediate aftermath of the demise of Democracy Wall: *The Legend of Tianyun Mountain* (1980), *A Corner Forgotten by Love* (1981), and *At Middle Age* (1982). I argue that the films resonated more with the concerns of the ordinary people who had participated in the Democracy Wall movement than with the worries of the insecure Party officials who ordered the crackdown on Democracy Wall. In effect, the chapter argues that the second cultural thaw engineered by the early post-Mao cultural bureaucracy was to some extent out of control in the early 1980s.

This assertion posed a problem. Since all these films were produced in the state-controlled film production sector (independent, nonstate film production was not an option at that time), was I really saying that oppositional cultural activity was possible within the state sector? I was clearly saying yes. These films connected to a real sense of hope that prevailed in society, a feeling that the system could perhaps reform itself in bold ways. The works projected very little that could be called cynicism. More than anything else, they were innocent, even idealistic.

This led to a debate about hope, a debate that continues to this day. I was obviously suggesting in the hopeful mid-1980s that some scholars gave the state too much credit with respect to its ability to control cultural production. I sided with those who saw more independence and agency within society, including film studios and other units of society under state control. Although the films of the early post–Cultural Revolution years are not studied or screened much these days, I was arguing that the amazingly popular films treated in chapter 9 chipped away at state legitimacy and qualified as quasi-dissident works produced by critical artists who functioned *within* the state sector, artists who had influential patrons *within* the cultural bureaucracy. But some scholars objected, saying that this analytical framework made excessive claims about the significance of forces of agency beyond the control of the state and was, therefore, a bit naive.

Chapter 10, "On the Eve of Tiananmen: Huang Jianxin and the Notion of Postsocialism," goes one step further by arguing that *The Black Cannon Incident* (1986), *Dislocation* (1987), and *Transmigration* (1989), three films produced in the state sector by Huang Jianxin in the mid- and late 1980s, moved well beyond the cathartic and destabilizing films of the early 1980s by sketching the contours of a China that is not socialist but distinctively postsocialist. The term *postsocialist* is used rather widely now as an analytical category, but I think I was the first person to apply it to the study of Chinese filmmaking. The concept of postsocialism was controversial when I first presented this chapter at a conference at UCLA in 1990. I asserted without hesitation that state socialist film studios were capable of producing postsocialist movies. This argument amounted to another round in the debate about agency. How could the socialist state be presiding over the crafting of postsocialist imagery?

The preparation of chapter 10 was inspired by two sharply contrasting political developments in China. If anything, the political atmosphere in China in late 1988 was even more electric and dynamic than it had been a decade earlier at the height of the Democracy Wall movement. I was already an admirer of Huang Jianxin's first two films when I was invited in December 1988 to attend a hastily arranged private screening of his not-yet-released third film, *Transmigration*, at the Film Archive in Beijing. Huang flew in from Xian to join us. Those of us who tended to stress the role of bottom-up agency found considerable evidence to support our views in the works of Huang and other young filmmakers laboring in the state sector. Less than six months later, however, our optimism was derailed by the bloody June 4 massacres. This chapter expressed my own anger, but it also reaffirmed my conviction that Huang Jianxin's films captured the postsocialist essence of China in the late 1980s and in some ways anticipated the Tiananmen crisis of 1989.

Chapter 11, "Velvet Prisons and the Political Economy of Chinese Filmmaking," looks at the issues of velvet prisons and self-censorship, and thus continues the discussion of postsocialism. Many wondered whether the Chinese film industry had a future in the wake of the violent crackdown in 1989 on dissent of almost any sort. It was easy to be pessimistic in the 1990s and to acknowledge, however reluctantly, the overwhelming power of the state to repress dissent and to direct cultural production in a variety of top-down ways. This raised the interesting subject of Miklos Haraszti's challenging writings about the role of velvet prisons in late state socialist Eastern Europe. Haraszti argued forcefully that the Hungarian state had contained significant dissent in the arts by making life more comfortable for artists rather than by resorting to violent and repressive Stalinist modes of management. That is, it was better and more efficient to buy off artists by placing them in well-appointed velvet prisons. Give them the illusion of artistic freedom, and they will censor themselves.

I wanted to understand the extent to which this theory applied to the post-Tiananmen Chinese film world. The stakes were familiar. Giving too much credit to the state ran the risk of failing to appreciate the impact of popular forms of resistance. Giving too little credit to the machinations of the state ran the risk of naively overestimating the influence of bottom-up societal forces. Haraszti's model is very useful and it has a great deal of explanatory power, but I concluded that it is too inflexible, excessively pessimistic, and wrongheaded about the apparent victory of cultural bureaucrats in Eastern Europe. For one thing, his paradigm failed to anticipate the sudden collapse of state socialist regimes in Eastern Europe and the Soviet Union. More importantly, it could not account for the diversity and quasi-subversive dimensions of the Chinese film industry both before and after the 1989 bloodbaths.

In the post-Tiananmen era, the Chinese state retreated in some important ways from the day-to-day management of the Chinese film world. First, market reforms led to the production of greater numbers of apolitical commercial entertainment films, which meant less space for crude and unpopular works of propaganda. Second, increasing numbers of art films by such young directors as Chen Kaige and Zhang Yimou were produced in small, provincial studios. Many of these works engaged in an intriguing sort of distancing by setting the narratives in prerevolutionary times. The films of Chen, Zhang, and others were often banned in China, but they were funded in new, globalized ways, won acclaim outside China, and boosted the morale of Chinese filmmakers who wanted to join the world. Third, new and inexpensive technologies of a sort unimagined by Harastzi led to the birth in the early 1990s of independent and underground filmmaking in China.

The final chapter of this book, "Social and Political Dynamics of Underground Filmmaking in Early-Twenty-First-Century China," looks at the ways in which this brave new world of independent filmmaking unfolded before and after 2000. This chapter was one of the first overviews of the colorful but fragmented underground sector. I know and admire some of the independent film artists. In 2003 the University of California, San Diego, my home institution, was one of the first in the world to host a large-scale Chinese underground and independent film festival, complete with visiting directors. I was very excited about the prospect of independent Chinese filmmaking. In some ways it seemed like the new movement might signal a return of sorts to the glory days of critical, private-sector filmmaking in the 1920s, 1930s, and 1940s. My hopes were high because much of my research on the socialist-era filmmaking of the 1950–1990 decades had explored the ways in which state-sector filmmakers tried to give expression to criticism of the Party and state. Imagine what Chinese filmmakers would do, I wondered aloud, if they could win a significant measure of independence from Party and state control! I think I was expecting the new post-1990 underground and independent sector to make large numbers of explicitly political films like Tian Zhuangzhuang's brilliant *Blue Kite* (1993).

Chapter 12 is a record of my initial reactions to the enormous wave of underground and independent productions that surfaced just before and just after 2000. Some of this work is magnificent, breathtaking, and bravely critical. But in general, I was disappointed and was fairly harsh in my first systematic survey of the material. So much of it seemed numbingly self-indulgent, even trivial. I think I was a bit too critical. I should not have been surprised that much of the early work was self-indulgent. After decades of Maoist collectivism and asceticism, Chinese artists had earned the right to be self-indulgent. Indeed, it is crucial for us to recognize the wondrous political dimensions of these self-indulgent expressions.

Introduction 17

I am writing these comments in late 2011 in the wake of the Jasmine uprisings that have shaken the Middle East. The all-too-apparent insecurities of the Communist Party have led to yet another cycle of political and cultural repression in China. Many excellent independent films have been made in China in recent years, though the nonstate sector is lying low at the moment. But if the political history of Chinese filmmaking in the last hundred years has taught us anything, it has shown us how these cycles of crackdown and opening come and go. International supporters and domestic patrons of independent Chinese filmmaking will not be discouraged. The creative impulses of Chinese film artists (amateurs and professionals alike) will continue to clash with the determination of Leninist-type cultural bureaucrats to control. At times the evidence compels us to be pessimistic. At times it allows us to be optimistic. I prefer optimism. Qian Zhongshu spoke approvingly in 1982 of "dangerous" people. The expanded Chinese film world of the twenty-first century, linked as it is to the Internet, is full of dangerous people.

NOTE

1. The New Culture and May Fourth movements were the two most important intellectual currents of early twentieth-century China. The hallmarks of the New Culture Movement, which began in 1915, were radical anti-traditionalism, anti-Confucianism, and receptivity to Western liberal culture. The May Fourth Movement, which began in spring 1919, continued to advance these tendencies, but also featured strident modern nationalism and openness to Marxism and other Western schools of radical thought that advanced fundamental criticisms of Western liberalism, capitalism, and imperialism.

1

Shanghai Twenties: Early Chinese Cinematic Explorations of the Modern Marriage

The new and "modern" marriages that were taking place in Shanghai and other metropolitan centers in China and elsewhere before and after 1900 are of enormous interest. Many young couples wanted modernity, but what sorts of issues arose once the honeymoon was over? By the 1920s, one wonders, what kinds of relationships did modern husbands and wives have? How do we know what day-to-day life was like in the new modern marriages? How much variation was there within the broad category of modern marriages? Were modern marriages the subject of a national discourse?

It is already too late to interview men and women who lived as modern married couples in the 1920s. One can read written accounts of modern marriage in the fiction, prose writings, and news accounts produced in the 1920s. Archival data are increasingly accessible. But what did new marriages look like? Are there any pictures, especially "moving pictures," produced in the 1920s that offer representations of modern married couples and the problems they faced? What about feature films? Were there feature films made in the 1920s about modern marriages?

The answer, of course, is yes. There was a booming movie industry in Shanghai in the 1920s. It makes great sense, therefore, to examine these films in an effort to find visual, indeed, moving-picture evidence of precisely how modern marriages were represented in an extremely popular and powerful entertainment medium. We want to do more than read about modern marriages. We want to see them in action.

Doing research on Chinese-language films produced in the 1920s is rather like doing archaeological research. Something very big and grand

and complicated was out there once, but now its physical remains are almost gone. If we were doing research on ancient Greece, Rome, or the Near East, it would be splendid to have direct access to all of the material culture produced by those societies when we seek to reconstruct in full detail the nuances and messiness of their social orders. But, alas, almost all of the physical remnants of those societies are gone. Archaeologists dig for years, hoping to find an intact artifact. Most often, however, all they come up with are shattered fragments. It is all very frustrating. But researchers have no choice. They are compelled to work with what they have.

It is the same for those who would like to make use of moving pictures produced in the 1920s in Shanghai to get a clear picture of what modern marriages or any other important social phenomena looked like when they were projected on the silver screen. By all accounts, well over five hundred feature films were produced in China (mainly in Shanghai) in the years between 1920 and 1929.[1] And this excludes newsreels, documentaries, and educational films. Unfortunately, as far as researchers have been able to tell, only eighteen feature films of the 1920s still survive.[2] Of these, ten are incomplete—that is, they are missing one or more parts. Only eight feature films have survived intact.

If we want to know about film culture and the film world in Shanghai in the 1920s, there is abundant published and handwritten archival evidence. These materials are indispensable. But if one wants to see and consider actual film artifacts, very little is available for viewing. Like the archaeologists, we should not be discouraged. We must work with enthusiasm with what we have in an effort to explore exceedingly rare visual sources on such topics as the modern marriage.

For those of us interested in visual sources on modern social and cultural phenomena, it is fortunate that three of the eighteen feature films of the 1920s that survive deal quite directly with the trials and tribulations associated with modern marriages. Though they offer us case studies of three modern marriages, the films are different in that they present three sharply contrasting narratives. The films were written by three different screenwriters, involve three different directors, feature three different sets of actors and actresses, and were made in three different local film studios. All approve of the modern marriage, but there is intriguing variation in the perspectives and the issues they treat on screen. That is, the films that survive do not present a single, unified, integrated view of the modern marriage. Instead, they show us a range of issues and problems that we can safely assume did in fact arise among many modern married couples in Shanghai in the 1920s. The films are attractive and informative precisely because they put human faces on the modern marriage and thereby allow us to get to know three very different modern couples—three very different men and three very different women.

A STRING OF PEARLS: XIUZHEN AND YUSHENG

We begin our search for the modern marriage by considering *A String of Pearls* (*Yi chuan zhen zhu*), a 1925 film written by Hou Yao and directed by Li Zeyuan for the Great Wall Film Company (Changcheng huapian gongsi). Hou Yao's views of modernity were shaped in part by the currents of the liberal May Fourth Movement, launched in 1919.[3] His movie gets off to a very fast start by providing a vivid and seemingly unproblematic portrait of an absolutely perfect modern marriage. What the audience appears to see is nothing less than a clear, though simple, definition of the modern marriage. The young husband, Yusheng, a white-collar accountant in an insurance company, is relaxing in his rather lavish Western-style living room dressed in a Western-style coat and tie. He is smoking a pipe and enjoying a newspaper. His stylish wife, Xiuzhen, is intelligent, nice-looking, beautifully dressed, and sporting a decidedly nontraditional hair style. Furthermore, the cosmopolitan, bourgeois husband and wife have a beautiful infant son.

What is wrong with this picture? Nothing. They have a lovely modern-style home. The two seem to love and respect each other. They seem to have chosen each other freely—in the modern way. Each has his or her own circle of friends. They seem to be quite comfortable in material terms and look like strong candidates for ongoing upward social mobility. In brief, the opening, set-up portion of this picture is designed to leave the clear impression that this modern marriage is solid, stable, and emotionally fulfilling. At no time in the film does Yusheng or Xiuzhen show even the slightest sexual attraction to a third party. They are utterly devoted to each other. The charming opening scenes strongly suggest that when it comes to the perfect modern marriage, there is a connection between conjugal bliss and material well-being. It is easy to like and emulate Yusheng and Xiuzhen. Nothing complicates their life as a couple: no meddlesome parents, no nosey in-laws, and no troublesome relatives.

Idyllic openings of this sort intentionally misrepresent. In truth, nothing is what it seems to be. Some naive viewers no doubt accepted this unrealistic portrait at face value. But less idealistic viewers were quite obviously being invited by the filmmakers to express a bit of skepticism. The picture is too good to be true. Does anyone really know a couple like Yusheng and Xiuzhen? Since real modern marriages are much more complicated and problem-ridden than the circumstances described at the outset of *A String of Pearls*, the filmmakers move quickly to reveal behind-the-scenes fragilities, uncertainties, and vulnerabilities.

Xiuzhen has been invited by a well-to-do former classmate to a lovely holiday party at a fancy home. Not only does she want to attend, she wants to dress in the modern, bourgeois way. She wants to wear a dazzling pearl necklace. For the first time, viewers are shown that our heroes are not really that well off. Xiuzhen, a bourgeois housewife, does not work. Yusheng's income is limited. There is no evidence that they have financial ties to family elders. These moderns are on their own, so they must be careful not to live beyond their means. There is certainly no money for a pearl necklace.

But Yusheng, the liberated New Culture husband, is sympathetic and wants to support Xiuzhen. He has a cultural investment in the way she looks. Both understand that their modern marriage must involve healthy doses of playacting. What is wrong with that? The filmmakers are asking the audience to be sympathetic to Xiuzhen and Yusheng. Why not support them? Modern husbands and wives should be able to go out alone in the evening to interact with friends. The pursuit of individual interests and individual social interactions outside the home is part of the definition of the modern marriage. Yusheng decides to borrow a pearl necklace from a friend who manages a jewelry shop. Xiuzhen is delighted and relieved. And she looks so beautiful.

Yusheng also readily agrees to engage in a bit of modern gender role reversal: he will stay home and take care of the baby while Xiuzhen goes out to party. How admirable. True, Yusheng's struggle in his role as surrogate "mother" provides comic relief at this point in the film. There is a bit of minor unease as the audience witnesses Yusheng trying to feed the baby and trying to put the infant to sleep. At one point he even drops the baby. Still, many moderns in the audience are on his side; he is giving it the old college try. He very much wants to be a modern husband, and the audience wants him to succeed. More conservative viewers likely asked themselves what Xiuzhen is doing out at night by herself and why her husband behaves like a mother. Differences in audience responses notwithstanding, what surfaces in this movie with great clarity are the many stresses and strains and pressures associated with maintaining the modern marriage.

Still, the audience is not prepared for a disaster. But disaster strikes nonetheless. A male guest at the party, another social-climbing playactor, notices Xiuzhen's pearl necklace. Xiuzhen lies and says her husband gave her the necklace. The male guest makes arrangements for a sneak thief to break into Yusheng and Xiuzhen's home that night under the cover of darkness to steal the necklace. The theft scene is of enormous interest because the audience actually gets to see the thief enter the bourgeois bedroom sanctuary of the modern couple. We actually view them lying in a large double bed under the covers. Something rather sacred has been violated by the invading stranger.

There is total panic in the morning when the necklace cannot be found. Yusheng hopes to solve the crisis by buying an identical replacement necklace, but he has no money. He tries to borrow money from friends—seemingly respectable middle-class people just like him—but they turn a harsh, cold shoulder. He is shocked and deflated. Then, in a touching effort to support his wife and protect his modern marriage and way of life, he embezzles funds from his company to buy a replacement necklace. The jewelry shop dealer is satisfied, but Yusheng's crime is discovered by a jealous coworker. He is arrested and sentenced to a multiyear prison term, much to the dismay of his wife and the film audience. Yusheng is a good man and loyal to his wife.

Xiuzhen's behavior is most interesting. She remains faithful to Yusheng while he is in prison, moves to a simple, low-cost hovel on the outskirts of the city, does a good job of raising their son, and takes in the clothes of others for cleaning and repair. No more urban glamour and upscale friends. A scary episode of catastrophic and overnight downward social mobility has unfolded before our eyes. And it looks like the downward mobility will be permanent. When Yusheng is released from prison, he has no job and no alternative but to live with his wife and son in the bare-bones hut. Disheveled and unsightly, he makes a feeble attempt to locate his old downtown friends, but all of them are embarrassed by his condition and refuse to acknowledge his presence.

The filmmakers could have decided to end *A String of Pearls* right here and thereby send a disturbing and depressing message about the fragility and illusory nature of the marital splendor enjoyed by Yusheng and Xiuzhen. But the film continues, and a very different message is delivered. First, in Yusheng's hour of need, a proletarian couple living next door (complete strangers who have never experienced fast-lane Shanghai) steps forward without explanation to find Yusheng a job in a modern factory, thus restoring his sense of dignity. The viewer is left to wonder whether *this* is the happy ending. The modern marriage will stay intact after all, but it will be a simpler and more down-to-earth proletarian modern marriage, not a materially and culturally splashy bourgeois modern marriage complete with big double beds, sofas, white-collar work, and pearl necklaces. Under the circumstances, this outcome would in fact have been a happy ending. There would be no second chance at a glitzy Shanghai existence, but the modern couple would have successfully dodged a bullet. An ending of this sort would have been agreeable, generous, and possible (even if implausible) in late-1920s Shanghai.

But the film goes on in ways that require one unconvincing coincidence after another. First, a white-collar accountant in the factory in which Yusheng labors is none other than the young dandy who hired the thief to steal the necklace. Second, the dandy is being blackmailed by the thief. Third, Yusheng accidentally stumbles upon one of the blackmail notes, follows the dandy to the payoff site where the thief attacks the dandy, and saves the dandy's life by giving the thief a trashing. The dandy's wife shows up in the hospital (where the dandy is recovering), wearing the stolen pearl

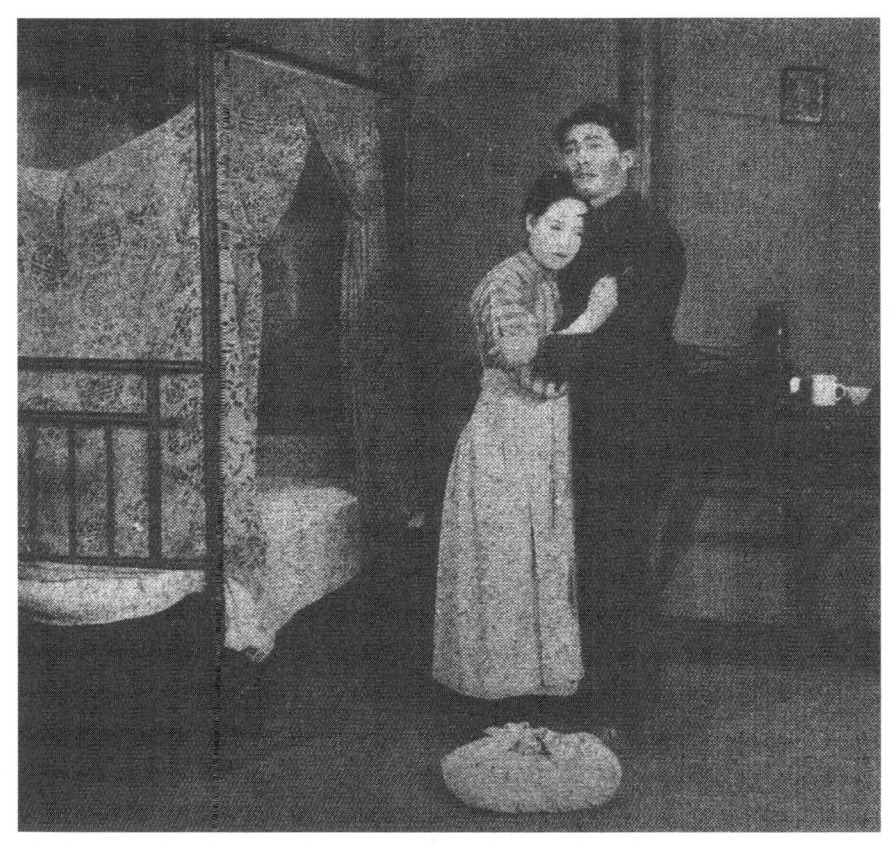

The devastated modern couple reunites after Yusheng's release from prison in *A String of Pearls* (1925, d. Li Zeyuan). China Film Archive

necklace. Since Yusheng does not know the dandy or his wife, he takes no notice of the necklace. But when Xiuzhen arrives, she recognizes her old classmate and the pearl necklace. The dandy promptly confesses everything and makes arrangements for Yusheng to get a good accounting job. Yusheng, Xiuzhen, and their son even get to move back into their bourgeois urban home (which the dandy has purchased for them!) and to dress once again in stylish middle-class clothing.

This second ending is, of course, preposterous and totally unconvincing. Few in the audience would have been taken in by a happy ending of this sort. The sudden downward social mobility of the couple is terrifying, and it has a ring of authenticity to it. The condition of middle-class families was indeed extremely fragile in 1920s Shanghai.[4] It is impossible to believe these people could miraculously recover everything they lost. How could anyone in the audience take this feel-good ending very seriously?

A *String of Pearls* is of course based directly on Guy de Maupassant's well-known short story "The Diamond Necklace."⁵ It is interesting to note, however, that the French original is far more critical, unforgiving, uncompromising, tragic, and, indeed, brutal than Hou Yao's extremely gentle Chinese screen adaptation. First, the downward social mobility of Maupassant's Xiuzhen character is permanent. Living in poverty, she and her husband are not allowed to recover what they have lost. Second, the diamond necklace borrowed and then lost in the French account was fake, not real. The French couple ruined their lives to beg and borrow enough money to buy a genuine diamond necklace to replace one that was worthless. In a word, the French story is far more poignant—and inflicts far more pain on protagonists and readers alike—than the Chinese version.

A *String of Pearls* is didactic, but it is not so clear what the moral message is. It would be wrong to argue that this film is a reactionary, anti–May Fourth, anti–New Culture text. The moral message quite clearly does not involve a denunciation of modern marriages. It is not a cultural warning inspired by Confucian ethical imperatives. The second ending may be utterly ridiculous and unrealistic, but it is interesting nonetheless for our purposes because it reconfirms the moral, ethical, social, economic, and cultural validity of modern marriages and those who seek them. Neither Yusheng nor Xiuzhen is ever cast in an unsympathetic or unfavorable light. Even when they exercise extremely poor judgment (such as Xiuzhen's desire for a one-night necklace and Yusheng's willingness to embezzle), the audience is on their side, understanding if not endorsing their every move. Further, the lovebirds remain faithful and loyal to one another through thick and thin. That is, their modern marriage has underlying substance and integrity. The didactic message of the film is that modern marriages of this sort are definitely worth pursuing, but that modern couples need to exercise caution and restraint when it comes to their material strivings. Newcomers to modernity must avoid getting carried away or going overboard.

Perhaps more important, there is a class dimension to the moral message. The filmmakers seem to be saying that modern love and modern marriage are intimately connected to social class and economic considerations. There is no such thing as a modern marriage divorced from economic and class realities. That is to say, there is not one single model of the modern marriage. Modern marriages will take on many forms, depending on a variety of material and cultural variables. Modern married couples need to function within the framework of class and economic constraints. In this respect, it is interesting that the only modern couple that comes forward to help Yusheng and Xiuzhen in their hour of greatest need is the proletarian modern couple. If it were not for their selfless assistance, Yusheng would not have gotten a job at the factory in the first place and the couple would not have recovered what they lost. The film does not deny that the proletarian couple constitutes one sort of model of the modern marriage, but it is clearly not the model being pursued by Yusheng, Xiuzhen, the filmmakers, and many in the film audience. Yusheng and Xiuzhen owe the proletarian couple a great deal, yet the moment our heroes are restored to their previous realm of bourgeois comfort, they completely forget about their proletarian friends. Indeed, they renew cordial relations with the very same people who either harmed them or ignored them when their middle-class marriage evaporated.

A String of Pearls constitutes a critique of the frantic material strivings of Shanghai moderns, but it is an exceedingly friendly critique. The material desires associated with the modern bourgeois marriage are affirmed here. If the didactic lesson was supposed to be that modern couples should refrain from conspicuous consumption and avoid making material desire a key element in their marital relationships, then the film should have ended with the couple appreciating the moral superiority of their temporary proletarian marriage and the righteousness of their new proletarian friends. But the fact is that they get everything back—and more. One wonders what they really learned from their harrowing experience. They seem fundamentally unchanged. All the film seems to be saying is, "Be careful!"

It is this fundamental affirmation of the modern bourgeois marriage that links *A String of Pearls* to decidedly modern New Culture and May Fourth currents and places it squarely in the anti-Confucian cultural camp. But if the film is so liberal, why do the filmmakers spend so much time scapegoating and bashing the key woman character—Xiuzhen? Surely this is a case of culturally conservative Confucian critics saying, "I told you so. This is what happens when time-honored ideas about the proper relationship between husbands and wives are violated." Does not the film explicitly blame the entire debacle on the vanity of modern women, women who are in a position to ruin their husbands and families?

The key to understanding this disquieting aspect of *A String of Pearls* is to remind ourselves that the modern marriage was nowhere defined in the film in utopian terms. With respect to bourgeois women, it is the prospect of *greater* individual freedom and liberation rather than *total, unqualified* freedom that is being offered. Precisely how much new freedom and liberation the modern woman gets is never stated with precision. This friendly critique of the modern marriage endorses modernity but points to dangers and temptations, especially in the material life of the modern couple. The harsh treatment of Xiuzhen is not inspired by premodern Confucian norms about the proper roles of wives but rather is consistent with modern, early-twentieth-century notions about the place of modern wives—primarily in the home, and not spending wildly. This is a modern critique of an apparently over-the-line modern marriage, not a "reactionary" Confucian critique. It is only when we assess the late 1920s by the new standards and expectations that took hold very slowly in the 1960s in Western middle-class societies that the bashing and scapegoating of Xiuzhen by the male screenwriter and male director seem hopelessly antimodern, even culturally reactionary. By the standards of the 1920s, the critique is well within the framework of emerging and evolving modernities.

OCEANS OF PASSION, HEAVY KISSING: LIJUN AND QIPING

If *A String of Pearls* is mainly about the material temptations that face modern married couples, then writer-director Xie Yunqing's sensational 1928 film titled *Oceans of Passion, Heavy Kissing* (*Qing hai zhong wen*)—produced at the Great China Film Company (Da Zhonghua baihe yingpian gongsi)— is about emotional and sexual transgressions and temptations. Modern husbands and wives have new material needs, but they also have new emotional needs. Once again, then, the limits of newly won freedoms and the boundaries of experimentation are being explored on screen.

One expects films made in China in the 1920s on the topic of extramarital sexual desire to deal with men who have strayed from the norms of marital fidelity commonly associated with the modern bourgeois marriage. What makes *Oceans of Passion, Heavy Kissing* so interesting is that it deals with an attractive young woman, Lijun, whose emotional and sexual needs are not being met by her faithful but boring husband, Qiping. Even his name ("Rising Peace") is boring. Furthermore, as in the case of Xiuzhen in *A String of Pearls*, the modern young woman is presented in an almost totally sympathetic light. The audience is invited to understand her needs. When it comes to sexual desire, how could any modern woman be satisfied with a weakling like Qiping?

Lijun's emotional unhappiness and sexual frustration have little to do with her material life. She and Qiping live in a comfortable, though not flashy, middle-class space. True, the film opens with a painful scene in which Qiping is fired from his white-collar office job due to bad work habits. But Lijun's passionate affair with a cosmopolitan college student predates by a significant degree Qiping's dismissal from his job.

Indeed, the dismissal scene is followed immediately by a fascinating sequence in which we see Lijun at home fantasizing about her lover, Mengtian ("Dreamy Days"). They write steamy love letters to one another and arrange secret liaisons in public parks and in Mengtian's trendy art-deco residence. We see Lijun speak to, caress, and kiss Mengtian's love letters. She even keeps a glossy photo of Mengtian hidden behind a prominently displayed photo of her husband. How exciting! How daring! Women viewers, one suspects, are being invited to participate vicariously in Lijun's adventure.

Nowhere is it said explicitly that Lijun and Mengtian have a sexual relationship, but it is implied throughout (and viewers could reasonably conclude) that they are sexual partners. For instance, almost every scene that takes place in Mengtian's residence centers near or actually on the large and alluring double bed that dominates his domestic space. When one recalls that as late as the 1950s it was impossible to show on American television a married couple anywhere near a large double bed, the centrality of Mengtian's inviting bed in 1928 in *Oceans of Passion, Heavy Kissing* is truly stunning. In this silent-era film, stereotypic notions of Chinese cultural prudishness are thrown out the window. Viewers are certainly not asked to approve of extramarital sex, but the strong impression is left that infidelity is not unusual in modern marriages in Shanghai. Indeed, it is important to notice that Lijun is definitely not being cast in the role of the predatory screen vamp, an unsavory villain who often figured prominently in Shanghai films of the 1930s (see chapter 2). Instead, Lijun is likable, sympathetic, and highly attractive. We want her to be happy.

Lijun's passionate fantasy world begins to unravel when Qiping intercepts one of Mengtian's love letters, dated July 1928, in which he proposes a "perfect, ideal" marriage. Qiping is further humiliated when he notices that Lijun has inadvertently placed the photo of Mengtian on top of rather than behind the framed photo of Qiping. Before Qiping can subject Lijun to physical abuse, she flees the home. Lijun shows up at Mengtian's residence only to learn that he is out with what appears to be one of his many fast-lane female friends. Hysterical, Lijun is heartbroken and wants to die.

A major difference between this film narrative and *A String of Pearls* is that while extended families appear nowhere in *A String of Pearls*, the larger, premodern patriarchal family structure is intimately involved in virtually all negotiations related to the various crises experienced by the modern married couple Lijun and Qiping. In brief, the search for the modern marriage takes place within a large and complicated social framework that includes the extended, premodern patriarchal formation. Indeed, for almost the entirety of the film, Qiping behaves like a weak, ineffective, incompetent, emasculated, sniveling mama's boy. He seems totally unprepared for a modern marriage. Time and again he is viewed crying—pathetically and uncontrollably.

Qiping's sturdy and formidable mother lives with the couple. No information is provided about his father. When she asks Qiping about his fight with his wife, he shows her the love letter and breaks down crying. It is the tough mother, not the weakling son, who goes over to confront Lijun's mother, another imposing senior female figure. The viewer sees right away that there is a difference between the two families: Qiping's mother represents basic middle-class comfort, but Lijun's mother is considerably more prosperous. Qiping's father is missing from the picture (and presumably dead), and Lijun's father, who surfaces late in the film as an apparent prototypical Confucian patriarch, is frequently absent from Shanghai on family business. Thus, it is the two senior women who battle over the wreckage of the modern marriage between Qiping and Lijun.

Lijun's mother swings into action by taking Lijun's side and summoning the playboy, Mengtian, to her house. Mengtian confesses to the affair and insists he wants to marry Lijun. Up until this point in the film, Mengtian has been characterized negatively as an irresponsible and superficial party animal, spiritually polluted by the worst of Western culture. He says he has a friend—a modern lawyer—who can arrange a modern divorce. The modern divorce, it seems, comes along with the modern marriage. Without consulting her husband, Lijun's mother agrees to the strategy. One suspects that divorce was not a common occurrence in Shanghai in the 1920s; thus it is remarkable that the divorce is agreed to so casually by the principal parties in *Oceans of Passion, Heavy Kissing*. Indeed, the scene in the lawyer's office is quite memorable. Qiping's mother continues to infantilize him. "Your wife has deserted you," she says, "so why all the tears? She is a cheap hussy, and people like her never change." Qiping's mom has no interest in forcing Lijun to come back. All she is interested in is getting back the money the family spent on the wedding! When it is time for Qiping to sign the divorce papers, he breaks down again and cannot do it. So his mother signs for him. By contrast, when it is time for Lijun to sign, she hesitates, showing some signs of pity for Qiping, but finally signs when her hand is enveloped and guided by Mengtian's.

Lijun and Mengtian now constitute yet another type of modern couple. Curiously, however, they never get married. Instead, Mengtian asks Lijun to move in with him (*tong ju*). Lijun is a bit nervous, but her mother does not object, and we know nothing about Mengtian's family. He swears he will change his ways. No more philandering. He calls her Honey. "With a fairy like you beside me, I would never think of leaving you and reentering the hectic life again," he asserts. The scenes that follow, all of which dwell on Lijun's modern emotional and sexual desires, and all of which take place in the vicinity of Mengtian's huge bed, are nothing short of riveting, especially when one recalls that *Oceans of Passion, Heavy Kissing* was made in 1928, more than eighty years ago. First, Mengtian offers Lijun alcohol and cigarettes, both of which she reluctantly accepts. Her days of boredom with Qiping seem to be over. Then Mengtian suggests that Lijun put on some smart and fashionable clothing. For reasons that are left unexplained, Mengtian's wardrobe is full of sexy women's clothing. Standing right beside Mengtian's big bed and in full view of an appreciative Mengtian, Lijun performs what can only be described as a partial striptease, as she removes her old clothing in favor of something new. "If the sky falls down," a delighted Mengtian blurts out, "I'll still be true to you."

Mengtian (*left*) and Lijun (*right*) experiment with cohabitation following her divorce in *Oceans of Passion, Heavy Kissing* (1928, d. Xie Yunqing). China Film Archive

Meanwhile, Qiping is seen alone and (of course) crying. Thanks to trick photography, he fantasizes that Lijun is still on his small bed, but soon the seductive image of Lijun is replaced by the threatening image of Mengtian. Tears continue to flow as Qiping rips up an old wedding photo.

The second part of *Oceans of Passion, Heavy Kissing*, the "resolution" portion, is not nearly as interesting visually and thematically as the first, set-up portion. The narrative fast-forwards three months. Presumably Lijun has been living an emotionally satisfying modern life with Mengtian. No evidence is offered to contradict this conclusion. Nor is there any evidence that Mengtian has been disloyal or reverted to his old "polluted" ways. But suddenly, the older and larger patriarchal order reaches out again to intervene. That is, the premodern form is seen in active negotiation and exchange with the modern mode.

Lijun's prosperous father appears on the scene for the first time. It is his fiftieth birthday and tradition demands an elaborate and sumptuous celebration. The audience learns that he was never told about his daughter's modern divorce and the new arrangement with Mengtian. Thus, he expects to see Qiping among the birthday celebrants. Lijun's mother frets about what to do, especially because Mengtian will be among the guests. She finally decides to invite Qiping, in hopes that he and Mengtian will keep their mouths shut so that the patriarch can leave Shanghai once again before discovering the truth. Qiping decides to attend the gathering, even though his mother strenuously disagrees. Worried that Qiping will not attend, Lijun's mother has told the old man that Qiping is ill and will most likely not be able to attend. She also buys a gift for the patriarch in Qiping's name.

As in the case of A *String of Pearls*, the conclusion of *Oceans of Passion, Heavy Kissing* is quite simply preposterous and utterly unconvincing. Lijun is deeply impressed by Qiping's displays of respect for her father. The father is surprised to see Qiping. "I thought you were sick," he says. Qiping has pawned some clothing to buy a gift. "I already have a gift from you," the old man says, "so why is there a second gift?" Then Qiping toasts the

Bewildered patriarch (*center*) expresses his disapproval of both daughter (*right*) and wife (*left*) in *Oceans of Passion, Heavy Kissing* (1928, d. Xie Yunqing). China Film Archive

patriarch multiple times. Moved by these expressions, Lijun asks Mengtian to go home ahead of her.

The patriarch requests a private meeting with Qiping later in the day. Qiping confesses everything, saying, "I am no longer your son-in-law." "Nonsense," the patriarch insists. The patriarch then leads a family delegation to confront Lijun and Mengtian. But Mengtian is not there. Why? This ultra-Westernized urban marriage-wrecker has been ordered home by his own parents. Their telegram to him, which we get to see line by line, says that since he is accomplishing nothing in Shanghai except wasting his time, having fun, and spending their money, he will have to suspend his studies and come home, where an arranged marriage has been set up for him. He immediately and obediently runs off with his tail between his legs. So much for the thoroughly modern Mengtian! Even he is far from being a one-dimensional character.

My argument is that *Oceans of Passion, Heavy Kissing* is essentially different from *A String of Pearls* in that *A String of Pearls* is mainly about material and economic aspects of the modern marriage, while *Oceans of Passion, Heavy Kissing* is mainly about emotional and sexual aspects of modern marriage. Still, it should not be assumed that the characters appearing in *Oceans of Passion, Heavy Kissing* show no concern about their material world. Issues of social class difference and access to money and resources are still important considerations. Mengtian scurries back to his parents because they are threatening to cut off the flow of money that funds his provocative cultural and social life. Qiping leads a fairly comfortable middle-class life, but he has lost his job and the divorce has cost him his access to Lijun's prosperous family. Viewers are allowed to believe that Qiping has never stopped loving Lijun, but it is also highly likely that his energetic cultivation of her father's affections is motivated at least in part by the ongoing prosperity of his ex-wife's family. Lijun is the one who seems to dwell exclusively on the emotional and sexual promises of the modern marriage.

When the family shows up at Mengtian's residence, they find Lijun lying unconscious on Mengtian's big bed. What is wrong with her? No one knows. A doctor is summoned. Suddenly there is a mysterious, modern pathology to consider. Will she be able to rally? The patriarch loudly asserts that his irresponsible wife—and she alone—is responsible for this ugly debacle. Of course the patriarch sends for Qiping to save the day. Again, Qiping's mother is stubbornly opposed, but in a rare act of defiance, he runs off to Mengtian's place. Miraculously, an agreement is reached between the patriarch and Qiping that sends Lijun back to Qiping's home. No one consults Lijun. The two mothers are advised by the patriarch to make up and "forget the past."

When Lijun regains consciousness, only to discover herself back in Qiping's home and small bed, she instantly sees all the errors of her ways and runs out to the waterfront determined to commit suicide. Qiping chases after her and at water's edge a sudden and complete reconciliation takes place. Despite his mother's view that Lijun could never be forgiven for her transgressions, Qiping forgives her. "Now you are repentant. It makes me love you all the more," Qiping gushes. For her part, Lijun laments, "Yes, I must atone for my sin."

Although this film is different in many important respects from *A String of Pearls*, it has much in common with the earlier work. For instance, despite the absurd and utterly unbelievable endings, the themes of repentance, forgiveness, and redemption in modern marriages are pronounced in both films. In the first film, material desire leads to disaster, while in the second, emotional desire results in ruin. But in both cases the modern marriage is salvaged when excessive, over-the-line desires are recognized and reigned in. In the real world of modern marriage in Shanghai, repentance, forgiveness, and redemption were probably much more difficult to achieve. In some cultures, the penalty for women who commit adultery is death. But the themes of repentance, forgiveness, and redemption are essential ingredients in films of this sort, because modern marriages continue to be steadfastly endorsed despite the various modern transgressions and betrayals that complicate them.

Modern women are scapegoated and bashed in these two films not because the filmmakers are anti–New Culture reactionaries opposed to the rise of new, modern women, but because modern marriage standards of the 1920s imposed severe limits on the conduct of women. In brief, blaming women for the problems that afflict the modern marriage is entirely consistent with modern international norms eighty years ago during the post–May Fourth era and does not constitute a conservative or reactionary attack on bourgeois modernity.

True, the larger, preexisting patriarchy plays a pivotal role in *Oceans of Passion, Heavy Kissing*, but this type of intervention and meddling was no doubt part of the harsh and complicated cultural realities faced by modern couples in Shanghai in the 1920s. Older forms and norms are quite clearly seen in negotiation with modern forms. Give-and-take ensues. Qiping is dominated by his old-fashioned mother, but he finally develops a backbone and rejects her advice in the end. Lijun's mother is a major actor in the crisis, but she supports her emotionally starved daughter, agrees to the modern-style divorce, and consents to the cohabitation arrangement with Mengtian.

Some might protest by arguing that the ability of the patriarch to engineer a reunion at the end of the film is a clear indication of the triumph of antimodern Confucian ethics in this film. But even here, the outcome depends on the willingness of the patriarch to sanction the possibility of forgiveness and redemption for a woman who has cheated on her husband, abandoned him, divorced him, and entered into a relationship of cohabitation with an unmarried man. More important, it is not necessary to take the preposterous happy ending seriously at all. The last-minute activities of the conservative patriarch are gratuitous, incredible, and absolutely unconvincing. It is the first two parts of the film that are socially and culturally engaging, not the final formulaic portion. The didactic message of this film is not "Avoid modern marriages." The didactic message is much better conveyed in the amusing English title of the movie provided by the filmmakers: *Don't Change Your Husband*. Interestingly, the official English title has nothing whatsoever to do with the sensational Chinese original: *Qing hai zhong wen*.

ORPHAN IN THE SNOW: CHUNMEI AND DAPENG

It is very difficult to classify *Orphan in the Snow* (*Xue zhong gu chu*), directed by the influential Zhang Huimin in 1929 for the China Drama Film Company (Hua ju yingpian gongsi), except to say that it centers on a very unhappily married woman, Chunmei; it highlights her multiple flights from abuse and oppression; and it features her ongoing quest for freedom and liberation in the post–New Culture era. Unlike both *A String of Pearls* and *Oceans of Passion, Heavy Kissing*, Zhang's brutally violent, even sadistic, film makes little or no effort to package itself as a "feels-and-looks-like-realism" melodrama. Indeed, one is tempted to classify *Orphan in the Snow* as a terrifying horror film. It is an urban film that largely takes place in an unrecognizable, nonurban fantasyland that looks more like Transylvania than Shanghai. From the first scene to the last, Chunmei's life amounts to hell on earth. One of the early inter-titles asserts that the beautiful Chunmei is "too weak to defend herself," but nothing could be further from the truth. This may be a horror film, but our heroine fights and resists from beginning to end, and in so doing functions as an inspiration to young women who want modern change.

Orphan in the Snow opens with a totalistic attack on what the viewer can plainly see is a traditional, Confucian-style marriage ceremony. Chunmei, the bride, has never seen her groom. Her parents, we are told, are dead. The marriage has been arranged. The goofy groom, Langen, is portrayed as nothing more than a fool, a laughingstock, and a buffoon. No respect whatever is shown for customary culture in this crude caricature. The only question is how Chunmei can achieve modern-style freedom. She is not Ibsen's Nora. She is a frightened and brutalized object of exchange in a decidedly premodern cultural arrangement.

As soon as they enter the traditional-style bridal chamber, the clumsy and ignorant groom wants to consummate the marriage. He wants sex. She declines and continues to hold out for many days. The groom, another infant-like mama's boy, complains to both his mother and his father's second wife, a concubine. They step in to pressure Chunmei. Though the concubine is described as "an intermediary between old and new ways," her approach is cruel and brutish. When Chunmei says, "No, I'd rather die than comply with his desires," the second wife beats her and subjects her to physical abuse that is quite literally hard to watch. It is relentless and vicious.

The second phase of the film begins when Chunmei (on the verge of suicide) takes flight. She wanders around in the wilderness and then collapses on some railroad tracks. She is saved from an oncoming train by the film's male protagonist, Dapeng, a handsome young man. If Chunmei's husband is the stuff of cultural backwardness and feudalism, Dapeng is a prime example of the best of modernity. He drives a shiny new car, he wears nice-looking Western clothing, and he has modern values. An intertitle describes Dapeng as "liberal and able to smooth out difficulties for others." When he learns that Chunmei is "homeless," he offers to bring her to his house to work as a servant. Chunmei conceals her recent past and the fact that she is legally married, and agrees to the offer.

At first glance, Dapeng's home seems like the complete opposite of Chunmei's old "feudal" home. It has a bourgeois look, not unlike the comfortable home featured in *A String of Pearls*. Dapeng lives with his mother, father, and two sisters. At first, Chunmei meets the mother and one of the sisters, both of whom seem supportive and welcome her with open arms. Their modernity is reflected in the fact that they enjoy listening to jazz on their ultramodern phonograph.

But the elder sister, puffing away on cigarettes, jealous of her brother's interest in the waif, and suspicious of Chunmei's intentions, turns out to be a monster. Chunmei, haunted by memories of her previous life, is not a very good servant. She is constantly making mistakes and breaking dishes and vases. The elder sister torments her with verbal and physical abuse that is worse than the torment she suffered in her feudal home. Again, the violence is prolonged and painful to view. Clearly, Dapeng and Chunmei are developing bonds of affection, but somehow Dapeng is unaware of the abuse that rains down on the young woman every day.

A crisis ensues when Dapeng's father returns home after a long absence. One afternoon, the whole family is outdoors having fun in the family garden. Chunmei helps by transporting water from a small pond. Dapeng tries to help her on the grounds that the water bucket is too heavy for her to handle. They sit down by the pond to rest, and a fascinating courtship scene follows. Dapeng puts his arm around Chunmei. He touches, caresses, and even fondles her hair and face. "Chunmei," he blurts out in the English inter-title, "out of pity for you, I seem to love you." The Chinese version of the inter-title is not quite so frank. The Chinese characters state that Dapeng finds Chunmei to be "lovable" (*keai*). "The hair on your head," he proclaims, "is as fair as that of the Westerners." This tender scene is designed to win the support of the audience, and in all likelihood, it did. After all that trouble, Chunmei deserves a break. And our handsome, modern, Westernized hero is there to show her the way to modernity.

But this is a horror film, and this fleeting moment of bourgeois bliss cannot be sustained. The mean sister, who cannot stand the idea of a mixed marriage (involving two different social classes), spots the innocent lovers, and summons her father and the rest of the family to see the scandalous scene with their own eyes. "Brother and Chunmei are making love," she howls in the English inter-title. Again the Chinese version is slightly different: there she says that they *"jiang qing hua"* ("engage in sweet/intimate talk"). The father says nothing to his son, choosing instead to scapegoat the young woman. "Chunmei, how dare you!" he yells. The father forbids Chunmei to have any further direct contact with Dapeng—though viewers know she had nothing to do with initiating the flirtation.

Chunmei remains in the employ of the bourgeois family, but she mopes about listlessly most of the time. The final eruption takes place on the auspicious occasion of the Lunar New Year celebration. Dapeng is away. While serving the meal, Chunmei trips and drops all the food on the floor. To the delight of the mean sister, the father promptly kicks Chunmei out of the house on a cold rainy night.

When Dapeng comes home, he is shocked to learn that his beloved Chunmei has been expelled. In an extraordinary scene of rebellion, far more militant than the instance in *Oceans of Passion, Heavy Kissing* when Qiping rejects the pleas of his mother, Dapeng confront his father: "Why haven't you pity on the poor, driving out such a helpless one?" Dapeng's mother is shocked at his disrespectful behavior. "Don't you know better than to talk to your Pa like that?" she asks. It is clear at this point that Dapeng is prioritizing love and emotion to the exclusion of almost everything else, including his material well-being. He is prepared to break from his family. "At all costs," he fumes, "I've to get her back. It's my desire to have it so, no matter what happens." His mother and one sister seem to be on his side, but he storms out of the house nonetheless—without any idea of where poor Chunmei has headed.

The final, and most horrific, portion of *Orphan in the Snow* starts out quite literally in the snow in a Swiss Alps–like setting. The viewer no longer cares that this mysterious place could not possibly be anywhere near Shanghai! Chunmei, clad only in skimpy household garments, wanders aimlessly in the mountains and finally collapses in a snow field where she has no chance to survive. Miraculously, she is discovered by Dapeng. This would have been a good place to end the film.

Instead, the picture moves even further in the direction of the horror, gothic, and fantasy genres. In fact, the movie comes full circle. At the very beginning of the film, during the feudal wedding scene, a pack of young guys dressed in Western attire takes great delight in ogling the young bride and mercilessly teasing her foolish groom. One of the young dandies, Xiaodi, is said to be "always crazy over a skirt." These dandies are a variation of Mengtian, the negative bourgeois character in *Oceans of Passion, Heavy Kissing*. Here, however, instead of exiting the narrative, by incredible coincidence the annoying "mods" reappear in the third and final portion of the film. They are hiking in the mountains and spot Dapeng giving comfort to a distressed Chunmei. Xiaodi, the leader, notices that Chunmei is the very same skirt he had his eye on at the wedding. When Chunmei and Dapeng decline Xiaodi's invitation to warm up in his nearby villa, a gang of eight men abducts Chunmei and throws Dapeng off a cliff into a lake.

The film comes full circle in the sense that Chunmei, desperate for freedom, liberation, and true love, finds herself in a prison-like environment once again. As it was in the beginning of the film, the issue is sex. "Be mine," Xiaodi says, "and you'll have enough to satisfy your wants as well as a respectable spouse." Again, Chunmei resists. A servant is instructed by Xiaodi to dress Chunmei in fashionable clothes and to "persuade her to do anything according to my wish." Before long the servant informs Xiaodi, "By no means will she comply with your wish." In fact, Chunmei starts smashing dishes and furniture and even slaps Xiaodi's face a few times for good measure.

Xiaodi's gothic villa comes complete with a dungeon. Chunmei, he orders, will be placed in one of the cells, along with two huge, poisonous lizards, until she agrees to Xiaodi's carnal demands. The audience is repulsed by the sight of the ugly lizards crawling closer and closer to the lovely Chunmei. Fortunately, our handsome hero Dapeng pulls himself out of the lake, finds his way to the villa, and manages to vanquish the eight dandies in the sort of extended martial arts scene for which director Zhang Huimin was known.[6] Indeed, Xiaodi ends up in the cell with the poisonous lizards moving up his body toward his face. He begs for mercy, but Chunmei and Dapeng just laugh.

Because the final portion of *Orphan in the Snow* is so fantastically ludicrous, no one is really expected to take the ending seriously. Still, it is interesting that the film does not just end with Chunmei's apparent victory in her quest for freedom and love. Though it is crystal clear that they will soon enter into a modern marriage (despite Dapeng's father's certain opposition), she is given one final speech. Looking into Dapeng's eyes, she coos, "You have for my sake braved dangers and the storm, taking no heed for your personal safety, and in this I am greatly affected by your love and henceforth am quite willing to submit to your commands." What?

Unlike the modern women in *A String of Pearls* and *Oceans of Passion, Heavy Kissing*, Chunmei has done nothing "wrong" by modern standards. She is not blamed for material or emotional excesses. She is the perfect victim. Thus it is all the more surprising when, in the end, she voluntarily submits herself to her modern love interest. Her modern happiness—both material and emotional—is entirely in the hands of her male savior. The audience is happy for her and the resolution of the film is satisfactory only because the audience, like Chunmei, has full trust in Dapeng, the only modern male figure in the three films under review here who is completely flawless. Chunmei's dependence on Dapeng, her submission to him, and her failure to push further for independence and freedom is definitely not presented in a critical or skeptical light in this film. According to the logic of the film, the ending of the film is not inconsistent with the cultural contours of modernity.

This raises the issue of the relationship between occupational independence and modern marriage. None of the three women in these films who desire modernity and strive for the modern marriage has occupational skills, a job, or independent means of support. The three case studies are quite different, but in all three the modern marriage is pursued well within the framework of the modern wife's economic dependence on the modern husband. All three women, Xiuzhen, Lijun, and Chunmei, are or will be stay-at-home housewives and homemakers. This does not mean that they are confined to the internal space of modern domesticity. On the contrary, their modern condition allows for considerable movement outside the domestic space, so long as they do not go out of bounds in their material or emotional lives.

The fact that these modern women do not have economic independence is not at all frowned upon by the filmmakers. The audience is asked to accept the reality of a modern marriage that does not usually come with professional or occupational roles for modern women. Again, one could argue that the ultimate submissiveness of the three women constitutes a victory for the premodern patriarchy, and that these films have nothing at all in common with progressive social causes and modern marital arrangements. But it is also possible to argue that the ending of *Orphan in the Snow* is consistent with global standards of modern marriage relationships in the 1920s. The film is saying that it is possible for women to be happily involved in a modern marriage without benefit of employment or economic independence. No doubt many in the audience in 1928 would have agreed.

THE AMBIGUITIES OF THE MODERN MARRIAGE

When we think about early Chinese feature filmmaking, we sometimes accept without adequate reflection the vague but politically charged suggestion that nothing very modern or socially progressive happened on Shanghai movie screens until 1931. Only after Japanese forces seized control of Northeast China in 1931 and attacked Shanghai itself in 1932 did filmmakers connect to the enlightening social currents associated with the New Culture Movement of 1915 and the May Fourth Movement of 1919. Before 1931 Shanghai filmmakers made martial arts films, costume dramas, and lightweight—often conservative or reactionary—butterfly dramas that held China back in the global community. According to more pointed versions of this account, it was not until leftists and agents of the Communist Party got involved in the Shanghai film world that a real connection could be made to the New Culture and May Fourth movements and to "progressive" causes.[7] In other words, leftists and Party cultural activists get all the credit for anything progressive that appeared on the Chinese silver screen. Scholars seriously interested in modernity should emphasize the films of the 1930s, not the 1920s.[8]

As this chapter on film representations of the modern marriage shows, we ignore the decidedly modern thrusts of 1920s films at our own peril. It is true, of course, that for those who want to focus on the film artifacts themselves, it is much easier to carry out research on the 1930s for the simple reason that there are many more films of the 1930s available for viewing. Still, the notion that entertainment films of the 1920s failed to address and endorse New Culture and May Fourth themes needs to be challenged. When it comes to domestic social and cultural issues, the New Culture and May Fourth tides included important anarchist, socialist, and Marxist currents, but the main tendency, especially in the realm of new social relationships, including all-important marital relations, was liberalism and liberal notions of modernity. It is not the least bit surprising, then, that highly sympathetic and supportive treatments of the modern marriage were prominent in popular feature films made in the 1920s.

A String of Pearls, *Oceans of Passion*, *Heavy Kissing*, and *Orphan in the Snow* are enticing artifacts not simply because each addresses the vicissitudes of the modern marriage. This grouping of three films is suggestive because one can detect thematic patterns that connect the trio. First, all three films clearly approve of and even promote modern-style marriages. An underlying assumption is that such marriages were superior to premodern marriages and, hence, better suited to urban people's needs at the beginning of the twentieth century. Second, no single model or single overarching definition of the modern marriage is articulated. Instead, the modern marriage is shown to be a moving target and a work in progress, with many variations and forms.

In this sense, these three films are not heavy-handed works of propaganda that peddle a one-dimensional truth about the modern condition.[9] In fact, the films strongly suggest the opposite. The viewer gets the impression that an exciting and open-ended adventure of exploration is under way. The characters are often presented in highly exaggerated ways, but there is significant variation among them. Among the men, Qiping is weak but Dapeng is strong, while Yusheng is somewhere in between. Among the culturally modern men, Mengtian represents the worst of the West, but Dapeng represents the very best, with Yusheng and Qiping occupying space in the middle. Westernized people are not singled out and scapegoated in a one-dimensional way in these films. With respect to premodern cultural traditions, Qiping has ties to the world of custom, while Yusheng seems to be largely independent of it. There is similar variation among the women. Xiuzhen behaves like a modern "material" woman disconnected from the old patriarchy. Lijun is an emotionally starved, modern free spirit who still has close links to a traditional family structure. Chunmei has terrifying encounters with the worst of both customary and modern cultural arrangements before being rescued by the best of the modern.

What we see, then, are individuals and couples who are confused by the complexities of the modern marriage. Multiple variables are in play as these young people actively negotiate with their cultural and social environments. The subject is new-style marriage relations. But issues of social class, income, and material life must be taken into account as the couples seek to shape their lives. Notions of marital bliss are linked in various ways to material abundance. The subject is the modern marriage, but the likable couples often have no choice but to interact with and negotiate with premodern forces and dynamics. The subject is modern change, but issues of gender arise once it is clear that in the early twentieth century, modern arrangements placed multiple restrictions and constraints on the newly won freedoms of women. The impositions of these boundaries, like the phenomenon of the submission of wives to husbands, had everything to do with modernity itself and should not be confused with premodern boundaries.

These films were not screened for a single audience; they were screened for diverse audiences. The situations of the people in the audience were as complicated and diverse as the situations of the characters in the films. There was something for everyone. The use of both Chinese-language and English-language inter-titles suggests that there was a clear market for these films (and the issues they addressed) outside Shanghai and outside China. The English inter-titles were not intended for American or British viewers, but rather for the millions of Chinese who lived in British-controlled areas of Asia, people who were Chinese but whose grasp of written Chinese was perhaps not as good as their control of English. These people, who lived in Singapore and elsewhere in Southeast Asia, were also interested in problems associated with the modern marriage. Differences between the Chinese and English inter-titles might have reflected differences between the experiences of viewers in Shanghai and viewers in Southeast Asia.

Indeed, one is tempted to argue that these "modern social issue" films of the 1920s were not national texts at all. In this sense they differ from the best-known films of the 1930s. Many of the celebrated films of the 1930s were overtly nationalistic. That is, they were consciously seeking to promote nationalistic consciousness and identity among film audiences that varied according to native place, culture, gender, class, age, and Chinese-dialect usage. Many of the most carefully studied films of the 1930s were explicit national allegories. They might have been about family, but the family unit was often an obvious stand-in for China.

By contrast, the films of the 1920s under review here were thoroughly modern, but they made little effort to function as national expressions. In fact, China is nowhere mentioned in any of these three films. These films were clearly modern in thematic thrust but operated as subnational cultural expressions. They contain no references whatever to the national political context of the late 1920s. But they do contain countless references to the complicated local and subnational cultural and social contexts of the late 1920s. In an important sense, China is not important in these films. Shanghai is important. Modern cities that happen to be in China are important. We may not learn much about China in these moving pictures, but we learn a great deal about the problems encountered by modern married couples in major metropolitan centers—centers that were more closely connected to the region and the modern world than they were to most of what constituted China in 1928.

These films are usefully viewed as subnational cultural artifacts, but somewhat paradoxically, they were also transnational. The films were not screened in very many places in China, but they were screened in Malaya, the Philippines, Singapore, and other places in Southeast Asia. The couples we see in these films had a lot more in common with couples in urban Southeast Asia than they had with couples in rural China. The films were successful and relevant at the subnational and transnational levels precisely because they were not about national identity and national consciousness. They were about the early stages of modern social transformations and thus were appealing to moderns throughout the region. The cultural globalization of which we speak so often today is not new. It was a fact of life long ago in Asia.

In many respects, these early—one might even say humanistic—film treatments of the modern marriage are concerned with modern temptations and modern seductions that come along with modern freedoms. No promises are made. Freedom means making choices. Some choices are good, some are bad. Many of our modern adventurers are shown to be suffering, but it is important to note that they are often complicit in the making of their own misery.

These films may be very old, but, curiously, they have a remarkable degree of contemporary relevance. After a long Maoist interlude in which conspicuous consumption, extramarital affairs, egoistic self-expression, and divorce were politically dangerous and thus not commonplace, starting in the mid-1980s metropolitan China once again discovered the subnational and transnational modern marriage, complete with all its ambiguities, stresses, and strains. As they did in the 1920s, young, modern, global married couples struggled with new freedoms, choices, and temptations, all of which involved complicated webs of negotiation.

Then and now, forgiveness, redemption, and reconciliation are by no means guaranteed to transgressors who have crossed sometimes invisible boundaries. No one is fooled by the artificial happy endings of *A String of Pearls*, *Oceans of Passion*, *Heavy Kissing*, and *Orphan in the Snow*. What will happen to our couples? How might new economic misfortunes affect the marriage of Xiuzhen and Yusheng? Will the "new" Qiping really be able to fulfill the emotional and sexual needs of Lijun? Will Dapeng get tired of Chunmei and will Chunmei forever be "quite willing to submit" to Dapeng's commands? What will happen if any of these modern women decides to get a job? Stay tuned.

NOTES

1. Cheng Jihua ed., *Zhongguo dianying fazhan shi* (Beijing: Zhongguo dianying chubanshe, 1998), 1:522–635.

2. Zhongguo dianying ziliaoguan, ed., *Zhongguo dianying ziliaoguan guanzang yingpian mulu* (Beijing: Zhongguo dianying ziliaoguan, 1995), 1–2.

3. Zhang Zhen, *An Amorous History of the Silver Screen: Shanghai Cinema, 1896–1937* (Chicago: University of Chicago Press, 2005), 159.

4. See Marie-Claire Bergere, *The Golden Age of the Chinese Bourgeoisie, 1911–1937* (Cambridge, UK: Cambridge University Press, 1989) for a discussion of some aspects of the vulnerabilities of the Chinese bourgeoisie.

5. Guy de Maupassant, "The Diamond Necklace," in *The Complete Short Stories of Guy de Maupassant* (New York: P. F. Collier and Son, 1903), 28–33.

6. Zhang Zhen. *Amorous History of the Silver Screen*, 214–15.

7. Cheng Jihua, *Zhongguo dianying fazhan shi*, 1:171–515. Cheng emphasizes the theme of Communist Party leadership of left-wing and progressive tendencies in the film world after 1931.

8. Two recent studies that focus on and perhaps unintentionally privilege the left-wing film movement of 1932–1937 are Laikwan Pang, *Building a New China in Cinema: The Chinese Left-Wing Cinema Movement, 1932–1937* (Lanham, Md.: Rowman & Littlefield, 2002); and Vivian Shen, *The Origins of Left-Wing Cinema in China, 1932–37* (New York: Routledge, 2005).

9. The films are consistent with the impression left by Leo Ou-fan Lee that people in Shanghai were experimenting with various forms of modernity in the early twentieth century. No single mode had surfaced to dominate in this early stage. Leo Ou-fan Lee, *Shanghai Modern: The Flowering of a New Urban Culture in China, 1930–1945* (Cambridge, Mass.: Harvard University Press, 1999).

2
The Theme of Spiritual Pollution in Chinese Films of the 1930s

The political campaigns launched by the Chinese Communist Party in 1981, 1983, 1987, and 1989 to eradicate foreign "spiritual pollution," a noxious by-product of "bourgeois liberalization," can be interpreted in a variety of ways. It is apparent, for example, that in each case the leadership was looking for a way to account for corruption, lawlessness, disorder, alienation, cynicism, and other nagging social problems without having to point to the failings of the Party itself. In the political realm, these campaigns provided opportunities for cultural conservatives to gain temporary strategic advantages over reformers inside the Party who, like their Eastern European counterparts in the 1980s, were eager to dismantle the traditional Stalinist cultural system. These initiatives, some of which were comical and some of which were deadly, can also be viewed as manifestations of Chinese nationalism, as products of the modernization process in a non-Western environment, and as attempts by the Party/state to achieve greater social control.

In spite of the novelty of the terms *jingshen wuran* (spiritual pollution) and *zichanjieji ziyouhua* (bourgeois liberalization) and the uniqueness of the social, economic, and political conditions that spawned these ideological and cultural crusades in the 1980s, the image of China as the innocent victim of foreign spiritual pollution is neither new nor the brainchild of post-Mao Chinese Communist theoreticians and propagandists. On several occasions during the late Qing, Republican, and socialist periods, political and intellectual elites sought to mobilize (and manipulate) ordinary people by issuing grave and sometimes hysterical warnings about the dangers of alien cultural contamination. For well over a century, it has been politically expedient to blame China's problems on the pernicious influence of foreign culture and the culture of the capitalist West in particular. Those who claimed to be protecting the Chinese people from Western spiritual pollution usually presented themselves as defenders of a vaguely defined but morally vibrant Chinese cultural essence. According to the logic of extreme elements, to embrace Western culture was to engage in cultural treason.

Of course, during the years of New Culture influence in the 1910s and 1920s, many defiant young Chinese intellectuals actively promoted the influx of Western culture. These radical iconoclasts claimed that outmoded traditional values and institutions had failed to meet the modern political and social needs of China. But Westernized New Culture radicals had great difficulty finding an effective way to communicate their message to the many who were disinclined to let go of conservative cultural moorings. By the early 1930s, during a period of neoconservative backlash, New Culture and May Fourth cosmopolitans were attacked from both the right and left by polemicists who argued that Western culture was polluting the minds of young people. May Fourth liberals paid little attention to such charges, but their critics were determined to find a forceful method of popularizing ideas about the dangers of alien spiritual contamination. The booming film industry, long ignored by bookish May Fourth intellectuals, soon attracted the attention of antiliberal enthusiasts. Ironically, it was the opponents of Western spiritual pollution who were among the first intellectuals in China to appreciate the extraordinary power of this thoroughly Western mass medium.

In no sense were the various efforts to raise questions about the threat of cultural contamination coordinated by a particular group or political party. Many groups and individuals, including some who were on opposing sides in the bitter civil war, participated in the drive. Indeed, the assault on Western bourgeois culture in China in the early 1930s was part of a global trend initiated in the West itself in the 1920s by fascists and Stalinists alike. Many films produced in China in the period between 1931 and 1935 were inspired by these developments but are distinctive nonetheless because they discuss the issue of bourgeois spiritual pollution in a non-European cultural environment. Furthermore, these films are significant cultural artifacts because, compared to May Fourth fiction, they involve a clearer intersection of elite and popular culture. An analysis of these works tells us almost nothing about the complex realities of Western bourgeois culture in the early twentieth century. But it does throw fascinating light on how those who were hostile to New Culture cosmopolitanism employed a mass cultural medium to fashion a simplistic but highly influential caricature of Western culture. Moreover, this caricature is remarkably similar to the stereotypical treatments of Western culture contained in a number of important Chinese films of the 1980s, another moment when calls for openness to Western culture threatened the interests of the ruling elite.

PEACH BLOSSOM WEEPS TEARS OF BLOOD: THE BUTTERFLY PROTOTYPE

By 1933, the young director Bu Wancang, a native of Anhui, was working closely with Tian Han and other members of a small leftist film group led by Xia Yan.[1] But his *Peach Blossom Weeps Tears of Blood* (*Taohua qixue ji*, 1931), made two years earlier, was the sort of maudlin love story that May Fourth intellectuals despised. Some film historians have refrained from attaching the mandarin duck and butterfly label to this important silent feature, preferring instead to argue that it resisted "feudal ethics." But on closer inspection it is hard to avoid the conclusion that it falls squarely into the butterfly category.[2] Yet, as Perry Link has argued so brilliantly, there is often much more to the butterfly genre than meets the eye.[3] Lurking just below the surface of this classic tearjerker, made more than three-quarters of a century ago, is an early cinematic attempt to explore the controversial issue of spiritual pollution in ways that were familiar to readers of late Qing and early Republican popular fiction. In fact, throughout the 1920s and early 1930s quite a few important butterfly novels were made into films. The structure of *Peach Blossom Weeps Tears of Blood* and similar types of work is utterly simple, but its influence on subsequent and more politically inspired discussions of the problem of spiritual pollution is unmistakable.

Peach Blossom Weeps Tears of Blood tells the story of a rich and handsome young man from the city, played by Jin Yan, a Korean-Chinese Valentino, who is attracted to a pure and simple country lass, played by Ruan Lingyu, the legendary master of melodramatic acting.[4] He invites her to visit his family in the city. Her father agrees because he has been on cordial terms with the lad's family and has been their employee for years. After arriving in the city, the youngsters declare their love for each other, but the young man's mother opposes the marriage. Urged on by several young city women who are unspeakably jealous, the mother asserts that the low-born, uncultured farm girl would be an embarrassment to the whole family.

Rather than break the bad news to his love, the young man tells her that his mother has agreed. On the assumption that the marriage will take place in the immediate future, the maiden agrees to move to a house occupied by the young man. When the father arrives in the city looking for his daughter, he is shocked to discover the couple living together, and to see his precious daughter dressed and made up in the urban way. He goes to the lad's mother to arrange a hasty marriage, but she sends the young woman and her father packing and places her son under house detention.

The girl, of course, is pregnant, and she finally gives birth to a daughter. All the attempts made by the young man to see her are foiled by the tough old woman. Just as the last petal of his magnificent peach blossom is about to fall, the young man pushes his mother aside, dashes from the house, and sprints to the deathbed of his true love. She forgives him and dies. He vows to cherish their child. At the funeral, the families are united. Even the old lady puts herself on the road to reform by confessing her role in the tragedy and vowing to change her ways.

Peach Blossom Weeps Tears of Blood set the standard for many subsequent films on spiritual pollution, including such works as *Country Love* (*Xiang qing*, d. Hu Bingliu and Wang Jin, 1981) produced in the tumultuous 1980s, by defining the problem in terms of a conflict between city and countryside. Corrupt, evil, and un-Chinese, the big city—especially Shanghai—is the symbol of an aggressive Western presence in China. The dubious moral conduct of the mother and son is linked directly to the alien and un-Chinese ways of the city. The pristine countryside, by contrast, represents the essence of China. Life in the unspoiled rural area is simple and pure. The young woman and her father are honest and hardworking. The village embodies the sacred past; the city exemplifies an uncertain and immoral present. In this respect, *Peach Blossom Weeps Tears of Blood* resembles the culturally conservative, antiurban popular fiction that surfaced in postrevolutionary France.[5]

Virtually no attention is given in this film to the economic, technological, or political aspects of the Western impact on China. *Peach Blossom Weeps Tears of Blood* focuses almost exclusively on the phenomenon of spiritual pollution. The underlying assumption is that Western cultural intrusion poses the most fundamental threat to China. Not only is Western spiritual culture alien and un-Chinese, it is corrupt and depraved. If this moral pollution can be averted, China can be saved. There is little need to reevaluate China's own cultural values and institutions.

Much of the emotional energy generated by this film (and many subsequent film treatments of the problem of spiritual pollution) is conveyed through powerful sexual imagery. The helpless young woman is China. Her innocent and childlike beauty is natural, she is a virgin, and she has never left the womb of the unspoiled countryside. But, like pure and innocent maidens everywhere, she is vulnerable and naive. The slick young man recognizes her Chinese virtues and the uniqueness of her beauty. "A city girl's beauty," he observes, "depends on powder and rouge." Yet, when he takes her to the city, she begins to wear fashionable clothes and to use makeup. When they first meet in the wholesome village environment, he declares, "How chaste and beautiful! You can never find such in the city!" But in the end, he seduces and corrupts the virgin. Thus, the film does much more than warn young people about the dangers of moral contamination; it projects the melodramatic but unforgettable image of an innocent virgin (China) defiled and left for dead by a smooth-talking outsider (the West).

Class is not an important analytical category in *Peach Blossom Weeps Tears of Blood*. Social stratification is portrayed in the film, and the economic division of labor is explained, but the class schema is strictly bipolar. The rich, for the most part, live in the city and are therefore more contaminated by alien culture. The poor live in the villages and personify the moral virtues of China. But the prosperous, it is crucial to point out, are not morally corrupt because they are rich, but because they live in closer proximity to the source of pollution. Similarly, the poor are not spiritually pure because they are poor. The film is effective, indeed frightening, precisely because it demonstrates that anyone, including the purest virgin, can be corrupted. Still, it is appealing to those it horrifies because it indicates that all those who have been exposed to spiritual pollution can be saved. Class origin does not determine one's fate. Poor people are not immune to cultural contamination; rich people who have contracted the foreign virus can be rehabilitated.

Peach Blossom Weeps Tears of Blood is an undistinguished film from an artistic point of view. Its main themes are poorly developed. It is naive and simplistic in conception, and it wastes Ruan Lingyu's screen talents. Its sensational and melodramatic narrative style badly distorts the nature of China's encounter with the West and misrepresents the condition of China's rural sector in the early Republican period. Director Bu Wancang offers no fresh vision of the future. Instead, he makes a superficial and sentimental appeal for the restoration of a vaguely defined traditional morality. Still, *Peach Blossom Weeps Tears of Blood* should be viewed as an important film for two reasons. First, the views of Westernized May Fourth intellectuals notwithstanding, it must be acknowledged that there was an enormous audience for this type of film, an audience whose fears and frustrations were not being adequately addressed by the writers of May Fourth–style fiction. Second, it is a prototypical work. Almost all the films of the 1930s that address the issue of spiritual pollution, including those made by both the right and the left, are only variations of the basic but spectacular approach adopted by Bu Wancang in his early work.

A DREAM IN PINK: THE "EARLY" CAI CHUSHENG

Standard treatments of the career of Cai Chusheng stress an important shift in his political thought that occurred in the early 1930s.[6] On January 28, 1932, while he was filming *A Dream in Pink* (*Fenhongse de meng*), Japanese forces attacked Shanghai. The twenty-six-year-old director, who was born in Shanghai and grew up in the Guangzhou area, stopped production at once, it is said, and became involved in anti-Japanese filmmaking activities. He eventually finished *A Dream in Pink*, but his new political concerns brought him into increasingly closer contact with the small leftist film group led by Xia Yan that had been organized after the Japanese assault. Cai did not join the Communist Party until 1956, but he emerged as one of the most important left-wing directors in Shanghai in the 1933-1937 period. As a result, his early work, including *A Dream in Pink*, is usually regarded as an embarrassment and ignored by early, mainstream Chinese Marxist film historians.[7] Indeed, Cai Chusheng himself wrote in 1936 that *A Dream in Pink* lacked "any insight or understanding."[8] In spite of Cai's objections, *A Dream in Pink* tells us much about the many ways in which prominent filmmakers, including leftists, were influenced by such early works on spiritual pollution as *Peach Blossom Weeps Tears of Blood*. Leftists did not invent the idea that Chinese society was being polluted by Western bourgeois culture; they expropriated it from people like Bu Wancang and Cai Chusheng who understood the dynamics of urban popular culture in the late Qing and early Republican eras.

A Dream in Pink is the story of the moral decline of a young writer, Luo Wen, who lives in Shanghai with his wife and daughter. Luo's wife, another pure and innocent female victim, is a paragon of traditional Chinese virtues—despite her modern appearance. She exudes what might be called moral virginity. She is a loyal and obedient wife, a devoted mother, and a respected schoolteacher. But Luo is restless. His work goes slowly because he likes to fantasize about life in Shanghai's glittering entertainment quarters.

Unable to resist temptation, Luo makes his way to a high-class nightclub where he meets a glamorous young woman who is surrounded by elegantly dressed playboys. She is, in every meaningful respect, the exact opposite of Luo's wife. She uses heavy makeup, smokes cigarettes, drinks alcohol, dances to Western music, and wears new-style clothing that exposes her breasts. In brief, she is worldly and seductive. In the end, he spends the night at her chic apartment.

Luo and the temptress pursue a hedonistic life of sexual excess in the months that follow. During one visit to her apartment, they amuse themselves by lying together on a studio couch and flipping through the pages of *London Life*. Each time she spots a glossy photo of a sexy British fashion model, she imitates the alluring facial expression of the fair-haired alien beauty.

In an effort to place the sordid relationship on a permanent basis, Luo divorces his quasi-traditionalistic wife and marries his exotic new love. His former wife is quite literally left with nothing, on a cold, snowy street. Inspired by his exciting new life, Luo now hopes to do some serious writing, but a series of unanticipated difficulties arises. His foreign-style wife wants to dance and party, needs lots of money to buy new wardrobes, and neglects Luo's lovely young daughter, who, with the exit of the mother, becomes what literary scholar Peter Brooks refers to as the primary "bearer of the sign of innocence."[9] Bored with Luo, his new wife goes back to the nightclub, meets a new lover, and runs away. Luo's demise is averted only when his former wife, who has been waiting patiently in the wings in a decidedly rural setting, offers to forgive and forget. In contrast to the heroine in *Peach Blossom Weeps Tears of Blood*, Luo's exposure to foreign spiritual pollution is not terminal.

The basic themes on spiritual pollution introduced in such classic butterfly films as *Peach Blossom Weeps Tears of Blood* are also present in *A Dream in Pink*. Cai Chusheng's film is different only because it provides a closer look at the source of moral contamination. Bu Wancang's work merely implies that the big city and Western culture generate corrupt morality. The male protagonist has already been corrupted when he appears on screen. One does not get to see exactly how he became so depraved. *A Dream in Pink*, by contrast, points to the urban and Western origins of spiritual pollution in explicit detail. Moreover, the film unfolds entirely within the context of the evil and un-Chinese metropolis, and the viewer is invited to observe precisely how the process of contamination occurs.

One has to go no further than the nightclub to understand the substance of Western culture. The *wu ting*, or dance hall, is presented by Cai Chusheng (and almost every subsequent cinematic commentator on spiritual pollution) as a microcosm of Western civilization. The people who inhabit the titillating world of the *wu ting* wear foreign clothes, utter "darling" and other foreign words, use foreign makeup, dance in the foreign way to foreign music, smoke foreign cigarettes, and drink foreign liquor. They are, in effect, what Mao Zedong and other Chinese Marxists writing in the 1920s regarded as internal foreigners who have shamelessly renounced their Chinese essence.[10] Their primary concern is hedonistic pleasure seeking, especially sexual gratification. The *wu ting* scene is transparently corrupt, decadent, and thoroughly alien to Chinese values. But for reasons that remain unexplained and mysterious, the morally corrupt culture of the *wu ting* nevertheless entices naive young people like a flame attracts moths.

The simple dichotomy of Chinese purity and Western moral degradation offers no middle ground. The audience must choose one or the other. Compromises with evil are impossible. Cai Chusheng, fine-tuning a style of editing that he later employed with great success in such leftist films of the late 1940s as *A Spring River Flows East* (*Yi jiang chun shui xiang dong liu*, d. Cai Chusheng and Zheng Junli, 1947), constantly cuts sharply back and forth between the moral world of the faithful schoolteacher and the depraved world of the glamour girl in order to heighten the stark contrast between good and evil.

The audience is able to witness a highly condensed version of the process of corruption from beginning to end: temptation, followed by a descent into hell, an awakening, confession, redemption, and finally rebirth. The film is structured in such a way that the viewer never doubts that the betrayed schoolteacher will forgive her husband's trespasses. All that is required of those who have been exposed to spiritual pollution in the 1930s (or to bourgeois liberalization in the 1980s) is a sincere confession. Once the prodigal son has confessed his sins, it is inconceivable that he will be denied absolution. This dimension of *A Dream in Pink* is a central ingredient in virtually all Chinese films on the theme of spiritual pollution.

QUEEN OF SPORTS: THE AMBIGUOUS LEGACY OF SUN YU

One of the most intriguing ironies of the attempt to expose the threat of Western cultural contamination in the 1930s is that the film world played any role at all. The moral character of film personalities had been suspect for some time. Many of the well-known directors and screenwriters of the 1930s, including some who were involved in making films that focused public attention on the issue of spiritual pollution, got their start in the 1920s, when a significant amount of filmmaking was only one step removed from popular but lowbrow *gewutuan*, or vaudeville, entertainment. Li Lili, Wang Renmei, and Zhou Xuan, three of the most popular film actresses of the 1930s and 1940s, began their careers as teenage performers on the vaudeville stage.[11] If a *gewutuan* program offered attractive young girls in scanty costumes, bare legs and arms, simple dance routines of the chorus line variety, catchy hit tunes, and a couple of comic buffoons, it stood a good chance of succeeding. Usually, the attractive young girls were enough.

Throughout the 1930s, the Chinese film scene was also strongly influenced by what was perceived to be the Hollywood model. Moviemakers and ordinary film fans alike possessed an amazingly detailed knowledge of American film culture. Newspapers and photo magazines were filled with sensational stories about scandal, sexual promiscuity, drug addiction, divorce, and suicide in the sparkling film world of Shanghai. Some filmmaking was financed by unsavory gangsters. But, curiously, the gossip did very little to diminish the popularity of movies and film personalities. On the contrary, the rumors tended to attract rather than repel the film audience.

The peculiar allure of this and other aspects of the foreign cultural model posed serious credibility problems for those in the film world who claimed they were warning the public about the threat of alien spiritual pollution. Even in films that clearly denounced foreign cultural contamination, foreign cultural modes were often presented in surprisingly tantalizing ways. It is by no means certain that the nightclub scenes in *A Dream in Pink* would discourage most viewers from fantasizing about what it would be like to spend a night on the town, or from actually doing so if an opportunity were at hand.

The problems of credibility and ambiguity of message are particularly apparent in the work of Sun Yu, an acclaimed director and screenwriter from

Chongqing, who in the 1920s studied drama and film at the University of Wisconsin and at Columbia.[12] *Queen of Sports* (*Tiyu huanghou*, 1934), made well after Sun Yu came under the political influence of Xia Yan's small Communist film group in Shanghai, is one of the first leftist attempts to explore the issue of spiritual pollution.

The story opens when the pure but high-spirited daughter of a wealthy rural family arrives in the big metropolis to attend a special school for female athletes. Inspired by the noble conviction that China will somehow be stronger if all people strengthen their bodies, she works hard to become an outstanding sprinter. But, alas, she is spoiled by success. She becomes arrogant, neglects her studies, applies makeup, wears fancy clothes, and begins to fraternize with slick, Westernized college lads who seem to spend all their time smoking, drinking, dancing, and fornicating. Rescued by her handsome but dedicated coach, she vows to change her ways. After seeing a classmate die following a grueling race, she decides that the pursuit of individual (i.e., bourgeois) glory is wrong, is no longer interested in the title "Queen of Sports," and resolves to serve others as an ordinary teacher of physical education.

In its basic concept, *Queen of Sports*, a leftist work, departs in no significant way from *Peach Blossom Weeps Tears of Blood* and *A Dream in Pink*. The unspoiled young woman represents the moral purity and honest simplicity of rural China; urban Shanghai is portrayed as unnatural, alien, and spiritually corrupt; the *wu ting* is used once again to capsulize the essence of foreign cultural priorities, and potent sexual imagery is employed to sharpen the emotional focus of the film. Social class is irrelevant. It is the Chinese people as a whole who are threatened by alien spiritual pollution.

But *Queen of Sports* is of enormous interest because Sun Yu's use of this traditional and formulaic approach to the problem of spiritual pollution produced ambiguous results. All the necessary ingredients are present, but the message gets lost. *Queen of Sports* titillates rather than educates. If one did not know that Sun Yu was a leftist director who had already made such important "social issue" films as *Daybreak* (*Tianming*, 1933) and *Small Toys* (*Xiao wanyi*, 1933), one would be tempted to conclude that *Queen of Sports* is a film that exploits the spiritual pollution issue for commercial purposes.

The problem is not Sun Yu's motive but the manner in which he executes the film. He understood better than most directors the appeals of the *gewutuan* and Hollywood formats. Thus, in *Queen of Sports* he tries to capture the attention of the audience by dwelling on the natural, robust sexuality of the rural heroine long before he introduces the problem of foreign spiritual pollution. In the opening scene, for instance, the energetic young woman, played beautifully by the vivacious Li Lili (known to many as Lily Li), is observed climbing the phallus-like smokestack of her ship, as the breeze whips her skirt to and fro. The camera is positioned in a way that

A perky small-town athlete (center) is led astray by hedonistic Shanghai playboys in *Queen of Sports* (1934, d. Sun Yu). China Film Archive

gives maximum exposure to her legs, thighs, and posterior. At the sports school, the female athletes dress in tight shorts and revealing T-shirts most of the time. In class, they suck on their pens as they sit wide-eyed before their dashing male teacher. An unusual shower-room scene, which includes soapy nude bathing and sensual close-ups of the brushing of teeth, is used to introduce aspects of daily life. In the morning, the young women are seen getting out of bed and dressing. Even the death scene at the end of the film seems designed to give the audience one final look at a partially clad young woman squirming and writhing on the training table.

Sun Yu's popularized tribute to the female body is, to say the least, a departure from the traditional concepts of femininity associated with the heroines in *Peach Blossom Weeps Tears of Blood* and *A Dream in Pink*. This is not to suggest that Sun Yu was a peddler of pollution. The problem is that he was trying to introduce a new and assertive model of Chinese innocence and purity at precisely the same time he was attempting to expose the evils of Western spiritual pollution. His heroine is wholesome, but she is also frisky and radiates a natural, spontaneous sexuality. In this respect, Sun Yu's model is meant to be a modern, YWCA-type progressive prototype. The underlying message, provocative in the Chinese cultural context even in the post-Mao era, is that a woman should not be ashamed of her body. The body can be developed in ways that can contribute to collective and national liberation. Yet the message is delivered in a way that tantalizes the male audience. Not only does the new social message get sidetracked, it can easily be confused with all that Sun Yu presumably seeks to discredit. The audience is asked to accept Sun Yu's new definition of wholesomeness, one that departs in no significant way from the definition that emerged during Chiang Kai-shek's New Life Movement of the mid-1930s, but to reject the culture of the dance hall that threatens to corrupt the young woman. The difficulty is that both models are new and alien. Those who are attracted to the heroine's natural sexuality are likely to be attracted by the glitter of the depraved *wu ting*. The problem of the unintended appeal of the negative model is especially acute in *Queen of Sports*, but it is present in virtually all films on cultural contamination and severely limits their effectiveness. In *Peach Blossom Weeps Tears of Blood*, *A Dream in Pink*, and, for that matter, many of the films produced in early post-Mao China, the heroines are virtuous but boring, while the villains are degenerate but engrossing.

A BIBLE FOR DAUGHTERS: A CASE OF IDEOLOGICAL CONFUSION

A Bible for Daughters (*Nüer jing*, 1934) was not simply a leftist film, it was a project of a small but influential Communist film group. The scenario was written by veteran Party members Xia Yan and Qian Xingcun, in collaboration with such prominent non-Party leftists as Zheng Boqi, Hong Shen, Shen Xiling, and Zheng Zhengqiu.[13] Although *A Bible for Daughters* was a Communist film, its target was not capitalism as an economic and social system. Instead, the focus was on the cultural dimensions of Western bourgeois liberalism, especially the phenomenon of spiritual pollution. It is not at all surprising that, as Marxists, these artists adopted a critical attitude toward the bourgeois culture of capitalism, but it is logical to expect Marxist critiques of liberalism to be fundamentally different from traditionalistic, precapitalist critiques of liberalism. The problem with *A Bible for Daughters* is that its approach to the problem of alien spiritual pollution differs in no significant way from the backward-looking and culturally defensive butterfly approach found in *Peach Blossom Weeps Tears of Blood* and *A Dream in Pink*.

Set in Shanghai in 1934, *A Bible for Daughters* features a small class reunion held on National Day for several affluent, Westernized women who have not seen each other in ten years. Virtually all of them have been corrupted in one way or another by foreign spiritual pollution. The first woman to speak, Xuan Shu, who placed too much faith in the ability of her physical beauty to guarantee the loyalty of her restless husband, is cruelly abandoned by the scoundrel as soon as her beauty begins to fade. Another guest, the calculating Yan Su, proudly describes the methods she uses to dominate and control her flirtatious husband. Gao Hua seems to have done well as a leading activist among Shanghai feminists. But, eager to discredit the women's movement, the male filmmakers soon reveal that Gao actually leads a morally corrupt and debauched private life. Instead of staying at home, where decent women, including modern women, are presumably based, Zhu Wen got a job in a department store and was immediately preyed upon by lecherous men. Xu Li has become a high-class courtesan. Gambling addict Xu Ling has destroyed her whole family.[14]

As in the other films on spiritual pollution, there can be no question about the source of the cultural disease that ruins the lives of young Chinese women. The host's home is elaborately decorated and furnished in the Western way; the cars, jazzy music, and dance styles are all Western, and the elegant jewelry, clothing, and hairstyles are Western. The only things Chinese about the women are their faces, and even these are painted, powdered, and plucked in the Western style. It is not wealth or bourgeois class status that account for the sad demise of the young women, it is the corruption of values associated with their reckless adoption of Western culture in the big metropolis and on the floors of infamous nightclubs. *A Bible for Daughters*, like the culturally conservative butterfly films discussed above, does not seek to explore the complexities and nuances of Western culture; its purpose is to exploit a crude but visually powerful caricature of Western bourgeois culture that was already deeply rooted in urban popular culture.

A Bible for Daughters, like *Queen of Sports*, manages unintentionally to convert the victims of spiritual pollution into objects of great fascination and mystery. But the profound political ambiguity one discovers in *A Bible for Daughters* is far more interesting than what one discovers in *Queen of Sports* because this film was a project in which Communist Party loyalists took (and still take!) much pride. The ideological confusion of its screen artists becomes even more apparent when one recalls the activities of the extreme right in the early 1930s. As Lloyd Eastman's fine scholarship has shown, the fascist Blue Shirt movement was gaining momentum in the early 1930s. One of the targets of its campaign of intimidation and violence was foreign, bourgeois spiritual pollution. Just before *A Bible for Daughters* was released, a Blue Shirt publication, *Qiantu*, complained that male students in Shanghai spent more time in dance halls than in libraries, while the females majored in cosmetics and foreign fashions. The Blue Shirts, according to Eastman, thought that "the pernicious influences of Western culture were the root cause of China's moral and cultural bankruptcy."[15] Of course, the Blue Shirt critique of bourgeois liberal culture was nothing new. The notion that liberal culture was decadent, corrupt, and exhausted was inspired, in large part, by the fascist evaluation of bourgeois culture that had gained currency in France, Italy, Spain, and Germany in the 1910s and 1920s.[16] In the European and Asian fascist perspective, communism and anarchism were perversions of thought associated intimately with the cultural cancer of liberalism.[17] Thus, at the same time the Blue Shirts were busy in polluted Shanghai—raiding dance halls and bookstores to root out the vestiges of New Culture and May Fourth liberalism and permissiveness—Nationalist military forces were hunting down Communists who had survived the 1927 counterrevolution. In the fascist view, liberalism and communism were inherently linked.

What is truly curious, however, is that these frightening and violent developments did not discourage the Communist underground in Shanghai from waging its own cultural war against May Fourth liberalism and Western bourgeois spiritual pollution. Qu Qiubai, the leader of the Communist cultural movement in Shanghai in the early 1930s, had been complaining for some time about the "Europeanized" condition of the Chinese literary world.[18] It is as if urban Communists, startled by the ferocity of the Nationalist Party's denigration of bourgeois liberalism, were anxious to compete with the right wing of the Nationalists for the leadership of the antiliberal trend by sinifying the emerging Stalinist critique of bourgeois culture. Needless to say, Chinese Marxists like Xia Yan should have recognized the fundamental difference between the classic Communist critique of bourgeois culture, conveyed in the writings of Marx, Engels, Plekhanov, and other European Marxists,[19] and the traditionalistic and reactionary fascist critique of bourgeois culture expressed in the works of Charles Maurras, Mussolini, and Hitler.[20] But in trying to reach a semiliterate mass audience that was comfortable with the butterfly caricature of Western bourgeois culture, *A Bible for Daughters*, the first Communist film to explore the issue of alien spiritual pollution in China, fails utterly to reveal the difference between socialist and fascist attacks on Western bourgeois culture. In Xia Yan's influential work, the two become blurred and, thus, virtually indistinguishable. When viewed together with such older but more visually compelling works as *Peach Blossom Weeps Tears of Blood* and *A Dream in Pink, A Bible for Daughters* leaves the distinct impression that there are no substantial differences between socialist and nonsocialist treatments of this explosive subject.

Nationalist censors liked *A Bible for Daughters*. They insisted only that one scene be added. At the end of the reunion, guests go outdoors to view a lantern parade staged for the New Life Movement, a short-lived neotraditionalist cultural campaign launched by Chiang Kai-shek in February 1934. Marxist historians miss the point when they protest that Xia Yan was forced to add this final scene.[21] In reality, the thrust of the film is logically and politically consistent not only with the New Life Movement, but also with the sensationalized and superficial portrayals of Western culture present in *Peach Blossom Weeps Tears of Blood, A Dream in Pink,* and other nonleftist treatments of the problem of alien spiritual pollution. It comes as no surprise, therefore, that an updated version of this film, bearing exactly the same title (*Nüer jing,* d. Bao Qicheng, 1987) and treating many of the same antiurban and anti–spiritual pollution themes, was released in Shanghai in the mid-1980s, during a Communist Party campaign against bourgeois liberalization.

Particularly interesting are the implications of *A Bible for Daughters* for Chinese women. The first guest, Xuan Shu, is told that her life is in a shambles because she entered into an untraditional "free marriage." The second woman, Yan Su, is successful in marriage only because she dominates her husband in what is represented as the Western way. Zhu Wen, who went out to work in a department store, has only herself to blame when she is preyed upon by lascivious men. The Westernized gambling addict, Xu Ling, is incapable of handling money. The feminist, Gao Hua, is a fraud. In brief, it is better for women to stay home and thereby avoid the agonies associated with spiritual pollution. The call for the liberation of Chinese women, a call inspired by Western liberalism, was one of the most radical elements of New Culture and May Fourth ideology. *A Bible for Daughters,* it must be said, seeks to discredit the women's movement by linking it to alien bourgeois values.

Research on Republican China, naturally enough, has tended to focus on the glaring differences between the main combatants, the Nationalists and the Communists, in the ongoing civil war, differences that account for the frequently expressed desire of each side to annihilate the other. But Sun Yu's *Queen of Sports* and Xia Yan's *A Bible for Daughters* suggest that it can be fruitful to consider the areas in which the ideology of the two parties overlapped, especially in the area of popular culture. Sun Yu's perky heroine, for example, learns to dedicate herself to self-sacrifice on the athletic field for the glory of the state, rather than for the glory of herself or her social class. Chiang Kai-shek undoubtedly condoned the sentiments expressed in this nationalistic film. Similarly, Xia Yan's rules of behavior for vulnerable young Chinese women could have been written by the antiliberal YMCA, an ardent supporter of the New Life Movement.

FILIAL PIETY: LUO MINGYOU, FEI MU, AND THE CONFUCIAN PERSPECTIVE

The backlash against May Fourth liberalism, including receptivity to Western bourgeois culture, took many forms in the 1930s. One of these was a revival of interest in Confucianism, a doctrine that had been mercilessly ridiculed by Lu Xun and other New Culture intellectuals in the 1910s. Throughout the 1920s and early 1930s, however, the film industry, a realm that was affected only in part by the May Fourth intellectual revolution, frequently sought to uphold traditional Confucian values. In the mid-1930s, there was a new surge of interest in Confucianism in the film world. Some of this activity was related to the activities of the colorful mogul Luo Mingyou, the founder and owner of the famous Lianhua Film Studio, which produced *Peach Blossom Weeps Tears of Blood*, *A Dream in Pink*, and *Queen of Sports*. Born in Hong Kong and educated in Guangzhou and Beijing, Luo allowed Cai Chusheng, Sun Yu, Wu Yonggang, and other important leftists to make films in his studio in the early 1930s.[22] But Luo was also on good terms with high officials in the Nationalist government and enthusiastically supported the various antiliberal and neoconservative campaigns launched by the state after 1931. Before long, he began expressing the view that Chinese films should propagate "national spirit" and serve the state.[23] One of Luo's favorite directors was the young Fei Mu, a meticulous artist who joined the Lianhua Film Studio in 1932. By the late 1930s, Fei Mu, like Cai Chusheng and Sun Yu, was actively participating in such leftist collective projects as *Lianhua Symphony* (*Lianhua jiaoxiangqu*, 1937), but his earliest work, especially the highly lyrical *Filial Piety* (*Tian lun*, 1935), which he codirected with Luo Mingyou, was Confucian to the core.

Filial Piety opens in the late Qing period as a filial son returns home on horseback on the eve of his father's death. The old man, breathing his last, encourages his son to excel in the rearing of his own offspring. The young man does his best, but twenty years later he realizes that his own son and daughter have been corrupted by heavy doses of spiritual pollution in the contaminated urban environment. "We came to the city," he tells his unrepentant son, "hoping that you might seek the path to prominence. Instead, you have chosen the road of pleasure." His son is a well-known figure who neglects his own son. The worried patriarch recalls his father's sound advice, and he promptly decides to move his family out of the depraved metropolis. In the morally invigorating rural setting he plans to open homes for orphans and the elderly. But his disrespectful son and daughter-in-law, addicted to urban life, refuse to cooperate. His daughter, soon bored with country life, sneaks away to join her slick lover in the city, in spite of the father's misgivings about the young man's questionable character. The old man is thus ignored by his shameless children.

Years later, the old man rejoices when his adult grandson wisely rejects the ways of his parents. The grandson subsequently arrives to help the old man run his charitable organizations. Before long, the old man's daughter also shows up, abandoned by her unreliable urban lover. The management of the orphanage is placed entirely in the hands of the grandson when the old man becomes ill. Although he is failing rapidly, the old man

A Confucian moralst (*left*), ignored by his pleasure-seeking son, returns to the pristine countryside and oversees the education of his grandson in *Filial Piety* (1935, d. Fei Mu, Luo Mingyou). China Film Archive

refuses to permit his grandson to use any money from the coffers of the orphanage to pay for medical expenses. Instead, he begs his filial grandson to dedicate himself to public service and to let "love for the individual extend to all humanity."[24]

As late as the early 1980s, Chinese Marxist film historians expressed nothing but contempt for *Filial Piety*, labeling it a "reactionary" work that seeks to disparage the theory of class struggle.[25] One suspects that this judgment is actually based on Luo Mingyou's open support of Nationalist Party calls for multiclass allegiance to the state. On the issue of spiritual pollution, however, *Filial Piety* is remarkably similar to the other films discussed here, including such poorly made leftist works as Xia Yan's *A Bible for Daughters*, which has been consistently praised in official Communist Party publications. The pristine rural setting represents positive Chinese values, while the big city symbolizes the evil West. As usual, the directors find no need to locate the story in a concrete socioeconomic environment. The assumption is that the problems of contemporary society have very little to do with economic, political, or social issues. Thus it is unnecessary to portray the socioeconomic system in any detail, or to provide much information about the concrete historical context. The film is offered as a timeless moral parable of universal significance. It is enough to draw a clear distinction between moral and immoral behavior, and to associate immorality, as *A Bible for Daughters* does, with the alien intruder. Moral corruption, it is suggested, not particular social or economic phenomena, is the source of China's weakness and lack of national unity. The only meaningful distinction that needs to be made among the Chinese themselves is between those who are associated with foreign ways and those who are faithful to time-tested Chinese values.

The main difference between *Filial Piety* and the other films on spiritual pollution analyzed here is that Luo and Fei propose a decidedly Confucian solution to the problem. Such earlier films on spiritual pollution as *Peach Blossom Weeps Tears of Blood* and *A Dream in Pink*, which were not openly associated with state political campaigns, refer only to vaguely defined traditional Chinese values. Quasi-leftist films, like *Queen of Sports*, that blur the difference between socialist and fascist critiques of bourgeois culture, advocate a forward-looking, albeit frighteningly totalitarian, alternative to purely traditional values. The Communist-inspired film *A Bible for Daughters* proposes no solution, other than simply warning innocent young women to avoid being tarnished by alien culture and suggesting, indirectly, that Chinese values (never adequately defined) are preferable. *Filial Piety*, on the other hand, openly advocates the superiority of Confucian morality.

Filial Piety is a misleading, even manipulative, work, not because it does not adopt the position on class struggle advanced by the Communist Party in the early 1930s, but because it fails to mention that many intelligent and decent Chinese had been questioning Confucian morality throughout the early Republican period. Like almost all the films of the early 1930s that deal with the problem of alien spiritual pollution, including leftist films, *Filial Piety* is logically incapable of taking a critical look at the failings of the Chinese cultural order that was dominant before the Western cultural mode began to take root. Films of this sort cannot consider the possibility that perceived faults in what was known as the traditional morality allowed Western cultural options to be viewed as attractive alternatives. Invariably, the sequential structure of such works is that a faultless, timeless, and utterly natural Chinese cultural order (sometimes labeled Confucian and sometimes left unlabeled) is intruded upon and subverted by an utterly hostile and sinister alien cultural virus.

Filial Piety, like other projects of the early and mid-1930s that deal with the threat of alien spiritual pollution, is best understood in the context of antiliberal and antibourgeois cultural trends that were both global and domestic. In the realm of elite culture, including modern fiction, liberal and antitraditional currents still ran deep. For instance, Ba Jin's *Family* (*Jia*), an angry New Culture and anti-Confucian assault on traditional values, was published in 1931. It was in the world of popular and commercial culture that antiliberalism and neotraditionalism fell on especially fertile soil. The main difference between *Filial Piety* and the other films discussed above is that it was quite literally produced for the New Life Movement. Chiang Kai-shek, a modern political figure, was not attempting to bring Confucianism back to full life, but he firmly believed that the moral cultivation of the individual and the acceptance of certain Confucian virtues, such as *li* (social propriety), were central to the resolution of the many social and political problems allegedly spawned by individualist and recklessly permissive liberal ways of thinking.[26] *Filial Piety* was a film that staunchly supported this view.

LITTLE ANGEL: THE PATHOLOGY OF SPIRITUAL DISEASES

In the tension-packed months prior to the 1989 Bejing massacres and the start of a long and repressive political campaign against bourgeois liberalization and spiritual pollution, the Beijing Film Studio released a film titled *AIDS Victims* (*Aisibing huanzhe*, d. Xu Tongjun). Educational units throughout China were required to arrange special screenings for their students. The movie tells the sensational, indeed inflammatory, story of three attractive young Chinese women who contract the HIV virus after having intercourse with a foreign teacher named Tony. The three women have two things in common. They live in a Special Economic Zone that is open to the alien world, and they each have frequent social and cultural interaction with foreigners. Foreign residents of China were reportedly offended by the not-so-subtle implications of the film and tended to conclude that it was a typical example of the crude, counterproductive, and xenophobic propaganda routinely turned out by the Chinese Communist Party.

In fact, the pathological conception of bourgeois liberalization as a highly contagious disease of the spirit that can be contracted after even brief exposure to alien cultural viruses is nothing new. Wu Yonggang, who was born in Wuxian, Jiangsu province, is another of those talented young directors of the 1930s whose work was, for a very brief time, designed to immunize Chinese youth against the dreaded infection of May Fourth liberalism. Sandwiched between Wu's *The Goddess* (*Shennü*, 1934), an excellent leftist melodrama (promoted by Tian Han and others in Xia Yan's Communist film group) that discussed prostitution, and *The Pioneers* (*Zhuang zhi ling yun*, 1936), an anti-Japanese picture that faithfully delivered the Communist resistance message, is a remarkably curious film titled *Little Angel* (*Xiao tianshi*, 1935) that is perfectly consistent with the main themes of the New Life Movement and, in its spectacular treatment of bourgeois culture as a contagious pestilence of the spirit, foreshadows such pre-Tiananmen representations of foreign culture as *AIDS Victims*.

Little Angel, which took first prize in a screenplay contest sponsored by the Nationalist Party's Department of Education in Jiangsu province, explores the decline of traditional family life in a small town. One household is of extremely modest means, but time-honored Chinese notions of moral conduct govern the interactions of its members. The head of the family is away serving his country as a member of the Nationalist military. By contrast, their affluent neighbors enjoy substantial material comfort, but there is no spiritual dimension to their family life. They have been contaminated by Western spiritual pollution. The children are neglected, the women sit around playing *majiang* all day, and the adulterous husband is, of course, constantly lusting after young women in the local nightclubs, where he smokes, drinks, and dances to Western music.

The film focuses on the exemplary behavior of an angelic young boy who belongs to the family of modest means. The household members have done everything they can to scrape together enough money to send the boy to primary school. Even his grandfather has taken a job, hand-copying texts, in spite of his bad eyesight. Deeply moved by a story he has read about an Italian boy who helps his father, the lad sneaks out of bed at night while the others are asleep to do some of the tedious copying for his grandfather. When the boy falls asleep in school one day, a note of reprimand is sent home. Still, the boy says nothing, continuing instead to carry on his nocturnal good deeds in secret.

The little angel gets most of his moral training from his sagacious grandfather, who is not at all like the superstitious and tyrannical patriarchs who appear so often in May Fourth fiction. The grandfather teaches the boy that he must always set a moral example. It is fine to associate with the spoiled children of the rich family, but he should avoid picking up their bad habits; instead, he should accept the responsibility of showing them the morally correct way of doing things.

The mother of the rich boy is the first in her family to see the light. On New Year's Eve her husband is out all night chasing seductive young women, while one of his children is sick in bed. The kindly neighbors, including the little angel, stop by the next day to show their concern and are shocked to see the condition of the drunken father. Frustrated and disgusted by the moral decay of her family, the wife of the rich man finally throws her *majiang* tiles out the window.

In an extraordinary and vivid final sequence (rich in Christian imagery) the little angel dashes into the street to push the rich boy out of the way of an oncoming car. The speeding auto, in which the rich boy's drunken father is riding, misses the rich boy, but strikes the little angel. At the hospital, the Christ-like cherub appears to be near death. The doctor announces that a blood transfusion might save him. Ashamed of his immoral and depraved conduct, the repentant rich man offers to donate his own blood, but, alas, the doctor discovers that the man's blood, like his spirit, has been contaminated by a mysterious but potent disease. The only solution is for the angel's spiritually clean elder sister, who is dressed in white like a nun, to provide unpolluted blood. After a miraculous recovery, the little angel is thanked by the members of the spiritually contaminated family for making their moral redemption possible. "You have given us spirit," says the rich man in his final confessional remarks.

Mainstream Marxist film critics long regarded Wu Yonggang's *Little Angel* as something of an embarrassment, and generally ignored it in discussions of Wu's career.[27] A fairly recent book-length discussion of Wu's long career does not even mention this work. But leftist objections to the film have less to do with its content than with the simple fact that it was linked so closely to the Nationalist Party's abortive effort to foster the New Life Movement. It is true that *Little Angel* does not treat the theme of class struggle. Yet it is clear that none of the films made by Wu Yonggang in the 1930s, including those influenced by Xia Yan's Communist film group, deals with class struggle. Wu acknowledges the existence of social classes, but his approach to social problems is consistently humanistic and culturalist. He recognizes the existence of evil, but he discusses it within the framework of individuals as members of the human race, rather than as representatives of particular social classes. His humanism, unlike the humanism found in Fei Mu's *Filial Piety*, is not explicitly Confucian, although it clearly contains some Confucian elements. The humanist perspective in *Little Angel* seems to have more to do with Christian humanism, a doctrine to which Wu was exposed as a student in a Christian middle school in Kaifeng in the 1920s. The point of all his early work is that members of the human community, regardless of class, are susceptible to the forces of darkness and spiritual pollution. Similarly, all those exposed to contamination can be cleansed. Wu Yonggang is obviously optimistic about the ability of human beings to transform their spiritual life. One way to immunize oneself against the alien cultural microbes that can infect the spirit is to emulate the behavior of such exemplary people as the little angel.

If, indeed, there is an element of Christianity in Wu Yonggang's approach to spiritual salvation, then it sets his work on alien cultural contamination apart from the other approaches discussed here, in at least one sense. He acknowledges, however indirectly, that contemporary Western culture has some redeeming qualities. That is, there were respectable people in the West (in this case, conservative Christians) who sought to combat what was regarded as the spiritual emptiness of liberal bourgeois culture.[28] And, of course, in this respect he was right. In France, Germany, and elsewhere in Europe during the 1920s and early 1930s, some Christian thinkers embraced the emerging fascist critique of bourgeois, liberal culture. In China,

Chiang Kai-shek converted to Christianity in 1930, and many in the foreign missionary community actively supported the New Life Movement.

The problem with *Little Angel* is not that it failed to treat the topic of class struggle. Respected leftist directors routinely made films that had little or nothing to do with the theme of class conflict. The problem, as this chapter has tried to suggest, is that when leftists turned to the subject of alien spiritual pollution, their work was very similar in conception and structure to noncommunist works that dealt with the same issue. It is not the least bit anomalous that Zheng Junli, a well-established leftist actor, played the part of the model Confucian grandson in Fei Mu's *Filial Piety*. Works on spiritual contamination, leftist and nonleftist alike, argue that it is the Chinese people as a whole, not individual social classes, who are threatened by Western spiritual pollution. Films on cultural pollution, including leftist works, do not present the wealthy as class enemies of the poor. They focus on the affluent for another reason. Because the prosperous live and work in closer proximity to Western culture, this pathological approach insists, they are the first to be exposed to the unseen virus of cultural subversion. Even the little angel, a diminutive Lei Feng (a Mao-era model soldier), is told that he might unwittingly catch the disease. Communist critics have ignored *Little Angel* because of the Nationalists' enthusiasm for the film. But if the project had been guided by the Communist film group and the Christian imagery had been dropped, one can easily imagine it being regarded by post-Tiananmen Chinese Marxist enemies of bourgeois liberalization as the centerpiece of early Communist attempts to combat the moral infection caused by alien spiritual pollution.

CHILDREN OF TROUBLED TIMES: SPIRITUAL POLLUTION AS TREASON

Children of Troubled Times (*Fengyun er nü*, 1935), a Communist effort, was made in the same year as *Filial Piety* and *Little Angel*. After writing the original story, Tian Han, a Communist Party member since 1932, was arrested. The screenplay was finally completed by Xia Yan, and the music, which includes the song "March of the Volunteers" (*Yiyongjun jinxing qu*), later adopted as the national anthem of the People's Republic, was composed by the young Communist Nie Er. The part of the protagonist, a young poet, was played by the talented Yuan Muzhi, who joined the Communist Party in 1940.

Children of Troubled Times, like many films that discuss spiritual pollution, is a disappointing work of art, but it is of interest because it is one of the few films of the 1930s that treats the problem of cultural contamination in relation to the deadly serious issue of national defense. In fact, it suggests that those who have capitulated to the subversive currents of foreign spiritual pollution have betrayed the nation in an ongoing cultural war. And traitors, as patriotic schoolchildren are often taught to believe, deserve to die.

As the story opens, a young poet, Xin Baihua, and his close friend, Liang, flee to Shanghai after the hated Japanese invade their Manchurian homeland in 1931. Although they live on the margins of Shanghai society, they are able to help a poor woman and her daughter, who are also refugees from the Northeast. But the poet is primarily interested in finding a way to meet the glamorous young widow who lives across the street. They finally meet in an elegant foreign-style club, full of beautiful women (*mei ren*) dressed in Western fashions. His friend warns the giddy poet about moral corruption and contamination.

A crisis occurs when Liang is arrested for associating with a man who engages in revolutionary activities. Fearing his own arrest, Xin runs away, and wanders the streets aimlessly before he gets up the courage to seek help from the lovely widow. She invites him into her house and into her bed. To avoid the police, the couple flees to Qingdao, which, like Shanghai, is a living symbol of corrupt foreign cultural presence in China. In lovely Qingdao, they pursue a decadent foreign way of life. She uses long cigarette holders; he wears spotless white gloves. They frequent European-style cafés. One day, as she is applying makeup, he reads that his friend Liang has been released from jail. She says it is no use to be concerned about national affairs. So they continue their own affair until Xin learns that Liang has been killed at the battle of Gubeikou, whereupon he suddenly rushes off to the front to join the resistance movement.[29]

The approaches of leftist, rightist, and independent filmmakers to the problem of spiritual pollution are similar in that they reflect common nationalist concerns. Western values are attacked not simply because they are inherently corrupt, but because they are foreign. They are the values of alien intruders who bully and insult the Chinese people as a whole. An underlying theme in all the films on spiritual pollution, including those made in the post-Mao era, is the notion that those Chinese who embrace the culture of the West are behaving in a way that is contrary to the national interest.

Children of Troubled Times is captivating because it takes films about alien cultural contamination one step further. The Confucian work *Filial Piety* and the humanist work *Little Angel* advocate the rejection of spiritual pollution as a means of attaining individual salvation. Such works assume that the national collective can benefit if sufficient numbers of contaminated individuals achieve individual redemption, but this argument is not made in an explicit way and the story is not located in a literal way in the context of a foreign military assault on China. Only in *Children of Troubled Times* does the audience see that the poet's decadent relationship with the foreign-style temptress is the only thing that is preventing him from defending the nation. Thus, those who adopt foreign cultural values are traitors or internal

A young poet (*left*) leads a decadent foreign-style life in Qingdao instead of resisting Japanese aggression in *Children of Troubled Times* (1935, d. Xu Xinzhi). China Film Archive

foreigners in two senses: they shamelessly reject wholesome Chinese ideas about love and family, and they refuse to defend the motherland against foreign military attacks.

SPIRITUAL POLLUTION, ELITE POLITICS, AND POPULAR CULTURE

In 1979, Sun Yu, the director of *Queen of Sports*, observed, "The revolutionary spirit of the May Fourth Movement was upheld and furthered in the cinema of the thirties."[30] This is a point of view that many assume to be true.[31] The general argument is that the maudlin love stories, martial arts adventures, and classical costume dramas that supposedly monopolized the Chinese screen in the 1920s finally gave way in the 1930s, and especially after the formation of the Communist Party film group in 1932, to "progressive," antifeudal, and patriotic films of the May Fourth variety. The reality of filmmaking in the 1930s, this chapter has argued, was considerably more complex.

Radical antitraditionalism and serious intellectual interest in the intricacies of Western liberal culture were two of the hallmarks of elite New Culture and May Fourth thought.[32] However, during the five years treated in this chapter, 1931 to 1935, a backlash against liberal May Fourth approaches to China's problems was under way. This trend was particularly evident in the realm of popular culture and was exploited by a variety of groups. Fascist Blue Shirts, like their European counterparts, railed at the pernicious influence of Western liberal culture, cultural Stalinists active in the Communist underground lamented the "Europeanized" condition of the modem literary movement, and the government's New Life Movement sought to foster renewed public respect for customary Confucian ideas about social relations.

Scholars who have written on Chinese cinema in the 1930s have paid relatively little attention to the films discussed in this chapter and to the general theme of spiritual pollution. Cheng Jihua and his collaborators do not raise the issue of spiritual pollution, preferring instead to focus consistently on problems related to class struggle and patriotic resistance to foreign military and economic intrusions. Jay Leyda generally follows Cheng Jihua in his choice of analytical categories, although, surprisingly, he does not even mention the name of Wu Yonggang, an extremely important director, in the main body of his book. The Soviet scholar Sergei Toroptsev discusses only one of the seven films treated in this article. Such oversights can be explained, in part, by the difficulty of analyzing these works within the ossified but still widely accepted categories of "feudal" and "progressive." This chapter contends that, at least on the explosive issue of the polluting influence of Western culture, the distinction between "feudal" and "progressive" approaches is exceedingly blurry. Films that are associated with leftists, like *Queen of Sports*, *A Bible for Daughters*, and *Children of Troubled Times*, bear a striking resemblance to works that were conceived by the right, like *Filial Piety* and *Little Angel*. Moreover, there is no significant difference between these efforts of the left and right and earlier traditionalist butterfly prototypes like *Peach Blossom Weeps Tears of Blood* and *A Dream in Pink*.

Although most of the films discussed here were not made under leftist political auspices, it is interesting that all the noncommunist film personalities associated with these works, including Bu Wancang, Cai Chusheng, Sun Yu, Fei Mu, and Wu Yonggang, ended up in the leftist camp and contributed in various ways to Communist filmmaking activities either before or after 1949. Most cultural historians have observed that the work of these filmmakers became more politically progressive after they came under the influence of the Party film group. To stress this transformation of consciousness is certainly a valid and useful way of understanding one aspect of the development of Chinese cinema in the 1930s. But this approach can leave the mistaken impression that directors like Cai Chusheng and Fei Mu totally abandoned their earlier ideas about filmmaking when they moved to the left. Insufficient scholarly attention has been given to the manner in which their preleftist notions about cinema and popular culture influenced the subsequent course of leftist filmmaking from the 1930s to the present day. A comparison of *A Dream in Pink*, a butterfly work, and *Children of Troubled Times*, a Communist effort, strongly suggests that the influence of the old-fashioned commercial filmmakers of the 1920s on the left was, in some respects, more profound than the influence of the left on the commercial filmmakers. Indeed, the impact of films like *Peach Blossom Weeps Tears of Blood*, made before the Party film group was formed, is quite apparent in the many films of the post-Mao era that warn Chinese youth about the dangers of spiritual pollution and bourgeois liberalization.

The idea that the spirit of the May Fourth Movement was upheld in the film industry of the 1930s is also misleading because it fails to take into account some of the basic differences between elite and popular cultural phenomena. In some important respects it was quite impossible for the May Fourth spirit of detailed inquiry to be upheld in the film industry. The New Culture and May Fourth literary movements were elite currents confined primarily to the ranks of intellectuals and students. New Culture intellectuals were interested in complexity and subtlety. Their medium was the printed page, and they felt most comfortable with such forms as poetry, the vernacular short story, critical essays, and, eventually, the novel. Modern stage plays (*huaju*) also catered largely to an educated audience. The film medium was very different. It belonged to the realm of popular culture and placed a premium on simplicity of message. In the 1920s, filmmakers had relatively little connection to the legacies of the May Fourth Movement. Their ties were to vaudeville, Hollywood, and the popular theatrical traditions of China, and their function was to provide mass entertainment for the marketplace. The illiterate and semiliterate film audience had little in common with sober-minded May Fourth intellectuals. There were exceptions (people like Tian Han who seem to have drifted rather easily between the literary and film worlds), but intellectuals tended not to regard filmmaking as a serious form of art, and they often found the personal lives of film people to be distasteful, even abhorrent. In brief, literary intellectuals, then and later, tended to look down on filmmaking and the simplistic, one-dimensional messages it conveyed to the masses.

In the 1930s the left and the right became interested in the astonishing power of the visual film image for reasons that were political rather than artistic. Xia Yan and Qu Qiubai, for example, suddenly discovered that films could be forceful "ideological weapons."[33] Filmmakers of all political persuasions were fascinated by the idea that they could use this new medium to shape the consciousness of the semiliterate masses. There was no grand, centrally directed conspiracy to bash European civilization. It is just that political interest in the popular film medium ripened at a time when propagandists of various and even competing political orientations found it useful to blame the problems of China on alien cultural subversion, a notion that was already deeply rooted in urban popular culture. The film medium demanded that ideas about truth, morality, and proper social relations be conveyed in packages that are simple, familiar, sensational, and highly entertaining.

Several basic points need to be made about the image of Western culture conveyed in films that seek to warn the masses about epidemics of spiritual pollution. First, the image amounts to an unadorned and manipulative caricature of Western culture. It suggests that the essence of Western culture is the narcissistic and decadent pursuit of pleasure. One has to look no further than the *wu ting* to comprehend Western cultural priorities. These dens of iniquity contain all the trappings of corrupt society, including shamelessly loose women who smoke cigarettes and dress in elegant but revealing clothing, and oversexed men who stumble around in a drunken stupor. The chaotic dance steps, the bizarre party hats, the seductive music, the exotic hairstyles, and the gleaming cars are always the same. Long-term moral commitments are impossible, and no one can be trusted. Even at work, presumably successful Western-style businessmen seem to do nothing but chase their secretaries and plan clandestine meetings with their lovers. In these films on spiritual pollution, the audience is told little else about Western culture. Virtually no attempt is made to introduce complex, subtle, or contradictory facets of Western cultural life.

Perhaps this sensational caricature of Western values was conceived of as a symbolic representation of Western culture. But when it was repeated time and again with little variation, the caricature undoubtedly created the impression in the minds of many that Westerners, and those Chinese contaminated by alien culture, lived in ways that were consistent with the popular stereotype. The urban film audience, in sharp contrast to intellectual elites, had limited access to information that conflicted with this potent caricature. Ironically, many of the highly popular Depression-era Hollywood films that were screened in Shanghai in the 1930s tended to reinforce the distorted image of Western culture contained in Chinese features.

Understanding the relationship between cinema and popular thought is one of the most imposing challenges facing those who study Chinese films. Clearly, it is not a matter of the film audience having totally accepted or totally rejected this contorted picture of Western values. Yet it is reasonable to assume that the constant repetition of this spectacular, one-dimensional image of Western values in the more than seventy-five years since the release of *Peach Blossom Weeps Tears of Blood* has caused aspects of the stereotype to seep into the consciousness of many viewers who know little else about Western society. In the early 1930s, Chinese political elites began to realize, as European fascists and Soviet Stalinists had already discovered, that the popular media could play a crucial role in mass mobilization and social control.

The films discussed here were supposed to generate popular acceptance of crude caricatures of Western spiritual culture. It is ironic, therefore, that acceptance of the image did not always lead to the adoption of a more wholesome mode of individual behavior. The intention of the filmmakers is clear: the audience should conclude that Western values are repugnant. Yet it is far from clear that the audience always reached such a conclusion. The reason is that even the most lurid and shocking images are, in some respects, highly tantalizing. Undoubtedly, some viewers enjoyed the films because they permitted one to fantasize about a glamorous foreign-style life without running the risks and suffering the consequences of such an existence. Others, when given the opportunity, actually experimented, in order to experience firsthand a bit of the "high life." Still others indulged in what was perceived as Western-style cultural life in order to break taboos. As Mark Twain said, Adam did not want the apple for the sake of the apple; he wanted it because it was forbidden. To the extent that moral codes were perceived as having been written and defended by illegitimate and unpopular wielders of power, breaking those codes was an act of rebellion.

In the 1930s, the campaign against alien cultural contamination was used, in part, by the government and right-wing political forces to turn public attention away from the social and economic problems of the regime. The aggressive penetration of liberal Western culture was made the scapegoat for almost everything that ailed China. Films on the theme of spiritual pollution generally did not take a critical look at the failings of the traditional and contemporary institutions, values, and politics of China itself. The motivations of leftist filmmakers are more difficult to understand, but their work was inspired, in part, by a nationalist desire to root out what they, like the extreme right, perceived to be a humiliating manifestation of popular psychological subordination to colonial rule. Leftist attacks on spiritual pollution were also greatly influenced by the ideologically rigid Stalinist critique of bourgeois culture fashioned in the Soviet Union in the late 1920s and early 1930s.

The campaigns against bourgeois liberalization and Western spiritual pollution launched by the Communist Party in 1981, 1983, 1987, and 1989 were hardly novel. Films like *A Small Street* (*Xiao jie*, d. Yang Yanjin, 1981), *The Herdsman* (*Muma ren*, d. Xie Jin, 1982), and *AIDS Victims*, which project the image of corrupted and drunken young people smoking, drinking, and dancing to the thumping rhythms of disco music, are closely linked to earlier works produced on both sides of the Taiwan Straight, such as *Soul of the Sea* (*Hai hun*, d. Xu Tao, 1957) and *Home Is in Taibei* (*Jia zai Taibei*, d. Bai Jingrui, 1970), and ultimately to such films of the 1930s as *Peach Blossom Weeps Tears of Blood*. All these works insist that the culture of the West is decadent and morally bankrupt, and strongly imply that those Chinese who adopt alien ways are a national disgrace. Those who are identified as people contaminated by a foreign liberal virus are, at the very least, subjected to official scorn and harassment. In moments of madness, however, they can become candidates for annihilation.

NOTES

An earlier version of this chapter appeared as "The Theme of Spiritual Pollution in Chinese Films of the 1930s," *Modern China* 17, no. 1 (January 1991): 38–75.

1. Shu Kei, ed., *A Comparative Study of Post-War Mandarin and Cantonese Cinema: The Films of Zhu Shilin, Qin Jian, and Other Directors* (Hong Kong: Hong Kong International Film Festival, 1983), 193.
2. Cheng Jihua, ed., *Zhongguo dianying fazhan shi* (Beijing: Zhongguo dianying chubanshe, 1981), 1:152–53.
3. Perry Link, *Mandarin Ducks and Butterflies: Popular Fiction in Early-Twentieth-Century Chinese Cities* (Berkeley: University of California Press, 1981), 1–78.
4. Liu Guojun, *Cong xiao yatou dao mingxing: Ruan Lingyu zhuan* (Chengdu: Sichuan wenyi chubanshe, 1986), 3–138.
5. Peter Brooks, *The Melodramatic Imagination: Balzac, Henry James, Melodrama, and the Mode of Excess* (New York: Columbia University Press, 1985), 88.
6. Zhongguo dianyingjia xiehui dianying shi yanjiu bu, ed., *Zhongguo dianyingjia liezhuan* (Beijing: Zhongguo dianying chubanshe, 1982), 1:338–49.
7. Cheng, *Zhongguo dianying fazhan shi*, 1:258–59.
8. Cai Chusheng, "Huikeshi zhong," *Dianying xiju* 1, no. 3 (December 10, 1936).
9. Brooks, *The Melodramatic Imagination*, 33–34.
10. Maurice Meisner, *Marxism, Maoism, and Utopianism: Eight Essays* (Madison: University of Wisconsin Press, 1982), 55.
11. Wang Renmei and Li Lili, "Mingyue gewutuan yu bensepai yan ji," *Zhongguo dianying yanjiu* 1, no. 1 (December 1983): 129–41.
12. Sun Yu, *Yin hai fan chou: huiyi wo de yi sheng* (Shanghai: Shanghai wenyi chubanshe, 1987), 35–40.
13. Hu Die, *Hu Die huiyi lu* (Taibei: Lianhe bao she, 1986), 216–18.

14. Chen Yuan-tsung and Stephan Horowitz, "Catalog of Chinese Films, 1905–1949" (unpublished manuscript, 1980).

15. Lloyd Eastman, "Fascism in Kuomintang China: The Blue Shirts," *China Quarterly* 49 (January–March 1972): 7–8.

16. Ernst Nolte, *Three Faces of Fascism: Action Francaise, Italian Fascism, and National Socialism* (New York: Holt, Reinhart and Winston, 1966), 10–21.

17. Karl Dietrich Bracher, *The German Dictatorship: The Origins, Structure, and Effects of National Socialism* (New York: Holt, Reinhart and Winston, 1970), 142–52, 247–72; Eastman, "Fascism in Kuomintang China."

18. Paul G. Pickowicz, *Marxist Literary Thought in China: The Influence of Ch'ü Ch'iu-pai* (Berkeley: University of California Press, 1981), 99–111.

19. Paul G. Pickowicz, *Marxist Literary Thought and China: A Conceptual Framework* (Berkeley: Center for Chinese Studies, 1980), 9–47.

20. Nolte, *Three Faces of Fascism*, 100–141.

21. Cheng, *Zhongguo dianying fazhan shi*, 1:315.

22. Zhongguo dianyingjia xiehui dianying shi yanjiu bu, *Zhongguo dianyingjia liezhuan*, 1:183–90.

23. Jay Leyda, *Dianying: An Account of Film and the Film Audience in China* (Cambridge, Mass.: MIT Press, 1972), 84.

24. Chen and Horowitz, "Catalog of Chinese Films, 1905–1949."

25. Cheng, *Zhongguo dianying fazhan shi*, 1:349–51.

26. Charlotte Furth, *The Limits of Change: Essays on Conservative Alternatives in Republican China* (Cambridge, Mass.: Harvard University Press, 1976), 203.

27. Zhongguo dianyingjia xiehui dianying shi yanjiu bu, *Zhongguo dianyingjia liezhuan*, 2:156–63.

28. Nolte, *Three Faces of Fascism*, 29–141.

29. Chen and Horowitz, "Catalog of Chinese Films, 1905–1949."

30. Sun Yu, "Cinema in the 1930s under the Influence of the May Fourth Movement," in *Electric Shadows: 45 Years of Chinese Cinema*, ed. Tony Rayns and Scott Meek (London: British Film Institute, 1980), T2.

31. Tuoluopucaifu (Sergei A. Toroptsev), *Zhongguo dianying shi gailun* (Beijing: Zhongguo dianyingjia xiehui ziliao shi, 1982); Leyda, *Dianying*; Cheng, *Zhongguo dianying fazhan shi*.

32. Lin Yusheng, *The Crisis of Chinese Consciousness: Radical Antitraditionalism in the May Fourth Era* (Madison: University of Wisconsin Press, 1972), 3–55.

33. Leyda, *Dianying*, 74.

3
Melodramatic Representation and the May Fourth Tradition of Chinese Cinema

The eventual recovery of the Chinese film industry from the ravages of the Cultural Revolution was nothing short of breathtaking. The obvious quality of works by veteran filmmakers like Xie Jin and irreverent newcomers like Chen Kaige forced Western scholars to take their first serious look at Chinese cinema. Unlike the field of contemporary Chinese literature, however, the newly emerging field of Chinese film studies is severely handicapped by the absence of a large scholarly literature that covers all the decades of the twentieth century. As a result, the new research on Chinese cinema is often narrowly focused. China specialists are inclined to locate recent Chinese films in the decidedly contemporary context of political and economic life in the post-Mao era, whereas film scholars trained in American and European studies tend to analyze Chinese films in terms of feminism, modernism, postmodernism, and other paradigms that were developed primarily for the purpose of criticizing the culture of the contemporary industrial world.[1] But practically no one looks at the accomplishments of post-Mao filmmaking in relation to the Chinese film traditions of the presocialist Republican era. Scholars of contemporary literature want to explore the relationship between post-Mao fiction and its May Fourth literary antecedents, but those who work on contemporary Chinese cinema rarely ask such questions. As a consequence, much of the new scholarship on Chinese filmmaking leaves the unintended but misleading impression that there is no meaningful connection between present-day and early-twentieth-century cinema and that serious Chinese filmmaking began around 1980.

The point of this chapter is to suggest that one of the most important developments in post-Mao cinema is linked, in terms of both form and content, to the rich legacy of Republican-era filmmaking. When scholars of literature refer to the legacy of Republican times, they are usually thinking of the May Fourth tradition of writing. But was there a corresponding May Fourth tradition of filmmaking that represented the best of Republican-era cinema? The answer to this surprisingly complex and politically sensitive question is yes and no.

It is clear that when the New Culture and May Fourth movements were fundamentally reshaping the world of letters in the 1910s and 1920s, they had almost no direct impact on filmmaking circles. In this narrow but crucial sense, we can say without hesitation that there was no May Fourth tradition of filmmaking. Most May Fourth literary intellectuals simply refused to take the film medium seriously. In spite of their professed interest in bringing about a democratization of culture (a modern culture for the masses), they generally expressed contempt for the cinema and made virtually no effort in the 1910s and early 1920s to bring the May Fourth movement to the film studios of Shanghai. Most regarded filmmaking as a vulgar commercial activity that had nothing to do with art.[2] Film pioneers, for their part, showed little interest in May Fourth currents. During the social and political upheavals of the 1910s and early 1920s, the film studios mainly concentrated on producing popular entertainment, which included musicals, light comedies, episodes from traditional fiction and opera, martial arts adventures, detective stories, and morality tales.[3]

This does not mean that filmmakers never treated contemporary subjects. Such works as *Romance of the Fruit Peddler* (*Laogong zhi aiqing*, d. Zhang Shichuan, 1922) and *A String of Pearls* (*Yi chuan zhen zhu*, d. Li Zeyuan, 1925) reveal a society in the throes of a disruptive, modern transformation; but as a rule, the emphasis was on the need to shore up rather than subvert traditional values. Early Chinese filmmakers felt most comfortable when they were dealing with the themes that were the mainstays of traditional and contemporary popular culture.

The notion that one cannot speak of a May Fourth tradition of Chinese filmmaking in the 1910s and early 1920s refers only to the issue of the basic intellectual and political content of May Fourth thought. To qualify as a May Fourth work, a film would have to embrace one or more of the following political positions: nationalist opposition to imperialist aggression, support for the political democratization of Chinese life, and rejection of traditional Confucian morality and values. With some exceptions, Chinese films of the 1910s and early 1920s did none of these things.

It is ironic, therefore, that in terms of form, early Chinese cinema was more thoroughly modern than May Fourth fiction. Making the transition from classical to vernacular literature was agonizing for modern writers. Filmmakers, however, did not have to make any emotionally wrenching transitions simply because there was no Chinese tradition of filmmaking to reject. They were commercial entertainers who accepted, without apology, the basics of the Hollywood approach to filmmaking because it made business sense. This does not mean that there was nothing Chinese about early Chinese films, that they were little more than crude copies of American originals. It simply means that Chinese filmmakers were making effective commercial use of an astonishingly popular cultural medium that everyone knew was foreign in origin.

It would be wrong, however, to suggest that mainstream May Fourth social and political thought had no impact whatsoever on the Chinese film industry in the 1920s. Writings on film history published in China after 1949 leave the mistaken impression that May Fourth thought did not reach the film world until the early 1930s. The veteran director Sun Yu once recalled that upon his return from the United States in 1927, "Eight long years had already passed since the birth of the May Fourth Movement, but none of its revolutionary spirit had penetrated the film world, controlled as it was by commercial entrepreneurs."[4] Actually, by 1925–1927 a few recognized May Fourth intellectuals, including Hong Shen, Ouyang Yuqian, and Tian Han, were writing screenplays and directing films. A small number of the films made in the mid-1920s advocated women's rights, criticized warlord rule, and described the hardships endured by factory workers. By this time there were also a few Chinese film adaptations of literature by Dumas, Maupassant, Ibsen, Molière, Wilde, and others. Moreover, state-of-the-art foreign films by such recognized masters as D. W. Griffith and Charlie Chaplin were well-known in China by the early 1920s.[5] But none of this added up to a May Fourth–type revolution in the film world.

It was not until the early 1930s, long after the original May Fourth movement had ended, that significant strains of basic May Fourth thought began to be reflected in highly simplified and popularized ways in Chinese silent films. We cannot speak of the direct participation of Chinese filmmakers in the original May Fourth movement, but basic ideas we associate with the May Fourth movement did, after all, begin to play a role in the partial reshaping of the film industry in the early 1930s.

The formation of the Lianhua Film Company in 1930 by Luo Mingyou was an important transitional event in the political history of the Chinese film industry.[6] Luo recruited a number of talented and relatively well educated young filmmakers, including Sun Yu, Cai Chusheng, Shi Dongshan, Zhu Shilin, and Bu Wancang, who were interested in making movies that treated social problems in an explicit way.[7] In part, Lianhua was looking for new ways to compete in the marketplace with the flood of American film exports. Between 1896 and 1937, more than five thousand foreign films, most of them American, were marketed in China.[8] Young Chinese filmmakers were now eager to discuss modern social issues in their work, but progress was frustratingly slow in 1930 and 1931.

Japan's occupation of Manchuria in September 1931 and its attack on Shanghai in late January 1932 changed everything. These frightening events were as central to the early political transformation of the film industry as the announcement of the humiliating terms of the Treaty of Versailles had been to the burgeoning new literature movement after 1919. Virtually overnight it became easier for Sun Yu, Cai Chusheng, and newcomer Wu Yonggang to inject overt modern politics into Lianhua films. In fact, circumstances had changed so much by early 1932 that the well-known Mingxing Film Company went so far as to encourage such May Fourth leftist intellectuals as Qian Xingcun, Xia Yan, Zheng Boqi, Yang Hansheng, Tian Han, and Hong Shen, some of whom were Communists, to submit screenplays. Most of these writers were Marxist romantics who had studied in Japan in the mid-1920s and founded the radical Sun Society in Shanghai in 1928 to advance the cause of proletarian literature.[9] For obvious political reasons, Chinese Marxist commentators have grossly exaggerated the significance of the activities of this small group of Party members.[10]

The presence in the film world of noncommunists and Communists sympathetic to May Fourth political traditions did not result in a May Fourth–type transformation of the Chinese film industry.[11] Neither the cultural and political environment of the 1930s nor the nature of the film medium itself would permit such a development. True, anti-imperialist patriotism, a hallmark of May Fourth political thought, became an increasingly important element in Chinese films. But the May Fourth themes of radical antitraditionalism and social democracy were much more difficult, if not impossible, to introduce at this time. The problem was not simply a matter of Nationalist Party censorship.[12] For one thing, May Fourth liberalism and socialism were on the defensive in urban China in the early 1930s. The new Nationalist government was building a base of social support in the urban sector and was advocating a type of nationalism that stressed respect for the Confucian cultural tradition. Some May Fourth intellectuals, including people who were affiliated with the Communist Party, were having second thoughts about the validity of the iconoclastic May Fourth analysis of Chinese culture.

Furthermore, no matter how much they genuinely subscribed to the complex May Fourth intellectual tradition, those who are often credited with bringing the May Fourth movement to the Chinese film industry in 1932 were confronted by a new commercial medium that placed little value on complexity and subtlety. They faced the challenge of having to please a vast new audience whose tastes were already well established. Making movies for the market was not at all like writing fiction for bookish intellectuals.

MELODRAMA AND THE MAY FOURTH TRADITION OF FILMMAKING

In order to understand vital aspects of the relationship between post-Mao Chinese filmmaking and the Republican cinematic tradition, it is necessary to challenge the myth that the Communist Party brought the May Fourth movement to the film studios of Shanghai in 1932. This interpretation implies that the Party had a coherent policy toward filmmaking that was systematically implemented by its operatives in the film world. Before 1932, it is often said, Chinese films were "feudal," "mercenary," and "reactionary"; after 1932, thanks to Xia Yan and the Party, "progressive" films that "reflected" social reality were finally being made in significant numbers.[13] As Sun Yu put it in 1979, "The film industry of the thirties, under the guidance of the Communist Party, managed to uphold and further the revolutionary spirit and ideology of the May Fourth Movement."[14]

The reality was quite different. Reformist political content began to appear in Chinese movies in the mid-1920s and early 1930s, before Xia Yan entered the film world. Individual Communists and leftists wrote screenplays and gave advice beginning in mid-1932, but the Party had no coherent policy toward filmmaking. Nothing at all like a multidimensional and rigorous May Fourth intellectual revolution unfolded at this time. The modern political content found in Chinese films before and after Xia Yan's arrival was a popularized and simplified version of such basic May Fourth ideas as anticapitalism, antiwarlordism, and anti-imperialism (some of which were consistent with official positions adopted by the Nationalists in the early 1930s). But the new themes were mixed in with political content that was old, familiar, and quite inconsistent with May Fourth thought. For instance, there is little evidence of sophisticated May Fourth radical antitraditionalism in the films of the 1930s. It is true that the censors did not encourage such content, but it is also the case that there was no meaningful popular audience for such messages and that the Nationalists' intellectual opposition (liberals and Communists alike) had backed away from the radical iconoclasm that one associates with the original May Fourth movement.

The film industry, one is tempted to say, ended up making a bigger impact on the former May Fourth intellectuals in its ranks than the intellectuals made on the film industry. Even if one gives such directors and screenwriters as Sun Yu, Cai Chusheng, Wu Yonggang, Shen Xiling, and Xia Yan the benefit of the doubt by assuming that they intended to introduce unadulterated May Fourth thought into Chinese films after 1930, it is hard to escape the conclusion that they became prisoners of the film medium. In particular, they became captives of melodrama, a multifaceted genre that dominated American and Chinese filmmaking in the 1910s and 1920s.[15]

To the very end of his life, Xia Yan insisted that he and the others who had May Fourth political pedigrees were fostering social realism in Chinese filmmaking. In fact, like the moguls of the early 1920s, they accepted without question the dominance of the melodramatic genre and thereby doomed to failure any chance they had to introduce complex May Fourth ideas.

Melodrama, as Peter Brooks and others have suggested, is characterized by rhetorical excess, extravagant representation, and intensity of moral claim.[16] It is an aesthetic mode of heightened dramatization that refers to pure and polar concepts of darkness and light, salvation and damnation. The melodramatic genre was developed first in the French theater in the immediate aftermath of the revolution, at a time when a significant postrevolutionary democratization of culture was taking place. Although melodrama is a distinctively modern form, its initial political thrust was conservative. The audience for melodrama included people from all social classes who were frightened and confused by the modern transformation of society. This new and powerful mode of representation had a major impact on European fiction in the mid- and late nineteenth century and was kept alive by filmmakers and television producers in the twentieth century.

The purpose of melodrama is not to deal with the monotony of daily life. Rather, it seeks to put an insecure and troubled mass audience in touch with the essential conflict between good and evil that is being played out just below the surface of daily life. In the melodramatic imagination, the world is essentially "a place of torment, where creatures of prey perpetually thrust their claws into the quivering flesh of the doomed, defenseless children of light."[17] The social mission of melodrama is to explain to the audience the nature of the fundamental moral confrontations that define an unfamiliar and threatening modern world. The petty conflicts of daily family life may seem trivial, the audience is constantly warned, but they are actually a manifestation of profound life-and-death struggles that confront the human community. The melodramatic mode is hostile to realism and naturalism because these modes of representation do not allow the narrative to "break through" to the plane on which moral polarities are visibly at war. The melodramatic artist must "pressure the details of reality to make them yield the terms" of the underlying and genuinely significant drama. Melodrama thus employs an inflated rhetoric that "can infuse the banal and the ordinary with the excitement of grandiose conflict."[18]

The political significance of the melodramatic mode lies in its insistence that ordinary people recognize and confront evil. But the message must be unmediated and irreducible if it is going to arouse the passions of the audience; the underlying "truth" about life must be kept simple. Consequently, melodramatists must rely upon such devices as moral polarization, excessive emotionalism, exaggerated expression, unusual human suffering, and extreme suspense.

It is surely no coincidence that melodrama, a popular cultural response to the anxieties and moral confusion caused by the revolution in France, became so entrenched in China just before and after the 1911 revolution. Although Perry Link does not use melodrama as an analytical category, something closely resembling melodrama was clearly central to the imagination of the "mandarin duck and butterfly" writers who were popular in urban China in late Qing and early Republican times.[19] These talented writers were well aware of the appeals of serialized newspaper fiction in late-nineteenth-century Europe. The fledgling Chinese film industry learned about the seductiveness of melodramatic representation from Hollywood and allowed the genre to dominate Chinese film production in the 1910s and 1920s.

Snobbish and high-brow New Culture and May Fourth literary intellectuals, interested as they were in systems of thought that were quite complex, naturally despised urban popular culture, including butterfly fiction and early Chinese commercial films. They missed the point by failing to see that melodramatic representation was, in its own way, addressing the crisis of twentieth-century Chinese culture and society. As Brooks points out, melodrama is popular in places where "the traditional imperatives of truth and ethics have been violently thrown into question, yet where the promulgation of truth and ethics, their insaturation as a way of life, is of immediate, daily, political concern." Melodrama, he reminds us, "starts from and expresses the anxiety brought by a frightening new world in which the traditional patterns of moral order no longer provide the necessary social glue."[20]

Melodramatic representation was appealing to low-brow, nonintellectual consumers of urban popular culture in the troubled early Republican period because it provided clear answers to nagging questions. As Brooks demonstrates, melodramatic good and evil are highly personalized and can be named as persons are named. "The ritual of melodrama," he suggests, "involves the confrontation of clearly identified antagonists and the expulsion of one of them."[21] There is no ambiguous moral middle ground. Melodramatic representation generally excludes the middle condition and gives little priority to subtlety or nuance. Melodrama is about the persecution of innocence; it teaches a morally confused audience how to recognize the difference between goodness and evil.

LEFTIST FILM MELODRAMAS OF THE 1930S: THE CASE OF SUN YU

When Xia Yan and other leftists sought to inject May Fourth notions about patriotism, Marxism, and progressive social change into Chinese films in the 1930s, the genre of melodrama was already deeply rooted in the industry. Their complaint about the film industry had nothing to do with the melodramatic form; it never occurred to them that there might be other ways to make films. They simply wanted to infuse larger doses of May Fourth political content into the popular melodramatic form. They accepted the genre without reservation and were perceptive in rejecting the idea that popular and commercial cultural forms, by definition, were incapable of conveying forward-looking political messages. Melodrama was appealing to them because it used clear language to identify and combat evil. They understood that a disadvantage of the genre was that it could be put to almost any political use, conservative or revolutionary. The melodramas of the 1920s (butterfly fiction and commercial films alike) often had conservative social implications; Xia Yan wanted to force the genre to serve revolutionary political ends. He liked the fact that melodrama was an inherently manipulative form of art. But what he and other leftists did not comprehend was that there would be no place for the complexities and subtleties, and most of the crucial middle ground, of May Fourth socialist thought in melodramatic representation.

When Chinese Marxists speak of the May Fourth tradition of filmmaking, they are not talking about anything that would strike Western scholars as a diverse, multidimensional, May Fourth–type intellectual revolution. The May Fourth tradition to which they refer is something much narrower. It amounts to a heroic, indeed melodramatic, legend that was tailored after 1949 to meet the political needs of the new socialist state, which, among other things, required the expropriation and manipulation of popular memories of the May Fourth movement. When they speak of the introduction of May Fourth thought in the film world in the 1930s, they mean the introduction of Marxism—which, to be sure, is a part, but only a part, of the original May Fourth tide. It refers to the now celebrated activities of such Communists and leftists as Xia Yan, Zheng Boqi, Qian Xingcun, Tian Han, Wang Chenwu, Shi Linghe, and Situ Huimin in the 1932–1937 period and to the films made by such "converted" veteran directors as Cai Chusheng, Sun Yu, and Wu Yonggang and such newcomers as Shen Xiling and Ying Yunwei.[22] The myth of Xia Yan and the May Fourth Communist Film Group was trampled upon during the Cultural Revolution, but it was revived with a vengeance by Xia and his backers in the late 1970s.[23] Pre- and post–Cultural Revolution Chinese writings consistently advance the cult of Xia Yan and other leftists by suppressing information about other developments and by failing to acknowledge the close connection between the May Fourth films of the 1930s and the popular melodramas of the 1920s.[24]

It is extremely difficult to challenge the conventional interpretation because the Chinese authorities control almost all the archival resources and, until recent times, have been inclined to allow ready access only to those films that appear to support the official view. But access to the films produced by the progressive camp after 1932 does at least provide us with an opportunity to evaluate the claim that they constitute a May Fourth tradition of filmmaking. What is most striking about these films is not their popularized May Fourth contents (although it is clear that new social and political themes emerged in the 1930s), but their melodramatic packaging. Sun Yu's *Daybreak* (*Tianming*, 1933), Wu Yonggang's *Goddess* (*Shennü*, 1934), Ying Yunwei's *Plunder of Peach and Pear* (*Tao li jie*, 1934), Shen Xiling's *The Boatman's Daughter* (*Chuanjia nü*, 1935), Cai Chusheng's *Lost Lambs* (*Mitu de gaoyang*, 1936), and Yuan Muzhi's *Street Angel* (*Malu tianshi*, 1937) are among the scores of May Fourth or left-wing films of the 1932–1937 period that so clearly belong to the broad category of melodrama. Melodrama was not the only genre that existed in the 1930s, but it was by far the most dominant. And it was a genre especially well suited to the task of popularizing and dramatizing basic Marxist ideas.

It is sufficient, for our purposes, to take a close look at one of these works, Sun Yu's leftist tear-jerker *Small Toys* (*Xiao wanyi*, 1933), a film that was praised by Xia Yan as soon as it appeared.[25] *Small Toys* contains precisely the type of rhetorical excess, grossly exaggerated representations, and extreme moral bipolarity that one finds in Chinese film melodramas of the 1920s and, for that matter, in the classic American film melodramas made by D. W. Griffith that were so well-known in China.[26] Sun Yu's work, like the work of almost all May Fourth filmmakers in the 1930s, constituted a mode of excess that had little in common with the original May Fourth respect for diversity, complexity, and subtlety of social analysis.

Set in the early 1920s, *Small Toys* tells the sad story of a virtuous and beautiful village woman who makes charming children's toys to support her family. Pastoral life is idyllic, and the woman is utterly devoted to her kind and unassuming husband. Suddenly, however, the handicraft industry and the tranquility of family life are shattered by an imperialist economic invasion of China. To make matters worse, the woman's husband dies, and her baby son is stolen and sold to a wealthy urbanite. When fighting between rival warlords breaks out, the woman flees with her innocent and lovely daughter to Shanghai where they live in a simple shanty.

Ten years later (1932) the mother and teenage daughter still try to eke out a living making wholesome and quaint folk toys, but their existence is threatened now by Chinese industrialists who are mass-producing such frightening but popular war toys as planes, cannons, and ships. Once again disaster strikes, when an unnamed but dastardly foreign enemy (the Japanese) attacks Shanghai. The woman's patriotic daughter volunteers to work in a first-aid unit and is killed in the fighting.

The pathetic woman wanders about aimlessly in the faceless and uncaring metropolis, trying in vain to sell her old-fashioned toys. On New Year's

82 Chapter 3

Day, a sacred time of family unity, she peddles a toy to a handsome rich boy. Of course, it is her long-lost son, but the woman fails to recognize him. A string of firecrackers explodes nearby. The half-crazed woman begins shouting: "The enemy is coming to kill us! Hurry up! We all must fight back! Save your country, save your families, save yourselves! Wake up, stop dreaming! Save China!" Some bystanders think she is insane, but others are beginning to listen.

On the one hand, we see in this classic leftist silent film virtually all of the elements of melodramatic representation that are present in the works of Bu Wancang (see chapter 2) and other leading melodramatists of the 1920s. The plain and innocent rural woman, a suffering victim of evil who represents Chinese purity, is played by the renowned starlet Ruan Lingyu, whose impressive mastery of the exaggerated style of melodramatic acting won her the adoration of the Chinese film audience in the early 1930s.[27] Shanghai, the wicked and corrupting modern metropolis, is correspondingly associated with murky and alien forces that prey on the virtuous. The confrontation, in short, involves clearly identifiable bipolar forces. Indeed, this tale conforms to mid-nineteenth-century French family melodramas

The idyllic life of a wholesome, but vulnerable, rural woman (*center*) is shattered by diabolical forces of evil in *Small Toys* (1933, d. Sun Yu). China Film Archive

that view the modern city as the "symbol of corruption lying in wait for peasant innocence."[28]

But in *Small Toys* we can also see the ways in which a streamlined and popularized Marxist political and economic analysis has been superimposed on the familiar and dominant melodramatic framework. For example, the struggle between good and evil is linked to class conflict. An important secondary plot in *Small Toys* involves the impossibility of a permanent love relationship between the folksy woman (who represents the innocent simplicity of preindustrial China) and a wealthy village lad who aspires to be a technologically sophisticated capitalist. Later in the film, the young man resurfaces as the owner of a modern toy factory that undermines the traditional handicraft industry but can do nothing to defend China against the real military strength of Japan. Apart from the loving bond that ties mother to child, the only healthy relationships the woman has in the city are with poor working-class people in the neighborhood who, like her, have fled the ravaged countryside. The evil metropolis is associated with the bourgeoisie much more clearly than it was in melodramas of the 1920s, while foreign economic and military threats are now explicitly labeled as imperialist. *Small Toys* is a lesson in elementary Marxism whose ability to reach the public depends on the rhetorical excesses of the melodramatic format.

Part of the reason that melodrama has been so successful in China is that it invariably focuses on family life. The assumption is that everything one needs to know about the bedrock moral confrontations that are shaping the new and unfamiliar modern world can be revealed in a dramatically heightened and sensationalized presentation of ordinary family life. Nothing is more central to Chinese life than the family. The crisis of nineteenth- and early-twentieth-century China was experienced by common people, in large part, as a family crisis. In the classic film melodramas of the 1920s, family crisis is precipitated by the erosion of traditional conceptions of morality, but we are not told why time-honored norms have broken down or what might restore them. In *Small Toys*, the accusing finger is pointed directly at the ravenous economic and political appetites of domestic and foreign class enemies, who are presented as dehumanized "others." Salvation—that is, the "new" family—will spring from the class solidarity of the persecuted and cruelly victimized poor.[29]

SADISM, MASOCHISM, AND MAY FOURTH MELODRAMAS IN THE 1940S: THE CASE OF TANG XIAODAN

The May Fourth–leftist film project came to an abrupt halt in 1937 when the war with Japan erupted. Most of the film personalities discussed here fled the Japanese occupation and engaged in other artistic and literary work in the interior. The people involved in making leftist melodramas were not able to regroup and recruit new talent until 1946, when they began at once to make films that revived the critical traditions of the 1930s. This time Xia Yan did not play a leading role. Consequently, the films of the late 1940s have not received the accolades that are reserved exclusively for the 1930s. In many respects, however, the films of the late 1940s, complete with detailed sound dialogues, are more interesting and complex than the mostly silent May Fourth films of the 1930s and probably did more to subvert the legitimacy and authority of the Nationalist state. Nevertheless, the genre adopted most often by postwar directors who had critical impulses was the leftist family melodrama pioneered by Sun Yu and others in the early 1930s.

A typical example of the May Fourth films of the 1940s is a work by Tang Xiaodan, *Heavenly Spring Dream* (*Tiantang chun meng*, 1947), one of the first postwar efforts of the state-owned China Film No. 2 studio in Shanghai. A native of Fujian, Tang Xiaodan learned how to make film melodramas after his arrival in Shanghai in 1929 at the tender age of nineteen. In the early 1930s he established close personal relations with Shen Xiling, a key leftist melodramatist, who, in turn, introduced Tang to Tian Han, Yang Hansheng, Situ Huimin, and other leading Communist film personalities.[30]

Heavenly Spring Dream tells the excruciatingly painful story of the engineer Ding Jianhua (whose name means "builder of China"), a virtuous and patriotic man who participated and sacrificed in the military resistance to Japanese imperialism. On the day the war ends, Ding is in Sichuan. His faithful and devoted wife proudly announces that she is pregnant. The ecstatic couple rushes back to Shanghai to start a new family, build a dream house, reunite with Ding's widowed mother, and help reconstruct a victorious China. Upon their return to Shanghai they are invited to stay in the home of a seemingly good-hearted contractor Ding knew before the war. But, we soon learn, appearances can be deceiving. During the occupation the contractor collaborated with the Japanese and became wealthy. After the war he bribed officials and obtained a falsified government document stating that he had been a patriotic underground operative during the war.

Naturally, multiple disasters strike before any of Ding's "spring dreams" can be realized. The postwar economy is in chaos, so he is unable to find a job rebuilding China. Since he has no money, he becomes increasingly dependent on the unsavory collaborator. Since Ding's wife is pregnant and his mother is sick, he agrees to sell the blueprint of his dream house to the collaborator, who is in need of suitable lodgings for his seductive mistress.

Ding can neither pay his wife's hospital bills nor support the son she bears. The rich traitor agrees to pay all costs, on condition that Ding gives up his newborn son. The traitor and his vicious wife have no children. (In

Chinese melodramas, evil people are often denied children of their own.) But the arrangement collapses when Ding's wife finds out about the plan and accuses the traitor's wife of abusing the infant. The Dings are then thrown out on the street to fend for themselves.

As they stagger along the highway, their dreams and hopes smashed to smithereens, the rich traitor pulls up in a shiny American car and talks in hushed tones with Ding, who once again, against the frantic protestations of his wife, surrenders his infant son. Farther down the road the suffering couple happens upon the home the traitor has built for his mistress with Ding's blueprints. Inside the house the traitor, the mistress, and the mistress's mother are blissfully playing with Ding's baby boy.

This sensational and exaggerated representation of the struggle between darkness and light in postwar China is remarkably similar, in terms of both form and content, to the Marxist melodramas produced by Sun Yu, Cai Chusheng, and others in the 1930s. The moral poles of vice and virtue stand out in stark, unmediated relief. Purity and innocence are represented by honest, hardworking people who love China. Greedy and lustful villainy is represented by the class enemy, bourgeois city slickers who are in league with foreign imperialism.

Sadistic agents of darkness shamelessly degrade decent folks in *Heavenly Spring Dream* (1947, d. Tang Xiaodan). China Film Archive

Heavenly Spring Dream opened on March 12, 1947, at two important Shanghai theaters, Huanghou and Guanghua. Its melodramatic essence is conveyed beautifully in emotionally charged advertising that appeared in local newspapers: "A great tragedy!" (*da beiju*), "Victory turns into tears!" (*shengli liu yanlei*), "Veterans are starving!" (*fuyuan e du pi*), "Crazed anger, incredible bitterness!" (*qi de fafeng, ku dao jidian*), "Anyone who wants to cry will have a good one here!" (*yao ku dajia ku yi chang*), "The poor are at the mercy of the rich, bones and flesh are ripped asunder!" (*qiong bu di fu, gu rou bei duo*), "Good can't compete with evil, gentlemen meet their doom!" (*hao buru huai, junzi lunluo*).[31] In both the 1930s and the 1940s, it was precisely this type of heightened and intensified rhetoric and highly polarized moral clarity that ordinary people expected to find in feature films. In public declarations in 1947, the director Tang Xiaodan used the same melodramatic language to describe the main themes of *Heavenly Spring Dream*: "Honest and conscientious government employees could barely survive, while crooked, traitorous former collaborators were instantly formed into 'underground workers.'"[32]

In films like *Small Toys* and *Heavenly Spring Dream*, the suffering of weak and upstanding people is always painfully intense and excessive. Virtuous and traditionalistic women (or feminized male surrogates like Ding Jianhua) must be insulted and humiliated, innocent children must die needless deaths, and the elderly must perish. Good people must be plagued by death and destitution. The point, of course, is that the forces of evil are sadistic. In melodrama, it is not enough to say that the agents of darkness inflict pain; they must be portrayed as demons who actually derive pleasure from tormenting their victims. But the dialectic of melodramatic representation also involves masochism. For the mode of excess to work on the audience, it is not enough to show that the representatives of virtue and goodness are weak and defenseless; they must be like Ding Jianhua, that is, people who endure staggering amounts of pain without registering a protest. Indeed, the terrible pain they endure in silence is, in a perverse way, welcomed by the persecuted, because it provides righteous victims with an unambiguous identity and thus gives meaning to their lives.

It is easy to understand why leftists were attracted to melodrama before and after the war. They wanted to find a way to make this popular genre serve revolutionary rather than conservative politics. They introduced basic Marxist notions of class struggle, capitalism, and imperialism to sharpen the vague images of good and evil that abounded in classic melodramas. But, as Robert Lang demonstrates in his fine study of American film melodrama, the genre demands drastic simplification and stereotyping. The entrenched operations of melodrama "turn on repetition and ritual." "As a temporal medium, the narrative requirements of which compressed real time," Lang observes, "films learned how to signify as much as possible by means of condensation, displacement, and new codes peculiar to the medium and the form."[33] Leftists may have thought they were bringing the May Fourth tradition of Marxism to the Chinese cinema, but in many May Fourth films of the 1930s and 1940s—movies that are still commonly referred to as works of "social realism"—Marxist ideas were swallowed up by the melodramatic genre and reduced to stereotypes and caricatures.[34]

Marxism, for instance, has a great deal to say about what motivates capitalists and imperialists. One might even say that it is crucial for any self-respecting Marxist to possess a sophisticated and nuanced understanding of what motivates the bourgeoisie. But the mode of excess has great difficulty explaining what motivates evil that is so utterly extreme and sadistic, or for that matter, virtue that is so masochistic. There are no logical ways to account for a villainy that is so profoundly diabolical. But as Brooks points out, "Evil in the world of melodrama does not need justification."[35] It is enough to know that it exists and must be combated. The audience does not need to know much and, melodramatists often assume, does not want to know much about the details of its origins. The purpose of melodrama is to arouse passions. Original May Fourth Marxism had to be distorted beyond recognition if it was going to be useful to melodramatists.

XIE JIN AND MAY FOURTH MELODRAMAS IN THE 1980s

An official biography of Xie Jin, without a doubt the most important Chinese filmmaker of the post-1949 period in terms of audience appeal, confidently states that he is "a realist artist."[36] Actually, his work has very little to do with realism. Xie Jin is one of the most renowned melodramatists in Chinese film history, a man whose films are clearly linked to the May Fourth tradition of the 1930s and 1940s. Although he is normally discussed within the framework of filmmaking in the socialist People's Republic, Xie received his basic training in stagecraft and filmmaking in the Republican 1940s. During the war he studied drama in a Nationalist school and did production work with Hong Shen, Chen Liting, and other leftists in Chongqing. After the war his former teacher Wu Renzhi, who began making film melodramas in the early 1940s, got Xie a job as an assistant director at the Datong Film Company in Shanghai. At Datong, Xie worked closely with such veterans as Tian Han, Zheng Xiaoqiu, and Hong Shen.

Xie Jin made a number of important films in the 1950s and 1960s, following his conversion to Marxism, but the purpose of this chapter is not to offer a detailed discussion of the fate of the melodramatic mode in the pre–Cultural Revolution and Cultural Revolution years. It would be misleading, however, to suggest that the advent of the socialist realist and Stalinist modes in China in 1949 spelled the end of melodramatic representation. Nothing could be further from the truth.

But in the thirty years between 1949 and 1979, melodrama clearly did not play the same critical role, in terms of politics and society, that it had played in the 1932–1937 and 1946–1949 periods and therefore does not belong to the May Fourth film tradition discussed here. May Fourth melodramas specialized in the criticism of contemporary society. Their criticisms may have had little in common with realism, but they were criticisms that subverted state authority nonetheless. The most memorable film melodramas of the 1950s and 1960s, by contrast, including Xie Jin's *Red Detachment of Women* (*Hongse niangzi jun*, 1960) and *Stage Sisters* (*Wutai jiemei*, 1964), did not focus on the new socialist society (see chapter 8). In thematic terms, film melodramas of the early socialist era were bogged down in the portrayal of the old Republican period. It was a propagandistic victor's cinema. Now that the Nationalists had been soundly defeated on the battlefield, the state-owned cinema industry could deal with the Republican era any way it wanted. The purpose of melodrama was now to legitimize the new rule of the Communist Party by portraying Republican times as hell on earth.

Film melodramas of the 1930s and 1940s are more interesting because they confronted forces of evil that were very much alive and kicking. These melodramas had an explicit contemporary relevance, whereas new socialist treatments of the wicked Republican era felt more like closely guided museum tours. One of the strong appeals of such classic melodramas as *Small Toys* and *Heavenly Spring Dream* was that, while they identified and confronted villainy, and in terms that were consistent with an elementary Marxist viewpoint, it was not compulsory that virtue and justice win out by the end of the picture. In the melodramas Xie Jin made upon his graduation in the early 1950s from the Political Research Institute of North China Revolutionary University, by contrast, the structure is always the same. First. the forces of evil (Nationalist Party operatives, landlords, traitors, Japanese) sadistically torment virtuous people (masochistic poor peasants, women, children, and old people). The Communist Party then routs the enemies of humankind and delivers their innocent victims to the promised land of socialism.

The point is that Chinese filmmakers in the 1950s and 1960s broke with the May Fourth tradition of the 1930s and 1940s by failing to make family melodramas that criticized contemporary social conditions and thus subverted state authority. Chinese filmmakers and the Chinese film audience slowly but surely began to lose touch with the May Fourth cinematic tradition. Classic leftist melodramas of the 1930s and 1940s were rarely shown. Socialist society itself could not be subjected to the direct and highly exaggerated critical reviews typical of the melodramatic genre. To the extent that new film melodramas discussed problems in socialist society, the problems had to be blamed on remnant evils (class enemies, bourgeois ideology, imperialism) associated with the Republican era.[37] Prohibited from looking for evil within the socialist system itself, self-respecting melodramatists were unable to play their proper role. I do not mean to suggest that filmmakers failed completely to produce works that pointed to the weaknesses of the socialist system. But, interestingly, most of the critical films that were made, such as Lu Ban's *Before the New Director Arrives* (*Xin juzhang daolai zhi qian*, 1956) and Xie Jin's own *Fat Li, Young Li, and Old Li* (*Da Li, Xiao Li, he Lao Li*, 1962), were satirical comedies, not melodramas.

It was not until Chinese society passed through the ordeal of the Cultural Revolution that the stage was set for the revival of melodramatic representation in Chinese films. The distinguished critic Shao Mujun is certainly right when he insists that the films made by Xie Jin after 1979 are "a contemporary expression" of the "tradition of Chinese progressive films which began to take shape in the 1930s, and became more and more mature in the 1940s." Shao refrains from using the term *melodrama*, preferring instead to perpetuate the idea of Xie Jin as a "realist." But even Shao, an arch-defender of the "Xie Jin style," resorts to the vocabulary of melodrama when he says that Xie Jin presses "close to reality by praising the good and denouncing the evil." "In the films made in the first three decades of New China," Shao observes, "this fine tradition vanished."[38]

Western observers, myself included, have shown the greatest amount of critical interest in the so-called Fifth Generation films of Chen Kaige, Tian Zhuangzhuang, Huang Jianxin, and others who, in their treatments of Republican and socialist China, thoroughly reject the melodramatic approach. By the mid-1980s, many of these young deconstructionist filmmakers were openly (and naively) proclaiming that the Xie Jin era was over. There is no question that the most creative artists to emerge on the Chinese film scene in the post-Mao period were the 1982 graduates of the Beijing Film Institute. Still, from the perspective of the early 1990s, it must be acknowledged that in many respects the most significant trend of the 1980s was the amazing revival of May Fourth melodramas. This conclusion is based in part on the behavior of the film audience, whose numbers rose from ten billion to eighteen billion between 1982 and 1988.[39] Melodrama, more than any other genre, positioned itself to meet the psychological needs of an emotionally drained and politically battered urban film audience. Xie Jin was the leader of the revival.

Xie Jin made so many award-winning family melodramas in the 1980s that one hardly knows where to begin (see chapter 9). *The Legend of Tianyun Mountain* (*Tianyun shan chuanqi*, 1980), *The Herdsman* (*Mumaren*, 1982), and *Garlands at the Foot of the Mountain* (*Gaoshan xia de huahuan*, 1984) are all excellent examples of critical melodramas that resonate with the nearly forgotten Republican-era May Fourth tradition. But Xie Jin's crowning achievement, released at a time when he was under enormous pressure from conservative political forces within the Communist Party and from young filmmakers and critics who were contemptuous of the Xie Jin mode, was *Hibiscus Town* (*Furongzhen*, 1987). Far from being a symbol of the end of the Xie Jin era, *Hibiscus Town* was selected by film professionals in January 1988 for first-place honors in four categories, including best picture, at the seventh annual Jinji Film Award ceremony and was also chosen by film fans for first place in four categories, including best picture, in the tenth annual Hundred Flowers film competition sponsored by *Popular Cinema* magazine. In the first ten Hundred Flowers competitions, Xie Jin films were voted best picture of the year five times by ordinary filmgoers.[40]

The novel by Gu Hua upon which Xie Jin's film is based is not an especially distinguished work of fiction. But in Xie Jin's condensed and dramatically heightened telling, the story moved millions of people and, like all his films of the 1980s, provided an opportunity for mass catharsis that no single work of fiction could provide. Melodramas of the Republican era, including May Fourth films, helped ordinary people deal with wrenching anxieties produced by the collapse of the customary Chinese moral universe. Xie Jin's melodramas of the 1980s were also produced in a context of profound cultural crisis, but this time it was the new socialist culture and morality that had taken root in the 1950s that were in crisis.[41]

Hibiscus Town opens in 1963 on the eve of the vindictive and destructive socialist education movement. The representative of the first polar extreme, goodness and virtue, is hardworking and honest Hu Yuyin, who also happens to be the most beautiful woman in town. Like the enterprising heroine of *Small Toys*, this symbol of virtue is vulnerable and innocent. The Chinese word *yu*, which appears in her name, means jade, a symbol of purity. Her privately run outdoor bean-curd stall is the most popular and lively place in Furongzhen. The picturesque setting of colorful people, cobblestone streets, and quaint houses seems idyllic.

It soon becomes apparent that something is dreadfully wrong with this pleasant scene For one thing, Hu's marriage is passionless. Her husband is a good and simple person, but like Ding Jianhua in *Heavenly Spring Dream*, he is an ineffectual and timid shadow of a man. They have a sterile and childless marriage of convenience in the socialist promised land. Her true love, a lost love, is the easygoing but virtuous local Party secretary. The couple was engaged at one point, but he was advised by heartless and calculating Party elders to break it off, lest he ruin his chances for a political career by marrying a peddler who has shaky class credentials. He then enters into a loveless marriage with a mean-spirited, grasping harpy.

There are other indications that the socialist system of class labeling is in serious disarray. On the one hand, a small and pathetic group of people, who have been branded "bad elements" by the Party, looks rather harmless.

On the other hand, a disheveled young man named Wang Qiushe, who begs for free meals at Hu's stall, is identified as a former poor peasant activist in the local Party-led land reform movement. Wang is a parasite who dreads hard work. Rather than sweat to earn an honest living, Wang sells to Hu Yuyin an old house that had been given to him by the Party.

Suddenly, a Party work team, headed by a cunning and vicious woman named Li Guoxiang, the primary representative of the second polar extreme, evil and villainy, shows up to implement the Socialist Education Movement. She is shocked to find the former poor peasant activist Wang Qiushe still living in poverty, while the private entrepreneur Hu Yuyin, who nourishes the people with her noodles and smiles, is celebrating the completion of a new house. "The rich get richer," she hisses, "while the poor get poorer."

All the local people are forced to attend a mass political meeting one dark night. Li Guoxiang frightens everyone by charging that the folksy old cadres, loved and respected by the common people, have neglected class struggle. Crazy Qin, an innocuous local bookworm who was branded as a rightist in 1957, is brought up on stage and publicly humiliated. There are only two choices, Li rants: either this class enemy "stinks" or he is "fragrant." There can be no middle ground.

To save himself, the young Party secretary betrays his former lover, Hu Yuyin. "In this world," he moans, "you've got to get others or they'll get you!" In rapid succession, Hu is declared a new rich peasant, her home and money are confiscated (though she has done nothing illegal), and her husband dies after attempting to kill the wicked Li Guoxiang. For the next three years Hu works alongside the other political lepers who are forced to sweep the streets before dawn every day.

When the disastrous Cultural Revolution strikes in 1966, local despot Li Guoxiang falls from power for a brief time and is made to stand alongside unsavory "bad elements." Before long, however, she is cleared and immediately forges a dirty political and sexual alliance with Wang Qiushe, the worthless, poor peasant buffoon.

Meanwhile, a spiritually healthy bond of respect and love develops between the still-radiant Hu Yuyin and Crazy Qin, the compassionate rightist who turns out not to be crazy at all. But their chance for happiness is crushed when Hu becomes pregnant. First, the sadistic leaders torment the couple by denying their request to get married, and then Crazy Qin is sentenced to ten years in prison. The torture continues as Hu Yuyin, late in her pregnancy, is still forced to sweep snow off the frozen streets. Finally, a sexually impotent but kindly old cadre who hates the dastardly (and childless) Li Guoxiang rushes pitiful Hu Yuyin to a military hospital, where she gives birth to a healthy son she calls Jun ("Army").

Ten years later, in 1979, it appears that evil has been vanquished, although the process by which it has been confronted and driven out is never

The virtuous Hu Yuyin (*right*), a fragrant blossom that attracts hornets as well as butterflies, is cruelly tormented by vicious Communist operatives in *Hibiscus Town* (1987, d. Xie Jin). China Film Archive

revealed. Hu Yuyin's house and money are returned to her, Qin (now her husband) is released from prison, and the family is united. Naturally, they reopen her lively and popular bean-curd stall. But, at the same time, the degenerate Li Guoxiang has somehow been promoted to a higher office. Wang Qiushe, reduced to the status of village idiot, runs about ominously shouting, "A movement is starting! A movement is starting!" People of virtue, we are warned, must remain on guard.

In technical terms Xie Jin is every bit as careful as his Hollywood counterparts. *Hibiscus Town* is a slick production that meets and in some respects surpasses international standards. But at heart it is still a melodrama that is linked to the classic nonleftist and leftist melodramas that were so popular in the Republican era. The prerelease publicity for *Hibiscus Town* could have been written in the 1930s for films like *Small Toys*. For example, *Shanghai Film Studio Pictorial*, making unabashed use of the rhetoric of excess, told its readers: "Hu Yuyin, a natural and fragrant hibiscus flower rooted in the good earth of Furongzhen, attracts many beautiful butterflies, but she also attracts ferocious and evil hornets. Battered by countless storms and icy chills, the petals of the hibiscus blossom wither and fall. For what seems like an eternity, this beautiful and kind-hearted rural lass endures an unjust fate of ridicule and devastation."[42]

Like *Small Toys*, *Hibiscus Town* is located in the vibrant rural heartland of China and involves a pure, innocent, and defenseless woman (the symbol of China) whose family is ruthlessly persecuted by a source of evil that is alien to everything that is Chinese. The polarization of virtue and villainy is absolute; no middle course is allowed. Pain and suffering are inflicted with sadistic pleasure and endured by their victims in a passive, even masochistic, fashion. The narrative is condensed, heightened, and exaggerated in a way that converts the banalities of daily family life into dramatic and highly significant events that symbolize the central moral confrontation of the era. The unspeakably sinister Li Guoxiang arrives in Furongzhen at precisely the moment when the innocent Hu Yuyin is celebrating the completion of her new house. The heavens open and torrential rains fall to earth at precisely the moment her defenseless husband is sentenced to ten years. A deeply rooted system of melodramatic signification is used by Xie Jin to identify the difference between darkness and light and thereby ease the anxieties of a mass audience that has been severely shaken and thrown into profound moral confusion by various cultural calamities. The melodramatic mode provides easy and comforting answers to difficult and complex questions. It offers moral clarity at a time when nothing seems clear. But by personalizing evil, the film leaves the impression that everything would be fine if only the "evil" people were removed from power and replaced by people of "virtue."

In spite of Shao Mujun's assertion that Xie Jin's post–Cultural Revolution melodramas are a "contemporary expression" of the "fine tradition" of critical filmmaking in the 1930s and 1940s, it is clear that Xie Jin's recent work departs from the leftist May Fourth tradition in one highly significant way. To the extent that the social and political sources of evil and villainy are established at all in May Fourth melodramas, they are associated with the agents of feudalism, capitalism, and imperialism. Similarly, virtue and innocence are invariably associated with the poor and oppressed classes of workers and peasants. The unspoken assumption of many of these classic films was that an anticapitalist, working people's socialist revolution would expel evil and save China. In Xie Jin's *Hibiscus Town*, however, this familiar conception is turned on its head. It is the demonic agents of the Communist Party and their poor peasant running dogs who represent evil, whereas hardworking entrepreneurs and "counterrevolutionary rightists" represent virtue and purity. Thus May Fourth–type melodramas were originally designed in the 1930s and 1940s to introduce simplified socialist politics, but Xie Jin's films are, in some important ways, designed to raise serious questions about the type of socialism that unfolded in China after 1949.

Chinese melodramatists like Xie Jin could get away with this type of blasphemous representation in the 1980s because it was consistent with the Party's own self-serving desire to identify the Cultural Revolution as an aberration. But Xie Jin's melodramas pushed far beyond the officially sanctioned condemnation of the Cultural Revolution. Xie and other melodramatists often begin with the Cultural Revolution in their films, but go on to lambaste the forced collectivization of agriculture, the Anti-Rightist Campaign, the Great Leap Forward, and the socialist education movement. Xie Jin never says that the Communist Party is hopeless and must be overthrown, but the viewer is left wondering whether the Party did anything right after 1949. It is for this reason that Xie Jin, a veteran Party member himself, was so disliked and distrusted by such Party elders as Deng Liqun and Hu Qiaomu.

Once Xie Jin and other loyal Party members began to use the popular melodramatic format to review the record of the Party in the entire post-1949 period, they became prisoners of the genre. The logic of melodramatic sensationalism dictates that the Party must be viewed as either good or evil. No matter how many unjustly persecuted and kindly old cadres and Party members are worked into the story and no matter how many happy endings are tacked on at the end, as they are in *The Legend of Tianyun Mountain* and *The Herdsman*, Xie Jin's films still assign the villain's role to the Party and thereby seriously subvert its prestige and reputation—just as such May Fourth films as *Small Toys* and *Heavenly Spring Dream* subverted Nationalist authority.

But there is another, and more important, sense in which Xie Jin is trapped by the melodramatic mode.[43] Melodrama may be appealing because it reveals to the audience the highly personalized human faces of virtue and evil and allows the audience to observe both the depraved intrigues of villainy and the pathetic suffering of its innocent and helpless victims. But aside from arousing righteous indignation, melodrama simply does not take its fanatically loyal audience very far. *Hibiscus Town* and Xie Jin's other melodramas, like their forerunners in the 1930s and 1940s, never tell the audience what motivates evil; they never explain why evil is evil. Evil simply exists and must be struggled against. Furongzhen, like the village portrayed in *Small Toys*, is a happy and tranquil place. Suddenly, and without explanation, the vile Li Guoxiang comes along to inflict pain and misery. Just as suddenly, the Cultural Revolution ends, Hu Yuyin's property and husband are returned, and the town seems tranquil once again. The role of the victims of evil is to suffer and sacrifice rather than resist. The victims do not seem to have a hand in their own salvation. Because Xie Jin's political melodramas, like May Fourth melodramas of the Republican period, focus so narrowly on the family unit, it is impossible for him to say anything significant about social and political forces that are at work outside the family.[44] This is why some scholars regard the family melodrama as an essentially petit-bourgeois form of art. Evil gets the attention of the audience when it can be observed bringing pain to the individuals who constitute a family unit. It is not necessary to know precisely why evil has appeared on the scene and why it works the way it does; neither is it necessary to know precisely how evil will be vanquished.

Xie Jin's films do a great deal to undermine the moral legitimacy of the Communist Party. To use the words of Shao Mujun, they "arouse emotions."[45] But it is exactly for this reason that Xie Jin has been attacked so vigorously by younger filmmakers who insist that it is time to move beyond sensational, melodramatic representation. Life is just not as simple as it appears in Xie Jin's films. One does not learn much about how the system "really" works by viewing films like *Hibiscus Town*. Chen Kaige's *Yellow Earth* (*Huang tudi*, 1984) demolishes the myth of the idyllic and harmonious rural village that is consistently portrayed in melodramas of the 1930s, 1940s, and 1980s. Huang Jianxin's *Black Cannon Incident* (*Hei pao shijian*, 1986) and *Transmigration* (*Lunhui*, 1989) forcefully reject the notion that absolute good and absolute evil exist anywhere in China. Where Xie Jin's melodramas deny the middle ground, Huang Jianxin's postsocialist films insist that the Chinese social and political arena is composed of nothing but middle ground. No one is pure or innocent (see chapter 10). The young filmmakers are interested in subtlety, nuance, and ambiguity, and that is why Western scholars are attracted by their works. Xie Jin is interested in the confrontation between clear moral absolutes. Western observers prefer Fifth Generation directors, but the undeniable fact is they had a very small audience in China. This is why the authorities never felt politically threatened by them. Xie Jin, the veteran melodramatist who sees the Chinese world in basic Manichaean terms of darkness and light, is the one who had the audience. "When people watch Xie Jin's films," Shao Mujun observed, "they don't have to rack their brains to think."[46]

It is highly ironic that backward-looking officials in the Chinese government have spent so much time hounding Xie Jin and subjecting his films to political censorship. The Communist Party comes off badly in his films because he insists upon using the exaggerated melodramatic format. In reality, Xie Jin is no dissident. He is a loyal Party member allied to an entity we might loosely define as the reform wing of the Party. There is no way to know right now if the massacres of June 1989 caused Xie to rethink his political views. The films he made before the massacres reveal that he advocates a fairly thorough reform of the Communist Party and socialist system, but not their overthrow. His films reject the idea that the Cultural Revolution was an aberration. To save itself and to save China, the Party must abandon the Stalinist and Maoist modes of operation that caused so much needless suffering in the 1949–1979 period.

More specifically, what Xie Jin opposes more than anything else is class struggle and mass mobilization politics. When one looks beyond the rhetoric of *Hibiscus Town*, the most politically daring of all Xie Jin's family melodramas, one does not find a plea for multiparty or pluralistic politics. Xie Jin's critics (and some of his defenders!) say that he is a Confucian Marxist. That is he believes there is nothing wrong with a one-party state, so long as it is an enlightened, benevolent despotism that renounces cruel class-struggle politics. Xie Jin disputes the view that there were significant numbers of class enemies of socialism in China after 1949. Entrepreneurs like Hu Yuyin and intellectuals like Crazy Qin are valued members of society. The Party, Xie believes, should be worrying more about allowing the various social classes to play their proper role and fostering multiclass harmony in China than about creating a classless utopia.

REFLECTIONS ON THE MAY FOURTH TRADITION OF CHINESE FILMMAKING

This chapter began by asking whether one can speak of a May Fourth tradition of Chinese filmmaking and whether Chinese films of the post–Cultural Revolution 1980s have anything in common with that tradition. My view is that we can, indeed, speak of a May Fourth tradition, so long as we carefully define it to mean the marriage between classic melodrama and elementary Marxism that took place in the 1932–1937 period and resurfaced in the 1946–1949 period. The union resulted in the birth of a popular tradition of critical and independent cinema that saw the crisis of contemporary China in terms of a spectacular moral struggle between the forces of darkness and light. But the partners in this marriage were not equal. The genre dominated the relationship and distorted the May Fourth politics. Still, the result was acceptable to the left. Whereas the political implications of classic film melodramas were, at best, unclear, May Fourth films implicitly subverted Nationalist rule and embraced the often vaguely defined cause of revolution.

The May Fourth tradition of filmmaking disappeared in the years between 1949 and 1979. This powerful "mode of excessive representation," which specialized in identifying degenerate villains who were responsible for the suffering of the innocent in contemporary society, was not tolerated by the architects of the new socialist China. Measured and friendly criticism was one thing, but melodramatic representation was anything but measured.

The Cultural Revolution catastrophe opened the door for the phenomenal revival of the forgotten May Fourth tradition of critical melodramatic filmmaking. It was finally possible not only to talk about socialist society in terms of darkness and light, but to identify the Party as the agent of darkness. But, once again, the genre overwhelmed and ultimately distorted the well-intentioned reform Marxism of popular melodramatists like Xie Jin. A cinema that represents Hu Yuyin, the heroine of *Hibiscus Town*, as a radiant flower that attracts both butterflies and hornets can provide opportunities for mass catharsis and thereby ease mass anxieties, but it cannot hope to unravel the confusing complexities and frustrating ambiguities of Chinese life.

Still, the melodramatic imagination is deeply rooted in Chinese life. It is a politically flexible mode that somehow manages to adapt and endure. This became apparent in the aftermath of June 4, 1989, the latest in a long series of modern Chinese political and cultural crises. The battered post-Tiananmen socialist state had no intention of allowing loyal but reform-minded artists like Xie Jin to make critical films that subject the 1989 crisis to the glaring light of melodramatic representation. It is equally clear that Deng Xiaoping and his followers decided to make the melodramatic mode serve their own political purposes. As they tell the story, "a tiny handful" of thugs, hooligans, rioters, and bourgeois parasites, all of them traitors in league with foreign imperialism, instigated a violent and immoral rebellion. Using the melodramatic rhetoric of excess that has become so common in twentieth-century Chinese political and social discourse, Deng Xiaoping told martial law troops, "We should never forget how cruel our enemies are. For them we should not have an iota of forgiveness." The "dregs of society" were opposed, of course, by virtuous and selfless Party loyalists and the heroes of the People's Liberation Army. Using concise language to refer specifically to the polar extremes of right and wrong, Deng said, "The PLA losses were great, but this enabled us to win the support of the people and made those who cannot tell right from wrong (*shi fei bu qing*) change their viewpoint." "If tanks were used to roll over people," Deng explained, "this would have created a confusion between right and wrong (*shi fei bu ming*) among the people nationwide."[47] In the aftermath of the massacres, Chinese publications scrambled to reveal the "true" nature of the saboteurs. Fang Lizhi was described as shameless "scum," Yan Jiaqi as a "contemptible scoundrel," and Wuer Kaixi as an unprincipled "pariah."[48]

By referring to such patently absurd characterizations, I do not mean to trivialize the tragedy that struck China in 1989. This type of melodramatic sensationalism is a familiar ingredient of what Joseph Esherick has referred to as Chinese political theater.[49] Jiang Qing, Lin Biao, Liu Shaoqi, and Deng Xiaoping himself have all been cast, in turn, as agents of darkness. The names change, but the melodramatic conception of the workings of the Chinese universe remains the same.

The problem with Xie Jin's popular melodramas is that they are hostages of a genre that severely limits the imagination. One can easily believe that Xie Jin was sickened by Deng Xiaoping's interpretation of recent Chinese history. Sooner or later, someone like Xie Jin will have a chance to tell the "true" story of the savage confrontation between darkness and light that occurred in spring 1989. Millions of distraught viewers will weep tears of blood as they observe the suffering of the innocent. And they will express boundless joy when the agents of evil are suddenly and miraculously routed on screen and replaced by leaders of "true" virtue.

NOTES

An earlier version of this chapter appeared as "Melodramatic Representation and the 'May Fourth' Tradition of Chinese Cinema," in *From May Fourth to June Fourth: Fiction and Film in Twentieth-Century China*, ed. Ellen Widmer and David Der-wei Wang (Cambridge, Mass.: Harvard University Press, 1993), 295–326.

1. Examples of both approaches can be found in Nick Browne, Paul G. Pickowicz, Vivian Sobchack, and Esther Yau, eds., *New Chinese Cinemas: Forms, Identities, Politics* (Cambridge, UK: Cambridge University Press, 1994).

2. For a discussion of the attitude of May Fourth literary intellectuals toward commercial filmmaking, see Paul G. Pickowicz, *Marxist Literary Thought in China: The Influence of Ch'ü Ch'iu pai* (Berkeley: University of California Press, 1981).

3. See Cheng Jihua, ed., *Zhongguo dianying fazhan shi* (Beijing: Zhongguo dianying chubanshe, 1963), 1:3–49.

4. See Sun Yu, "Cinema in the 1930s under the Influence of the May Fourth Movement," in *Electric Shadows: Forty-Five Years of Chinese Cinema*, ed. Tony Rayns and Scott Meek (London: British Film Institute, 1980), T3.

5. See Li Xiao, Li Kezhen, and Li Jiansheng, "Zhongguo dianying zong mulu (1905–1937)" and Wang Yongfang and Jiang Hongtao, "Zai Hua faxing waiguo yingpian mulu (1896–1924)," *Zhongguo dianying yanjiu* 1, no. 1 (December 1983), 184–259, 260–82.

6. For a biography of Luo, see *Zhongguo dianyingjia liezhuan*, ed. Zhongguo dianyingjia xiehui dianying shi yanjiubu (Beijing: Zhongguo dianying chubanshe, 1982–1987), 1:183–90. (Hereafter this multivolume source will be referred to as *ZDL*.)

7. For biographies of Shi and Cai, see *ZDL*, 1:15–23, 338–49. For a discussion of Zhu, see Lin Nien-tung, "Zhu Shi-lin," in *A Comparative Study of Post-War Mandarin and Cantonese Cinema: The Films of Zhu Shi-lin, Qin Jian, and Other Directors*, ed. Shu Kei (Hong Kong: Hong Kong International Film Festival, 1983), 22–25.

8. Wang and Jiang, "Zai Hua faxing waiguo yingpian mulu," 260.

9. For information on Qian (who was known as A Ying), Xia, Zheng, and Hong, see *ZDL*, 1:76–83, 261–77, 196–201, 214–21; for Yang and Tian, see *ZDL*, 2:115–30, 55–65. See Pickowicz, *Marxist Literary Thought in China*, for a discussion of the Sun Society romantic Marxists.

10. See Zhongguo dianying yishu yanjiu zhongxin, Zhongguo dianyingjia xiehui, and Beijing dianying xueyuan, eds., *Xia Yan de dianying daolu* (Beijing: Zhongguo dianying chubanshe, 1985), 6–7.

11. Ke Ling argues that it did. See "Shiwei 'Wusi' yu dianying hua yi lunkuo," *Zhongguo dianying yanjiu* 1, no. 1 (December 1983), 4–19.

12. For an argument that stresses censorship, see Jay Leyda, *Dianying: An Account of Films and the Film Audience in China* (Cambridge, Mass.: MIT Press, 1972), 88–89.

13. This is the basic view put forward in Cheng, *Zhongguo dianying fazhan shi*.
14. Sun Yu, "Cinema in the 1930s under the Influence of the May Fourth Movement," T6.
15. The term *melodrama* is used here in its broadest possible sense. I recognize, of course, that there are many different types of melodramas and that each has its own characteristics. By referring to the direct impact of American film melodrama on Chinese cinema, I do not mean to suggest that Chinese film melodramas did not have their own national characteristics or that they were not influenced by Chinese traditions of narrative and stagecraft. For recent applications of melodrama theory to contemporary Chinese filmmaking, see E. Ann Kaplan, "Melodrama/Subjectivity/Ideology: The Relevance of Western Melodrama Theories to Recent Chinese Cinema," *East-West Film Journal* 5, no.1 (January 1991), 6–27; and Stephanie Alison Hoare, "Melodrama and Innovation: Literary Adaptation in Contemporary Chinese Film" (PhD diss., Cornell University, 1989).
16. The following discussion of melodrama draws heavily on Peter Brooks, *The Melodramatic Imagination: Balzac, Henry James, Melodrama, and the Mode of Excess* (New York: Columbia University Press, 1985).
17. Brooks, *The Melodramatic Imagination*, 5. These words were used by Theodora Bosanquet to characterize the way in which Henry James viewed the world outside his study.
18. Brooks, *The Melodramatic Imagination*, 40.
19. Perry Link, *Mandarin Ducks and Butterflies: Popular Fiction in Early-Twentieth-Century Chinese Cities* (Berkeley: University of California Press, 1981).
20. Brooks, *The Melodramatic Imagination*, 20.
21. Brooks, *The Melodramatic Imagination*, 17.
22. For biographical sketches, see *ZDL*: Wang Chenwu (1:4–9), Shi Lingle (1:47–52), Situ Huimin (1:53–64), Sun Yu (2:81–87), Wu Yonggang (2:156–63), Shen Xiling (1:84–91), Ying Yunwei (1:102–10).
23. For a detailed Red Guard denunciation of Xia Yan and the 1930s "Communist film group," see Shanghai hong qi dianying zhipianchang hong qi geming zaofan bingtuan, ed., *Dianying xiju sishinian liang tiao luxian douzheng jishi* (Shanghai, 1967).
24. The most important pre–Cultural Revolution book that presented this point of view (Cheng Jihua, *Zhongguo dianying fazhan shi*) was reprinted without revision in 1981.
25. Cai Shusheng [Xia Yan], "Kan le 'Xiao wanyi' zhi Sun Yu xiansheng," *Shen bao*, October 10, 1933.
26. The text of *Small Toys* is contained in Sun Yu, *Sun Yu dianying xuanji* (Beijing: Zhongguo dianying chubanshe, 1981), 91–126.
27. See Zhongguo dianyingjia xiehui dianying shi yanjiu bu, ed., *Ruan Lingyu* (Beijing: Zhongguo dianying chubanshe, 1985); and Liu Guojun, *Cong xiao yatou dao mingxing: Ruan Lingyu zhuan* (Chengdu: Sichuan wenyi chubanshe, 1986).
28. Brooks, *The Melodramatic Imagination*, 88.
29. Sun Yu places the emphasis on the class solidarity of the poor, but it is clear that the unity of the people portrayed in *Small Toys* is also related to the fact that they are from the same hometown in rural Jiangsu. Emily Honig argues that native place identity was far more important to many women factory workers than

their class identity. See *Sisters and Strangers: Women in the Shanghai Cotton Mills, 1919–1949* (Stanford, Calif.: Stanford University Press, 1986).

30. For a sketch of Tang Xiaodan, see *ZDL*, 2:100–109.

31. *Shen bao*, February 26–March 9, 1947.

32. Tang Xiaodan, "Jituo yu xiwang—daoyanzhe de hua," in *Tiantang chun meng* (Shanghai, 1947).

33. Robert Lang, *American Film Melodrama: Griffith, Vidor, Minnelli* (Princeton, N.J.: Princeton University Press, 1989), 47, 24.

34. See Leo Ou-fan Lee, "The Tradition of Modern Chinese Cinema: Some Preliminary Explorations and Hypotheses," in *Perspectives on Chinese Cinema*, ed. Chris Berry (Ithaca, N.Y.: Cornell University East Asia Papers, 1985), 1–20, for a discussion of late-1940s cinema that emphasizes its "social realism."

35. Brooks, *The Melodramatic Imagination*, 33.

36. See *ZDL*, 6:481–95.

37. See Paul Clark, *Chinese Cinema: Culture and Politics since 1949* (Cambridge, UK: Cambridge University Press, 1987).

38. Shao Mujun, "Chinese Films: 1979–1989," *China Screen* 3, no. 11 (1989).

39. *Beijing Review* 33, no. 8 (February 19–25, 1990), 46.

40. *China Screen* 2, no. 3 (1988).

41. For a discussion of early 1980s melodramas, see Ma Ning, "Symbolic Representation and Symbolic Violence: Chinese Family Melodrama of the Early 1980s," *East-West Film Journal* 4, no. 1 (December 1989), 79–112.

42. See *Shang ying huabao* 1, no. 1 (January 1987). Similar advertising can be found in *Dazhong dianying*, no. 4 (April 1987).

43. For another discussion of *Hibiscus Town*, see Nick Browne, "Society and Subjectivity: On the Political Economy of Chinese Melodrama," in *New Chinese Cinemas*, ed. Browne et al., 40–56.

44. Another analysis of Xie Jin's melodramas is contained in Ma Ning, "Spatiality and Subjectivity in Xie Jin's Film Melodrama of the New Period," in *New Chinese Cinemas*, ed. Browne et al., 15–39.

45. Shao, "Chinese Films: 1979–1989," 11.

46. Shao, "Chinese Films: 1979–1989," 11.

47. *Zhong gong shisan jie si zhong quan hui* (Beijing: Xin xing chubanshe, 1989), 11–13.

48. *Beijing Review* 32, no. 49 (December 4–10, 1989), 23–26.

49. Joseph W. Esherick and Jefferey N. Wasserstrom, "Acting Out Democracy: Political Theater in Modern China," *Journal of Asian Studies* 49, no. 4 (November 1990), 835–65.

4

Never-Ending Controversies: The Case of *Remorse in Shanghai* and Occupation-Era Chinese Filmmaking

Completed in late 1944, *Remorse in Shanghai* (*Chun jiang yi hen*) is perhaps the most controversial Chinese movie ever made. Yet one looks high and low in the scholarly literature for a sustained discussion of this extraordinarily interesting work. There are many fleeting references to *Remorse in Shanghai*, almost all of which hint at controversy—controversy that surrounds all films made in occupied China during the 1937–1945 war years. With the exception of Poshek Fu, scholars of Chinese cinema (including myself) have not written much about occupation-era cinema. Yet it seems unreasonable simply to ignore this period. Either the films of the occupation years are part of Chinese film history or they are not. Scholars should not avoid controversy. Everyone should take a stand. My own view is that those who are interested in the entire one-hundred-year history of Chinese filmmaking should have informed opinions about the movies made under conditions of occupation and the legacies of those films during the postwar era.

The various brief references to *Remorse in Shanghai* raise more questions than they answer. Jay Leyda writes a few lines about *Remorse in Shanghai*, Zhang Yingjin and Xiao Zhiwei make a passing reference to it, and Poshek Fu devotes a few useful paragraphs to it, though he makes it clear he was not able to see the film.[1] Virtually all these brief accounts contain factual errors. Some blurb-writers express great passion. Cheng Jihua, taking great care (for reasons that will be explained later) not to reveal the names of any of the Chinese associated with *Remorse in Shanghai*, savages the film in a few lines, and steadfastly refuses to recognize it as an authentic Chinese movie.[2] That is, he deliberately declines to list the movie in his comprehensive filmography of movies made between 1905 and 1949. The China

Film Archive, however, includes *Remorse in Shanghai* in its official catalog of Chinese films.[3] It is easy to see that considerable confusion, and even a bit of mystery, have always surrounded the movie.

Given its obvious notoriety, why has no one written in detail about *Remorse in Shanghai*? In part, it is because very few scholars have had an opportunity to see the film. For decades researchers feared that no copy of *Remorse in Shanghai* had survived the various traumas that shook China in the half century after 1945. In 2001, however, a copy turned up in an archive in Russia. Thus, more than sixty years after its release, it is finally possible to sort out many of the controversies related to the notorious *Remorse in Shanghai*. In doing so, we are able to learn something about four distinct historical moments: the Taiping Rebellion (the time in which the film is set), the Japanese occupation of Shanghai (the time when the film was made and released), the Civil War (the time when some of the people associated with the film were singled out for harsh criticism by the Nationalist government), and the postrevolutionary era (the time when the film was inaccessible to researchers but functioned nonetheless as a focal point of passionate Communist discourses on anti-Japanese and nationalist themes).

CONTROVERSIAL CONTEXT

In May 1943 the Wang Jingwei government in Nanjing agreed with the Japanese occupation authorities in Shanghai that the Chinese film world was not doing nearly enough to support the war effort.[4] Wang wanted to see political propaganda films that supported Japan and embraced the Greater East Asian Co-Prosperity Sphere, movies that explicitly denounced Anglo-American imperialism.

Wang Jingwei took action by having his operatives set up Huaying (Zhonghua dianying lianhe gongsi), a new unit that was to regulate all film-making, distribution, and exhibition. Huaying was part of Wang's Ministry of Propaganda, and its managing director was Feng Jie, the head of the Shanghai bureau of the Ministry of Propaganda. Feng was a hardliner, but considerable artistic control remained in the hands of Kawakita Nagamasa and Zhang Shankun, extremely interesting and hard to categorize people who had worked well together at Zhonglian (Zhongguo lianhe zhipian gufen gongsi), the Sino-Japanese film group that was dissolved to make way for Huaying. Kawakita and Zhang were firmly committed to Sino-Japanese cooperation, but they believed that feature films, by definition, needed to have artistic and entertainment dimensions.[5]

Huaying made thirty-six features in 1943. Economic conditions were deteriorating steadily in this period as the war drew to an end; thus it was necessary for the films to have entertainment and market appeal. Otherwise, no one would go to see them. As a consequence, Chinese and Japanese observers who were primarily concerned with the political role of films expressed renewed disappointment about concessions made to entertainment priorities. Huaying's films were insufficiently political. They failed to offer enough explicit propaganda support for the Greater East Asian Co-Prosperity Sphere. Some officials felt that political goals might be easier to achieve in films that were Sino-Japanese coproductions. Huaying was thus urged to get involved with its Japanese counterparts. But only one coproduced film was actually turned out during the war: *Remorse in Shanghai*, a film also known by its Japanese title, *Noroshi wa Shanhai ni agaru*. The project, which involved Huaying and Great Japan Productions (Dai Nippon eiga kaisha), began in late 1943 with a Japanese screenplay that was carefully reviewed and revised by Tao Qin, an important Huaying scriptwriter. The production was well funded, and the actual filming took more than six months.[6]

Remorse in Shanghai was an unprecedented coproduction in many respects. Not only was the screenwriting cooperative, there were two directors, one Chinese (Yue Feng, later replaced by Hu Xinling) and one Japanese (Inagaki Hiroshi). Yue Feng made a number of occupation-era films (both before and after the end of the "Orphan Island" period in late 1941), and Hu Xinling had been trained in Japan. Inagaki, according to Peter High, was well-known in Japan.[7] The cast included a veteran Japanese star, Bando Tsumasaburo, and many of the brightest wartime and postwar Chinese stars: Mei Xi, Li Lihua, Wang Danfeng, Han Langen, and Yan Jun. Actor Liu Qiong and cinematographer Huang Shaofen, both of whom were active in occupation-era filmmaking, declined invitations to join the project.[8] In aesthetic terms, the film integrated Chinese and Japanese approaches. As a consequence, it has a fascinating hybrid (or regional, as opposed to national) look. The Chinese production staff was apparently greatly impressed by the equipment and technological support provided by the thirty technicians who arrived from Japan to help.

CONTROVERSIAL HISTORY

Remorse in Shanghai, a historical film, is based loosely on events that occurred in the mid-nineteenth century. After the declining and isolated Tokugawa *bakufu* lifted bans on foreign travel, a Japanese ship named the *Senzaimaru* arrived in Shanghai on June 7, 1862. The boat contained fifty-one passengers, and it was Japan's very first semiofficial mission to China. China and Japan had no formal diplomatic relations. On the surface, the reason for the visit was to look into commercial conditions in China in the aftermath of the Opium War (1839–1842) and the opening of various

Western-dominated treaty ports on the China coast. Japan had been forcibly opened by Commodore Matthew Perry and the U.S. Navy in 1853, so the Japanese, concerned that Western nations would seek to set up treaty ports in Japan, were naturally curious about conditions in China. In effect, the Japanese aboard the *Senzaimaru* were on an intelligence-gathering mission to a part of the world they understood poorly. As Joshua Fogel has pointed out, the Japanese on board the *Senzaimaru* "wanted to see what happened when an East Asian country was forcibly opened to trade by the West."[9]

Many of the Japanese who arrived in Shanghai in June 1862 had another, less public, agenda. They hailed from domains in southern Japan such as Choshu and Satsuma that were hostile to the ruling Tokugawa *bakufu*. Indeed, a number of those proto-nationalists who boarded the *Senzaimaru* were later prominent in the Meiji Restoration that overthrew the Tokugawa in 1868. In fact, one of the major historical figures portrayed in the 1944 Chinese film *Remorse in Shanghai* was Takasugi Shinsaku, a young militant from Choshu who was a loyal disciple of Yoshida Shoin, a highly influential Japanese political activist who stridently opposed any flexibility on the issue of compromises with the West. In the film, Takasugi's role is played quite effectively by Bando Tsumasaburo. Takasugi kept a diary that, to this day, remains one of the key sources on the 1862 voyage of the *Senzaimaru*.

The Japanese visitors were at once impressed and repulsed by what they saw in Shanghai. As Fogel has shown, there was a gap between the respect for Chinese culture they had gained by reading books in Japan and the shock they experienced when they witnessed the poverty of the Chinese they saw on the streets of Shanghai.[10] The power, technological sophistication, and wealth of the West was very much on display in Shanghai, but it was painful for the Japanese to see Chinese elites as well as commoners reduced to a subordinate status. The Japanese met Chinese from various walks of life and even paid visits to private homes. The Japanese travelers were quite a novelty. At that time, there was no reason for anyone to express hostility toward them. The Japanese communicated with the Chinese by means of "brush conversation" (*bi tan*)—the exchange of notes written in classical or literary Chinese. The Japanese also met with Westerners, including British, French, and American residents of Shanghai. "The Chinese have become servants to the foreigners," Takasugi Shinsaku lamented in his diary. "Sovereignty may belong to China but in fact it's no more than a colony of Great Britain and France."[11]

One of the many remarkable things about the visit of the *Senzaimaru* is that by coincidence its passengers got to see the great Taiping Rebellion that was shaking Qing rule to its foundations. Indeed, the Japanese travelers actually heard gunfire exchanged between Taiping and Qing forces outside Shanghai. This refers to the attempt made by Taiping forces under the command of Li Xiucheng to attack and occupy Shanghai beginning in January 1862. By the time the *Senzaimaru* arrived in summer 1862, the Taiping assault had been largely repulsed, though there were still skirmishes taking place outside Shanghai.[12] Takasugi's diary reveals that he was highly sympathetic to the Taiping rebels, whose activities were badly understood back home in Japan. What was important to Takasugi was not the Christian theology of the Taipings, which he downplayed, but the fact that the rebels opposed British forces that were helping the Qing.

In further *bi tan* conversations with Chinese contacts in Shanghai, Takasugi was shocked to learn that Lin Zexu, the imperial commissioner who did his best to resist the British in Guangzhou on the eve of the Opium War, was not adequately appreciated by the Chinese Takasugi met. He was also puzzled as to why so many Chinese seemed to accept British and French domination. In historical terms, China was "ahead" of Japan in 1862 when the *Senzaimaru* reached Shanghai. While Japan was just beginning its contact with the West, China had been interacting with the West for more than twenty years. Takasugi had no way of knowing about long-term patterns of economic, social, and political decline in China. He thus wrongly concluded that the demise of the Chinese government and the poverty of its people were solely the result of Western aggression. He convinced himself that the same thing would not happen to Japan. The sense of China being "ahead" of Japan at this time and of Japan needing to learn from China's experiences was well captured in his diary.

Fogel argues convincingly that when Takasugi left Shanghai in the summer of 1862, he continued to believe that Japan and China shared many aspects of a common culture, a culture that had originated in China. Though he respected Chinese culture, and thus regarded China and Japan as comparable (and thus equal) cultural entities, he concluded that China was losing its fight with the West. He was disappointed, even stunned. In a perfect world, it would be satisfying to see China and Japan standing side by side in that fight, but Takasugi was mainly concerned about Japan and how Japan might avoid the problems that faced China. Japan needed to make political and military reforms. It did not occur to Takasugi that Japan had any special role to play in assisting China in its struggle to cast off the yoke of Western imperialism.[13]

CONTROVERSIAL WARTIME RE-NARRATION

By spring 1944, when production of *Remorse in Shanghai*—the story of the 1862 voyage of the *Senzaimaru*—commenced, the war was not going well for Japan. In fact, it was the beginning of the end. By the time the film was completed in late 1944, American B-29s were already flying bombing missions over Japan. The question confronting Zhang Shankun, Kawakita Nagamasa, Yue Feng, Inagaki Hiroshi, Hu Xinling, and all the others associated with this one and only Sino-Japanese coproduction of the war era was how to tell the story of the first Sino-Japanese encounter of 1862 after the *Senzaimaru* arrived in Shanghai.

In a very general sense, the film narrative is faithful to the history of the *Senzaimaru* mission. But, like virtually all historical movies, it creates many fictional characters and situations, takes liberties with its plot development, and thus distorts in order to craft a compelling and focused human story. In the film version, Takasugi and the others reside in a small inn in Shanghai. Their initial encounters in Shanghai cause them to see a sharp distinction between Chinese culture and Western culture. The group is hosted by Qing officials who speak of the need for Sino-Japanese cooperation. One official says that Chinese and Japanese should overcome old conflicts, tensions, and mistrust. In fact, there had been no meaningful diplomatic contact between China and Japan for centuries, so there could not have been any mistrust. This speech was undoubtedly inserted for the benefit of audiences viewing the film in 1944. After this formal reception, the Japanese are then taken to a Beijing opera performance, which they very much enjoy and respect. In fact, they regard it as a prime example of first-rate Asian art. On another occasion they are hosted by Western residents of Shanghai, who treat the Japanese to an evening of ballroom music and dancing. The Japanese are deeply disturbed by the superficiality and decadence of the evening gathering.

Back at the inn they meet and befriend a beautiful and intelligent young staff member, Yu Ying, played by the famous actress Li Lihua (who was only twenty years old at the time). The Japanese guests are stunned to learn that she can speak Japanese. She explains that she spent some time in Nagasaki, the only Japanese port open to Chinese trade during the late Tokugawa period. She offers to function as their guide and translator in Shanghai. Yu Ying is, of course, a fictionalized character.

By the time the film is over, it is clear that Takasugi and the Li Lihua character, Yu Ying, have affection for each other. But this relationship is developed slowly and with extreme care in the film. The dimension of mutual sexual attraction is present, but it is extremely muted and understated so as not to give offense to the film audience in China. Takasugi is extraordinarily respectful and admires the intelligence and clear-headed rationality of the young Chinese beauty. Their many conversations focus almost entirely on politics. It is clear that the Li Lihua character detests the British and other Western aggressors. She also supports the Taiping rebels and tells Takasugi as much as she can about the rebel movement. She is also contemptuous of the Qing, who, for various reasons, have lost control of the situation in China. The young woman then takes the Japanese visitors on a tour of

Shanghai, during which they see desperate war refugees as well as British artillery emplacements.

Strolling along the streets of Shanghai looking at Chinese antiques, Takasugi meets another fictionalized character, a young Chinese woman, Xiao Hong, played by the famous actress Wang Danfeng (who was only nineteen years old at the time). She and a household servant sell Takasugi a family heirloom, an antique Chinese ink stone. The treasure is being sold to raise money for her upcoming marriage. Takasugi, who demonstrates deep knowledge and respect for the splendid artifact (knowledge the British could never have), buys the ink stone. It turns out that the young woman's father, the head of a better-off family that is in decline, served in the Chinese military at the time of the Opium War and has deeply rooted anti-British instincts.

The old man's son, Shen Yizhou, played by the famous and handsome wartime actor Mei Xi, is an officer in the Taiping rebel army. He is in Shanghai on a secret mission. Speaking excellent English, the Mei Xi character visits the British consulate and is assured by a sympathetic, mid-level British official (all the non-Asian parts in the film are apparently played by Europeans who were residing in Shanghai during the wartime occupation) that the British will not resist the entry of Taiping forces into the city. He then visits an American arms dealer who agrees to sell modern weaponry to the Taipings.

Here the filmmakers are taking liberties with the historical record. The impression is left that in June 1862 the Taiping attack on Shanghai has not yet begun in earnest and that the Taiping leadership is still counting on support from the British, French, and Americans. In reality, the Taiping attack was launched in January and by June, when the Japanese were visiting, had already been beaten back by combined Qing and Western forces.[14] But the film is clearly made more dramatic if the events of January (a time when there were still some Western voices of support for the Taiping crusade) are said to be happening in June.

There is no evidence that the Japanese visitors met with anyone associated with the Taiping movement, but in *Remorse in Shanghai*, the young Taiping leader, chased by Qing soldiers, is given refuge by Takasugi and his lovely Chinese interpreter. One of the many high points of this surprisingly well-done film is a long discussion between the two men. Takasugi is highly respectful and supportive of the Taiping leader, but he asserts that the British and Americans are not reliable. They have exploited China since the time of the Opium War and will betray the Taipings. Indeed, Britain has already reduced India to a "slave" nation and wants to do the same to China. The Taiping leader is emotional and indignant. He retorts that Britain and America are "civilized" nations, incapable of betrayal. Moreover, since the Taipings are Christians, they have a special religious bond with the Westerners.

Japanese and Chinese unite in a righteous cause in *Remorse in Shanghai* (1944, d. Hu Xinling, Inagaki Hiroshi). China Film Archive

In linguistic terms, this scene, like many others in the film, is mesmerizing. Takasugi speaks Japanese, while the character played by Mei Xi speaks Chinese. The Li Lihua character speaks both Japanese and Chinese in her role as interpreter. At one point, though, she puts aside the role of translator and tries, in her own Chinese voice, to convince the Taiping leader that the British brought opium and the Opium War to China and continue to exploit China in various ways, including exercising control over the highly profitable Chinese customs office. "Reason" and "clarity of political vision" are very much gendered female in this film. The Li Lihua character is cool, calm, and astute, while the views of the male Taiping leader are clouded by his emotions. He storms away, refusing to continue the dialogue. The figure of the strong Chinese woman, it should be noted, is widespread in prewar, wartime, and immediate postwar Chinese cinema.

The Taiping attack on Shanghai is depicted in glowing terms. It is as if Shanghai has been liberated. The people go out into the streets to welcome their heroes. Strict prohibitions are enacted, including a total ban on opium consumption and trafficking. A joyous family reunion brings together the old man, his Taiping rebel son, his attractive daughter, and her fiancé. The old man is troubled, however, by his son's views of the British. He cannot quite believe that the British are going to do anything to help China. In the old days, he says, "the British were our enemies." But both of the young Chinese men present in the room—the son and the future son-in-law—tell the old man he is wrong. That was then; this is now. When the old man mentions to his son that he has invited the Japanese over for a visit, the son abruptly departs, saying he does not want to see the Japanese.

A young couple learns the hard way that dastardly British imperialists seek to subjugate Asia in *Remorse in Shanghai* (1944, d. Xu Xinling, Inagaki Hiroshi). China Film Archive

When the Japanese guests arrive, another fascinating discussion, undoubtedly the single most interesting and effective scene in the film, ensues. In a word, the meeting is a love fest. The old man deeply appreciates Takasugi's profound knowledge of Chinese culture. Moreover, the Japanese visitor shows Confucian-like respect for the wisdom and dignified bearing of the older man. Writing *bi tan* notes, the old man tells of the bad old days of the Opium War, the heroics of Lin Zexu, and the pain of witnessing Indian soldiers kill Chinese. Imagine the horror of it, he laments, "Asians killing other Asians." There is no evidence that the Japanese actually discussed the fate of India with their Chinese contacts. Repeated references to the unacceptable colonial status of India and its people were obviously inserted for the edification of viewers in 1944. The old man then asks if he can take a close look at Takasugi's sword. He is overwhelmed by the magnificence of the sword. "It is a weapon," he declares, "but it is also a work of fine art!"

This meeting of new friends is disrupted when the Japanese are informed by mail that there is trouble back in Japan. In Choshu, the home domain of Takasugi, an initial exchange of fire between Japanese coastal forces and Western naval vessels has led to a French landing and the destruction of Japanese fortifications. The incident described in the film actually happened, but it occurred in June 1863, not in June 1862.[15] Again, to heighten dramatic impact the scriptwriters took liberties with the chronology of the period to suggest that the Chinese and the Japanese, then and now, are in the same boat. In the film, the Japanese visitors to China are seen rejoicing because, they proclaim, this outrage will unite all Japanese and create a national consciousness.

The film then cuts to a scene in the British consulate. The decision has been made to support the Qing and help defeat the Taipings. In a scene that highlights the explosive issue of racial difference, a single voice of conscience on the British side, a diplomat named Medhurst who had earlier met with the Taiping rebel leader, asserts that the British cannot break their promise to the "King of the Taipings." After all, he says, the Taipings are Christians. His superior laughs. "It's a pity that the King of the Taipings doesn't have white skin, like us," he retorts. That is, it all comes down to race. As for religion, he insists that the Taipings are nothing but a bunch of "fanatics." In any case, he quips, "God knows nothing about what happens east of the Cape of Good Hope!"

Meanwhile, in the Taiping camp, the highest leaders insist that the British will never engage in acts of betrayal. The Shen Yizhou character is sent to the British consulate to reconfirm the neutral stance of the British. But he is quickly thrown out of the compound by security personnel. Only then does he understand that the Japanese and Yu Ying, the Chinese woman, were right all along. The Westerners, working with the Qing, then launch an attack on Taiping forces.

A squad of British troops arrives at the old man's house looking for Shen Yizhou. They loot the home, burn it to the ground, and kill the old man. In response, the old man's future son-in-law kills a British soldier. One of the Japanese friends slays a British soldier who is about to fire on Xiao Hong, the old man's daughter. The Japanese then stand together with the family to mourn the old man in the time-honored way. The fiancé vows to join the Taiping army. The daughter, burning with hatred for the British, says she will await his return.

The final portions of *Remorse in Shanghai* are infused with multiple expressions of cultural and even political solidarity between China and Japan. For instance, one of the Japanese visitors makes an effort to speak Chinese in order to console the young woman, Xiao Hong, who has lost her father. During the chaos of the counterattack on the Taipings, the young Taiping leader, Shen Yizhou, shows up at the residence of the Japanese looking for Takasugi. His purpose is to acknowledge the wisdom of the well-meaning Japanese and to pledge his friendship. Unfortunately, Takasugi is absent when Shen arrives. This sets up the final sequence.

When Takasugi returns, he is distraught to learn that he missed seeing Shen Yizhou. Takasugi's friends tell him it is time to get out of Shanghai and return to Japan. It is too dangerous with so much fighting. Takasugi steadfastly refuses to leave. He declares that he must go out and find Shen. In a Japanese language conversation, Takasugi gives the following reason: "I have to go to him because he came to see me. Sincerity. That is at the heart of Asian morality." The Li Lihua character insists on going with Takasugi. It is only at this point that their mutual affection is made crystal clear, though they are still much more comrades-in-arms than they are a romantic couple.

On the outskirts of Shanghai, they encounter a column of retreating Taipings. Takasugi and Shen finally spot each other and they engage in a brotherly reunion, with each praising the other. By this time, the Japanese view the Qing authorities as the hopeless running dogs of foreign power. Shen resolves to drive out the Western imperialists "even if it takes a hundred years." They clasp hands, and Takasugi shouts, "When you start fighting against the foreigners, we Japanese will start fighting against them too." As the Taiping forces march forward, a song titled "Miya-san, Miya-san" plays in the background. This marching song was actually composed at the time of the Meiji Restoration for Japanese imperial troops. Thus, a rousing effort is made in the end to link the Taiping anti-foreign, anti-Qing agenda to the anti-foreign, anti-Tokugawa cause of the still unfulfilled Meiji Restoration. This use of "Miya-san, Miya-san" in *Remorse in Shanghai* was not the first time the tune was borrowed. One can find variations of it in Gilbert and Sullivan's *Mikado* (1885) and Puccini's *Madame Butterfly* (1904).[16]

In the final scene of *Remorse in Shanghai*, Takasugi is out at sea on the *Senzaimaru* headed back to Japan (without the Li Lihua character). A long sequence of Shen Yizhou leading an attacking force of Taiping rebels is superimposed on a facial shot of Takasugi. Of course, the 1944 audience knew that the Taipings were defeated shortly after 1862 and that the Japanese were losing the Pacific War of the 1940s, but on screen the Taiping rebels and their Japanese comrades certainly looked like winners.

CONTROVERSIAL RECEPTION

The original plan was for *Remorse in Shanghai* to premiere in Shanghai, Nanjing, and Guangzhou on December 7, 1944, the third anniversary of the outbreak of the Pacific War. But severe economic and political turmoil stood in the way.[17] The film was released in both China and Japan but screened under extremely unfavorable circumstances. To this day, it is hard to know much about popular response to the film. It is difficult to estimate the number of people who had a chance to see the film. There certainly was systematic press coverage of the project in *Hua bei ying hua*, a popular occupation-era film monthly controlled by the cultural authorities in Shanghai. Indeed, *Hua bei ying hua* published a number of articles on the film over a nine-month period in 1944.[18]

Not surprisingly, *Hua bei ying hua* had nothing but praise for the movie. Providing a summary of the story line for readers, one article stated that the film told the true story of the British-American invasion of East Asia and thus inspired Chinese and Japanese people to work together to fight their common enemy. Like all film magazines, *Hua bei ying hua* also offered up gossip and tidbits of interest to film fans. Some of the Japanese, it was said, tried their best to speak a "stumbling" brand of Chinese. Li Lihua, by contrast, made rapid progress in acquiring a working knowledge of Japanese. She often volunteered to translate for Bando Tsumasaburo, the main Japanese star. Wang Danfeng, required to speak a bit of English in the film (a scene in which she denounces the British squad that intends to burn her father's house), was said to have spent all her spare time practicing.

According to *Hua bei ying hua*, the Chinese and Japanese technicians and staff worked well together, stopping to discuss every scene. Other sources suggest that there was strife from time to time, but Kawakita Nagamasa intervened on occasion to keep the project moving ahead.[19] Special mention was made of the dramatic scene in which Takasugi meets Shen Yizhou for the first time. A garden and a study were meticulously designed to serve as a dignified backdrop to their serious discussion of politics in the Pacific region. The scene worked, it was said, because both China and Japan were on the side of "righteousness" at the time of the visit of the *Senzaimaru*. The actor Mei Xi, who played Shen Yizhou, was said to have matured as an artist, no longer playing the role of the "handsome and rich" young man in order to meet the challenge of playing the part of an experienced middle-aged man.

But in a matter of weeks following the release of *Remorse in Shanghai*, Sino-Japanese partnerships of any sort were in deep trouble. Wang Jingwei died in Japan in January 1945. In spring 1945, American B-29s were bombing Tokyo and other Japanese cities. On the evening of March 8–9, 1945, at least eighty-five thousand residents of Tokyo were killed in a single fire bombing.[20] In August, atomic bombs were dropped on Hiroshima and Nagasaki. Japan surrendered unconditionally. Back in China, the Nationalist government, based in remote Chongqing during the war, returned to power in Nanjing and Shanghai by the end of 1946. "Takeover" officials, some of them corrupt and merciless, were looking for opportunities to confiscate the property of people said to have behaved as "traitors" during the war. Almost all those who had resided in occupied Shanghai during the war were suspect. Some of those arrested or charged were indeed guilty of treason—that is, they had worked hand in glove with the Japanese occupiers. Many who were innocent were nonetheless jailed and/or stripped of their property. Some who were guilty, but well connected, escaped without a blemish. It all seemed unfair and arbitrary.[21]

Due to the unusual public visibility of film personalities, there was much talk in the immediate postwar period about their wartime activities. But from the outset, public opinion was divided. Writing in 1946, a commentator named Hu Yan pointed specifically to *Remorse in Shanghai* and one other highly controversial wartime film, *Eternity* (*Wan shi liu fang*), produced in 1943, as examples of films said by some to be the work of collaborators and traitors. Hu disagreed, refusing to condemn as "traitors" the actors and actresses associated with the projects. According to Hu, clearly a fan of stars like Li Lihua and Mei Xi, their "cooperation" is understandable. During the occupation era, he claimed, if an actor or actress refused to cooperate, he or she might have been arrested and tortured. What were actors and actresses supposed to do? Commit suicide? Hu also pointed out that treatments of Western imperialist aggression during and after the Opium War were basically accurate. The thrust of Hu's article suggested that those who were looking for scapegoats should leave the actors and actresses alone.[22]

A very different approach was adopted in an unsigned article that appeared in *Zhongguo yingtan* in 1946. This polemic not only singled out screen artists, it focused exclusively on female stars. Chen Yunshang, the talented Cantonese actress who played strong female roles in *Mulan Joins the Army* (*Mulan cong jun*, 1939) and *Eternity*, was said to be in "deep trouble" and hiding out in Hangzhou following her husband's arrest. Chen Yanyan (the "Chinese Bette Davis"), who had made a number of wartime films, including the 1942 production of *A Waste of the Best of Times* (*Huanghua xudu*), directed by Yue Feng, was said to have been abandoned by all her friends. Li Lihua, the article declared, had lost her soul because in *Remorse in Shanghai* she actually spoke Japanese and condemned Britain and the United States. Now she was shamelessly running around trying to make friends with Westerners.[23]

This postwar gossiping and sensationalism seems trivial. But it was followed by an official Nationalist government investigation. According to archival sources, on November 19, 1946, Shanghai's first postwar mayor, Wu Guozhen, was authorized by municipal Party and military authorities to conduct an investigation of the wartime film industry. Only two films were singled out: *Remorse in Shanghai* and *Eternity*. Those who had opinions about these two films were invited to attend an investigation meeting to be convened at the Huguang cinema in Shanghai.[24]

By early 1947 a report prepared by one of Mayor Wu's top aides summed up the evidence gathered in the investigation. The report agreed that of all the Chinese films produced during the war years, only *Eternity* and *Remorse in Shanghai* needed to be taken seriously. The other films did not have meaningful political content. After viewing the two controversial films, investigation committee members, who included officials as well as journalists, wrote down their views. Mayor Wu's aide said that in his own view there was a difference between *Eternity* and *Remorse in Shanghai*. *Eternity* was made under Japanese supervision, but it was well made in terms of plot and style. Not only did it "not distort the historical facts of the Opium War, to a certain degree it can even inspire national consciousness." By contrast,

Remorse in Shanghai was indeed a work of collaboration carried out by traitors. It engaged in "all out propaganda" for Japan's Pan-Asian agenda, and it badly distorted "the image of Britain and the United States."[25] The investigation committee found evidence that the Japanese who promoted the production of *Eternity* were greatly disappointed by the result. That is, the film was insufficiently propagandistic. Thus, the Japanese moved on to *Remorse in Shanghai* and took a more hands-on (coproduction) approach to get the desired political result.

These and other materials were sent along to the Shanghai Municipal Court. Beginning on October 4, 1947, and continuing on November 11 and December 9, a total of approximately thirty people, almost all of them formerly employed by the Huaying group set up by the Wang Jingwei government in early 1943, were summoned to testify before the court, one group at a time. Chen Yanyan and Li Lihua were in the third group to appear. According to a newspaper report, Chen Yanyan confirmed that she played roles in several movies, but insisted that none of them were "collaboration" (*funi*) films. Moreover, she wanted to know why the women were being singled out. "Why was I interrogated," she asked, "while my male counterpart in those films, Liu Qiong, was not subjected to any charges?" Li Lihua, still only twenty-three years old in 1947, claimed she joined Huaying "against her will." She insisted that even now in 1947, she had no idea about the "gist of *Remorse in Shanghai*." Making use of a play on the words "*yi hen*" in *Remorse in Shanghai* (*Chun jiang yi hen*), she said that she definitely "regretted" (*yi hen*) her involvement in the movie. "I don't want to be an actress anymore," she added.[26]

According to interviews I conducted with Li Lihua in the mid-1980s, the cases against Chen Yanyan and her, along with the charges made against others, were not pursued in the Shanghai courts. The main reason was that the civil war between the Nationalists and the Communists was at a critical point and the Nationalist state had more important things to do. Indeed, both the Nationalists and the Communists were interested in winning the support— overt or covert—of leading personalities in the cultural world. Nothing was to be gained by moving ahead with the scapegoating of a few actresses.

As for the film personalities who were active during the occupation era, some chose to leave China. Li Lihua went to Hong Kong (where she made *China Girl* [*Hua guniang*] and many other films) before emigrating to the United States (where she had interacted earlier with John Wayne, Victor Mature, and others). Chen Yanyan, older than Li Lihua, went to Hong Kong and then to Taiwan. Liu Qiong went to Hong Kong in 1948. Wang Danfeng, the young actress who played Xiao Hong in *Remorse in Shanghai*, also went to Hong Kong in 1948.

Many of the occupation-era Shanghai stars who worked in the Hong Kong Mandarin-speaking film industry in the late 1940s monitored mainland Chinese politics very closely. Some, noting the success of the Communists on the civil war battlefield, even sought to open a dialogue with Party representatives about a future return to Shanghai after it was taken over by the Communists. Others who had risen in the Shanghai film world during the occupation simply remained in Shanghai. For example, Sang Hu, a young occupation-era screenwriter, had an extremely successful career in the Shanghai film world after 1945 and after 1949.

CONTROVERSIAL LEGACY

From 1949, the first year of the People's Republic of China, to the present day, official attitudes toward occupation-era film production have been somewhat inconsistent. The people who took over the film industry after 1945 with the Nationalist return to power, as well as the people who took it over after 1949 with the Communist victory, tended to be film artists who had not remained in Shanghai during the Japanese occupation. This does not mean they were in Yan'an, the Communist wartime base. Most spent the war years in Chongqing working in some cultural capacity for the resistance movement organized by the Nationalist government (see chapter 5). One suspects that, at a personal level, they had nothing against their colleagues who had remained in Shanghai during the Japanese occupation. After all, they had worked together in harmony prior to 1937. Old networks of support and bonds of friendship had meaning. But it was clearly in the personal interests of those who had departed from Shanghai during the war to offer little resistance to the immediate postwar idea that occupation-era films and film personalities were tainted. The cloud that hung over people involved in the occupation-era industry made it easier for those returning to Shanghai from the interior in 1946 to assume control after the war.

When one examines the list of leading film personalities who joined the Communist Party between 1949 and 1958, it becomes apparent that most were people like Zhao Dan, Bai Yang, and Zheng Junli who had worked in the interior during the resistance war. Thus it continued to be in their interests, even after 1949, to allow a dark cloud to hang over occupation-era film workers. But their willingness to perpetuate such ideas was far from total. Archival sources show that in the early years of the People's Republic, films made during the occupation era, including Yue Feng's 1941 picture *Family* (*Jia*) and even Maxu Weibang's *Begonia* (*Qiu Haitang*), made for Huaying in 1944, were still being shown in public in China. *Begonia*, for instance, was screened 223 times in Shanghai alone in 1950 (to a total audience of more than a hundred thousand). Needless to say, *Remorse in Shanghai* was not among the occupation-era films screened at that time.[27]

In the early years of the People's Republic, it was rare for a film personality who had risen to fame in the occupation-era film industry to be admitted to the Communist Party. But many of these people prospered and led privileged lives in socialist China. In part, this is because their levels of collaboration with the Japanese were insignificant. People who ran hotels and restaurants before the occupation also ran them during (and after) the occupation. The same is true of most in the occupation-era film industry. They made movies. Another reason for their acceptance following the establishment of the People's Republic is that they were popular and their skills were badly needed by the new regime. Wang Danfeng, who played a role in *Remorse in Shanghai* almost as important as Li Lihua's, seems to have lived a charmed life. She appears not to have been caught up in the ugly *Remorse in Shanghai* scapegoating that occurred after the war. She went to Hong Kong in 1948 but voluntarily returned to socialist China in 1951, after the start of the Korean War and a new wave of anti-Americanism. She appeared in ten films in the 1950s and early 1960s. She even survived the Cultural Revolution. Like Wang Danfeng, the occupation-era actor Liu Qiong returned to socialist China from Hong Kong in 1952 to become something of a matinee idol. Liu also survived the Cultural Revolution and even played a lead in *The Herdsman* (*Mumaren*), a leading 1980s film. Sang Hu, an important occupation-era screenwriter whose credits include *Devotion to Love* (*Nong ben duoqing*), a film produced by Huaying in 1943, had a distinguished directorial career after the founding of the People's Republic. A lifelong noncommunist, not only did he survive the Anti-Rightist Campaign of 1957 and the Cultural Revolution, he actually made films during the Cultural Revolution.

Thus, it is true that many of the people who worked in the occupation-era film industry were not discriminated against or victimized either after the war or after the founding of the People's Republic. They flourished. Yet it is also true that the films they made during the war remained under a cloud—never screened, never studied in a serious way, and, on occasion, denied recognition as "Chinese" films by Cheng Jihua and other influential film historians. Even now, the China Film Archive is reluctant to make these films and related research materials accessible to serious scholars. As for biographical information about occupation-era actors, actresses, directors, and screenwriters who stayed in China and had successful careers after 1949, state-controlled publications have consistently covered up their involvement in Huaying and similar wartime organizations. I interviewed Wang Danfeng and Sang Hu on a couple of occasions in the 1980s, and they were disinclined to say much about their work in the occupation period. The stigma persists.

What conclusions can one reach, then, about *Remorse in Shanghai*? We know that the China Film Archive still does not want to screen the film.

Indeed, the archive does not even have a videotape or DVD copy of the film. Its only copy seems to be a 35 mm print that is stored in an inaccessible off-site film vault (*pian ku*). There is official hostility to the film because it is hard, after all, to avoid the conclusion that *Chun jiang yi hen* is indeed a work of collaboration. Poshek Fu has argued quite eloquently and with good reason that scholars should refrain from arbitrarily placing occupation-era films into the "collaboration" category. He rejects the resistance/collaboration binary and the notion that anything that was not actively "resisting" the occupation must have been actively "collaborating" with the occupation. Fu asserts that virtually all occupation-era films fall primarily into a middle zone, neither resisting nor collaborating. The films made at that time were light entertainment and they kept the industry alive under difficult circumstances.

In the case of some films, however, Fu goes one step further and makes a convincing case that a work like *Mulan Joins the Army* (1939) can actually be read as an anti-Japanese patriotic narrative. He also states that more controversial works like *Eternity* intentionally subverted Japanese efforts to make them more explicitly propagandistic. Thus, in the end, Fu finds that most films are middle-zone, light entertainment works, but that some actually qualify as resistance works or come very close to qualifying. I agree fully with his conclusions and his implied critique of those who want to place all occupation-era work in the "collaboration" and "treason" categories, super-patriots who continue to discredit occupation-era film workers, discourage research on these films, and even deny the films status as Chinese movies.

Fu does not, however, find any examples of middle-zone works that clearly spilled out in another direction, close to the collaboration category. I would argue that the *Remorse in Shanghai* project involves an almost unambiguous case of collaboration, especially considering that it was made at a time when the Japanese cause was headed for defeat. Fu states clearly that he did not have a chance to see *Remorse in Shanghai*. This is a pity, because one senses that he might agree that this work does not fit very well into the noncollaboration, middle-zone category.

Of course, one must concede that all sorts of alternative readings are possible when one is dealing with a diverse film audience. Unfortunately, in the case of *Remorse in Shanghai* we are not likely to know with precision how the audience reacted. But it seems to me that the possibility of various readings does not do much to undermine the conclusion that *Remorse in Shanghai* was a work of collaboration. Certainly the Chinese film world leaders involved in the production were fully aware of the nature of the narrative and its clear expression of support for the Japanese war cause and the Japanese vision of a Greater East Asian Co-Prosperity Sphere. Postwar Nationalist investigators tended to be quite flexible, but even they concluded that there was a clear distinction between *Remorse in Shanghai* and *Eternity*.

Even if *Remorse in Shanghai* was a work of collaboration (and I think it was), it is hard to support the idea that it is not a Chinese film. If it is not a Chinese film, what is it? It appears that Japanese commentators have never claimed that the film is Japanese. So, what does a film have to be to qualify as Chinese? If a film is made in China, set in China, has a Chinese director, has a Chinese scriptwriter, has famous Chinese film stars, makes overwhelming use of the Chinese language, is released in China, is regarded at the time of release and later as a Chinese film, and is funded, at least in part, by Chinese sources, is it not a Chinese film? If the coproduction aspect of the project disqualifies *Remorse in Shanghai* as a Chinese film, then many of the best movies made in China after 1984, including some of the Fifth Generation and most of the Sixth Generation works that have received so much international acclaim, have to be disqualified as well. These days we are fond of speaking of innovative new films that are intimately connected to processes of globalization and transnational cultural production. But that does not stop us from regarding them and writing about them as Chinese films. We assume that the phenomenon of globalization is brand-new. Perhaps we need to think of how different *Remorse in Shanghai* would seem if we thought of it as a very early example of transnational filmmaking.

The tangled legacy of *Remorse in Shanghai* is further complicated by another problem. If one looks closely at the analysis of Chinese history from the Opium War to the time of the Taiping attack on Shanghai in 1862 that is conveyed in *Remorse in Shanghai,* and pays special attention to its critique of Western imperialism, the conclusions it reaches about the toll that Western aggression took on the Chinese people, and its indictment of the failings of a declining Qing state, one sees that the overview is essentially accurate, even though highly simplified. Commentators noticed this problem as early as 1946. Nonetheless, critics of the film, ever eager to marginalize the work, invariably avoid discussion of this issue.

Not only is the overview accurate, it is a view of mid-nineteenth-century Chinese history that was embraced almost entirely by post-1949 Communist filmmakers in the People's Republic. Anyone who doubts this assertion need only take a close look at such famous Mao-era films as *Lin Zexu* (d. Zheng Junli, 1959). The British were ruthless exploiters. The Chinese people suffered miserably. The Qing government was incapable and at times even unwilling to do anything about the threat. Peasant rebels were decent and patriotic. To this day, these are the lessons that every Chinese schoolchild learns. When it comes to mid-nineteenth-century history, all that *Remorse in Shanghai* says is that there were both Chinese and Japanese who recognized these facts in 1862.

There is another irony associated with the various attempts to discredit *Remorse in Shanghai* in the People's Republic. By contemptuously dismissing the Qing state as running dogs of foreign imperialism, incapable and perhaps unwilling to do anything to protect Chinese national dignity, the makers of *Remorse in Shanghai* were clearly sending a political message to the film audience in 1944: the former Nationalist government, exiled now in Chongqing, is no better than the Qing state. The Nationalists are dominated by the Western imperialists and care little about the sufferings of the Chinese people. Present-day historians of China do not accept this view, but for many decades propaganda organs in the People's Republic repeatedly delivered precisely such a message.

It is true that in recent times the Communist Party has taken a softer, gentler approach to the Nationalist Party and its history. But that tendency is driven by the dynamics of present-day Taiwan politics. During the Mao years, patriots in the People's Republic were willing to ignore the anti-imperialist, pro-peasant uprising and anti-Nationalist thrusts of *Remorse in Shanghai* in order to focus all attention on the film's pro-Japanese (and hence, treasonous) essence. In the post-Mao years, some Chinese nationalism has turned into Chinese ultranationalism, an ultranationalism that loves to target Japan and Chinese who are seen as soft on Japan.[28] In the postrevolution, postsocialist era of globalization, fewer people than ever in China (including film scholars, one suspects) would have any interest in the anti-British, anti-Qing, anti-Nationalist, and pro-peasant elements of *Remorse in Shanghai*. Indeed, even more than they did in the past, critics in China are likely to dwell exclusively on the pro-Japanese nature of *Remorse in Shanghai*, and thus continue to deny the film its rather unique place in the controversial history of Chinese cinema.

NOTES

1. Jay Leyda, *Dianying: An Account of Films and the Film Audience in China* (Cambridge, Mass.: MIT Press, 1972), 146–47; Yingjin Zhang and Zhiwei Xiao, *Encyclopedia of Chinese Film* (London: Routledge, 1998), 195, 228; Poshek Fu, *Between Shanghai and Hong Kong* (Stanford, Calif.: Stanford University Press, 2003), 126–29.

2. Cheng Jihua, ed., *Zhongguo dianying fazhan shi* (Beijing: Zhongguo dianying chubanshe, 1981), 2:118–19.

3. Zhongguo dianying ziliaoguan, ed., *Zhongguo dianying ziliaoguan guanzang yingpian mulu* (Beijing: Zhongguo dianying ziliaoguan, 1995), 11.

4. The following paragraphs rely heavily on the excellent and path-breaking research of Poshek Fu. See Fu, *Between Shanghai and Hong Kong*, 108–32.

5. See Yingjin Zhang, *Chinese National Cinema* (New York: Routledge, 2004), 88–89.

6. See Fu, *Between Shanghai and Hong Kong*, 126–29.

7. Peter B. High, *The Imperial Screen: Japanese Film Culture in the Fifteen Years' War, 1931–1945* (Madison: University of Wisconsin Press, 2003), 81, 151, 157, 180.

8. See Zhang and Xiao, *Encyclopedia of Chinese Film*, 195, 228.

9. This discussion of the voyage of the *Senzaimaru* borrows heavily from the excellent pioneering research done by Joshua A. Fogel. See his "The Voyage of the *Senzaimaru* to Shanghai: Early Sino-Japanese Contacts in the Modern Era," in Joshua A. Vogel, *The Cultural Dimension of Sino-Japanese Relations* (Armonk, N.Y.: M. E. Sharpe, 1994), 79–94.

10. Fogel, "The Voyage of the *Senzaimaru* to Shanghai," 82.

11. Fogel, "The Voyage of the *Senzaimaru* to Shanghai," 86.

12. See Jonathan Spence, *God's Chinese Son* (New York: Norton, 1996), 298–309, for a discussion of the early 1862 Taiping assault on Shanghai. Spence also mentions the *Senzaimaru* (page 309).

13. Fogel, "The Voyage of the *Senzaimaru* to Shanghai," 92–94.

14. Spence, *God's Chinese Son*, 302.

15. Rhoads Murphey, *East Asia* (New York: Longman, 1996), 264–65.

16. I am indebted to Nishimura Masato for this information.

17. Fu, *Between Shanghai and Hong Kong*, 129.

18. See the following articles in the journal *Hua bei ying hua*: "*Chun jiang yi hen* lishi ju pian," no. 48 (1944); *Chun jiang yi hen* zhipian quzhi," no. 48 (1944); "Xuanchuan bu zhongshi wenhua yingpian," no. 48 (1944); "*Chun jiang yi hen* kai pai huaxu," no. 49 (1944); "*Chun jiang yi hen* bujing fuli tanghuang," no. 50 (1944); "Yi nian lai Shanghai yingpian tongji ji shezhi," no. 52 (1944); "*Chun jiang yi hen* jingcai yimu," no. 56 (1944); "Nanxing shumiao—Mei Xi," no. 56 (1944).

19. Fu, *Between Shanghai and Hong Kong*, 129.

20. John Hunter Boyle, *Modern Japan* (New York: Harcourt Brace Jovanovich, 1993), 258–60.

21. Suzanne Pepper, *Civil War in China* (Lanham, Md.: Rowman & Littlefield, 1999), 7–42.

22. Hu Yan, "Chun jiang bu yi hen, wan shi yong liu fang," *Ying yi hua bao*, no. 2 (1946).

23. "Bukan huishou de nü mingxing," *Zhongguo yingtan* 1, no. 1 (1946).

24. Wu Guozhen, "Zhongguo Guomindang," Shanghai shi danganguan, Q1-12-1464.

25. "Shanghai shi zhengfu baogao," Shanghai shi danganguan, Q1-12-1464.

26. "Li Lihua, Chen Yanyan shenxun qingxing," *Zhongguo dianying*, no. 4 (1947).

27. Shanghai shi danganguan, B-171-1-35.

28. For an example of a "new nationalist" and "anti-Japanese" tract that recycles old and familiar information about Japan's involvement in China's occupation-era film industry to make easy political points in an anti-Japanese political environment, see Tian Ye and Mei Chuan, "Riben diguozhuyi qin Hua qijian de dianying wenhua qinlue," *Dangdai dianying* (January 1996): 91–94.

5
Victory as Defeat: Postwar Visualizations of China's War of Resistance

There was an extraordinary amount of violence in China during the first fifty years of the twentieth century, but the War of Resistance was by far the worst instance. Tens of millions experienced that conflict as nothing less than a holocaust. Death, destruction, privation, and persecution were daily occurrences. Communities were ripped apart. Individual incidents of terror and agony were reported in the press, but so long as the struggle was still unfolding, it was difficult for participants to evaluate the devastating impact of the war on Chinese society. Not until the defeat of Japan was it possible to craft epic narratives that reflected critically on the national meaning of the endless nightmare.

Elite nation-builders had their own grand interpretations of the meaning of the war. Their views, embodied in a variety of official mythologies, have been studied quite carefully. One wonders, however, how ordinary people, including those who lived in the vast areas under direct Japanese occupation and were cut off from detailed news about the course of the war, thought about the hardships they had suffered during the long ordeal. Once the struggle was over, many prominent Chinese, including politicians, historians, novelists, and journalists, were eager to tell the people about the ultimate meaning of their sufferings. But few were as successful in the role of "voice of the people" as the leading filmmakers. In a word, they captured the imagination of the urban population. Visual images produced at this time were so potent that many decades later, elderly and middle-aged Chinese still remembered the holocaust in the vivid terms spelled out in highly popular postwar film epics.

THE POSTWAR FILM SCENE

In the mid-1930s the Chinese film industry was flourishing. Everything changed when the war spread to Shanghai in August 1937. Many film personalities fled into the interior to aid the resistance. Those who stayed behind did the best they could to make "Orphan Island" films in Shanghai in the foreign concessions, which were beyond direct Japanese control, from 1937 to late 1941. For obvious reasons, however, these works did not deal explicitly with war-related themes.

Throughout the war, and particularly after the attack on Pearl Harbor, Chinese films were made under Japanese auspices in Shanghai and elsewhere. This work had entertainment value but was incapable of considering the impact of the war on ordinary citizens. By late 1944 and early 1945, as the Allies closed in on Japanese forces, relatively few Japanese-sponsored works were produced. Chinese who worked in that sector of the film industry were afraid of being accused of collaboration when the war was over. During the war the Nationalist government tried to encourage filmmaking in the interior. Due to poor production environments and inadequate means of distribution, however, these works, almost all of which fell into the category of patriotic mobilization propaganda, attracted little attention.[1] In short, none of the films made in China between 1937 and 1945 took a comprehensive look at the war and its social consequences. By the end of the conflict, Chinese filmmakers in both the interior and the occupied zones were almost completely idle.

Once victory was in hand, there was an enormous demand for new Chinese-made films, especially works that talked about the war. But the film world responded very slowly. In the twelve months that followed the Japanese surrender on August 14, 1945, not a single Chinese film was completed. Consumers demanded, but did not get, new Chinese productions. Instead, they got old Chinese films and American films.

The situation was so tense that in early June 1946 a riot broke out at the Strand Theater (Xinguang da xiyuan) on Ningbo Road in Shanghai, when patrons violently protested yet another screening of an old Charlie Chaplin movie.[2] Consumers looked forward to seeing *new* Hollywood films, but ticket prices were exceedingly high and lines unbearably long. As a result, there was a booming black market for tickets to the most popular American movies.[3] Local papers demanded to know why there were no new Chinese films.

The lack of new film production activity was related to the threat of full-scale civil war and frustrating delays in the takeover of Shanghai and other Japanese-occupied cities. It is sometimes forgotten that the government did not make an official return to its prewar capital in Nanjing until May 5, 1946.

Ordinary film fans had no way of knowing that both the state and private sectors had ambitious agendas for the postwar film industry. For the state, the first step involved nationalizing the Japanese-controlled film studios in Shanghai and Beijing and confiscating their equipment, by far the best moviemaking hardware available in China. By nationalizing these units and refusing to make the equipment available to private sector filmmakers, the state was declaring its intention of going into the postwar motion picture business. This was a first for China. The Nationalist state had been largely uninvolved in the sprawling prewar film industry. When the state began taking over Japanese studios in late 1945, its filmmaking experience was limited to a few crude and highly forgettable wartime propaganda works turned out in Wuhan and Chongqing.

Two of the new state-owned units, China Film No. 1 and China Film No. 2, were located in Shanghai, and one studio, China Film No. 3, was set up in Beijing. To increase its chances of success, the state retained (and thus monopolized) the services of the Chinese technicians and production crews of the former Japanese studios.[4] Lists of Chinese stars who had worked with the Japanese were published, and a few high-profile arrests were made, but no one was tried for treason. Film workers who had cooperated with the Japanese were generally spared after the war.

The new state studios also offered employment to the many stage and film workers who had served the resistance so valiantly in the interior. With the war at an end, these people now needed jobs. As a rule, however, directors and film workers who had served in the interior were kept apart from those who had remained in Shanghai.

Filmmakers who desperately wanted to revive the private sector after the war had a hard time competing with the state. They had difficulty attracting investors, they had to order new equipment from abroad, and they were unable to offer immediate employment to film workers, most of whom had families to support.[5]

Well before any state or private-sector films were actually produced, there was a good deal of discussion in the popular press about the hopes of postwar filmmakers. Using time-honored neo-Confucian standards, some commentators argued that both state and private filmmakers had a moral obligation to play an uplifting role in the postwar industry. In general, there was a greater awareness of the extraordinary power of the film image than there had been before the war. In May 1946, for instance, one film writer asserted that there was "no agency in the world so capable of being used for adult education as the motion picture." The "propaganda possibilities" of film, he solemnly concluded, "make it one of the strongest and most penetrative influences in human history."[6]

Those who emphasized educational goals (and there were both conservatives and liberals in this camp) tended to be critical of the purely commercial orientation of most prewar private-sector filmmakers. When the overriding concern was moneymaking, critics said, the result was often worthless trash that weakened public morals. It was necessary to look upon films "as something aside from a means of entertainment."[7] In a word, filmmaking was too important to be left exclusively in the hands of greedy merchants and capitalists.

Although the rhetoric was high-minded, the first few postwar films, almost all produced in the new state-owned studios, failed to offer anything new or innovative. Disillusionment and despair were already facts of postwar life, but none of the new works confronted the problem of urban malaise and its connection to the dislocations of war. The very first state-funded postwar production, *Loyal and Virtuous Family* (*Zhong yi zhi jia*), released on August 27, 1946, was written and directed by Wu Yonggang, a well-known leftist whose prewar work had been praised by Communist critics. A one-dimensional story of the wartime sacrifices of a patriotic Shanghai family, it differed in no significant way from the simplistic pro–Nationalist Party and pro-American propaganda films produced by the state during the war. Another early postwar state project was *Songbird on Earth* (*Ying fei renjian*), directed by Fang Peilin and released on November 7. It was precisely the sort of formulaic entertainment musical churned out in large quantities by prewar commercial studios.

The box office success of some of these early postwar films was due, in large part, to their novelty. They were advertised in the newspapers as the "first" postwar this or the "first" postwar that, and people naturally turned out to take a look. Some critics complained that the films were poorly made imitations of Hollywood originals, but the film-hungry audience was understandably curious.

Only a relative handful of film-world insiders knew that, even as these disappointing early postwar movies were making the rounds, startlingly different works were already in production in the state-owned studios and, shortly thereafter, in the private studios. These stunning works, fashioned without exception by filmmakers who had worked in leading Nationalist cultural organizations during the war, boldly asserted that the social disruptions caused by the war were so severe that victory felt like defeat. Despite the depressing nature of these postwar epic narratives, the films were phenomenally popular. Indeed, they caused a sensation that propelled the film industry to the forefront of the Chinese cultural world in early 1947.

PREWAR CONNECTIONS, WARTIME PASSAGES, AND POSTWAR NETWORKS

Chen Liting, Shi Dongshan, Cai Chusheng, and Zheng Junli were especially prominent among the screenwriters and directors responsible for the astonishing surge of creativity that swept through the Chinese film world in late 1946 and early 1947. The four men shared much in common. All four were veterans of the robust stage and screen worlds of prewar Shanghai. Chen Liting and Zheng Junli were leaders of the Shanghai Amateur Experimental Drama Troupe (Shanghai yeyu shiyan jutuan) in the late 1930s, while Shi Dongshan, Cai Chusheng, and Zheng Junli were well-known film personalities associated with Shanghai's glamorous Lianhua Film Studio (Lianhua dianying zhipianchang) in the prewar years. All four had contacts in Nationalist government offices, in the business world, and in left-wing cultural circles. All four held moderate political views and refrained from joining political parties. All four fled Shanghai prior to the Japanese occupation in November 1937 and passed many difficult years in the interior working for various Nationalist cultural organizations engaged in resistance activities. All four spent considerable time in wartime Chongqing, returning to Shanghai by early 1946 to breathe life into a postwar reincarnation of the old Lianhua Film Studio called Kunlun (Kunlun yingye gongsi).[8] Most important, all four had ambitious plans to film unsettling accounts of the holocaust experience.

A native of Shanghai, Chen Liting, the most intellectual of the group, was swept up by the post–May Fourth surge of interest in modern drama. In 1931, while attending Daxia University in Shanghai, Chen translated *The Rising of the Moon*, a highly influential early-twentieth-century play by the noted Irish dramatist Lady Gregory.[9] This famous work helped launch a renaissance in Irish drama; it featured lively, direct, and powerful dialogue that was rooted in Ireland's rural folklore. Chen directed and acted in the first Chinese production of *The Rising of the Moon*.

In late 1931 and early 1932 Chen worked as an elementary schoolteacher in rural Nanhui county, east of central Shanghai. Chen began at once directing experimental "street theater" (*jietou ju*) that dispensed with stages, sets, artificial lighting, and other conventions. Actors and audience were in direct contact. Inspired by Lady Gregory's example, Chen emphasized simplicity and clarity of message. His most famous production, *Lay Down Your Whip* (*Fang xia ni de bianzi*), caused an immediate uproar. Years later, during the War of Resistance, it was performed countless times throughout China.[10]

Back in Shanghai by mid-1932, Chen worked for several years organizing and directing amateur theater groups that were loosely affiliated with the League of Left-Wing Dramatists. He also wrote film reviews for *Chen bao* and *Ming bao*, and translated a number of Soviet books on filmmaking, including Vsevolod Pudovkin's *On Film Acting* (*Dianying yanyuan lun*).[11] It was in the mid-1930s that Soviet films began to be screened in China.

When the war erupted, Chen was one of the primary leaders of the Shanghai Amateur Experimental Drama Troupe. His company immediately joined the resistance by breaking into two groups to form the third and fourth brigades of the Shanghai Salvation Drama Troupe (Shanghai jiuwang yan ju). Chen served as the leader of the fourth brigade. After putting on numerous street performances, including *Lay Down Your Whip*, the troupe fled Shanghai before it fell, in September. For the next three years Chen and his compatriots traveled under harsh conditions through central and southwest China, performing innumerable patriotic plays.

In 1941 Chen arrived in Chongqing and was immediately invited by the Nationalist authorities to join the state-run China Film Studio (Zhongguo dianying zhipianchang) and the Central Cinematography Studio (Zhongyang sheying chang). But Chen's main contribution continued to be in the theater world. As a member of such state-sponsored groups as the China Art Theater Society (Zhongguo yishu ju she), Chen directed leading plays by Wu Zuguang, Xia Yan, and Chen Baichen. Chen Liting's most impressive wartime effort was his staging of Guo Moruo's famous 1942 play, *Qu Yuan*.

Chen Liting was back in Shanghai by early 1946. He was invited to join the state's new China Film No. 2 studio, and he began at once to write and then direct *Far Away Love* (*Yaoyuan de ai*), the first in a series of controversial epics on the social dislocations caused by the holocaust. The premiere, held in Shanghai's well-known Huanghou Theater on January 18, 1947, was a landmark event in postwar filmmaking. Such prominent actors and actresses as Zhao Dan, Qin Yi, and Wu Yin, all of whom had worked with Chen before or during the war, were recruited by the state-run studio to play leading roles. The Ministry of Defense supported the production by putting units of uniformed soldiers at Chen's disposal.

Chen Liting made a second film at the China Film No. 2 studio, Chen Baichen's *A Rhapsody of Happiness* (*Xingfu kuangxiangqu*), in late 1947, before moving on to Kunlun, the new private studio, to direct *Women Side-by-Side* (*Liren xing*) in early 1949, a work based on a screenplay cowritten by Chen and the noted dramatist Tian Han. After 1949 Chen served the new socialist regime in many capacities, including a long stint as director of the Haiyan Film Studio in Shanghai from 1957 to 1966. There is no evidence that Chen Liting ever joined the Communist Party, even though many leading film personalities did so in the 1950s.

Shi Dongshan, whose original name was Shi Kuangshao, was raised in Hangzhou. His father was an accomplished local artist and musician, but the family was of modest means. Shi left Hangzhou in 1922, finding work as a set designer at the Shanghai Yingxi Film Company (Shanghai yingxi gongsi).[12] He directed his first film for Yingxi in 1925, at the age of twenty-three, and in 1930 Shi began working for the legendary Lianhua Film Studio, one of the two most important film companies of the 1930s. Prior to the Japanese occupation of Manchuria, Shi's finely crafted works did not have a particular political orientation. On the contrary, one of Shi's specialties was directing the sort of flashy martial arts thriller that was so popular in the late 1920s.

Beginning in 1931, however, his films took on a more pronounced patriotic tone as the Japanese threat intensified. In 1937 he fled Shanghai for Wuhan and later Chongqing, where he, like Chen Liting, worked for the China Film Studio, an arm of the Political Bureau of the Nationalist government's Military Affairs Commission (Junshi weiyuanhui zhengzhi bu). Shi produced a number of highly patriotic wartime propaganda films and directed a few stage plays.

In 1946 he returned to Shanghai and helped found the Kunlun Film Studio. In August 1946 he completed the controversial screenplay *Eight Thousand Miles of Clouds and Moon* (*Ba qian li lu yun he yue*), a narrative thematically consistent with Chen Liting's *Far Away Love*. It was Kunlun's first postwar production. This film, directed by Shi himself, was released simultaneously at the Carlton, Huguang, and Huanghou theaters in Shanghai on February 21, 1947, a month after the triumphant appearance of *Far Away Love*.

Shi resided in Hong Kong in 1948, returned to Beijing in 1949 after the revolution, and was appointed head of the Technology Committee of the Ministry of Culture's Film Bureau (Wenhua bu dianying ju jishu weiyuanhui).[13] After 1949 Shi's directorial activities were limited. Shi never joined the Communist Party, and by late 1951 he became the target of political criticism. On February 23, 1955, at the age of fifty-three, Shi Dongshan committed suicide. According to one of his sons, his farewell note was confiscated on the orders of Zhou Enlai, and news of the suicide was suppressed.

Cai Chusheng was born in Shanghai, but returned with his parents to their native place, Chaoyang, Guangdong, when he was six. His formal education was limited to four years in an old-style private school. At age twelve Cai was sent by his father to Shantou to learn a trade, first in an old-style bank (*qian zhuang*) and then in a small shop. Cai was far more interested, however, in amateur theater activities. In 1926 he helped make local arrangements for a Shanghai film company that was shooting a movie in Shantou. In 1929 he moved to Shanghai and, like Shi Dongshan before him, worked at a number of odd jobs in the film industry. Cai's big break came in 1929, when at the age of twenty-three he met the famous actor and director Zheng Zhengqiu, who was also a native of Chaoyang. Zheng immediately brought his compatriot into the well-known Star Film Company (Mingxing yingpian gongsi), where Cai directed six pictures. In summer 1931 Cai Chusheng began working at the Lianhua Film Studio, where he met Shi Dongshan.[14] Like Shi's, Cai's films of the early 1930s had no pronounced political characteristics. Works like *A Dream in Pink* (*Fenhongse de meng*, 1932) were the sort of mainstream, culturally cautious works that Cai's mentor, Zheng Zhengqiu, had mastered years before. Some of his films were criticized by leftist writers.

It was only after the Japanese attack on Shanghai in 1932 that Cai's films became overtly patriotic. By the mid-1930s he was making a greater impact on the film world than Shi Dongshan was. Cai's masterpiece, *Fisherman's Song* (*Yu guang qu*, 1934), written and directed when he was twenty-eight, was the first Chinese film to win an international award.[15]

In 1937 Cai fled the occupation of Shanghai and spent more than four years making Cantonese-language resistance films in Hong Kong. Following the occupation of Hong Kong he fled to Guilin, and finally to Chongqing in late 1944, where he met up with his old friend Shi Dongshan. Cai was seriously weakened by tuberculosis following his departure from Hong Kong, but by February 1945 he was able to serve as a member of the committee on writing and directing of the Nationalists' Central Cinematography Studio. Chen Liting also served on that committee.

In January 1946 Cai returned to Shanghai to help organize the privately run Kunlun branch of the old Lianhua Film Studio. Kunlun's second film, *A Spring River Flows East* (*Yi jiang chun shui xiang dong liu*, 1947), a spectacular two-part account of holocaust dislocation released in three Shanghai theaters (Lidu, Huguang, and Meiqi) on October 9, 1947, on the eve of National Day, was written primarily by Cai Chusheng. The film was so popular it played continuously in Shanghai for almost a year.

Like Shi Dongshan, Cai Chusheng went to Beijing in 1949 and assumed a number of leadership positions in the new cultural organizations, including the vice directorship of the Film Bureau under the Ministry of Culture (Wenhua bu dianying ju). Cai did not join the Communist Party until 1956. Owing to harsh treatment during the Cultural Revolution, Cai Chusheng died on July 15, 1968, at the age of sixty-two.

Zheng Junli, whose family hailed from Zhongshan county, Guangdong, was born in Shanghai. Fond of art in his early years, Zheng dropped out of middle school during his second year and eventually enrolled in the theater department of the famous Southern Art Institute (Nanguo yishu xueyuan). In the 1930s Zheng established himself as one of China's leading stage and screen actors. In 1932 he joined the Lianhua Film Studio, came into close contact with Shi Dongshan and Cai Chusheng, and appeared in many outstanding films. Some films, like *The Big Road* (*Da lu*, d. Sun Yu, 1934), were associated with the left, while others, like *Filial Piety* (*Tian lun*, d. Fei Mu, 1935), were associated with neoconservative causes. There can be no doubt, however, that Zheng was ardently patriotic. On the eve of the war Zheng, like Chen Liting, was a leader of the Shanghai Amateur Experimental Drama Troupe, which formed the third and fourth brigades of the Shanghai Salvation Drama Troupe once the war was under way. Zheng

Junli was leader of the third brigade, which also included the well-known actor Zhao Dan. Chen Liting was in charge of the fourth brigade. After doing considerable propaganda work in Shanghai proper, these groups moved into the interior to do long-term resistance work once Shanghai fell.

At Guo Moruo's urging, Zheng served in Chongqing as director of China's wartime Children's Theater Troupe (Haizi jutuan). From 1940 to 1942 he worked outside the wartime capital on a documentary film project for the Nationalist government's China Film Studio, returning to Chongqing and the stage as a director and actor in the last few years of the war.[16]

Zheng Junli returned to Shanghai in 1946, joining immediately in the effort to establish the Kunlun branch of the old Lianhua Film Studio. There he worked with Cai Chusheng on the epic film *A Spring River Flows East*. The screenplay, written primarily by Cai, was finished in the summer of 1946. The direction of the film was left primarily to Zheng.

After 1949 Zheng Junli continued making films at the Kunlun Studio. In 1951 his movie *Husband and Wife* (*Women fu fu zhi jian*) was severely criticized for presenting a "distorted view of life in the liberated areas" after 1949, and Zheng was forced to write a self-criticism titled "With Deep Remorse I Must Reform Myself" (*Wo bixu tongqie gaizao ziji*). Zheng was allowed to continue working, and he eventually joined the Communist Party in 1958. In 1961, however, his film on the life of Lu Xun was banned before its release, and in 1967, at the outset of the Cultural Revolution, Zheng was jailed. Owing to mistreatment, he died in prison in 1969 at the age of fifty-eight.

FAR AWAY LOVE: A MEANINGFUL FABRICATION

The remarkable postwar works of Chen Liting, Shi Dongshan, Cai Chusheng, and Zheng Junli pose a major question: How was it possible for films that treated victory as defeat to be so popular? To answer this question, it is extremely important to go over almost every detail of their elaborate narrative reconstructions of the war years. This method allows us to appreciate patterns of appeal that link the texts to the popular audience. As Robert Darnton has pointed out, reconstructions of this sort are not objective, historically accurate, or "true" in any strict sense.[17] We study them because they are "meaningful fabrications" that often reveal much about popular perceptions. The point about these works is not that they were historically accurate accounts of the holocaust years, but rather that they were extremely influential and came to be accepted as valid representations by millions of ordinary urbanites in the postwar period. In a word, the films captured a psychological reality that was pervasive in urban society after the war.[18]

The first narrative, an amusing satire called *Far Away Love*, begins in Shanghai in late 1927. Chen Liting believed that a full understanding of the disruptive social dynamics of the war years required a grasp of prewar conditions. As the account opens, the audience sees a respected young professor named Xiao Yuanxi lecturing on the subject "women and society." Xiao presents himself as a modern-minded intellectual who supports the cause of women's rights.

One day Xiao catches a female servant named Yu Zhen taking a book from his study. She claims she is only borrowing it. Given her rural background, Xiao is amazed the young woman can read. Later he tells a female colleague named Wu Ya'nan that he has a grand experiment in mind. Xiao proposes to take personal charge of the servant's reeducation. He is confident he can mold such fine raw material into a "modern young lady" (*modeng xiaojie*). At first Yu Zhen misunderstands. When she was still in her village, a landlord's son wanted to convert her to a *xiaojie*, that is, his concubine. The two intellectuals convince her that Xiao has nothing but the best intentions.

Yu Zhen finally agrees, and Professor Xiao lectures her on the role of women in modern society. Since "modern" is defined primarily as "Western," the servant is taught Western table manners and the correct way to shake hands with men. Her peasant garb is exchanged for modern, urban clothes. Still, throughout her rigorous training, Yu Zhen continues to function as a servant. For example, Xiao insists that Yu Zhen sit with him at the breakfast table, but he still expects her to serve the meal.

The professor eventually writes a book titled *On New Women* (*Xin funü lun*) about his experiment, and his fame spreads. He confesses to Yu Zhen, however, that her progress has not been totally satisfactory. She is not an "ideal" woman, he proclaims, because she is insufficiently "independent." Xiao complains that she obeys his commands a bit too mechanically. That problem is addressed, however, when Wu Ya'nan, known throughout the picture as Big Sister Wu, convinces Yu Zhen to go to a public meeting (on the Japanese threat) that the busy professor has no time to attend. Yu Zhen goes in order to show more "independence."

The narrative leaps ahead to 1931. Xiao has married his "ideal" woman and a son is born. Unfortunately, their domestic tranquility is disturbed by the Mukden Incident. Influenced by Big Sister Wu, Yu Zhen attends ever more meetings. She also enrolls in a class that provides her with some leadership training. Xiao begins to resent the fact that his wife is never home. She justifies her absences by referring to his earlier remarks about the need for women to show "independence." When Japanese forces attack Shanghai in January 1932, Yu Zhen's father is killed in a bombing raid. Her brother joins the Nationalist army and is killed in the fierce fighting. Throughout the struggle Yu Zhen works as a volunteer nurse. When an armistice brings the fighting to an end in May, the professor is delighted that Yu Zhen will be returning home. But Yu Zhen is depressed because there was no clear victory. She says her brother "died for nothing." Eager to regain control of his wife, Xiao orders Big Sister Wu to stay away from the family.

The narrative leaps ahead to July 1937. The couple has another son and war threatens once again. And once again Big Sister Wu shows up to recruit Yu Zhen for war preparation. Xiao claims that the war will never reach Shanghai, and when it does he is shaken to the core. When a friend offers him a comfortable military desk job in Hankou, Xiao agrees to flee the city. Yu Zhen insists on staying in Shanghai as long as possible to do dangerous work at the front. Husband and wife separate, but Xiao refuses to take either of the children, even though he is headed for a safe rear area.

Xiao lives a life of great comfort in Hankou. He wears a fancy Nationalist uniform and lives in a spacious home once occupied by Japanese residents. He has servants and an expense account. When he is not attending meaningless meetings, he plays cards in his office. Enthusiastic young people plead for a chance to go to the front, but Xiao urges them to be "logical" and refuses to process their papers. At night Xiao spends his time in Hankou's best nightclubs.

When the Japanese occupy Shanghai, Yu Zhen retreats with other resistance activists. Along the way her infant child is killed in a Japanese strafing assault. Yu Zhen later joins a Nationalist military unit and puts on the crude uniform of infantry regulars. Every day she hikes along with the troops, helping wounded soldiers, refugees, and orphans.

One of the most visually interesting sequences in the film involves the reunion in Hankou between Xiao and Yu Zhen. The gap that now separates them is apparent in everything that happens. She is wearing rough straw sandals and a tattered uniform; he has expensive leather shoes and a full cape. He wants to pay for a rickshaw; she prefers to walk. He wants her to wear women's clothing; she insists on staying in her battle fatigues. He takes her to Hankou's most elegant restaurant; she says she is not hungry.

The restaurant scene is especially effective. Xiao spends a small fortune on a wasteful dinner while starving children gape through the window. Yu Zhen is appalled by the decadence of the restaurant culture. She asks Xiao when he started smoking and drinking so much. When the bill comes, Yu Zhen says that a soldier at the front could live for a month on what Xiao has spent.

Back in his lavish home, Xiao tries to tell Yu Zhen that life in the rear is different from life at the front and urges her to adjust. But even Xiao's pet dog does not like Yu Zhen. The dog smells Yu Zhen's feet and immediately begins an angry bark before jumping up on Xiao's lap. One evening they go out to a dazzling nightclub for an evening of drinking and dancing to Western music. The party ends abruptly when Yu Zhen slaps a man who is harassing her.

Wearing battle fatigues and straw sandals, an embarrassed Yu Zhen (*left*) enters an elegant Hankou restaurant with her corrupt husband (*center*), in *Far Away Love* (1947, d. Chen Liting). China Film Archive

As the war gets closer to Hankou, Yu Zhen wants to return to the front. Xiao is opposed to her plan. Late one night her thoughts return to the warm feelings of community she enjoyed with her comrades in the army. Before dawn she slips out and returns to the women's work brigade at the front, leaving a note that tells Xiao she will return whenever she can.

The war drags on and the paths of husband and wife do not cross. With the fall of Hankou, Xiao drifts to Guilin, where he takes up a minor teaching post. Xiao's dignity continues to slip away. Students sneak out of his meaningless lectures, and a new article of his, titled "Women's Heaven and Earth Is Still in the Family," is severely criticized in the press.

Yu Zhen, it seems, has a new family. She is working feverishly on the outskirts of Guilin with Big Sister Wu and many others who comprise a wartime Nationalist military collective. The group treats the elderly like parents, soldiers like brothers, and orphans like its own children.

The film ends when a Japanese assault on Guilin leads to a mass exodus of terrified refugees, including Professor Xiao, who looks quite pathetic. His clothes are disheveled, his glasses are broken, and he has lost almost all his personal possessions. Worst of all, he is not getting the respect he thinks he deserves. He complains that being in a refugee column is like being in the army: "There is no individual freedom!" Actually, the column consists primarily of women, children, and the elderly. Xiao is one of the few adult males in the group.

The refugees finally make it to an evacuation center where Yu Zhen's women's brigade has arranged for a caravan of trucks to take the women and children to safety. It is here that Big Sister Wu spots the wretched Professor Xiao among the women and children. She then brings Yu Zhen and Xiao together in the final scene of the movie.

Xiao wants to get back together with Yu Zhen. He says he needs her and cannot understand how she can get along without her husband and family. He wants her to go to Chongqing with him. When she declines, he asks if she has another man. She answers that she "loves all of those who have died and all who are still fighting." She pities him because he "loves only himself." His is a "selfish love." Still, she promises to talk to him about their relationship once the war is over. Xiao then jumps on a truck and goes off with the women and children.

EIGHT THOUSAND MILES OF CLOUDS AND MOON: THE ILLUSION OF REALITY

The second narrative, *Eight Thousand Miles of Clouds and Moon*, begins in Shanghai in the summer of 1937, immediately following the Japanese invasion.[19] Like *Far Away Love*, this account of the holocaust is particularly interesting because it dwells on the experiences of a young woman, this time a seventeen-year-old college student named Jiang Lingyu. Inspired by the patriotic appeals of actors who visit her campus, she wants to join a mobile drama troupe being put together by resistance organizers. She is both innocent and idealistic, and never asks how she can gain by actively supporting the war effort.[20]

Lingyu, a native of Jiangxi, lives in Shanghai with her aunt (her mother's sister), uncle, and two cousins (one is a female, a bit younger than Lingyu, and the other, Zhou Jiarong, a male, is older). The problem for Lingyu, played by the famous actress Bai Yang, who spent the war doing cultural work in the interior, is that her relatives firmly oppose her plan to join the troupe and leave Shanghai. Lingyu's uncle expresses negative stereotypes of actors and stage people. He protests that it is immoral for young men and women to be thrown together in this fashion beyond the supervision of their families, and sternly warns that "good people will be transformed into bad people" in such circumstances. Lingyu's aunt asserts that the theater people have unacceptably low social and cultural status. Lingyu insists that they are people of "learning" (*xuewen*) and "standing" (*diwei*). Even her cousin, Jiarong, is opposed. He says the issue is not patriotism ("We are all patriotic"), but rather the illogic of running off with a bunch of "stars" (*mingxing*).

But the narrative strongly suggests that the issue is, in fact, patriotism. The choice seems to be between family and country, an extremely complicated choice for most people. In this blatantly manipulative account, as in *Far Away Love*, the characterizations of the family members are so uniformly negative that the choice is easy. The narrative applauds Lingyu, a teenage female, when, to the shock and dismay of her relatives, she sneaks out to run away with the troupe of actors, a group that is clearly linked to the Nationalist government and military. Indeed, during much of the story troupe members wear Nationalist military uniforms. They regard themselves as "cultural soldiers" (*wenhua zhanshi*).

The story follows the troupe as they move from Shanghai to Suzhou, Wuxi, Changzhou, and Wuhan. Although the material living conditions of the troupe are austere, its sense of solidarity is great. In a word, the troupe is Lingyu's new family, a surrogate family born of wartime privation. The group tirelessly performs outdoor skits (including a fascinating production of Chen Liting's *Lay Down Your Whip*) to arouse the anti-Japanese indignation of the masses. They also do indoor patriotic plays for the enjoyment of infantry soldiers. Great pains are taken to show that the actors are not at all like the stereotypes imagined by Lingyu's relatives. They are cultured, disciplined, and selflessly dedicated to national salvation.

During the course of the struggle a love relationship develops between Lingyu and a classmate named Gao Libin, who also joined the drama troupe. It is a special love, born of war and sacrifice. Their bond is based on mutual respect and their united contributions to the resistance. As they move farther inland the couple experiences every imaginable war-related hardship. One time they see a member of their troupe shot dead by the enemy. Another time Lingyu falls ill and is cared for by Libin and the group.

After the troupe arrives in Chongqing, Lingyu receives a letter from her father in rural Jiangxi. In sharp contrast to the maternal relatives in Shanghai, her father writes approvingly of her patriotic activities and her relationship with Libin. He agrees that they should marry but urges them to wait until the war is over. The couple accepts his view. "China's victory will be our victory!" they say. Libin, played by the popular actor Tao Jin, who spent most of the war doing cultural work in Chongqing, fantasizes about what China will be like when victory is achieved. The country, he predicts, will be peaceful (*heping*), democratic (*minzhu*), and free (*ziyou*), and the people will be happy (*xingfu*). Filial to the core, they plan to invite her father to live with them, and to produce a grandson for his enjoyment.

Suddenly Lingyu's cousin, Jiarong, played by the young actor Gao Zheng, shows up in Chongqing.[21] He claims that he, too, is participating in the resistance, but it is clear from his comments that he is enriching himself by engaging in war profiteering. He even offers to supply Lingyu with coffee, powdered milk, candy, and other delicacies. Jiarong is shocked to find that Lingyu and Libin are not benefiting personally from the war. He cannot understand their selfless dedication. For her part, Lingyu is repulsed by Jiarong's animated description of Chongqing's lively (*renao*) dance and party scene. Interestingly, the growing gap between the two cousins has pronounced national and cultural dimensions. The filmmakers take pains to show that Jiarong and his corrupted friends (like Professor Xiao and his cronies in *Far Away Love*) live, dress, and socialize in what is portrayed as the Western manner, while the members of the Nationalist drama troupe (like Yu Zhen's medical team in *Far Away Love*) live and work in ways that are shown to be consistent with essentialistic Chinese customs and morality.

As soon as Japan surrenders in August 1945, Lingyu and Libin get married in a ceremony attended by all their resistance-war comrades. Jiarong stumbles, uninvited, into the wedding party, dressed in a Western suit and tie. Disappointed to learn that Lingyu has married Libin, he invites Lingyu to join him on a special early flight back to liberated Shanghai, where new postwar business opportunities await. Needless to say, Lingyu declines.

But the end of the war brings nothing but difficulties for the newlyweds. First, dressed in simple Nationalist military uniforms, they travel to Jiangxi to see Lingyu's father. The couple is shocked to discover that Lingyu's father is dead and the family property has been sold. Morale in her native village is low.

Later, in Shanghai, they visit her aunt and uncle, who now live with Lingyu's cousins in a splendid foreign-style house that Jiarong got from a German national whom he protected just after the war. The reunion does not go well. Jiarong is now dressed in a fancy Western-style military uniform that suggests he is an officer involved in the postwar government takeover of Shanghai. His new girlfriend, shallow and stupid, spends most of her time applying makeup. Lingyu's female cousin has married a well-dressed businessman.

Lingyu and Libin are embarrassed by the comments of their relatives. During a *majiang* game, Lingyu's aunt asks how much money they made during the war performing plays. Jiarong says that people like them who got nothing for "serving the people" (*wei renmin fuwu*) were fools. The uncle adds that many people who lived in the interior (*houfang*) made money. The couple missed one golden opportunity during the war, he points out, but they should not miss another one in postwar Shanghai. Jobless and without the means to secure housing of their own, Lingyu and Libin are forced to live with their relatives for a time, but their relations with the family steadily decline.

One of the most interesting aspects of this film is its perspective on the lives of people who remained in Japanese-occupied areas during the war. With the important exception of Lingyu's relatives and their circle of friends, the portrayal of those who lived under the occupation is surprisingly sympathetic. For instance, Lingyu and Libin are thrilled when they reestablish contact with a group of former classmates who remained in Shanghai during the war. A number of them now work as respected journalists and teachers. Indeed, their close relations with this group of people who suffered under the occupation remind one of the intimate collectivistic bonds that united resistance activists in the interior. In the end, Lingyu takes a job as a journalist and Libin works as a primary school teacher.

In an especially graphic episode, Lingyu shows great compassion for a desperate widow whose home and property have been confiscated by Lingyu's cousin, Jiarong, in the postwar takeover. Because the widow's husband died at the end of the war, she is now easy prey for people like Jiarong, who use any excuse to charge that people who lived in Shanghai during the occupation are traitors (*hanjian*) who deserve punishment. The homeless widow insists that her husband was not a collaborator. "You think that anyone who remained in Shanghai must have been a traitor!" she cries. Jiarong responds that the old man sold goods to Japanese consumers in his shop and rented rooms to Japanese tenants. The issue in the narrative is not so much the innocence or guilt of the accused traitor's family, but the perspective that the audience is being encouraged to accept. The morally upright Lingyu and Libin show compassion for the plight of the woman. They seem to be saying that ordinary people who remained in Shanghai and who encountered the Japanese every day ought to be viewed sympathetically, while those like Jiarong who pretended to participate in the resistance in the interior deserve to be scorned.[22]

Lingyu and Libin decide to move from their relative's luxurious home to a dilapidated one-room flat. Still, their postwar difficulties mount. Lingyu's work as a journalist gets her involved in the effort to expose people like Jiarong and, thus, intensifies family conflict. At one point she confronts her cousin: "Even though you are a relative, I'll write about all your activities unless you return the things you took." Libin works hard as a teacher, but weakened by years of wartime hardship and postwar scarcity, he contracts tuberculosis.

Toward the end of the narrative Lingyu discovers she is pregnant. Normally this would be a joyous way to begin postwar life. But given the unexpected circumstances, she wonders whether it is a good thing. For a time, their spirits are buoyed by the return to Shanghai of the rest of their comrades in the drama troupe.

The narrative ends months later when Lingyu, alone at night, collapses on a rain-soaked street. Libin panics when she fails to return, and mobi-

Lingyu (*center right*) and Libin (*center left*) are among disillusioned youth who experience hopelessness in postwar Shanghai in *Eight Thousand Miles of Clouds and Moon* (1947, d. Shi Dongshan). China Film Archive

lizes the wartime veterans, most of whom are still wearing rough military garb, to fan out through the city to find her. They finally locate her and bring her to a hospital. The cost for her care and the delivery of the baby is 500,000 yuan. The leader of the troupe has 200,000 yuan, and the rest of the members contribute the remainder. Libin finally arrives at the hospital as a healthy baby is born. But the story closes on a highly ambiguous note. It is not at all clear that Lingyu will survive. The doctor says her only hope is to rest for a year in "a place where the air is clean." The group resolves to care for the baby. "This child is our child," they pledge. Still, the final image is a huge question mark on an otherwise blank screen, followed by a text that invites the audience to participate in the resolution of the problem. It asserts that the actions of the audience will determine whether people like Lingyu live or die.

A SPRING RIVER FLOWS EAST: COMMUNITIES AND IDENTITIES IN FLUX

The third and most powerful narrative, a two-part film titled *A Spring River Flows East*, features many of the same lead actors and actresses, but this account of the holocaust experience heads in a number of new directions.[23] The first part, *Eight Years of Separation and Chaos* (*Ba nian li luan*), begins not in 1937, but on National Day, October 10, 1931, in the immediate aftermath of the Japanese occupation of Manchuria. As in *Far Away Love*, a serious effort is made to locate war-related issues in the broader context of prewar conditions. In this story the protagonist is a young man named Zhang Zhongliang, who works as a night-school teacher in a class attended by female textile workers in Shanghai.

Zhang, an ardent patriot who advocates immediate resistance to Japanese aggression, has organized a gala National Day talent show in a factory union hall. At the end of the show he is urged by young workers to make some patriotic remarks. His passionate anti-Japanese speech elicits two different responses. The majority applauds wildly and throws money on the stage; one female worker, Sufen, idolizes the dashing and heroic teacher. But a small minority seated at the front, consisting of management and staff, is alarmed by the spontaneous political demonstration. Zhang (played by Tao Jin) is summoned by the factory's manager, who claims to be as patriotic as the next fellow. He insists, however, that Zhang's political activities will irritate the Japanese and bring unwanted attention to the factory, thus threatening the livelihood of the workers.

After this opening tone is set, the narrative turns to the romantic relationship between Zhang Zhongliang and Sufen. Showing the utmost respect for the family matriarch, Zhang invites Sufen to come home for dinner one night to meet his mother. Naturally, the mother takes an immediate liking to the shy and highly traditionalistic young woman (played by Bai Yang). Zhang proposes marriage to Sufen later that night and, as he presents her with a ring, is heard promising that the couple will "be together forever" (*yongyuan zai yiqi*). The couple gets married and before long a son is born.

Unfortunately for them, full-scale war breaks out in mid-1937, and Japanese forces are fast approaching Shanghai. Their dreams of family unity are smashed. Determined to join a Red Cross unit, Zhang tells his mother and wife that they should stay behind in Shanghai, but that if the situation becomes intolerable, they should flee to their native village in the countryside, where Zhang's father and younger brother, Zhongmin, are living. "I'm leaving you only because of the resistance war," Zhang tells Sufen.

Zhang's Red Cross group gets caught in the middle of the bloody struggle for Shanghai and then retreats west when the city is lost. His family flees to the countryside and links up with Zhongmin and his fiancée, who belong to a guerrilla unit based in the hills. Zhongmin, played by Gao Zheng (the evil cousin in *Eight Thousand Miles of Clouds and Moon*!), is a paragon of Confucian virtue. When the Japanese close in on the village, Zhongmin respectfully asks his father's permission before escaping with his fiancée to the guerrilla base.

In 1938–1939 Zhang travels with Nationalist units to Hankou and then Nanchang, all the while doing exhausting and dangerous Red Cross work. But life is much worse for his family in the countryside under the Japanese occupation. Japanese forces confiscate grain, property, and livestock and require the people to do backbreaking forced labor. When a merciless new grain tax is announced, villagers plead with Zhang's father, the village school principal, to appeal to the enemy. Instead of reconsidering, the Japanese execute the old man. The local guerrilla unit gets revenge by wiping out the Japanese post in the village, but Sufen, her son, and her mother-in-law decide to return to Shanghai to wait out the war.

Meanwhile, Zhang Zhongliang has been captured by the Japanese in the interior and forced to do slave labor. He escapes, however, and, dressed in rags and penniless, arrives in Chongqing in 1941. He tries to find resistance-related work but fails. He is also frustrated in an attempt to secure factory work in one of the war industries. In a deep depression, he looks up an acquaintance from Shanghai by the name of Wang Lizhen, played by the famous actress Shu Xiuwen, who made resistance movies in Chongqing during the war. Wang offers to let Zhang live in her spacious house and promises to use her influence with a wealthy businessman named Pang Haogong to get him a meaningful job.

Zhang is shocked to discover, however, that Pang's company is not helping the resistance at all. Pang is a war profiteer. His employees hang around all day, while his lieutenants enjoy a carefree life of dancing, partying, eating, drinking, and romancing. Zhang complains to Wang Lizhen that "there's not an iota of resistance spirit at the company." Wang laughs hysterically and tells him he needs to relax and adjust to life in Chongqing. His spirit weakened, Zhang finally gives in to temptation. Not only does he accept her advice, he also succumbs to her seductions. After several rounds of heavy drinking, Zhang ends up in Wang's bed. Wang is unaware that Zhang is married.

At the end of part one the story returns briefly to Shanghai, where Sufen and Zhang's son and mother are struggling to survive under a cruel occupation. Even though they live in a simple shack and have barely enough to eat, Sufen and her mother-in-law help out at a school that tends to war orphans. One night, at a moment when Zhang is in bed with Wang in Chongqing, Sufen wonders why the family has not heard anything from him for years.

Unlike the first part of this epic narrative, which covers the period from 1931 to 1944, the second part, titled *Before and after Dawn* (*Tian liang qian hou*), takes place almost entirely in the summer and autumn months of 1945. The beginning of this segment is dominated by the story of Zhang Zhongliang's meteoric rise in the ranks of Pang Haogong's elaborate business organization. Before long he becomes Pang's chief aide, fully complicit in a web of corrupt wartime profiteering and influence peddling. While Zhang and his new friends and cohorts feast on lobsters and crabs flown into Chongqing from occupied Shanghai, Zhang's mother, wife, and son are barely managing to make ends meet under the Japanese occupation. To make matters worse, toward the end of the war Zhang decides to marry Wang Lizhen at a lavish wedding ceremony in Chongqing. During the wedding feast a letter addressed to Zhang arrives from his wife. Fearful that his prewar past will be revealed, he destroys the letter.

In his capacity as Pang's most trusted assistant, Zhang is among the first to fly back to Shanghai when the war ends. Pang has used his influence to get Zhang designated as a "takeover official" (*jieshou dayuan*). Their goal is to get off to a fast start in exploiting postwar economic opportunities. In liberated Shanghai, arrangements have been made for Zhang to live in the home of Wang Lizhen's cousin (*biaojie*) He Wenyan, played by the famous actress Shangguan Yunzhu. At first, He Wenyan courts Zhang's favor because she wants him to help get her husband, who has been arrested for collaborating with the Japanese, released from jail. Later she discovers that her husband has been seeing other women, so she allows him to languish in prison while she focuses on yet another seduction of Zhang, the rich newcomer from Chongqing. Zhang instantly agrees to the new arrangement but asks Wenyan what they will do when Lizhen arrives from Chongqing. Wenyan says it will be no problem: Lizhen will be his "resistance-war wife" (*kangzhan furen*); she will be his "secret wife" (*mimi furen*).

Zhang's first wife, Sufen, and his mother and son are worried sick because they have heard nothing from him in the first few weeks of the postwar period. Although the war is over, the family's economic situation steadily worsens. Desperate for work, Sufen looks for a job as a domestic servant. As fate would have it, she gains employment as a day worker in the large house run by He Wenyan. Indeed, her husband is in bed with Wenyan on the morning Sufen arrives to be interviewed for the job. The lipstick-stained bedclothes she will have to hand-wash belong to her own husband, who once promised her that they would be together for eternity.

Soon thereafter Wang Lizhen arrives from Chongqing and takes up residence with Zhang at Wenyan's house. Now, for the first time, all three of Zhang's women are under the same roof. Wenyan knows about Lizhen, but not about Sufen. Lizhen knows nothing of Zhang's connections to Sufen or Wenyan. Sufen knows nothing about her husband's presence in the house. Zhang, of course, is unaware of Sufen's work in the servants' quarters.

A major crisis explodes at a sumptuous National Day banquet held at the house on October 10, 1945. The guest of honor is Pang Haogong. Just as Pang is about to force Zhang and Lizhen to do a tango for everyone, Sufen, who is serving drinks to the guests, spots Zhang. A major scandal then erupts in front of all the guests. Sufen collapses on the dance floor, Lizhen screams

Postwar dreams are shattered when Zhang Zhongliang's 'prewar' wife (*center right*) discovers that he has a 'wartime' wife in *A Spring River Flows East* (1947, d. Cai Chusheng, Zheng Junli). China Film Archive

hysterically, and Wenyan cracks a wicked smile when it becomes clear that Zhang is indeed married to the servant. Lizhen runs upstairs, threatening suicide if Zhang does not divorce Sufen. Zhang promises her he will get a divorce. Sufen runs home to break the bad news to her son and mother-in-law. The mother is numbed by Sufen's disclosures. By coincidence, the old lady has just received a letter from her younger son, Zhongmin, the upright guerrilla fighter who sacrificed for the nation throughout the war. He has written to announce his marriage to his prewar sweetheart, who worked alongside him throughout the difficult years of national struggle. Zhang's mother pulls her grandson over and tearfully tells him to learn from the example of his uncle Zhongmin rather than his father.

In a highly emotional final sequence, the old lady takes Sufen and the young boy to a confrontational meeting with Zhongliang, who is now caught in the middle; his mother, wife, and son are downstairs, while his second wife and his mistress are upstairs. At this point the narrative centers on the issue of Zhang's choice. Will he go back to his old life or continue to embrace his new life?

Disgraced by her husband's conduct, Sufen commits suicide by jumping into a nearby river. The old lady and the young boy rush to the waterfront, but it is too late. A distraught Zhongliang arrives on the scene but seems incapable of assuming responsibility for his grieving family members.

Before long, Lizhen and Wenyan arrive in a fancy American automobile to urge Zhongliang to leave with them. Viewers are not allowed to learn what Zhongliang decides to do. As the story ends, his mother looks into the camera, as if addressing the audience, and wails, "In times like these, decent people can't survive, while villains live for a thousand years!"

FAMILY NARRATIVES AS NATIONAL ALLEGORIES

One of the first (and rather odd) things one notices about these popular resistance-war narratives is that very little is said about the massive violence of the war itself. The enemy is almost never seen. No Japanese appear in either *Far Away Love* or *Eight Thousand Miles*. In *A Spring River*, Japanese atrocities are shown in detail only in relatively brief episodes involving Zhang Zhongliang's capture, the occupation of his native village, and the closing of the school for orphans in Shanghai. Postwar Japanese films like *The Human Condition* (*Ningen no joken*, d. Masaki Kobayashi, 1959) contain many more details about the brutality of Japanese forces in China.

The most obvious explanation for such an omission is that postwar filmmakers simply did not have the budgets or the technical means to re-create the sort of large-scale battle scenes one normally associates with war epics. Instead, the directors of these works skillfully inserted bits of wartime documentary footage in a few strategic places to give a graphic sense of the terror that engulfed combatants and noncombatants alike. But it is not these explicit treatments of violence that make the three films successful and convincing as holocaust narratives.

Rather than focus on violence, these directors, and the many who followed their lead in 1947 and 1948, decided to emphasize the social consequences of protracted war. This appears to be what the postwar audience wanted. More specifically, all three films dwell almost exclusively on the fate of the family unit in the holocaust environment. Telling the story of the war in the form of family histories made sense in basic production terms. Postwar filmmakers had the means of executing such a plan. More important, however, the decision resonated with a long family-centered tradition of Chinese cinema.[24] Nothing was more important in the mid-twentieth-century social structure of China than the family unit. And more than anything else, ordinary people experienced the war as members of family groups.

All three films adopt the view that in experiential terms it was not the nation as a whole that suffered during the war, it was Chinese families that suffered. And the losses were staggering. Families were ripped apart and then reconfigured in a variety of unfamiliar ways. In *Far Away Love*, Yu Zhen loses her father, her brother, and her son. Moreover, the war forces her to confront issues of legitimate and illegitimate authority in family life. In the end her marriage is destroyed. In *Eight Thousand Miles*, Jiang Lingyu's family disintegrates before her eyes. When she returns to her native village, her father is dead and the family dwelling has been sold. During the course of the war she loses all respect for her relatives in Shanghai, who fail to support her plan to join the resistance. Her cousin Jiarong becomes a war profiteer.

Wartime dreams about reuniting families are dashed when the war is over. Lingyu's family exists in name only. When Lingyu learns of her family's corrupt and exploitative postwar activities, she moves out and rejects her relatives. Indeed, when she turns to journalistic work, her own family becomes a target of her scathing investigative reporting.

Lingyu's attempt to start a family of her own is frustrated. She has a child, but it is by no means clear that she will live to see the child grow up. The prewar Chinese family seems to have no future. For people like Yu Zhen (in *Far Away Love*), Lingyu, and Libin, its role has been assumed by the collective surrogate family of friends and comrades that evolved in the interior during the war. It is this group that plays the nurturing and support roles normally associated with the consanguine family, and that commands the loyalty and respect of people like Yu Zhen, Lingyu, and Libin.

The account of wartime family breakup in *A Spring River* is even more devastating. This is because the intriguing protagonist, Zhang Zhongliang, is markedly different from the positive characters (Lingyu and Libin) that one encounters in *Eight Thousand Miles*. The story of Zhang Zhongliang and his family is more interesting and more painful precisely because Zhang appears first in "Eight Years of Separation and Chaos" as a heroic figure. His heroism has two interrelated dimensions. First, he is an ardent patriot, willing to sacrifice to defend the nation from Japanese aggression. Second, despite his youth, he is an old-fashioned, Confucian-style family man. He is devoted to his equally traditionalistic wife and son (promising that they will be together forever) and profoundly filial in his interactions with his kindly mother. Zhang's excellent relations with his family are central to the subsequent development of the narrative. He is willing to sacrifice for the nation-state because, by doing so, he will be protecting and defending his family way of life. In this film (and in *Eight Thousand Miles*) the dominant vision that positive characters have of postwar life entails a "great reunion" that will bring decent families back to where they were in the prewar period. Victory meant family restoration.

One of the greatest tragedies of the war is that for millions of people the "great reunion" never happened. There was no return to prewar modes. Indeed, in *Far Away Love*, hopes for a family reunion are dashed well before the end of the war. The case of Zhang Zhongliang in *A Spring River* is particularly poignant (and more complex than the cases of Lingyu and Libin in *Eight Thousand Miles*) because he is a "good" man who went "bad" during the war itself. The visions he had of a "great reunion" are not simply denied to him (as they were to Lingyu and Libin), he actually abandons them once he becomes entangled in a web of wartime corruption, greed, and moral depravity. Most disturbing of all, it is by no means clear at the end of the narrative that the corrupted hero can be reformed and returned "home" to his mother and son. The whole meaning of the term "family" has been distorted beyond recognition when Zhang, confused and panicky, is shown together on (of all days) National Day with his prewar wife, his wartime wife, and postwar "secret wife."

DEFINING THE AUDIENCE AND ITS NEEDS

These three family narratives, and especially *Eight Thousand Miles*, were clearly inspired by the personal wartime experiences of the screenwriters and directors who had joined the resistance. Shi Dongshan, for instance, worked in a traveling theater troupe during the early years of the war and eventually reached Chongqing, just like the characters in his movie.[25] It does not follow, however, that the primary audience for these films was people like themselves who had traveled to the interior.

By failing to ask questions about the audience, scholars have failed to note the obvious. The primary target audience for these films was people who stayed behind and endured the harsh Japanese occupation. In large cities like Shanghai, most people had stayed behind. After the war they were by far the largest potential audience for the new epic accounts of the war. They may not have participated in the resistance, but they too experienced the war as separation and deprivation. They too experienced the immediate postwar period as disappointment and disillusionment.[26] Victory did not feel like victory when families remained fragmented and when innocent people were accused of collaboration.

People returning from the interior had much to learn about how ordinary citizens had suffered under the occupation, and the movies under review provided such information. But it appears that these films primarily addressed the needs of the people who had stayed behind. Cut off from reliable news during the war, they had many questions about events that had unfolded out of view in the interior. Therefore, they were strongly attracted to epic narratives that re-created the war and thus allowed them to see the disorienting social forces it had unleashed. They needed answers to nagging questions about family defeats that followed national victory.

After the war many ordinary Shanghai residents felt stigmatized by their decision to remain in Shanghai during the years of conflict. Many were defensive about their personal histories. Some of the people who returned from the interior felt superior and treated those who had remained behind in a condescending fashion. One of the most striking things about the grand holocaust narratives under review here, and especially *Eight Thousand Miles* and *A Spring River*, is that they view the ordinary people who lived under the Japanese (the very same people who made up the audience for these films) in a sympathetic light. These narratives firmly rejected the view that people who had stayed behind were unpatriotic collaborators. It is easy to understand why such films were so popular.

This is not to say that these films contained no criticism of those who lived under the occupation. In *Eight Thousand Miles* the portrait of Lingyu's aunt and uncle is most unflattering. They are clearly greedy war profiteers. But more important are the sympathetic characterizations of the old woman (whose property is seized by Jiarong on the pretext that her husband was a traitor) and the patriotic classmates who are reunited with Lingyu and Libin after the war.

In *A Spring River* the brief representations of traitors like He Wenyan's husband are striking, but far more vivid are the visual portraits of those who were victimized by the foreign aggressors. Zhongliang's father and the other patriotic villagers are exploited mercilessly by the Japanese, and his mother and wife suffer unspeakably in urban Shanghai. They have atrocious housing, they lack adequate food supplies, and they are humiliated by the enemy time and again. These compassionate accounts of the misery of Sufen and her mother-in-law were warmly welcomed by postwar moviegoers. It was gratifying to see their own story on screen.

But postwar film fans saw much more on the screen than sympathetic images of their own wartime sufferings in occupied Shanghai. They also learned from these powerful narratives that not all the people who traveled to the interior were motivated by selfless patriotism. Professor Xiao Yuanxi is presented in *Far Away Love* as a cowardly man whose acceptance of a government desk job in Hankou is motivated more by fear than patriotism. The detailed accounts of the activities of Pang Haogong and his corrupt associates in *A Spring River* revealed a disgraceful life of wartime comfort and privilege. The tales of the moral decline of people like Zhang Zhongliang in *A Spring River* and Xiao Yuanxi in *Far Away Love* are particularly gripping because they make it clear that many well-regarded citizens who traveled to the interior did not behave patriotically. One of the most effective editing techniques used in *A Spring River* to accentuate the failings of people like Zhang Zhongliang in the interior involved a constant cutting back and forth from scenes of brutality and hardship in occupied Shanghai to scenes of luxury and decadence in Chongqing. This allowed the audience to see what was blocked from view during the war. After viewing these movies, it was easy to conclude that people who lived in the occupied areas sacrificed more than those who sat out the war in the interior.

146   Chapter 5

ISSUES OF CLASS AND GENDER

Characterizations such as good and evil, strong and weak, selfless and selfish had definite class and gender dimensions in these popular family narratives. In terms of social class, intellectuals (with the important exception of Professor Xiao), artists, factory workers, and peasants are cast in an exceedingly positive light in all three films. The urban bourgeoisie, however, is treated very harshly in all three narratives. It is to this class that Professor Xiao is assigned in *Far Away Love*; he is cast as a self-centered, petty bourgeois snob. In *Eight Thousand Miles*, Jiarong, his parents, and his friends are revealed as wartime and postwar profiteers who have no patriotic inclinations whatsoever. In *A Spring River*, the factory owner who is upset by Zhang Zhongliang's patriotic speech on National Day, the businessman Pang Haogong, and, finally, Zhang himself are portrayed as greedy and heartless opportunists who prey on the poor and defenseless. None of the films offers even one example of a patriotic capitalist. Most interesting of all, the bourgeoisie is indicted as a class not because it is incompetent in professional terms, but rather because of its moral failings. In the end, the problem of the bourgeoisie in Chinese society is treated more as a moral problem than as an economic or political problem. The individualism of businessmen and petty bourgeois professors prevents them from behaving patriotically. These sorts of representations of class are, of course, quite familiar. Prewar films and fiction were filled with similar images of upright working people, patriotic students, and selfish bourgeois elements.

A far more provocative aspect of these grand narratives is their treatment of gender issues. Indeed, the characterizations of men, and particularly men in the prime of life, are highly critical. The narratives seem to hold men responsible for China's plight: men were not able to prevent the Japanese invasion and, after the war, were not able to reunite the nation. The failings of China, in this controversial reading, are the failings of its men. Some men, like Jiarong, the young businessman, are greedy and corrupt. Some, like Pang Haogong, are crude bullies. Some, like Professor Xiao, are shameless hypocrites. Others, like Zhang Zhongliang, are simply weak, indecisive, and ineffectual until they link up with people like Pang. They value a social life that stresses the pleasures of wine, women, and song.

According to patriarchal norms, men are ultimately responsible for the well-being of the family and, by extension, the nation. But in these family narratives most of the males who are central to the stories are not seen in such time-honored roles. Very little information is supplied about their family life: nothing is known about Professor Xiao's background, Jiarong has no wife or children, nothing is known about Pang Haogong's family, and Zhang Zhongliang's relations with women are motivated primarily by lust once he leaves his family. In short, the viewer is led to believe that wartime conditions brought out the worst in China's men. There are positive portrayals of men in these narratives, including the characterizations of Libin in *Eight Thousand Miles* and Zhang Zhongmin in *A Spring River*, but in both films these attractive male figures are of secondary importance.

If war brought out the worst in China's men, it appears to have brought out the best in China's women, at least according to these popular postwar visualizations. On the whole, women seem stronger and more capable than men under wartime circumstances. In *Far Away Love*, Yu Zhen, a rural servant trained to be a middle-class housewife, sacrifices everything for the resistance while her cowardly husband runs away. In *Eight Thousand Miles* the entire story of the holocaust and its social consequences is seen from the perspective of a remarkably resilient and persistent young intellectual woman, Jiang Lingyu. In *A Spring River*, the most important women, Sufen and her mother-in-law, are not at all like the modern and progressive-thinking Lingyu, but like Lingyu, they have a remarkable ability to endure hardship and survive without the help of their husbands and adult sons. These images of strong, independent, and patriotic women are among the most intriguing aspects of postwar cinema. Characters like Yu Zhen, Lingyu, and Sufen stand in sharp contrast to the negative and threatening images of the femme fatale that were so prevalent in prewar cinema.

Even the negative female figures, the bourgeois women, are not exactly a recycled version of the 1930s screen vamp. They too seem stunningly independent and resourceful in the harsh wartime environment. Confused and weak, Zhang Zhongliang is no match for the tough-minded Wang Lizhen. Similarly, He Wenyan proves to be unusually capable of adjusting and adapting to a wartime and postwar world in which relations with men are fleeting and unreliable.

Given the highly patriarchal norms of Chinese society in the mid-twentieth century, it is striking to see the extent to which cultural decency, wartime strength, and anticolonialism are gendered female in these films, all of which were written and directed by men. Similarly, it is surprising to see the extent to which cultural degeneration, weakness under wartime conditions, and the failure to resist colonialism are gendered male. This picture of wartime China shows patriarchal norms and the family institution itself to be in serious disarray. With a couple of important exceptions (Libin and Zhang Zhongmin), men are irresponsible and unpredictable, while women are strong and capable.

THE CULTURAL POLITICS OF POSTWAR HOLOCAUST EPICS

For decades the classic films *Far Away Love*, *Eight Thousand Miles of Clouds and Moon*, and *A Spring River Flows East* have been thought of as leftist works fashioned by filmmakers who supposedly were under the control of the Communist Party. Critics close to the Nationalist Party accepted this view and thus questioned the credibility of the filmmakers and dismissed the films.[27] They never attempted to explain the astounding popularity of the movies or, more important, to appreciate the extent to which the filmmakers had close links to the Nationalist state and the Nationalist Party during and after the war. Critics close to the Communist Party accepted the view that the films were leftist and celebrated the progressivism of the artists, thereby claiming these important artifacts as their own.[28]

In fact, the cultural politics of these holocaust narratives are not so clear-cut. The political and cultural content of the films is neither as pro-Communist nor as anti-Nationalist as most observers would have us believe. The films have a highly critical tone, but the social criticism is consistent with perspectives associated with both the Nationalist and Communist parties. *Far Away Love* was made by the Nationalists themselves in a state-run studio. All three movies were officially reviewed and approved by Nationalist state censors.[29] In recent years, industry personalities familiar with these films have asserted that state censors had been bribed. But this is not a very convincing explanation of why they were passed by the censors. Daily advertising in local newspapers reveals that all three films had extremely long runs in Shanghai and other major cities. The state certainly had the means to shut down theaters that showed offensive films, but no serious effort was made to discourage repeated screenings of the three epics under review here.

Communist and Nationalist cultural historians have failed, each for their own reasons, to mention that *Far Away Love*, *Eight Thousand Miles*, and *A Spring River* were among the ten films made in 1947 that received the coveted Zhongzheng Culture Prize, named in honor of Chiang Kai-shek himself. All recipients got a cash award and a handsome Oscar-like trophy. *A Spring River*, the most critical of the three films discussed here, was listed first among the ten "glorious" winners by *Shen bao*, hardly an antigovernment newspaper.[30] Actress Bai Yang, who joined the Communist Party in 1958, won the first Chiang Kai-shek Best Actress Award in 1947 for her performances in *Eight Thousand Miles* and *A Spring River*. For nearly fifty years the two sides in the civil war have been too embarrassed to acknowledge this unsettling fact.

Scholars in the People's Republic accounted for the production and public release of these films by emphasizing the ability of the filmmakers to outsmart Nationalist bureaucrats who were eager to crush works critical of wartime and postwar social disarray. Actually, the critical thrust of these movies was well-known. There was no revolutionary conspiracy. Spectacular newspaper advertising that appeared long before the films were first shown was remarkably explicit. Ads for *Far Away Love*, a government-made movie, proclaimed, "All males are selfish; women struggle for liberation!" (*nanren dou shi zisi; nüzi lizheng jiefang*), "How will women of today find a way out?" (*shidai nüxing chulu hezai*), and "The ideal wife turns out to be more than anyone imagined!" (*lixiang taitai chuchu chaochu lixiang*). Ads for *Eight Thousand Miles* declared, "So many sorrows and tears before and after victory!" (*shengli qianhou xing suan lei*) and "See never-ending waves of ugliness; curse never-ending and ferocious corruption!" (*kan wuwan de jieshou choutai; ma wuwan de tanwu ezhuang*). Ads for *A Spring River* stated, "An epic production that shakes the Chinese film world" (*zhenhan Zhongguo yingtan de wenyi ju zhi*) and "A beacon that can be seen for ten thousand miles; eight years of separation and chaos; heaven is in distress, earth is in misery; ghosts and spirits are moaning!" (*fengyan wanli; ba nian li luan; tian cho di can; gui shen wu yan*).[31] Advertising campaigns, some of which were funded with government money, underscored rather than concealed the critical thrust of these painful narratives.

The praise heaped on these films by the mainstream popular film press suggests that the community was acutely aware of the critical and controversial approach to the war taken by Chen Liting and other postwar directors. For instance, the April 1947 edition of the popular film magazine *Dianying*, a nonpolitical publication that normally concerned itself with the divorces of film stars, the number of kissing scenes in American movies, the shape of Bai Guang's legs, and the kinds of cosmetics used by Hollywood matinee idols, boldly asserted that *Far Away Love, Eight Thousand Miles*, and *Heavenly Spring Dream* (*Tiantang chun meng*, d. Tang Xiaodan, 1947; see chapter 3), another controversial war-related film produced in a state-run studio, were fine examples of postwar films that "illustrated reality and gave voice to the people."[32]

The *Dianying* article, which appeared before the release of *A Spring River*, asserted that these films were popular because the screenwriters were attuned to "the inner feelings" of the film audience. By contrast, many veteran screenwriters were said to be out of touch. They had the connections to get their stories made into films, but they were interested in cinema only as "a tool to make a fortune." They exploited the postwar demand for films, but their scripts were "terrible." The magazine called explicitly for more films like *Eight Thousand Miles*, which it claimed was the "first postwar Chinese film" purchased by foreign buyers for distribution in Europe. As for the money-grubbers whose films failed to deal with the real concerns of the audience: "These scum who hurt the Chinese film industry should be sent to the gallows that has been set up by the people. They should be purged!"[33]

Nationalist authorities allowed the films to be screened in part because they were consistent with critical perspectives held within the Nationalist Party and government.[34] Disillusioned elements within the Nationalist movement realized that the cultural and political messages of the films struck a responsive chord among the millions who had resided in enemy-occupied areas during the war. This was an audience that desperately wanted to see, and thereby "experience," events that had taken place in the interior. These were people who wanted to understand the connection between wartime dislocations and the bitter disappointments that ordinary people experienced immediately following victory. The films ask: Why did victory not feel like victory? Why did the people who sacrificed the most seem to benefit the least? and Why did those who sacrificed least seem to benefit the most?

It is time to look at such works not solely in terms of the highly polarized politics of the civil war era and after, but also in terms of the complex relationship between commercial filmmakers working in the state and private sectors and their vast film audience. When the films are analyzed from this perspective, it is possible to see that the cultural politics of these epic narratives were far from radical or progressive. They were decidedly conservative. All three films argue that certain core Chinese values, especially those governing social relations within the family, were broken down and forgotten during the long years of wartime separation and dislocation.

Without exception the positive characters in all the films (Yu Zhen, Lingyu, Libin, Sufen, Zhongmin, and even Zhongliang before his moral decline) were people who cherished traditional family values: respect for parents and devotion to spouse and children. Their patriotism and unselfish public-spiritedness were natural extensions of their old-fashioned, neo-Confucian cultural orientation. There is nothing left-wing about the mores of these people.

The negative characters (Professor Xiao, Jiarong, Pang Haogong, Lizhen, Wenyan, and Zhongliang after his moral decline) are people who betrayed time-honored family values and adopted alien, spiritually polluting ways that make them decadent, irresponsible, and greedy. Their wartime behavior, according to the logic of these narratives, was also an extension of their immoral family relations. They are incapable of acting patriotically, it seems, because they do not accept "real" Chinese cultural values. Some are cowards, and some actually betray the nation, while others participate in the resistance only because they are motivated by personal gain.

The audience is being told that people who were faithful to traditional Chinese family values sacrificed selflessly in the interior or suffered unjustly in the occupied territories. People who abandoned old-style family values were hedonistic profiteers, shameless collaborators, or cowards. After viewing narratives of this sort, the audience, comprised essentially of ordinary people who suffered under the occupation, knew whom to blame for their wartime and postwar miseries. The underlying argument of these films, one usually not associated with leftists, is that the erosion of traditional family values during the war was a destructive phenomenon that weakened the entire society. Nowhere is the state or the Nationalist Party blamed for the moral decline. Still, it is hard to avoid the conclusion that these films eroded public confidence in the postwar state.

It is not enough, however, to point out that the family values embraced by the negative characters are simply untraditional. They are foreign. Every effort is made in these works to show that the negative characters responsible for much of the wartime and postwar misery of common people behave, look, and even dress in a Western, bourgeois manner. Their culture is an alien, capitalist culture of merchants. The narratives seek to deny these people their essential Chineseness. Stripped of their Chinese identity, these personalities behave, not surprisingly, in ways that are incompatible with the national interest. The films, therefore, are anticolonial in two senses: they resist Japanese imperialism, and they reject Western bourgeois culture.

It is inadequate, however, simply to dismiss these characterizations as so much Marxist anticapitalism. There is something very Confucian and culturally conservative about the antimerchant thrust of these popular visualizations. When it comes to denouncing capitalism and the bourgeoisie, there is much that Chinese Marxism of the 1930s and 1940s shared in common with the neoconservative approaches that surfaced in urban China in the 1930s (see chapter 2). In August 1948, ten months after the release of *A Spring River*, Chiang Ching-kuo, a top Nationalist leader, blasted Shanghai's big-money interests: "Their wealth and their foreign-style homes are built on the skeletons of the people. How is their conduct any different from that of armed robbers?"[35]

But what about the image of the collective family that emerges so prominently throughout *Far Away Love* and at the end of *Eight Thousand Miles*? Surely this is a revolutionary vision of the new socialist society that awaited China. Surely it justifies the view that these films are the work of leftists. The problem is that while the image is definitely "collective," it is far from revolutionary. The "collective" or surrogate family espouses most of the old family values advocated by the positive and patriotic characters! The audience is told there is a need for drastic social change, but it should be a transformation that will restore real Chinese family values rather than reject them.[36] It will be a change that eradicates the pernicious influence of the alien culture of greedy merchants.

Women appear in these films as remarkably strong and independent survivors of the holocaust experience. These images were undoubtedly welcomed by women viewers, said to comprise a majority of the audience for postwar Chinese films.[37] Yu Zhen and Lingyu are "liberated" from oppressive families, and find happiness and fulfillment in wartime Nationalist collectives. But their liberation is from the unpatriotic, bourgeois, foreign-style family, not from patriarchal authority in general. The new surrogate families to which they bond allow for an active role for women, but they remain essentially patriarchal. Women who liberate themselves from alien bourgeois families have only one option: to resubmit to the Chinese-style patriarchal authority of the patriotic collectives. These collective groupings embrace what are viewed as essentialistic Chinese family values. They are values linked to the rural pasts of Yu Zhen, Lingyu, and Sufen.

China won the war. China defeated Japan. But the social consequences of the holocaust were most profound. When the war was over, victory felt like defeat, not only for many of those who joined the resistance, but especially for those millions who endured the hardships of enemy occupation. *Far Away Love, Eight Thousand Miles,* and *A Spring River* were early postwar attempts to explain that feeling.

DEFEAT AS VICTORY AND VICTORY AS DEFEAT

During the early phases of the war there was a tactical need for a popular culture that mobilized people and showed how defeat could be turned into victory. As Chang-tai Hung has pointed out, wartime popular culture made a significant contribution to the resistance effort.[38] Personal and family losses were staggering, but millions of people were determined to sacrifice for national salvation. Of course, most wartime popular culture was state-directed propaganda. It resisted Japanese imperialism quite effectively by building a strong sense of community, but its approach to Chinese society was largely uncritical.

The popular culture of the immediate postwar period discussed in this chapter headed in new directions because it was responding to different needs. Now the challenge was to explain why victory felt like defeat. Even though cultural workers in the state sector were among those who addressed this question, the most vibrant postwar popular culture can hardly be characterized as state-directed propaganda. In fact, those who produced the new popular culture took pride in their relative independence from the state. Some directors accepted state financial support but continued to function as independent-minded and critical artists nevertheless.

One is tempted to say that controversial postwar films are better characterized as an example of popular culture directed by intellectual elites who had close ties to the literary world. But the story of postwar popular culture is more complex (and more interesting) than that. Most popular postwar films, including state and private-sector productions, are interesting examples of top-down and bottom-up cultural cross-fertilization. Intellectual elites like Chen Liting and Shi Dongshan definitely did not pull the victory-as-defeat theme out of thin air and then impose it on a politically docile public in a top-down manner. The popular culture they produced fed on the discontent that was already a pronounced fact of postwar life. The filmmakers did not create the disaffection.

But just because postwar filmmaking was not a clear case of top-down cultural imposition by the state or by independent cultural elites does not mean that it was a matter of filmmakers blindly chasing public opinion. That is to say, the most popular postwar productions cannot be regarded as instances of purely commercial activity in which filmmakers contribute little or nothing of their own, preferring instead to give the masses whatever they seem to want. Postwar filmmaking involved an intersecting of elite and mass cultural currents. The ideas and concerns one finds expressed in these works are a combination of elite and popular views.

The Nationalists claimed in the immediate postwar period that they wanted a high-minded, morally engaged, and educational film industry. They wanted a curtailing of what they viewed as degenerate pulp filmmaking. Ironically, the response to this plea was *Far Away Love, Eight Thousand Miles of Clouds and Moon,* and *A Spring River Flows East*—films that destabilized Chinese society.

The movies discussed here were surprisingly independent and critical, but they were not intended to be revolutionary. Their original purpose was to address injustices and stimulate reform. But as the political situation in China spun out of control, these films had the longer-term, but unintended, effect of being oppositional and even subversive.

The case of postwar filmmaking is more complicated and ambivalent than writings by Nationalist and Communist scholars allow, because there was a clear connection between the Nationalist state and the production and distribution of controversial films. Some of the most disturbing films made in 1947, pictures like *Far Away Love, Heavenly Spring Dream,* and *Diary of a Homecoming* (*Huan xiang riji,* d. Zhang Junxiang), were produced in government studios, funded with government monies, and distributed with government support.

The state had ample means of cracking down on these and the most disturbing private-sector films. But the fact is that the state did little or nothing to prevent production and distribution, and its failure to get tough had little to do with bureaucratic inefficiency or corruption. A more convincing explanation, but one that has been resisted by Nationalist and Communist scholars alike, is that the sentiments of despair and disillusionment conveyed by the films were consistent with the views of many state and Nationalist Party insiders. Clearly, in early 1947 there were state cultural elites who regarded these works as constructive calls for reform rather than as conscious attempts to subvert state and Party authority. Like the filmmakers themselves, they had no idea that these popular films would serve to deepen the mood of disillusionment and cynicism and thus further undermine government credibility.

In brief, the case of popular culture under review here does not fit into any ready-made analytical paradigm. The lines between official and unofficial, state and private, elite and popular, commerce and art, and loyalty and disloyalty are too blurry here to be accounted for by any ready-made theory of popular culture, including that of the influential Frankfurt school. As Chandra Mukerji and Michael Schudson observed, Frankfurt school thinkers "perceived mass culture as aesthetically and politically debilitating, reducing the capacities of audiences to think critically and functioning as an ideological tool to manipulate the political sentiments of the mass public."[39] Postwar Chinese films definitely fall into the category of commercial mass culture, but their critical/democratic essence cannot be accounted for by the Frankfurt school model.

These popular films also fail to fit into any single aesthetic format. Chen Liting called *Far Away Love* a tragicomedy (*bei xi ju*), but it is better characterized as a rare example of film satire. *Eight Thousand Miles of Clouds and Moon*, *A Spring River Flows East*, and *Heavenly Spring Dream* were classic melodramas (*tongsu ju*), and *Diary of a Homecoming* was a playful farce. But, in sharp contrast to what Chinese Marxist scholars have said, none of these works had much to do with cinematic realism. They distorted, collapsed, and simplified events in a variety of highly sensational ways. They are the "meaningful fabrications" referred to by Darnton. But while the images may not have been realistic, they were incredibly powerful. In the end, it is their power that intrigues. The filmmakers discussed here were successful (in ways they could not be after 1949) because they knew the anxieties and concerns of their audience (that is, they were in touch with the psychological realities of those troubled times), they knew how to distill, process, and package the information that was "coming up from below," and they knew how to "sell" the final product. Their epic holocaust narratives were not a mirror reflection of popular opinion, but neither were they unconnected to the mood of postwar bitterness and despair.

Alfred Hitchcock supposedly said, "Movies are life with the boring parts cut out." This is another way of saying that movies are not real life at all. The popular films under review here may not have been realistic, but they clearly captured the public imagination. They created the illusion of reality. They were powerful and, ultimately, subversive because they explained why ordinary people felt defeated after the victory over Japan. In late 1946 the director Shi Dongshan referred explicitly to the new challenges of postwar filmmaking when he wrote that he and his friends found "reason and justification" for the hardships suffered during the war. "It was more difficult," Shi confessed, "for us to understand why, in the months after victory, we felt defeated."[40]

NOTES

An earlier version of this chapter appeared as "Victory as Defeat: Postwar Visualizations of China's War of Resistance," in *Becoming Chinese: Passages to Modernity and*

Beyond, 1900–1950, ed. Wen-hsin Yeh (Berkeley: University of California Press, 2000), 365–98.

1. Some important wartime films produced in the interior include *The Light of East Asia* (*Dong ya zhi guang*, d. He Feiguang, 1940), *Young China* (*Qingnian Zhongguo*, d. Su Yi, 1940), *Storm on the Border* (*Saishang fengyun*, d. Ying Yunwei, 1940), and *Japanese Spy* (*Riben jiandie*, d. Yuan Congmei, 1943), all completed at the China Film Studio (Zhongguo dianying zhipianchang) in Chongqing.

2. "Strand Theater Incident," *China Weekly Review* 102, no. 3 (June 15, 1946): 51–52.

3. *Dianying* 1, no. 6 (October 20, 1946): 19.

4. *Dianying* 1, no. 6 (October 20, 1946): 19.

5. *Dianying* 1, no. 6 (October 20, 1946): 19.

6. V. L. Wong, "Motion Pictures Today Important Agency in Education—of Old and Young," *China Weekly Review* 101, no. 11 (May 11, 1946): 230.

7. Wong, "Motion Pictures Today," 231.

8. For an account of the Lianhua Studio in the early postwar period, see You Ming, "Lianhua dianying zhipianchang xunli," *Dianyi huabao* (December 1, 1946): 8.

9. Zhongguo dianyingjia xiehui dianying shi yanjiubu, ed., *Zhongguo dianyingjia liezhuan* (Beijing: Zhongguo dianying chubanshe, 1982), 2:237–44.

10. Chang-tai Hung, *War and Popular Culture: Resistance in Modern China, 1937–1945* (Berkeley: University of California Press, 1994), 55–64.

11. *Zhongguo da baike quanshu: dianying* (Beijing, Shanghai: Zhongguo da baike quanshu chubanshe, 1991), 51.

12. *Zhongguo da baike quanshu: dianying*, 357–58.

13. Zhongguo dianyingjia xiehui dianying shi yanjiubu, *Zhongguo dianyingjia liezhuan*, 1:15–23.

14. Zhongguo dianyingjia xiehui dianying shi yanjiubu, *Zhongguo dianyingjia liezhuan*, 1:338–49.

15. *Zhongguo da baike quanshu: dianying*, 44.

16. Zhongguo dianyingjia xiehui dianying shi yanjiubu, *Zhongguo dianyingjia liezhuan*, 2:286–97; *Zhongguo da baike quanshu: dianying*, 482.

17. Robert Darnton, "Workers Revolt: The Great Cat Massacre of the Rue Saint-Severin," in *Rethinking Popular Culture: Contemporary Perspectives in Cultural Studies*, ed. Chandra Mukerji and Michael Schudson (Berkeley: University of California Press, 1991), 100.

18. I would like to thank Professor Tu Wei-ming for suggesting the use of the term *psychological reality*.

19. A published text of *Eight Thousand Miles of Clouds and Moon* can be found in Zhongguo dianying gongzuozhe xiehui, ed., *Wusi yilai dianying juben xuanji* (Xianggang: Wenhua ziliao gongying she, 1979), 2:1–81. The dialogue in the film itself does not always follow the text of the screenplay. The title of the film is taken from a line in the famous poem titled "Man jiang hong" by Yue Fei (1103–1141).

20. For a contemporary review of the film, see Man Jianghong, "Ba qian li lu yun he yue," *Dianyi huabao* (December 1, 1946): 2–3.

21. For a sketch of the young actor Gao Zheng, see Xi Zi, "Lianhua wu xin ren," *Dianyi huabao* (December 1, 1946): 14–15.

22. For a sensitive and sympathetic portrait of people who lived under the Japanese occupation of Shanghai, see Poshek Fu, *Passivity, Resistance, and Collaboration: Intellectual Choice in Occupied Shanghai, 1937–1945* (Stanford, Calif.: Stanford University Press, 1993).

23. A published text of *A Spring River Flows East* can be found in Zhongguo dianying gongzuozhe xiehui, *Wusi yilai dianying juben xuanji*, 2:85–230. The dialogue in the film does not always follow the text of the screenplay, especially in the concluding scenes. The title of the film is taken from a line in a poem by the famous Tang poet Li Bai.

24. Zheng Junli's own lengthy discussion of *A Spring River Flows East* is contained in his book *Hua wai yin* (Beijing: Zhongguo dianying chubanshe, 1979), 1–18.

25. See Jay Leyda, *Dianying: An Account of Films and the Film Audience in China* (Cambridge, Mass.: MIT Press, 1972), 166.

26. One of the best studies of the immediate postwar mood of Shanghai is Suzanne Pepper's *Civil War in China: The Political Struggle, 1945–1949* (Berkeley: University of California Press, 1978).

27. See Du Yunzhi, *Zhongguo dianying shi* (Taibei: Taiwan shangwuyin shuguan, 1978), 2:96–101.

28. See Cheng Jihua, ed., *Zhongguo dianying fazhan shi* (Beijing: Zhongguo dianying chubanshe, 1963), 2:210–14, 217–23.

29. For a study that sheds light on the complexities of the censorship institution, see Xiao Zhiwei, "Film Censorship in China, 1927–1937" (PhD diss., University of California, San Diego, 1994).

30. *Shen bao*, February 15, 1948. See the Sunday supplement titled *Mei zhou huakan*.

31. All of these advertising texts can be found in the film advertising sections of *Shen bao* in 1947, especially in the January, February, and October issues.

32. *Dianying* 1, no. 8 (April 1, 1947): 16–18.

33. *Dianying* 1, no. 8 (April 1, 1947): 16–18.

34. For a powerful discussion of the antimerchant, antibourgeois sentiments of both Chiang Kai-shek and Chiang Ching-kuo in the postwar period, see Lloyd Eastman, *Seeds of Destruction: Nationalist China in War and Revolution, 1937–1949* (Stanford, Calif.: Stanford University Press, 1984), 172–215.

35. Quoted in Eastman, *Seeds of Destruction*, 182.

36. Leftists in the Chinese countryside in the 1940s also espoused traditionalistic cultural criticism of postwar society. See Edward Friedman, Paul G. Pickowicz, and Mark Selden, *Chinese Village, Socialist State* (New Haven, Conn.: Yale University Press, 1991).

37. *Dianying* 1, no. 9 (June 1, 1947): 3.

38. Hung, *War and Popular Culture*, 270–85.

39. Mukerji and Schudson, *Rethinking Popular Culture*, 38.

40. This statement by Shi Dongshan is contained in a handout distributed to all ticketholders when they entered the theater to see *Eight Thousand Miles of Clouds and Moon* in 1947. An original copy of the handout survives in the China Film Archive (Zhongguo dianying ziliao guan) in Beijing.

6

Acting Like Revolutionaries: Shi Hui, the Wenhua Studio, and Private-Sector Filmmaking, 1949–1952

SHI HUI AS "SON OF A BITCH"

I first saw Shi Hui on screen in 1977 at Hong Kong screenings of *Fake Bride, Phony Bridegroom* (*Jia feng xu huang*, 1947) and *Sorrows and Joys of Middle Age* (*Ai le zhongnian*, 1948), important civil war–era productions. Both films are marvelous comedies made by the Wenhua Film Studio in Shanghai, the best in China in the postwar years. Shi Hui starred as an impish but lovable con artist in the first and as a wise and caring school principal in the second. I jumped to the conclusion that Shi Hui was the most versatile actor in Chinese film history. It was clear, though, that whenever Shi Hui and Wenhua were mentioned, other key names were almost always linked to their success. With respect to *Fake Bride, Phony Bridegroom*, the screenwriter was Sang Hu (a rising talent in the wartime and postwar theater and films worlds and a close associate of Shi Hui), the director was Huang Zuolin (a former Cambridge student who had served as Shi Hui's mentor in wartime Shanghai), and the cinematographer was Huang Shaofen (whose legendary camera work dominated Chinese cinema).[1] In the case of *Sorrows and Joys of Middle Age*, Sang Hu was both the screenwriter and director.

In an effort to learn more about Shi Hui and Wenhua, I began an oral history project that included interviews with Sang Hu, Huang Zuolin, and Li Lihua (who played opposite Shi Hui in *Fake Bride, Phony Bridegroom*). The most interesting remarks about Shi Hui came from his old friend Huang Zongjiang:

> Shi Hui had a huge chip on his shoulder. If I made 600 yuan a month in the 1940s, he wanted to make 601. When he was young he had worked at a lot of

odd jobs—such as service worker on a train—where he was pushed around. People with money and position abused him, and he never forgot it. He hated the world, and he was incredibly cynical. He had no interest in politics. He didn't believe in anything. But he hated rich people nevertheless. He felt no pity for the Nationalists when they fell.

Among his friends he was very haughty with his nose up in the air. But at the same time, he had lots of experience mingling with low-life [people], including prostitutes, people in bars, and so forth. So, when he had trouble after the Anti-Rightist Campaign began [in 1957], no one felt sorry for him or was willing to come to his rescue. In 1980 when Li Lihua [came back to China and] saw me, she was still referring to Shi Hui as a "son of a bitch."

Shi Hui was quite irreverent. One time he sat down at a fancy piano in a nice home and mockingly began to play some classical music, punctuating it every so often with a loud fart.

Just before he fell in the Anti-Rightist Campaign, he and I were leaving a screening of Chaplin's *The Great Dictator*. Shi Hui said, in dejected tones, "We haven't laughed like that in eight years." He was always making comments like that—which later got him into trouble. If others made the same kinds of remarks, no one cared. But when Shi Hui did it, people reported his words.

After 1949 Shi Hui was an outsider. There was a new system and political structure. To get into the mainstream, you had to join the Communist Party. It was for this reason that Shi Hui showed some interest. He wasn't used to life out in the cold. But his chances of being admitted to the Party were just about zero.

SHI HUI AS "KING OF THE STAGE" IN OCCUPIED SHANGHAI

Sanitized official biographies of Shi Hui offer more systematic, but much less colorful, accounts of his life.[2] Shi Hui was born in 1916 near Tianjin. Though he achieved fame in Shanghai, he never lost his strong northern accent or his affection for northern culture, including old-style theater and other popular art forms such as *xiangsheng*. When Shi Hui was one year old, his father moved the family to Beijing. When he was in middle school, his father was out of work, and Shi Hui had to quit school and enter a Beijing-Shenyang railway training program in 1930. He worked on a train and in the Shanhaiguan station until late 1931 when he returned to Beijing, where he ended up selling odds and ends at the Zhenguang Cinema. This provided him with an opportunity to see many foreign and domestic films. He studied English in an extension class and pursued his amateur interests in Beijing opera and the *erhu* (a two-stringed Chinese musical instrument). Thanks to a friend, Shi Hui got his start as an actor in the China Traveling Theater Troupe (Zhongguo lüxing jutuan), and this led to work in Chen Mian's prewar Salon Troupe (Shalong jutuan).[3] His early performances included parts in such famous Cao Yu plays as *Thunderstorm* (*Lei yu*) and *Sunrise* (*Richu*).

In 1940 when Shi Hui was twenty-five years old, Chen Mian introduced him to theater contacts in Shanghai, where Shi Hui worked throughout the wartime occupation. His passionate performances were soon noticed. The wartime flight of many leading Shanghai actors created opportunities for newcomers such as Shi Hui. He performed in *Family* (*Jia*) and other progressive plays put on by the Shanghai Theater Art Society (Shanghai ju yi she), said to have loose affiliations with the Communist Party underground, but he moved on in summer 1941 with Huang Zuolin (his new mentor), Wu Renzhi, and others to launch the Shanghai Professional Theater Troupe (Shanghai zhiye jutuan).

In December 1941, Japanese occupation forces in Shanghai took control of the International Settlement, and Huang Zuolin's new group was shut down. In early autumn 1942 Huang and others formed the famous Kugan Players (Kugan jutuan), a group that brought Shi Hui to the very pinnacle of the Shanghai theater world. Under the careful patronage of both Huang and Fei Mu, Shi Hui soon emerged as the most popular actor in wartime Shanghai. He got leading roles in *The Big Circus* (*Da maxituan*), which enjoyed a spectacular 40-day run in October and November, and *Begonia* (*Qiu Haitang*), which broke all records by running for 135 days between December 1942 and May 1943.[4] Theater fans began heralding Shi Hui as "King of the Stage" (*huaju huangdi*) at the tender age of twenty-eight.

After the war Shi Hui remained in Shanghai. He continued to perform onstage, but like many others, he became increasingly involved in the film world. In 1947 he joined his old friends Huang Zuolin and Sang Hu in forming the Wenhua Film Studio, a private company that specialized in decidedly humanistic film projects that had more than the usual amount of artistic value. Four roles that propelled Shi Hui to postwar film stardom deserve special mention. In the delightful comedy *Fake Bride, Phony Bridegroom*, written by Sang Hu and directed by Huang Zuolin, Shi Hui played a struggling Shanghai barber. In both *Long Live the Missus* (*Taitai wan sui*, 1947), written by Zhang Ailing and directed by Sang Hu, and *Night Lodging* (*Ye dian*, 1947), written by Ke Ling and directed by Huang Zuolin, he played nasty old men.[5] In *Bright Sunny Days* (*Yan yang tian*, 1948), written and directed by Cao Yu, Shi Hui played a lawyer. Things were going so well during the filming of *Fake Bride, Phony Bridegroom* that the American periodical *Life* magazine published an attractive photo spread on Shi Hui and the postwar Chinese film scene.

In late 1948, on the eve of the collapse of the Nationalist regime in Shanghai, Shi Hui began writing and directing for the first time. The movie was titled *Mother* (*Muqin*, 1949). But he remained best known for his acting, nevertheless, and his unique box-office appeal was indisputable. In early 1949 Sang Hu recruited him to play the lead in *Sorrows and Joys of Middle Age*, a heartwarming comedy written and directed by Sang Hu about a gentle primary school principal who finds love late in life. Both *Mother* and *Sorrows and Joys of Middle Age* revealed that there were problems in contemporary Chinese society, but both films adopted a light, optimistic tone. Outside the gates of the Wenhua Studio in April 1949, however, society was unraveling, and the revolutionary forces of the Communist Party were poised to enter Shanghai.

SHI HUI AS LIBERATION CELEBRANT

When Luo Xueqian, head of the leading state-owned film studios in Shanghai, fled on May 3, 1949, it was clear to most in the film world that the days of Nationalist rule were almost over.[6] Few in Shanghai's glittering movie industry had much sympathy for the departing Nationalists. Film personalities had ample opportunity to flee, but almost none made the move. Still, few moviemakers had knowledge of the Communists or working relations with their representatives.

There was widespread agreement in film circles on the sad state of the domestic film industry. Many believed that the Nationalists had done far too little to protect the postwar film industry from the aggressive marketing strategies of the American movie industry. Hollywood competition, many felt, threatened to destroy the domestic industry. There were calls throughout the late 1940s to control the number of American films imported to China. Actors, actresses, screenwriters, and directors called for government intervention and protectionism. The Nationalist response had been disappointing, but there was reason to believe that the Communists would be more assertive. Shanghai filmmakers had their own reasons for embracing the anti-American position associated with the Communist Party.

Communist forces occupied Shanghai on May 25, 1949. Six days later, on May 31, film and theater people held a hastily convened conference as part of the "liberation" celebrations taking place throughout the city. The next day movie and stage personalities took to the street in a colorful parade. Closed down for two weeks beginning in mid-May, Wenhua, Kunlun, and Guotai, three of the most important private studios in Shanghai, reopened for business on June 2.[7]

The Communist Party, for its part, made it clear that the political support of theater and film people was welcome. Indeed, in sharp contrast to the behavior of the Nationalists, the Communists actively recruited film professionals to their cause. This does not mean that the Party did not harbor suspicions about the ideological orientation of bourgeois film stars, many of whom, like Shi Hui, had remained in Shanghai throughout the Japanese occupation and had continued with their glamorous careers during the bloody civil war. But given its often-expressed interest in the cultural and intellectual spheres and its strong desire to consolidate its rule in urban centers, the Party was in desperate need of the mass media expertise of urban filmmakers.

The Party formally took over the Nationalists' two major film studios in Shanghai on June 2, 1949, putting veteran Party member Yu Ling in charge of these state filmmaking units, now merged and renamed the Shanghai Film Studio (Shangying).[8] But the message went out that, especially in Shanghai, the heart of China's prerevolution film industry, the new state studio would need time to gear up and that the private studios, including Wenhua, were needed.

To better control the Shanghai arts world, the Shanghai Theater and Film Association (Shanghai xiju dianying xiehui) was set up on June 18. An election was held to determine its leadership. It is not clear precisely how the election was organized, but the number of votes received by the top twenty-seven candidates was published.[9] The leading vote-getters, with 586 and 554 ballots, respectively, were veteran Party members Yu Ling and Xia Yan. The rest of the list was composed primarily of famous non-Party figures who clearly wanted to cooperate with the Party and play a leading role in the postrevolution art world of Shanghai. Shi Hui's mentor Huang Zuolin came in fifth with 450 votes, the popular actor Zhao Dan came in seventh with 356, followed by director Chen Liting (ninth with 342), director Ying Yunwei (tenth with 287), director Wu Yonggang (eleventh with 274), actor Lan Ma (twelfth with 252), and director Zheng Junli (fourteenth with 235). Shi Hui ranked sixteenth with 215 votes.

The tally was good news for Shi Hui because his strong desire to be acknowledged as an enthusiast of liberation was recognized by his appointment to the executive committee of the association. But it was disappointing news because many of the people higher on the list were not his equals, and only a few votes separated him from relatively unknown figures such as the politically ambitious twenty-four-year-old actress Huang Zongying (who came in twenty-first with 180 votes).

The Nationalists had done little to cultivate the support of theater and film people, thus perpetuating the caricature of actors and actresses as empty-headed and oversexed prima donnas. Shanghai film personalities were flattered to be courted by the Communists. In summer and fall 1949 many in the film world, acutely aware of an important opportunity, worked very hard to be noticed by the new authorities and perceived as revolutionary activists. This competitive jockeying for position had practical implications. It was assumed that those who could establish revolutionary credentials would be in a position to play a leading role in the postrevolution film world, while those who failed to attract political attention would be pushed aside. In the early months, this high-energy climate gave rise to a mood of optimism. It was widely known that all the film stars had unconventional personal histories and a poor track record of political activity. But none of that seemed to matter in mid-1949. What mattered was acting revolutionary. Thus, one of the first major activities supported by the new theater and film association was a massive parade of performing artists held on July 4 to honor the People's Liberation Army (PLA).[10] Almost all the big stars were there.

A few days later the association promptly announced that its members were determined to clean up the film world by preventing unhealthy Chinese films from being screened. Calling for both censorship and self-discipline, Xia Yan urged veteran film workers to sign a pledge to maintain high standards. *Qingqing dianying* published photos of both Shi Hui and Huang Zongying signing the pledge.[11] A few movies were subsequently banned, but in fact, despite the solemn pledges, in the two-year period from April 1949 through May 1951 many hundreds of prerevolution Chinese films were shown in Shanghai, along with a very small number of new, postrevolution works. Films from the prewar 1930s, the controversial Japanese occupation period, and the civil war period were widely shown, along with movies from Hong Kong. There were approximately forty-eight movie theaters in Shanghai in 1949, twenty-two of them higher-quality first-run venues.[12] Virtually all of them were privately owned and operated. In the two-year period mentioned above, these theaters scheduled more than forty-six thousand screenings of Chinese films for more than 24 million customers.[13]

Shanghai film veterans actively supported the various movements against "poisonous" Hollywood films that were launched in late summer 1949 and later.[14] In their youth, many of them were addicted to Hollywood film culture; now it was in their artistic, economic, and political interest to denounce films from capitalist countries. But in 1949 and most of 1950 it was still necessary to show American and British films in order to satisfy public demand for movies and to ease the transition to the postrevolution era. In the eighteen months from April 1949 to October 1950 when Chinese forces entered Korea, there were more than thirty-three thousand screenings of 646 American and British films (virtually all of them pre-1949 titles) to a total Shanghai audience of more than 14 million.[15] Western film culture was still very much a part of the immediate postrevolutionary scene.

Shi Hui was especially active in mid- and late 1949 in showing enthusiastic support for the new regime. On August 1, celebrated as the founding day of the PLA, Shi Hui and a friend performed a *xiangsheng* comedy routine as part of a radio fund-raising event to benefit army veterans. Five days later he sold autographed paper fans (*shanzi*) to help raise funds for veterans who had helped disaster victims. On October 1 he and the popular silent screen matinee idol Jin Yan led the largest march ever of stage and screen personalities, this time in support of the formal establishment of the People's Republic.[16]

Other stars, with better political connections to the new regime, engaged in higher-profile public activities. In late July, Zhao Dan went to Beijing to participate in the first meeting of the China Film and Theater Workers' Association (Zhongguo dianying xiju gongzuozhe xiehui), an organization that was to help coordinate filmmaking nationwide. Bai Yang (who had traveled to Beijing from Hong Kong with politically active director Zhang Junxiang to pay homage to the Party even before the fall of Shanghai) was included in a Chinese delegation that went to Moscow in late October to celebrate the anniversary of the October Revolution. Only two years earlier, in 1947, she had been honored as the first recipient of the Chiang Kai-shek Best Actress Award! Now she was one of the most visible film world supporters of the Communist Party. Back from Moscow in December, she was assigned to work at the state-run Shanghai Film Studio, where she presented a glowing report of her visit to the Soviet Union. On December 21, 1949, she even recited a poem in honor of Joseph Stalin's seventieth birthday at a public gathering in Shanghai.[17]

Beginning in July 1949, the newly established Shanghai Literature and Arts Office (Shanghai wenyi chu), a state organ led by Yu Ling and Xia Yan, convened several conferences and meetings attended by both state and private-sector filmmakers, including representatives of the four leading private film studios.[18] The new ground rules were spelled out in general terms, but many questions went unasked. Who, among the ranks of the prerevolution Shanghai film veterans, would be able to enter the Party and the government? How would they prove themselves?

In early November 1949, Shi Hui raced off to Beijing to plan Wenhua's first postrevolution film. The relationship between the new government and the private-sector filmmakers of Shanghai was far from clear, but movie production leaped ahead anyway.

SHI HUI AS KINDLY COP

Wu Xingcai, Wenhua's principal financial backer, was still in Hong Kong in fall 1949. But he was soon convinced by the new Film Bureau in Beijing to renew his interest in the company. The first Wenhua picture initiated after the occupation of Shanghai by PLA forces was a grand film adaptation of Lao She's novella *This Life of Mine* (*Wo zhei yi beizi*), originally published in

1939.[19] Production began in late fall 1949 with an eye to completing the project in time for the lunar New Year holiday season in early 1950. *This Life of Mine* was directed by Shi Hui and starred Shi Hui in the title role of an old-fashioned Beijing policeman.[20]

This undertaking provided Wenhua with an excellent chance to get off to a good start in the new postrevolution era. *This Life of Mine* had several advantages. It was an important piece of May Fourth–type fiction crafted by a highly respected noncommunist writer, Lao She, who had returned to China after the revolution and showed initial enthusiasm for the new order. Very few works of May Fourth fiction had been adapted for the screen prior to 1949. Wenhua would be doing the regime a favor by demonstrating that the new society was the legitimate heir to the May Fourth cultural legacy. The film would highlight the softer, flexible side of the new order.

This Life of Mine was also promising because it had an epic quality. Rather than taking a microscopic look at a particular moment in time (as most films did), it showed dramatic changes in Beijing over a long period. Lao She's original novel covered the period from 1909 to 1921. To make the film even more sweeping in historical terms, screenwriter Yang Liuqing, working closely with Shi Hui, extended the story all the way to 1949 and the Communist victory.

Most scholars regard *This Life of Mine* as a directorial and performance tour de force for Shi Hui. Filled with rich details of local life in Lao She's beloved Beijing, the movie traces the life of an ordinary neighborhood cop. The film is especially effective in conveying in a strikingly sentimental way the colorful language and street customs of Beijing folk. The hero of the story is a decent, morally upright, gentle, unassuming man who spends most of his time mediating minor disputes. People trust and respect him. As a twenty-two-year-old cop, he takes great pride in his work and is full of enthusiasm. But he is naive and knows nothing about politics. He is confused when the Qing dynasty suddenly collapses in 1911.

Our hero stays on the job during the warlord regime that follows. But he and his partners are given degrading jobs (such as guarding the entrance to the homes of corrupt government officials) or forced to harass patriotic students who take to the streets, first to protest the Twenty-one Demands in 1915 and later to advance the May Fourth Movement in 1919. Our cop, still naive, sympathizes with the students and cannot understand why the government suppresses them. Meanwhile, the local economy stagnates, and policemen struggle to hold their families together. The first half of the film covers the material contained in Lao She's original novella and takes considerable pains to remain faithful to the text.

The second half of the film picks up where Lao She left off and is quite disappointing in that there is less Beijing local color and more politics—

Shi Hui (*right*) as kindly Beijing cop in *This Life of Mine* (1950, d. Shi Hui). China Film Archive

politics consistent with the late 1940s Party perspective on the recent history of China. Thus, Beijing is shown to be in decline in the Nanjing decade after the capital is moved south by the Nationalists. Our hero's wife has died, and his daughter has married into the family of another policeman. Only his son, who also becomes a cop, remains behind. Like his father, he is a decent person, but he is more politically conscious and befriends a number of revolutionary students.

The Japanese occupation of Beijing is treated in a highly emotional but predictable manner, highlighted by an episode of popular outrage in response to a sexual assault (a familiar trope found in both pre- and postrevolution Chinese films). The cop's son is engaged to a sweet local girl. Monstrous-looking Japanese arrive at the home one day in the company of Chinese collaborators looking for any Chinese girl who can be pressed into service as a sex slave for Japanese troops. The cop and his son do their best to trick the villains but are reduced to looking on in horror as the lass is dragged away, kicking and screaming. The son then resolves to leave Beijing to join the guerrilla fighters. The father allows him to do so but points out that without the son he will be alone in the world with no one to help in his old age.

The final sequence involves the civil war period and the return of the Nationalists. The regime, not surprisingly, is shown to be totally corrupt. A former traitor, who now works for the Nationalists, mercilessly tortures the old man to get information about his son's Eighth Route Army activities. In prison, the old cop meets a young revolutionary who was once a friend of his son. He watches helplessly as the young man is executed.

The old cop is then forced into a labor gang before being tossed away like a piece of trash. He is reduced to begging, wanders the streets of Beijing trying to find shelter and food, and finally dies one night in a back alley. Images of his son in a PLA uniform, fighting to win national victory, appear briefly on the screen, but it is too late for the old man.

This Life of Mine is both predictable and propagandistic in the second half, but it must be acknowledged that the film did a credible job of fusing the prerevolution Wenhua legacy of soft, humanistic, highly aesthetic filmmaking with the postrevolution demand for harder, overtly political narratives that reinforced the Party's version of history. If the point was to make a united front film that contained a little of the old and a little of the new, then *This Life of Mine* and Shi Hui were certainly successful. The only minor concern involved the final scene. Should the old man be allowed to die alone on the street without seeing his son and the happiness of the new society? Or should he be shown welcoming his son and joining in the victory parades? The original screenplay contains the happy ending. But Shi Hui came up with a variety of excuses for his decision to end the film on a tragic note. At a conference convened in Shanghai on February 13, 1950, and attended by numerous film world luminaries, Shi Hui explained rather defensively that he wanted very much to do the shot according to the script, but a mass scene involving troops entering the city would be too expensive for a private film company. He said he tried to rent an airstrip in Shanghai to shoot the last mass scene, but Nationalist pilots were still dropping bombs in the region.[21] To this day, summaries of the film invariably contain the rosy ending that was never filmed.[22]

Reviews were quite favorable, and the audience clearly regarded it as a wonderful gift for the 1950 lunar New Year. The film was screened in Shanghai 575 times before a total audience of 314,389 in 1950, a record that Wenhua's subsequent efforts in 1950 would not be able to match.[23] The new government was so pleased with the film that it decided to send it to a film festival in socialist Czechoslovakia.

Shi Hui expressed only one reservation in public about the artistry of the film. He told a number of film insiders that the character of the revolutionary youth who appears throughout—and is executed in the end—was not present in Lao She's original novel. Shi Hui expressed some regrets about imposing this character on the narrative because in his view the representation was stiff and unconvincing.[24]

SHI HUI AS GOOD-HEARTED SMALL-TOWN TAILOR

The second postrevolution film produced by Wenhua was *Peaceful Spring* (*Taiping chun*). Released in late spring 1950, it brought together many pivotal members of the old Wenhua team, including director Sang Hu and master cinematographer Huang Shaofen. It starred Shi Hui in the complicated role of Liu Jinfa, a kind-hearted old-style tailor in a small town in eastern Zhejiang in the years from the Japanese occupation to the arrival of the PLA.

Meticulously photographed, expertly edited, and nicely performed, the movie was simple and compelling, reminiscent in many respects of late-1940s Wenhua productions. The main character is tailor Liu, played by Shi Hui in a highly nuanced manner. Liu is a decent, good-hearted, kindly, nonconfrontational figure who does not want to hurt anyone's feelings. Indeed, he does what he can to please everyone around him. The portrait of the tailor is vintage Wenhua humanism: Liu is a profoundly sympathetic character whose gentle disposition is viewed in a positive light.

Early in the film, Liu takes in a poor rural boy, Genbao, as a long-term apprentice. As time goes by it becomes obvious that the hardworking Genbao is a perfect match for Liu's daughter, Fengying, played nicely by the legendary postwar actress Shangguan Yunzhu (who failed to gain entry to the Party in the 1950s and ended up committing suicide in the Cultural Revolution by jumping from a building in Shanghai).[25] Tailor Liu thinks the best of everyone, but the two young people are more politically astute.

The only other main characters are Zhao Laoye and his wife, prosperous local elites who have been good customers of Liu for many years. Liu appreciates their patronage, but his daughter and Genbao are vividly aware that Zhao collaborated with the Japanese and then worked closely with local Nationalists after the war. Liu values his old-style relationship with the Zhaos, while the young people remain suspicious. Nevertheless, Fengying and Genbao are extremely respectful of the old tailor and do nothing to question his authority. In brief, they love and admire the kind old man in ways consistent with Confucian codes, though they worry that ill-intentioned people might take advantage of him.

Two crises are featured toward the end of the picture. First, since Zhao Laoye still has no son, he wants to take tailor Liu's daughter as a second wife. Liu has no alternative but to decline on the grounds that the girl is already committed to apprentice Genbao. Zhao then secretly arranges to have Genbao drafted into the army and jailed when the lad refuses to serve. Zhao, a wily manipulator, knows Liu will come to him for help, at which point a deal is arranged. Zhao will use his influence to get Genbao released if Liu agrees to give over his daughter to Zhao in marriage. Liu goes along in order to save the young man. But before the marriage takes place, the two young people, without Liu's knowledge, run away.

Denying knowledge of the escape plan, Liu is jailed. Before long, however, PLA forces arrive on the outskirts of the town. Zhao Laoye's wife shows up at the jail to tell Liu that she feels sorry for him and will pull some strings to get him released. Once Liu is out, however, Zhao's wife asks for a favor. She pressures Liu to store several boxes of valuables "for safekeeping" and pays him for his assistance. Given their long-term business relationship and his belief that Mrs. Zhao saved his life, Liu foolishly agrees.

The second crisis occurs after the PLA arrives. At first, things go well when Liu's daughter and Genbao return to the house and everyone in the joyous community welcomes the advent of the "new society." But then Fengying discovers by accident that her father is hiding valuables that belong to the Zhaos. In a fascinating sequence toward the end of the film, Fengying confronts her father, but the old man asserts he has done nothing wrong. The Zhaos helped him in the past, and they were good customers. He gave his word, and his word must mean something. Defying her father, Fengying tells Genbao the story. Genbao is still very respectful of his future father-in-law, but he has become politically involved in the community and argues that the only moral thing to do is to hand in the valuables to the new government. Tailor Liu strenuously objects, clinging to the notion that his word and customary human relations stand for something.

The rejoinder of the young people contains both moral and practical components. First, they say there is a new morality. The Zhaos were exploiters and collaborators, so turning their property over to the people is morally justified. Second, since the Zhaos are reactionaries, anyone who helps them will also be branded a reactionary. The young people understand what this means, but old Liu sticks to his ethical guns.

When a family friend who was drafted by the Nationalists shows up at the shop missing a leg, tailor Liu is deeply troubled. His daughter tells him he must turn over the valuables. But Liu continues to balk. It is only when Genbao gets a letter from his home village saying his dear mother has been killed in a Nationalist air raid that old Liu becomes enraged and turns over the valuables. Liu says he now knows what an inhuman reactionary is and that he wants to be a human. A local government cadre tells Liu he is entitled to a reward, but Liu says he will not take it. The cadre insists. In the final shot, Liu is praised at a large public meeting for buying government bonds with his reward money.

In many respects *Peaceful Spring* was a notable success in that, like *This Life of Mine*, it almost seamlessly bridged the gap between the prerevolution and postrevolution Shanghai cultural scene. The film stands in clear political opposition to both Japanese wartime aggression and Nationalist postwar bungling. It also reveals the class structure of society and shows the class enemy (the Zhaos) to be in league with foreign and domestic oppressors. The victory of the revolution and the masses of laboring people is explicitly applauded. From this point of view, there is little difference between *Peaceful Spring* and Wenhua's first postrevolution film, *This Life of Mine*.

All of this was accomplished in *Peaceful Spring* without Wenhua sacrificing its artistic integrity. Shi Hui, director and screenwriter Sang Hu, and cinematographer Huang Shaofen dominate the show in almost exactly the ways they did in prerevolution Wenhua films. The film's overt praise for the revolution notwithstanding, *Peaceful Spring* looks and feels a lot like *Sorrows and Joys of Middle Age*. This film, also written and directed by Sang Hu and starring Shi Hui, was released by Wenhua in early 1949 in the final days of the old regime. Indeed, *Sorrows and Joys of Middle Age* was screened in Shanghai for many months after the arrival of revolutionary forces in May 1949 (including 322 postrevolution screenings in 1949 and 14 screenings in 1950).[26]

The humanism of *Peaceful Spring* overshadows the attention it pays to human conflict, including class tensions and international conflict. *Peaceful Spring* tries very hard to be revolutionary but ends up a humanistic work. The most interesting characterization is Shi Hui's portrayal of Liu Jinfa, the kindly tailor. Thanks to Shi Hui's brilliant acting, Liu is utterly convincing and sympathetic. The audience likes him, even though he seems oblivious to the evil that swirls around him. Not only does he not resist abusive people, he completely fails to recognize injustice when it stares him in the face. The issue is not simply that Liu is naive and entirely too trusting; it is that he remains attractive as a character in spite of his sentimentality. The young people are far more aware of harsh realities that the old man consistently fails to grasp, but they too are clearly paralyzed by their Confucian devotion to the patriarch. They defer to his authority throughout the film and thereby reveal the extent to which they too are invested in "old" social relationships.

Given the popularity of *Peaceful Spring* (188,577 people viewed 467 screenings in Shanghai alone in 1950), Shi Hui and his old friend, writer-director Sang Hu, must have been shocked by the hostility Party critics expressed toward the work.[27] In its June 24, 1950, edition, *Wen hui bao* carried two blistering attacks on the film. One critic said that director Sang Hu had ignored warnings about the need to make changes. Much of this fanciful story, he charged, would be misinterpreted by the film audience. The class enemies slipped away quite easily without being made to suffer for their crimes. And the reward given by the revolutionary cadre to the old tailor at the end was totally inappropriate. Conduct like his should not be rewarded.[28]

A more serious attack was offered by Mei Duo, the editor of *Wen hui bao*'s biweekly theater and film supplement. She argued that the problems with the film centered on the backward nature of screenwriter Sang Hu's mind. It was ideologically misguided to have the film revolve around the life of a hopelessly "empty" character like the old tailor. The relationship between the tailor and the local class enemies is illogical, Mei said, and the film does not do nearly enough to expose the exploitative nature of Zhao Laoye, the local elite. Sang Hu had an attitude problem, she wrote, and was in urgent need of thought reform.[29]

Sang Hu knew there was trouble even before these attacks were published. His response was printed in the second issue of the new journal *Dazhong dianying*.[30] Assuming a humiliating posture, Sang Hu simply surrendered without a fight. In line after line of self-flagellating prose, he confessed that his mentality was indeed petit bourgeois to the core and that the whole story was an irresponsible fabrication. All the criticisms of *Peaceful Spring* were on target, he stated. In fact, he wrote, the film was "a total failure." The criticism was devastating: the film was pulled from distribution and rarely mentioned thereafter.

SHI HUI AS CULTURAL REVOLUTIONARY

In July 1950, not long after the appearance of the stern criticisms of *Peaceful Spring*, Shi Hui published a highly political and self-congratulatory article titled "The Shanghai Film and Theater Worlds in the Year since Liberation."[31] Nowhere in the essay did he mention the *Peaceful Spring* debacle or his connection to it. Referring instead to general developments between June 1949 and June 1950, he began by saying that the film and theater world wanted to "thank the Communist Party and thank the People's Liberation Army" for the chance to start a new life. Using the new political jargon, Shi Hui said that in the past the film and theater scene served relatively few people because Shanghai was controlled by imperialists and reactionary Nationalist bureaucratic capitalists who squeezed out the "sweat and blood of the laboring people." True, Shanghai was rich in dance halls, restaurants, and theaters, but, upon reflection, he could now see that people in the film and theater worlds got little more than leftover scraps.

In the year following liberation, Shi Hui proclaimed, artists had abandoned a misguided sense of pride in their privileged positions in Shanghai society. Given new life, the stars of old worked hard to accomplish as much as possible. "Within three days of liberation," he wrote, "we formed scores of performance troupes" that went out to the factories to put on shows for "worker brothers." Moreover, he reminded readers, theater and film people also participated enthusiastically together with soldiers and ordinary citizens in a grand victory parade. Even though it rained that day, the "stars" still went out "to dance in the streets." According to Shi Hui, soldiers said that "what you've done is just as heroic as what we do at the front."

Organizationally speaking, Shi Hui observed, the formation of the Shanghai Theater and Film Association was an unprecedented event because it united the performing arts world for the first time and thereby allowed for the "collectivization" of cultural activity. The association sponsored a massive liberation parade for performing arts workers and organized a spectacular six-day fund-raising event held outdoors during summer 1949. Tens of thousands of people mobbed the park to see their favorite stars. Owing to this direct contact between entertainers and the masses, the theater and film world was able to make ideological progress, Shi Hui claimed. This gala was followed by a successful radio fund-raising marathon to benefit old soldiers and disaster victims. Shi Hui describes such events as "miracles" that could never have happened in the old society. The "petty bourgeois feeling of superiority" that had caused so many artists to behave in "self-indulgent ways" had disappeared.

The transformation of the arts world was so profound, Shi Hui reported, that "many comrades, including all types of artists, joined the army, went to the countryside, and enrolled in revolutionary universities" that offered crash courses in the new politics. Artists no longer wanted to be admired as a privileged class; they wanted to be "good revolutionary workers" who "wholeheartedly served the people." They did this in the first year, he said, by turning out several short public-service films urging patriotic citizens to buy government bonds. Ironically, buying bonds is exactly what old Liu Jinfa did in the now-discredited film *Peaceful Spring*.

At the end of his article, Shi Hui paid homage to theater workers who had turned out two new plays, *Song of the Red Flag* (*Hongqi ge*) and *Ideological Problems* (*Sixiang wenti*). The first of these, he said, dealt with the working class and required stage people to become familiar with proletarian life. The second play, *Ideological Problems*, was for educated people. Shi Hui concluded by saying that the film and theater world would undoubtedly face many challenges and problems in the future. But, he insisted, a good start had been made in the first year. The important thing was that people in the cultural arena wanted to "transform" (*fanshen*), had merged with the "people," and were willing to use "criticism and self-criticism" to make further progress.[32]

It is notable that Shi Hui's self-promotional article referred to the alleged contributions of the heavy-handed play *Ideological Problems*. The third feature film produced by Wenhua after the revolution (and the first after the *Peaceful Spring* controversy) was in fact a movie version of *Ideological Problems*. Released in August 1950 (with 446 screenings and an audience in Shanghai of 220,516 in 1950), this frightening work had almost nothing in common with *This Life of Mine*, *Peaceful Spring*, or the humanistic Wenhua tradition.[33] Shi Hui himself was totally uninvolved in the production.

No doubt it made political sense for Wenhua to be associated with the filming of *Ideological Problems*, especially in the aftermath of the criticism of *Peaceful Spring*. Shi Hui's mentor, Huang Zuolin, the leading figure at Wenhua, oversaw the production but is designated in the credits as one of eight people in a direction "collective" that linked Wenhua to the Shanghai People's Art and Theater Institute (Shanghai renmin yishu ju yuan). Huang's artistic genius notwithstanding, *Ideological Problems* is quite simply a disaster, though a disaster with very sharp teeth. The acting and cinematography are terrible, the characterizations are wooden, and the story line is quite mechanical. Worse still, it featured an unprecedented orgy of intellectual-bashing.

Ideological Problems deals with one of the many "revolutionary universities" set up in China in 1949, in this case East China People's Revolutionary University on the outskirts of Shanghai. Ostensibly, the university provided noncommunist educated people with an opportunity to reorient their "thinking" in preparation for a suitable job assignment in the new society. Owing to their shaky class backgrounds and cultural bearings, all the students have an attitude problem. The school functions as a thought reform camp. Indeed, in some respects it resembles a prison for ideological sinners. All the internees are spiritual transgressors who require cleansing before they can be returned to society. Indeed, conditions at the school strongly resemble the circumstances of penal detention in the early 1950s described in Allyn Rickett and Adele Rickett's classic book *Prisoners of Liberation*.[34]

A few students are zealots determined to prove to the authorities that they are pure and ready for leadership positions in the new society. One such activist is also motivated by the fact that he has a serious case of venereal disease and thus is obsessed with getting the Party to notice his "clean" ideological disposition. These unsparing activists spend most of their time bullying the other backward students and threatening to mount "struggle meetings" against them.

Most students are people who have been contaminated by feudal or bourgeois values, the most important of which is selfish individualism. They are sinners who do not yet understand the extent to which they are in serious need of redemption. They include such stock characters as the American-style bourgeois intellectual, the party girl, and the landlord's son.

The progress of this study class is overseen by yet another stock character, a masculinized, slightly plump, ever-smirking, always calm, self-righteous, middle-aged, female Party cadre who wears baggy Maoist unisex fatigues and a worker's cap in every scene. The movie consists primarily of one criticism/self-criticism meeting after another in which the actors and actresses, standing stiff and straight, appear to be reading their lines from posters held to the side of the camera.

At the outset of *Ideological Problems*, one gets the impression that the dual problems of harsh zealotry and bourgeois backwardness will be given equal attention by the wise Party cadre, so that both issues can be resolved at the same time. But as the picture progresses, the problem of ultra-leftism is neglected, and all the emphasis is placed on the bourgeois backwardness of non-Party intellectuals. One never gets to see the sort of "struggle session" that the zealots threaten at the beginning because the Party cadre prefers to advance the thought transformation process in a more congenial way, but the option of resorting to a struggle meeting, once mentioned at the outset, is never repudiated. The transgressing students are fully aware that "struggle" is still an option.

Most students are in denial about the full extent of their ideological sins. But long sermons and longer meetings make it clear that confession is the only way to salvation. One by one, all the students see the error of their ways and willingly "convert" to the new morality.

Given the thrust of Sigrid Schmalzer's research on Chinese interest in the early 1950s in the issue of human origins and the criteria that define the "human" condition, it is useful to note that *Ideological Problems* definitely addresses this topic.[35] The logic of the film builds on the basic idea that there is no middle path. Either you are with the revolution and the people or you are opposed to the revolution. Furthermore, a concerted effort is made in the film to "dehumanize" those who are not clearly inside the revolutionary camp. By this logic, a nonrevolutionary is a counterrevolutionary, and a counterrevolutionary is nonhuman. Since no one wants to be seen as inhuman, it is essential to position oneself solidly within the revolutionary camp. When the students at the revolutionary university recognize that they do indeed want to be saved by reforming their thought, what they are really saying is that they want to be included in the "human" category.

Understanding the politics of *Ideological Problems* makes it easier to comprehend the shrill criticism directed in mid-1950 at Shi Hui's vivid portrayal of Liu Jinfa, the kind-hearted tailor. Sang Hu's script and Shi Hui's acting, not to mention Huang Shaofen's deft cinematography, humanized a nonrevolutionary. By contrast, the viewer of *Ideological Problems* is given no way to admire the ugly people who have "thought" problems. Tailor Liu has just as many problems as they do but remains attractive and respected nonetheless, even in the eyes of the progressive young people in his life. *Peaceful Spring*, unlike *Ideological Problems*, pays attention to the ways in which a decent man like tailor Liu can be full of contradictions but still thoroughly human.

Ideological Problems states quite explicitly that it is not just thought reform that makes a person human. Thought reform cannot be achieved without labor—hard physical labor. One of the bourgeois intellectuals in the film protests to the masculinized female cadre that he already has his mind right and that there is no need for him to work in the fields since he can make a better contribution elsewhere. This remark prompts another long-winded lecture by Baggy Pants about the sacred nature of labor.

Ideological Problems and its Wenhua producers received rave reviews in the press. The Ministry of Culture organized a symposium and stated that it was extremely satisfying to know that a private film studio had turned out a work of such enormous "educational significance."[36] Much was made of the seemingly impressive attendance figures nationwide and in Shanghai. For example, in the last three months of 1950, *Ideologial Problems* was screened 446 times in Shanghai to an audience of more than 220,000. But these totals are misleading. The numbers were high because a serious effort had been made to orchestrate group attendance. Huge discounts of up to 80 percent were offered to units that applied for collective admission three to four days in advance.[37] When the campaign was over, screenings and attendance plummeted—18 screenings in Shanghai in 1951 for 6,500 viewers.[38]

SHI HUI AS PIMP

Wenhua's willingness to help with the filming of *Ideological Problems* was rewarded. In late summer and early fall 1950, just before the entry of Chinese forces into the Korean War, Wenhua began production on a relatively soft film that was more in keeping not only with *This Life of Mine* and *Peaceful Spring* but also with the longer-term Wenhua artistic legacy. Based on a May Fourth–type novel titled *Corruption* (*Fushi*), originally published in 1941 by the celebrated writer Mao Dun, this film was adapted for the screen by the respected Shanghai literary figure Ke Ling and directed by Huang Zuolin, who had recently worked so hard on the *Ideological Problems* disaster.[39] *Corruption*, identified by the Wenhua leadership as a priority (*zhongdian*) project closely tied to its desire to emulate "the filmmaking experiences of the Soviet Union," was released on December 15, 1950.[40]

Set in 1940, the story deals with a self-centered young bourgeois woman in wartime Chongqing who breaks with her socially responsible husband to pursue a life of adventure. She falls in with the wrong crowd and ends up functioning as a spy for the dark forces of Nationalist reaction linked to American intelligence agencies. Her ex-husband, a Communist, is played by Shi Hui in his first role since *Peaceful Spring*. Throughout his career Shi Hui specialized in playing a variety of colorful ordinary people, including low-life characters. Playing the part of a clean-cut revolutionary youth was new to Shi Hui. His performance was credible but lackluster.

In the story, the young, corrupted woman provides information about her former husband. After he is arrested, the authorities ask her to help make him talk. But she admires his resolve and refuses to cooperate. She soon befriends a young woman who is trapped in a situation quite like her own. Later, the protagonist is shocked to learn that her ex-husband has been executed. Reading a farewell letter from him that begs her to get out of her dreadful circumstances, she sees the light and runs away to the liberated areas, taking the younger woman with her. Mao Dun seems to have expressed no objections to the screen adaptation of his novel, though the original work is more introspective than political and contains no final sequence about the two women heading off to a Communist Party base area.

Shi Hui played a much more memorable part in the fifth Wenhua production since the Party's victory in Shanghai, a gut-wrenching movie titled *Sisters Stand Up* (*Jiejie meimei zhanqilai*) that explored the unsavory subject of prostitution in Republican China. Filmed in late fall and early winter 1950 and released in early 1951, *Sisters Stand Up* was written and directed by newcomer Chen Xihe, who had researched the topic by visiting a Women's Labor Training Institute in Beijing to which former prostitutes had been assigned. To provide himself with political cover, Chen also convened a number of "discussion sessions" in which he respectfully requested the "advice" of various political and cultural authorities.[41]

Set in Beijing in 1947, the first half of the film takes a highly dramatized, but still strikingly ethnographic, approach to the sordid business of prostitution. Focusing on the sad story of Daxiang, an illiterate peasant girl whose mother was tricked into selling her into prostitution, it offers an extremely detailed look at the ways in which prostitutes were recruited, bought and sold, trained, controlled, and marketed in late Republican Beijing. In addition to being introduced to the various personal stories of seven prostitutes, the audience gets a close look at a number of specialists in the industry, including terrifying procurers of young women, older men who handle the finances, older women who take responsibility for disciplining the prostitutes, and heartless young men who actually run the brothels. Equally important, the film offers portraits of male customers, parents, and loved ones of the prostitutes, as well as corrupt policemen who are paid for their support.

Though the first half is intriguing, the film still must be regarded as one-dimensional in that it presents few of the nuances and gray areas of the industry discussed by Gail Hershatter in her study of prostitution in China.[42] In the movie, the people who run the industry are monsters, and the prostitutes are ruthlessly oppressed victims. There is little middle ground. The picture is graphic, disgusting, and powerful. But, given these distortions, one is surprised in the first half to see at least some prostitutes who appear

176   Chapter 6

to adjust to their fate and bond to some degree with "Mother," the controlling older woman who feeds them carefully selected bits of information about the outside world. For instance, when word circulates that the PLA is on the outskirts of the city, the older woman has no trouble convincing the women under her control that the Communists regard prostitutes as inhuman trash. The Communists will round them up and murder them.

Shi Hui, a man who by some accounts was personally familiar with the pre-1949 world of prostitution, gives a brilliant performance as the loathsome Ma San, a thoroughly despicable procurer of innocent young women. As he did so successfully in *This Life of Mine*, Shi Hui speaks in the rich and colorful Beijing dialect in order to allow the distinctively local character of Beijing to surface. The image of Ma San is genuinely bone chilling.

The second part of the film, which coincides chronologically with the early weeks and months of the Communist occupation of Beijing, is quite disappointing and rather predictable—and Shi Hui plays almost no part in this portion of the film. Indeed, the second part is a lot like *Ideological Problems*. In fact, the *very same* always smirking, always correct, masculinized, baggy pants, Mao-capped woman cadre who appears in *Ideological Problems* shows up in *Sisters Stand Up* to reeducate the prostitutes.

The women, scared to death, are sent to a reeducation center (one that, like the "revolutionary university" in *Ideological Problems*, has the look and feel of a prison) where they are cleaned up and organized in study groups. Baggy Pants guides them every step of the way. Gradually, after countless meetings and lectures, the women tell their horrible stories and come to understand the exploitative nature of the old society. Daxiang, our heroine, becomes an activist and is appointed head of her group.

Once again, the issues of humanity and labor come into play. The Party repeatedly tells the women that prostitution work was "not their fault" but, rather, the fault of the evil class enemies. Yet there is no escaping the conclusion that they are in a detention center and that their status is something less than human. Otherwise, why is there a need for reeducation? Baggy Pants makes it clear that thought reform cannot be achieved without participation in labor. Naturally, she does not regard prostitution as real labor. And of course, the ex-prostitutes want to become human by participating in honest work. In fact, many of them, including Daxiang, "volunteer" for prostitute reeducation work in Subei (and forsake reunification with families and loved ones, including, in Daxiang's case, a fiancé) once their own course of study is complete. The film audience in Shanghai could not have missed the less-than-flattering reference to Subei, the region believed by many to have been the native place of most lower-class Shanghai prostitutes.[43]

Sisters Stand Up was shown widely in Shanghai in early 1951. Surpassing the standard set by *This Life of Mine* one year earlier, it was screened 657 times in 1951 to an audience totaling 344,521 people in Shanghai alone.[44] Even though the virtuoso performance by Shi Hui as the dastardly Ma San completely overshadowed the uninspired performance of Ding Wen as Baggy Pants, the film was warmly received by critics.[45]

One explanation for this reception is that Wenhua had learned its lesson with *Peaceful Spring*. That is to say, it was necessary to show the militancy of the aroused masses and the suffering of the class enemies before the film could end. Thus, *Sisters Stand Up* has what *Peaceful Spring* did not have: a large-scale struggle meeting. A stage is set up, the masses of prostitutes in the camp are gathered together, the class enemies are dragged forward, and Baggy Pants orchestrates the struggle session. Emboldened by their new consciousness, the former prostitutes denounce and spit on the old brothel owners. The prostitutes then charge the stage in an attempt to beat the class enemies to death. Baggy Pants intervenes, saying that the new society requires that these cases be handled "according to the law." But then she asks the enraged throng, "What do you think their punishment should be?" The women scream out, "Execution!" Baggy Pants shouts back, "OK!" Scenes of this sort made *Sisters Stand Up* immune to criticism.[46]

SHI HUI AS PEASANT SOLDIER

Wars require war movies, and the Korean War was no exception. Veteran film personalities wasted no time in showing enthusiastic support for the war effort. In mid-December 1950, shortly after Chinese forces entered Korea, a photo appeared in a popular film magazine featuring the famous actresses Bai Yang and Shangguan Yunzhu singing anti-American songs at a troop support rally.[47]

Immediately following the filming of *Sisters Stand Up*, Wenhua and Shi Hui quickly began work on *Platoon Commander Guan* (*Guan lianzhang*), a war film based on a propaganda novel by Zhu Dingyuan. This effort reunited the creative team that completed *This Life of Mine* in early 1950, including Yang Liuqing as screenwriter and Shi Hui as both director and lead actor in the title role. *Platoon Commander Guan* was released in spring 1951. It was Shi Hui's first attempt to play the part of a peasant soldier. Huang Zuolin and other leaders of Wenhua undoubtedly concluded that it was good for the studio to do its patriotic bit. It would be a safe and noncontroversial agitprop (agitation-propaganda) film. They were wrong.

Platoon Commander Guan was one of the unfortunate political casualties of the aggressive campaign launched by the Party press in May 1951 against another film, *The Life of Wu Xun* (*Wu Xun zhuan*), a private-sector Shanghai movie involving two film world icons, veteran director Sun Yu and leftist actor Zhao Dan.[48] In superficial terms, criticism of the film was directed at the wrongheaded, and thus counterrevolutionary, mass education activities of a mid-nineteenth-century intellectual. In reality, the attack was part of a frightening nationwide "rectification" campaign targeting the alleged bourgeois ideological orientation of writers and artists in mid-1951—a campaign entirely in keeping with the political agenda spelled out in Huang Zuolin's disturbing film *Ideological Problems*, released the previous summer. This time, however, the Party's critique of bourgeois intellectuals could not be ignored, blunted, or circumvented: the *Renmin ribao* (*People's Daily*) editorial spearheading the campaign was written by Mao Zedong himself.[49]

At one level, *Platoon Commander Guan* was, indeed, unproblematic. Set in rural Jiangsu in the weeks leading up to the final PLA march on Shanghai, the movie tells the simple story of Commander Guan, a poor peasant from Shandong who had risen through the ranks during the civil war. Guan has the common touch and is respected by his troops and the higher-ups.

All of this is established in a number of extremely interesting opening scenes in which a highly educated college student, now on active duty in the military, is sent to Guan's unit to offer cultural instruction to rank-and-file peasant soldiers, many of whom are illiterate. In addition to raising the cultural level of the troops, the student is expected to be modest and learn about the hard life of those who have been sacrificing at the front.

The student gets off to a bad start by speaking in ways that are highly abstract and thus cannot be comprehended by the common soldiers. But this tension is worked out early in the film, and the student goes on to have cordial relationships with the troops. In the second part of the film, the entire focus is on the heroism of Guan's unit as they take a key Nationalist position just west of Shanghai. The cowardly Nationalists are holed up in a building that contains women and orphans, so Guan must figure out a way to vanquish the enemy without putting the innocents at risk. The unit is successful, but Guan loses his own life in the final showdown.

Platoon Commander Guan was shown widely in Shanghai in 1951 (347 screenings and a total audience of almost two hundred thousand people), but much to Shi Hui's dismay, the film was not at all appreciated by urban, intellectual Party critics in the immediate wake of the Wu Xun campaign.[50] The problem was that Shi Hui's portrayal of peasant soldier Guan was too vivid for its own good. When playing the roles of local cop, old tailor, and pimp, Shi Hui tried his best to bring out the color and complicated truth of these memorable characters. The same was true of his rendition of the peasant soldier. Guan and his men are shown to be peasant soldiers from the north (Shandong) fighting in the unfamiliar environs of the south. Their Shandong accents are extremely heavy, they employ exotic Shandong colloquialisms when they speak, and they use vulgar curses. In short, Guan and his men have a strong local identity. This was unacceptable to critics at

Shi Hui (*center*) as earthy peasant soldier having fun with bookish Communist intellectual in *Platoon Commander Guan* (1951, d. Shi Hui). China Film Archive

the time of the Korean War, who wanted to see China and Chinese troops presented as unified and culturally sanitized "national" subjects who spoke perfect *putonghua*.

Urban ideologues were embarrassed by the colorful, rough-and-tumble representation of peasant warriors in *Platoon Commander Guan*. Their criticisms of the film reveal a complex love-hate relationship with peasants. On the one hand, according to the official Party line, peasants were heroes of the revolution worthy of deep respect. But it was embarrassing to show peasants as they really were. It was fine to represent peasants in folksy ways, but it was dangerous for characterizations to get too close to reality. As Jeremy Brown has shown in his research on late-Mao era urban intellectual contempt for peasants, it is often the case that profound disgust and revulsion lurked just below the surface of patronizing Party images of the peasantry.[51] From this urban intellectual perspective, the peasant soldiers in *Platoon Commander Guan*, and especially Guan himself, look and act like a bunch of ignorant yahoos and yokels. This was not the image of heroic Chinese fighters the leadership wanted the world or even the nation to see.

Shi Hui thought he was doing his job, but the critics made it clear that he was taking his job much too seriously.[52]

Another problem with *Platoon Commander Guan* was that it failed to adhere to Leninist notions of hierarchy and discipline. In one of the earliest scenes, Guan cannot be located by the urban student because he is rolling in the dirt, playing with local children who have stolen his cap. To make matters worse, Guan's relationship with his troops seems much too casual. From the Party's point of view, Guan does not behave like an official with power, and his underlings are insufficiently respectful of his authority. There is not enough structure in the unit.

In one particularly interesting scene, a major battle commences, and senior officers tell Guan to hold his troops in a rear area and wait for instructions. Guan is repeatedly seen complaining to his superiors and urging them to send the unit into battle. Critics pointed out that it was totally inappropriate for a junior officer to be raising questions about the wisdom of those higher in the chain of command. One critic went so far as to say that it was not clear whether Guan's troops were fighting for the nation or fighting out of loyalty to Guan himself.[53] In effect, the critics were charging that the ignorant and undisciplined peasants from Shandong under Guan's personal command looked more like an old-fashioned bandit gang than a unit in the national army.

Rather than straighten out the peasants, the urban intellectual in their midst adjusts to the situation by joining the primitive gang. Films such as *Ideological Problems* made it clear that it was fine for Party elites (like Baggy Pants) to bash bourgeois urban intellectuals, but it was not fine for urban intellectuals (like the university student in *Platoon Commander Guan*) to lose their identity by merging with an undisciplined and uncultured band of crude illiterates.

As he had in his previous roles, Shi Hui worked hard to "humanize" his multifaceted character. Once again, the problem was that he succeeded. That is, he created a sympathetic, likable, flesh-and-blood human character complete with warts at a time when the Party's definition of humanity called for homogenized and disciplined uniformity. The Party's hypersensitivity to characterizations like Shi Hui's Commander Guan revealed serious insecurities within the ruling elite. The victors in the civil war, including Mao himself, spoke with very heavy regional accents, a fact that was often concealed from the public. They had regional identities and were linked to regional networks and regional power bases, but they wanted ordinary citizens to think in terms of national unity. They talked about the organic and open relationship between the revolutionary leadership and the masses but very much demanded the respect and deference that came along with strict Leninist hierarchies of power.

SHI HUI AS AMERICAN CAPITALIST

By the end of 1951, following the problematic reception of *Platoon Commander Guan*, it became clear that Wenhua's days were numbered. A plan was in the works to integrate all private-sector studios into the state sector. Wenhua's final attempt to serve the new society was a rather remarkable movie titled *Window on America* (*Meiguo zhi chuang*), another anti-American, Korean War–era work that has been systematically ignored by film scholars in China, many of whom find it embarrassing. The film was shot in winter 1951–1952 and released in early 1952 as yet another expression of film world political support for the Chinese war effort.

Adapted for the screen by Huang Zuolin from an original Soviet text, codirected by Huang Zuolin, Shi Hui, and Ye Ming, and filmed by Huang Shaofen, all of them important members of the Wenhua team, *Window on America* is the only movie in Chinese film history set entirely in the United States and featuring Chinese actors and actresses in the roles of white and black Americans.[54] Shi Hui, complete with fake nose, plays the lead role of Mr. Butler, a New York capitalist whose business is in trouble owing to economic disruptions caused by the Korean War. This long-forgotten movie is a work of wartime propaganda, but it is unusually memorable nonetheless, in part because it is a surprisingly effective comedy and in part because Shi Hui is masterful in the challenging role of Butler.

The entire film takes place during a two- to three-hour period on the forty-second floor of a Manhattan skyscraper. Butler and his voluptuous secretary fret because the stock market news is alarming. Business is bad because the economy has shifted to a wartime footing. Their deliberations are interrupted by the sudden appearance of a lowly thirty-two-year-old window washer named Charley Kent, who enters their office through an open window. Startled, Butler offers the young man a fancy cigarette and listens attentively to his story.

Recently laid off from a factory job owing to the restructuring of the wartime economy, Charley asks a favor. Deeply depressed, he has decided to commit suicide by jumping out the window. But he wants his final pay packet, meager as it is, to be handed over to his mother. The hilarious Shi Hui character, Butler, agrees to help, saying that since America is a free country, Charley certainly has the freedom to kill himself. But he argues that Charley is missing a great moneymaking opportunity. For instance, if Charley agreed to make a public statement to the effect that his final wish before jumping was to enjoy a famous brand-name cigarette one last time, he could earn $300, which of course would be passed along to his poor mother.

When Charley agrees to the scheme, Butler becomes quite excited and offers to serve as Charley's agent. The poor worker, whose brother was drafted

Shi Hui (*right*) as Butler, the greedy American capitalist, in *Window on America* (1952, d. Huang Zuolin, Shi Hui, Ye Ming). China Film Archive

to fight in Korea, is then asked to wait for a couple of hours before jumping. Butler explains that Charley's reasons for committing suicide have absolutely no market value and sound like "commie propaganda." He needs to think like a Hollywood filmmaker and tell a romantic story about an unhappy love affair. When a confused Charley agrees to the new plan, Butler scrambles to line up sponsors of the suicide: a men's clothing dealer wants Charley to wear one of its fine suits, a famous whiskey distillery wants him to take a final gulp of its product before jumping, and a manufacturer of "unbreakable" sunglasses (who looks exactly like American president Harry Truman!) wants him to put on the glasses before leaping.

Butler, now thinking of starting a new business as a suicide agent, writes up a formal contract for Charley, and makes arrangements for the big event to be broadcast on radio. When Charley notices that Butler gets three-quarters of the profits, Butler responds indignantly by saying that Charley has the easy part: all he has to do is jump.

The riotous fun continues when a team of workers (including a "black" man) arrives to set up the broadcast equipment. All belong to a trade union. Once the workers learn what is happening, they do verbal battle with Butler and slowly convince Charley that he is being exploited. Indeed, Charley soon discovers that the capitalists need him more than he needs them. Insisting now on being called "Mr. Kent," Charley begins making various demands. In the end, he decides to cancel the suicide altogether. With the suicide scheme in ruins, Charley and the workers depart in victory.

The film ends with Butler being hounded by all the sponsors he had lined up and with the workers standing on a hill outside the city, pointing to the horizon and referring to the good society that exists in "another country" far away (the Soviet Union).

It would be a mistake to dismiss *Window on America* as a low-budget propaganda film. Its significance resides in the fact that it was successful and that it could not have been made in state studios that lacked directors such as Huang Zuolin, multitalented actors such as Shi Hui, and top cinematographers such as Huang Shaofen. With the Wu Xun campaign still unfolding, Shi Hui and Huang Zuolin were asked to make an anti-American film based on an original Soviet text, and they did so with enthusiasm. Indeed, looking at the entire Wenhua postrevolution production record, one wonders what more these filmmakers could have done to serve the new society. To win the favor of the new political elites and to seek entrance to the Party, Shi Hui had played a humble cop, an old-fashioned tailor, a patriotic youth, a sadistic pimp, a revolutionary soldier, and finally, a New York capitalist.

But his work always fell short of Party standards. His characters, including Butler, were never mere cardboard caricatures of good or evil. The positive characters, like Commander Guan, always exhibited character flaws. The "middle characters," like the Beijing cop and the Zhejiang tailor, were often befuddled and confused. The negative characters, like Ma San the pimp and Butler the New York capitalist, consistently revealed an undeniable humanity. Nothing that Shi Hui did was good enough for Party critics.

By the time *Window on America* was released, the Party had already given up on Shi Hui. In the end, the Party was incapable of distinguishing between Shi Hui the man and Shi Hui the Shanghai film-world bad boy. It was incapable of seeing the difference between Shi Hui and the colorful characters he played. In the end, the verdict was that Shi Hui, only thirty-seven years old in 1952, could not be trusted and had outlived his usefulness.

SHI HUI AS RIGHTIST

After Wenhua released *Window on America*, the eight private film studios still functioning in Shanghai were shut down and their staffs integrated into the expanding web of state-sector filmmaking. Shi Hui, officially categorized as a director and an actor, was placed at first in the Shanghai Film Studio.[55] But in the state sector, the studio heads made all the decisions. It was no longer a matter of directors and screenwriters coming up with their own ideas. It was a command economy. From the outset, Shi

Hui was marginalized at Shangying, and his career rapidly deteriorated. After *Window on America*, he was never again invited to participate in a movie that had anything to do with the serious topic of revolution.

His work—when he got any—took him out of the world of contemporary society (where he had been a dominating force since 1942) and into a world of fantasy and retreat. In 1952 and 1953 he had no work at all. In 1954 he directed a charming children's movie for Shangying called *A Letter with Feathers* (*Jimao xin*) about a cute little boy who uses his wits to help the Red Army during the resistance war. In 1954 he made a cameo appearance in a mediocre historical film titled *The Rebels* (*Song Jingshii*), about a Qing-era peasant rebellion. In 1955 he directed an exotic fairy-tale opera titled *A Heavenly Match* (*Tian xian pei*), written by his old friend Sang Hu. Shi Hui, the most accomplished actor of his time, was only forty years old in 1955. No doubt he felt underappreciated and wondered whether his celebrated career was over. After a four-year engagement, Shi Hui married actress Tong Baoling in 1955. They had no children.

The Hundred Flowers liberalization campaign launched in 1956 raised Shi Hui's hopes. In an effort to shake up the film world, directors at Shangying were encouraged to form small creative collectives. Shi Hui immediately led a group that included the noted young director Xie Jin, veterans Xu Changlin and Chen Baichen, and screenwriter Shen Ji. Qu Baiyin, the deputy head of Shangying, dubbed the group the Five Flowers (Wu hua she). They became affiliated with a smaller state-sector film studio in Shanghai called Tianma.

Xie Jin and Chen Baichen worked on the screenplay for *Woman Basketball Player No. 5* (*Nü lan wu hao*). Xu Changlin produced a script called *Endless Passion, Deep Friendship* (*Qing chang yi shen*). To support his old colleague, Shi Hui agreed to make a cameo appearance in the film. He played the role of a worker who gradually loses his sight. No one knew it at the time, but the sightless worker would be Shi Hui's final role.

Shi Hui's own project was a daring screenplay titled *Night Voyage on a Foggy Sea* (*Wu hai ye hang*). Thanks to the Hundred Flowers cultural opening, filming on this thinly veiled piece of political criticism was approved. The story involved the fate of a group on a boat trip from Shanghai to Ningbo. The ship was called *Democracy No. 3* (*Minzhu san hao*). When the ship runs into a dense fog, the people on board are required to work together to save themselves. The political message was not hard to figure out: to avoid a "shipwreck" the Chinese people had to swing into action, bypassing incompetent leaders.

Just as the filming of *Night Voyage on a Foggy Sea* was completed, Shi Hui, veteran director Wu Yonggang, and actress Wu Yin were summoned to Beijing in late spring 1957 and criticized as rightists. Chen Baichen, another member of the Five Flowers group, was also identified as a rightist. The enormously destructive Anti-Rightist Campaign was under way.

Back in Shanghai, Shi Hui was ordered to attend a "big criticism meeting" (*pipan da hui*) organized for the special purpose of "examining his thought" (*sixiang jiancha*). Shi Hui had always loved the spotlight, but the struggle meeting directed at him was not the sort of attention he was accustomed to in his days as a big star. It was pointed out that one of the negative characters in *Night Voyage on a Foggy Sea* was explicitly identified as a "Party member." This character was said to be selfish and doing things only for personal gain. The appearance of this character, the attackers said, was proof that Shi Hui was putting the Party down. No one, especially friends from the late 1940s who had finally made it into the Party or still had hopes of winning Party membership, stepped forward in his defense.

Shi Hui was ordered to appear at a second criticism meeting. But after returning home, he disappeared the next day. In a final and carefully planned performance that can be regarded as either a case of "life imitating art" or an instance of "art imitating life"—the distinction was now entirely unclear—Shi Hui boarded the same ship (*Democracy No. 3*) featured in his "rightist" movie and began the trip from Shanghai to Ningbo. Many of the sailors knew Shi Hui because he had taken the trip many times as a way of better understanding life at sea. Right on cue, one of the deck hands recognized him as the ship pulled away on that fateful day. "Are you here again to experience life?" he asked. Shi Hui nodded. Yes, indeed, he was there to experience Chinese life in mid-1957.

Not long after this encounter, the forty-three-year-old Shi Hui committed suicide by jumping overboard and drowning.

Days later Public Security officers were summoned to Wusongkou, south of Shanghai, to examine the body of an adult male that had washed up on the beach. The face of the corpse had deteriorated beyond recognition, but a subsequent inquiry identified the body as Shi Hui's.

To this day, no published source in the People's Republic has acknowledged that Shi Hui committed suicide.[56] His final performance was ingenious. Suicides committed by prominent people were not reported because they made the Party look bad. Shi Hui, finding a way to silence the critics, got the last word. It would not be easy for the Party to explain why Charley Kent chose life in capitalist America, while Shi Hui chose death in socialist China.

Huang Zuolin and Sang Hu survived the Anti-Rightist Campaign but were among the many prerevolution film luminaries who were kept outside the Party for the remainder of their careers. A few eventually got what they wanted. Huang Zongying was admitted to the Communist Party in 1956, Zhao Dan in 1957, and Bai Yang in 1958.[57]

NOTES

An earlier version of this chapter appeared as "Acting Like Revolutionaries: Shi Hui, the Wenhua Studio, and Private-Sector Filmmaking, 1949–1952," in *Dilemmas of Victory: The Early Years of the People's Republic of China*, ed. Jeremy Brown and Paul G. Pickowicz (Cambridge, Mass.: Harvard University Press, 2007), 256–87.

1. For short biographies of Sang Hu, Huang Zuolin, and Huang Shaofen, see *Zhongguo dabaike quanshu: dianying* (hereafter cited as *ZGDBK*) (Beijing: Zhongguo dabaike quanshu chubanshe, 1991), 338, 197, 195.
2. See Wei Shaochang, ed., *Shi Hui tan yishu* (Shanghai: Shanghai wenyi chubanshe, 1982). This volume includes a useful essay by Ye Ming titled "Yi Shi Hui," 527–38.
3. *ZGDBK*, 238.
4. See Edward Gunn, *Unwelcome Muse: Chinese Literature in Shanghai and Peking, 1937–1945* (New York: Columbia University Press, 1980), 111–50.
5. For a discussion of *Night Lodging*, see Paul G. Pickowicz, "Sinifying and Popularizing Foreign Culture: From Maxim Gorky's *The Lower Depths* to Huang Zuolin's *Ye dian*," *Modern Chinese Literature* 7, no. 2 (Fall 1993): 7–31.
6. "1949 ying tan jian shiji," *Qingqing dianying* (hereafter cited as *QQDY*) 18, no. 1 (January 15, 1950).
7. "1949 ying tan jian shiji."
8. See Zhongguo dianyingjia xiehui dianying shi yanjiubu, eds., *Zhongguo dianyingjia lie zhuan* (hereafter cited as *ZGDYJLZ*) (Beijing: Zhongguo dianying chubanshe, 1982), 2:9, for a discussion of Yu Ling's activities.
9. "Xiju dianying lianhe qilai," *QQDY* 17, no. 15 (August 1, 1949).
10. *QQDY* 18, no. 1 (January 15, 1950).
11. *QQDY* 17, no. 16 (August 15, 1949).
12. "Quan Shanghai dianying yuan diaocha biao," *QQDY* 17, no. 19 (October 1, 1949).
13. Shanghai Municipal Archives (hereafter cited as SMA), B172, 1–35.
14. See Zhiwei Xiao, "The Expulsion of Hollywood from China, 1949–1951," *Twentieth Century China* 30, no. 1 (November 2004): 64–81.
15. Xiao, "The Expulsion of Hollywood from China."
16. *QQDY* 18, no. 1 (January 15, 1950).
17. *QQDY* 18, no. 1 (January 15, 1950).
18. *QQDY* 18, no. 1 (January 15, 1950).
19. Lao She, *Huoche ji* (Shanghai: Shanghai zazhi gongsi, 1941), 101–95.
20. The screenplay is in Lao She, *Wo zhei yi beizi* (Beijing: Jiefang jun wenyi chubanshe, 2001), 120–99.
21. Lao She, *Wo zhei yi beizi*, 199–200.
22. *Zhongguo yishu yingpian bianmu* (hereafter cited as *ZGYYB*) (Beijing: Wenhua yishu chubanshe, 1981), 1:55–56.
23. SMA, B172, 1–35.
24. Lao She, *Wo zhei yi beizi*, 200.
25. For a post-Mao reevaluation of this important artist, see Wei Xiangtao, *Yi ke yingxing de chenfu: Shanguan Yunzhu zhuan* (Beijing: Zhongguo dianying chubanshe, 1986). Interviewees insist that Shangguan's Cultural Revolution suicide was related

to a pre–Cultural Revolution intimate relationship with Mao Zedong. Wei Xiangtao (110–13) describes a private meeting between Mao and Shangguan set up by Shanghai Mayor Chen Yi on January 10, 1956, at which Mao admitted to being a fan of the famous actress.

26. SMA, B172, 1–35.
27. SMA, B172, 1–35.
28. Li Yuangang, "Dui *Taiping chun* de ji dian yijian," *Wen hui bao*, June 24, 1950.
29. Mei Duo, "Ping *Taiping chun*," *Wen hui bao*, June 24, 1950.
30. Sang Hu, "Guanyu *Taiping chun*," *Dazhong dianying* 1, no. 2 (1950): 14.
31. Shi Hui, "Jiefang yinian lai de Shanghai ying ju jie," *QQDY* 18, no. 13 (July 1, 1950).
32. For an extended discussion of the meaning of the term *fanshen*, see William Hinton, *Fanshen: A Documentary of Revolution in a Chinese Village* (Berkeley: University of California Press, 1997).
33. SMA, B172, 1–35.
34. Allyn Rickett and Adele Rickett, *Prisoners of Liberation* (San Francisco: China Books, 1981).
35. Sigrid Schmalzer, "The People's Peking Man: Popular Paleoanthropology in Twentieth-Century China" (PhD diss., University of California, San Diego, 2004).
36. "Sixiang wenti," *Dazhong dianying* 1, no. 7 (1950).
37. "Sixiang wenti."
38. SMA, B172, 1–35.
39. Mao Dun, *Fushi* (Shanghai: Hua xia shudian, 1949). The screenplay is in Ke Ling, *Ke Ling dianyingjuben xuanji* (Beijing: Zhongguo dianying chubanshe, 1980), 125–210.
40. Shi Bangshu, "*Fushi* de 'pai hou pai' zhi," *Dazhong dianying* 1, no. 13 (1950).
41. See Chen Xihe, "*Jiejie meimei zhanqilai* de choubei jingguo," and Su Chun, "Shanghai minzhu fulian tongzhi tan *Jiejie meimei zhanqilai*," *Dazhong dianying*, no. 16 (February 1951): 26–29.
42. Gail Hershatter, *Dangerous Pleasures: Prostitution and Modernity in Twentieth-Century Shanghai* (Berkeley: University of California Press, 1997).
43. See Emily Honig, "Pride and Prejudice: Subei People in Contemporary Shanghai," in *Unofficial China: Popular Culture and Thought in the People's Republic*, ed. Perry Link, Richard Madsen, and Paul G. Pickowicz (Boulder, Colo.: Westview Press, 1989), 142.
44. SMA, B172, 1–35.
45. Yao Fangcao, "Li Linyun de chouhen," *Dazhong dianying*, no. 16 (February 1951): 30.
46. For a typical positive review, see Tian Yin, "Zhu fu xin sheng de jiemeimen," *Xin min bao*, February 17, 1951.
47. *QQDY* 18, no. 20 (December 15, 1950).
48. For a collection of critical articles on *The Life of Wu Xun*, see *Guanyu yingpian "Wu Xun zhuan" de pipan*, 2 vols. (Beijing: Zhongyang dianying ju, 1951).
49. For discussions of the Wu Xun campaign, see Jay Leyda, *Dianying: An Account of Films and the Film Audience in China* (Cambridge, Mass.: MIT Press, 1972), 197–98; and Paul Clark, *Chinese Cinema: Culture and Politics since 1949* (Cambridge, UK: Cambridge University Press, 1987), 45–50.
50. SMA, B172, 1–35.

51. See Jeremy Brown, "Staging Xiaojinzhuang: The City in the Countryside, 1974–1976," in *The Chinese Cultural Revolution as History*, ed. Joseph W. Esherick, Paul G. Pickowicz, and Andrew G. Walder (Stanford, Calif.: Stanford University Press, 2006), 153–84.

52. For a brief discussion of the criticisms of this film, see Clark, *Chinese Cinema*, 51.

53. Zhao Han, "Ping *Guan lianzhang*," *Dazhong dianying*, no. 20 (April 10, 1951): 24–25.

54. *ZGYYB*, 1:97.

55. Wei Shaochang, *Shi Hui tan yishu*, 536.

56. *ZGDYJLZ*, 2:76–77, a watered-down version of the article prepared by Ye Ming for Wei Shaochang's book on Shi Hui, offers a typical account of his death that avoids use of the term "suicide." Shi Hui's rightist designation was reversed in 1979. Official sources still fail to identify Shi Hui as the screenwriter of *Night Voyage on a Foggy Sea*. See *ZGYYB*, 1:284–85.

57. See *ZGDBK*, 24–25, 196; and *ZGDYJLZ*, 2:245.

7

Zheng Junli, Complicity, and the Cultural History of Socialist China, 1949–1976

The most powerful sequence in *East Palace, West Palace* (*Dong gong, xi gong*), Zhang Yuan's provocative 1996 underground film, involves a tense confrontation between a young transvestite and a Beijing policeman. Moments before receiving a vicious beating at the hands of this obvious symbol of Party and state power (an authority figure who is nevertheless terrified by his own conflicting emotions of attraction and revulsion), the transvestite calmly, almost seductively, says: "In this desperate situation, the thief falls in love with her executioner. The love she feels is a kind of perversion. . . . She can already feel the blade against her neck. At that very moment, she throws herself into his arms and gives herself completely to her executioner." "The convict," the transvestite insists, "loves her executioner. The thief loves her jail keeper. We love you. *We have no other choice.* I love you. Why don't you love me?"[1]

This episode offers useful ways of thinking about the fate of run-of-the-mill film director Zheng Junli and thousands of other cultural workers who enthusiastically engaged in creative accommodation with the Communist Party during the Mao years. Zheng did not survive all the way to 1976. He died in prison in 1969 at the age of 58.[2] The abuse he suffered amounted to a slow and painful execution. Zheng's situation was indeed desperate, and he had experienced desperation on more than one occasion. His status constantly shifted back and forth from privileged insider to distrusted outsider. The evidence suggests, however, that from beginning to end Zheng loved the Party and never questioned the legitimacy of his tormentors. Perhaps he felt he had no other choice. But he could not understand why the Party did not love him in return. Zheng believed he did everything the Party wanted him to do. Still, he failed to fathom why it did not acknowledge his devotion. Since, in

Zheng's view, the Party was always right, his many problems must have been the result of his own failings. It is impossible to know what Zheng thought privately about his awful plight. But his masochistic public utterances are quite clear: he deserved what he got every step of the way.

Zheng Junli, like many other little-known and similarly abused cultural workers, was posthumously "rehabilitated" in the late 1970s, long after both he and Mao were dead. The glowing, one-dimensional, and always uncritical accounts of his life that suddenly appeared were as distorted and ultimately as dishonest as the harsh attacks on his character circulated in the 1950s and 1960s. During the Mao years, the Party had on occasion cast Zheng as a disgusting bourgeois degenerate. In the post-Mao years, it preferred to think of him as a progressive and enlightened saint. He was neither.

The truth is that Zheng Junli, like most of the artists who populated the state-controlled cultural world of China after 1949, had a very interesting, though highly untidy, background. For example, in the late 1920s and early 1930s, Zheng faced the challenge of accommodating himself in political and cultural terms to Nationalist Party rule and the brave new world of the Nanjing decade. He did extremely well in those days, moving freely between the foreign-controlled international settlement in Shanghai and the national space controlled by the new government. In 1932, a time when the film world was expanding rapidly, Zheng made the transition from stage to screen by joining the famous Lianhua Film Studio. He was not a big star in the mid-1930s, but his contacts in the stage and film worlds were extensive.[3]

Zheng's immediate post-Mao biographers stress his connections to Xia Yan, Chen Baichen, and others loosely described as leftists. Standard accounts of his 1930s film career dwell exclusively on roles he played in such vaguely defined progressive films as *Big Road* (*Da lu*, d. Sun Yu, 1934).[4] They never mention that there was much in "progressive" films, including portrayals of gender and class relations, that was not progressive. Emphasizing the "white terror" environment that supposedly prevailed during the Nanjing decade, biographers fail to point out that Zheng and "progressives" like him had cordial relations with artists who, in the Mao and early post-Mao periods, were seen as pro-Nationalist and even reactionary. For instance, in 1935, the year after he acted in *Big Road*, Zheng played a prominent part in *The Spirit of the Nation* (*Guo feng*, d. Luo Mingyou), a film produced for Chiang Kai-shek's neo-conservative New Life Movement. In 1935 he also played an important role in *Filial Piety* (*Tian lun*), a Confucian-oriented film by Fei Mu that was also made expressly for the New Life Movement. Fei Mu's co-director, Luo Mingyou, expressed open support for the Nationalist regime (see chapter 2). Although these types of Republican-era contacts were left out of post-1949 sketches of people like Zheng, cultural bureaucrats and senior Party leaders never forgot.

Zheng Junli and many in his circle who later rose to prominence in Mao's China also adjusted remarkably well to the new circumstances created by the Japanese invasion in 1937. For instance, before and after the Japanese attack on Shanghai, Zheng and numerous other Nanjing-era actors formed theater troupes devoted to the Nationalist-led resistance cause. Zheng led the third brigade of the Shanghai Salvation Drama Troupe, which included the famous actor Zhao Dan, whose life would intertwine with Zheng's in many fascinating ways after 1949.[5]

With the Japanese takeover, Zheng Junli left Shanghai, arriving in Chongqing in 1938. There, he and many others with multifaceted backgrounds went to work for Chiang Kai-shek's Nationalist government. Although there was nothing unusual about this type of activity, early post-Mao biographers did not mention it, referring instead to vague "resistance" activities in the interior. In fact, Zheng functioned as the director of the government's Children's Theater Troupe (Haizi jutuan) and then in 1940–1942 worked on documentary film projects for the state-run China Film Studio, including one titled *Long Live the Nation* (*Minzu wan sui*, 1942).[6]

Zheng and many of his associates of the Nanjing decade and resistance war era, including those who had worked for the government, grew increasingly disillusioned with the Nationalists during the 1945–1949 civil war. There is no convincing evidence that Zheng was attracted to the Communist Party, but as a film director in Shanghai's privately owned Kunlun Film Studio, he made films that reflected poorly on the government. The best of these was the astonishingly popular melodrama titled *A Spring River Flows East* (*Yi jiang chun shui xiang dong liu*, 1947), discussed in detail in chapter 5. His treatment of the demoralization that was sweeping postwar China was bold because it was by no means clear when the film was released which side would emerge victorious in the civil war. His second film, *Crows and Sparrows* (*Wuya yu maque*, 1949), is frequently referred to as a classic progressive work, but in reality it was made at the tail end of the civil war when the outcome of the conflict was obvious to all, and when cultural workers who were disinclined to flee Shanghai with the Nationalists were already positioning themselves for favorable treatment in the postrevolutionary era.

Zheng Junli's civil war activities were later acclaimed by the Communist Party, but *A Spring River Flows East* posed problems for Party cultural bureaucrats. For one thing, the film's success complicated the notion that cultural production in the late Nationalist era was subjected to ruthless, state-sanctioned, white terror repression. If there was white terror, how could such a critical and destabilizing film be openly produced and widely distributed? And how could it win a Chiang Kai-shek Prize (Zhongzheng jiang) after its release in 1947?[7]

Zheng Junli was typical of the middle-level cultural personalities with complex and even politically embarrassing Republican-era backgrounds who remained in place after the Communist takeover and looked forward to working with the new regime. Zheng, like many others, was a survivor who grew up in a world that was adjusting to the shift from monarchy to republic, and who, as a young adult, adjusted in rapid succession to the advent of Nationalist rule in Nanjing, the golden age of foreign domination of Shanghai's international settlement, life in Chongqing during the resistance war, and the agonies of the civil war. Zheng was only thirty-seven years old in spring 1949 when Communist forces occupied Shanghai. He and most of his associates had every intention of accommodating themselves to and even playing a leading role in the new cultural order, even though they knew almost nothing about the Party, its policies, and its plans for China. They were eager to serve a powerful state and looked forward to surviving and even prospering by learning the new rules of the game and working to strengthen preexisting networks that bound like-minded friends. The Party, based for so many years in the rural sector, actively courted the support of urban cultural personalities whose skills and notoriety were badly needed during the transition. Messy personal histories could be ignored.

On June 18, 1949, the Shanghai Theater and Film Association was set up by the Party. An election was then held among stage and screen professionals to select its leaders. Zheng Junli was undoubtedly happy with the results. Of the top twenty-seven vote-getters, veteran Communist Party members Yu Ling and Xia Yan got 586 and 554 votes. The rest of the list consisted mainly of well-known non-Party personalities, including virtually all of Zheng's best Republican-era friends: writer and director Shen Fu with 547 votes, writer Chen Baichen with 459, actor Zhao Dan with 356, actress Wu Yin with 224, and actress Huang Zongying with 180. Zheng himself was fourteenth with 235 votes, finishing ahead of such gifted actors as Shi Hui, Zhang Fa, and Shi Yu.[8] Zheng was also pleased that his two civil war–era films continued to be shown. *A Spring River Flows East* was screened 137 times in Shanghai in 1949 and 135 times in 1950. *Crows and Sparrows*, which Zheng reworked in the months following the Communist takeover of Shanghai, was screened 577 times in Shanghai in 1950 to an audience of 287,000.[9] It was all very exhilarating and promising. Zheng and his old friends must have felt like insiders.

Zheng Junli continued to work for the privately run Kunlun Film Studio in the early years of transition. The new state allowed private sector cultural activity. His first screenwriting and directorial project was a low-budget political film titled *Husband and Wife* (*Women fu fu zhi jian*), based on a propaganda novel by Xiao Yemu. It became a common practice in socialist China to base films on theatrical scripts or works of fiction that had already been passed by censors. The production was initiated in late 1950 at about the time of China's entry into the Korean War, and the film was released in spring 1951.

Husband and Wife starred Zheng's old friend Zhao Dan, who had just finished playing the title role in Kunlun's much more expensive production of *The Life of Wu Xun* (*Wu Xun zhuan*, d. Sun Yu, 1951), a film about a legendary Qing dynasty education reformer who tried to help rural people. *Husband and Wife*, a far more modest work, concerns a Shanghai intellectual, Li Ke, who serves the revolution in rural Shandong during the civil war. He meets and marries an illiterate peasant woman, Zhang Ying, who has been cited as a labor hero. They have a son, and things go well until the couple is assigned to Shanghai after the revolution. He is thrilled to return to the urban environment; she feels awkward and out of place. In fact, issues of this sort were not uncommon in the early 1950s years of transition.

Various stresses and strains soon drive a wedge between the two revolutionaries. Often confrontational and shrill, she complains that he has changed. Enjoying the good life in the city, it seems he has forgotten the peasants. He responds that she is inflexible, mired in the ways of the past and unable to appreciate China's modern future. Naturally, the film ends on a happy note. Thanks to Party intervention, the two reconcile, with each admitting shortcomings and a need to make ideological progress. The film was fairly harmless. Movie fans liked it. In the first five months of 1951 it was screened in Shanghai 236 times to an audience of 106,500. *Platoon Commander Guan* (*Guan lianzhang*, d. Shi Hui, 1951), a somewhat similar, though more polished, film released at about the same time by Wenhua, another private film studio, was shown 347 times to an audience of 199,000.[10]

Initial reviews of *Husband and Wife*, which appeared in mid-April 1951, were encouraging. *Dazhong dianying* (*Popular Cinema*), the leading film fan magazine, ran a nicely illustrated and friendly report that contained no hint of problems. *Xin min bao*, a Shanghai news daily, published three reviews, all praising it.[11]

Then Zheng Junli got the first political shock of his post-1949 career when the apparently politically correct film was criticized harshly in the press beginning in late April and continuing into July. Zheng and Zhao Dan were quite upset. Hard-line critics like Zhao Han, writing first in *Dazhong dianying* and then in *Wen hui bao*, claimed that Zheng's portrait of Li Ke, the revolutionary urban intellectual, was much too sympathetic.[12] Li's petty bourgeois essence was inadequately denounced. The depiction of the peasant woman Zhang Ying was, by contrast, unflattering and harsh. The peasants shown in the first part of the film seemed excessively backward and buffoon-like. When the conflict between husband and wife is resolved, it seems to be mainly on his terms. Another critic worried about the negative impact the movie would have on the film audience in places that had only

Tensions related to the "mixed" marriage of an urban intellectual (*right*) and an illiterate rural woman (*left*) are explored in *Husband and Wife* (1951, d. Zheng Junli). China Film Archive

recently been taken over by the Communists. Party cadres—indeed the Party itself—looked bad in it. Li Ke, a Party official with eight years experience, seemed like a condescending and self-centered petty bourgeois element; Zhang Ying, a labor hero, looked ignorant and petty.[13] Zheng Junli, the critics implied, suffered from the same petty bourgeois afflictions that plagued the protagonist, Li Ke. How else to explain his glorification of the bourgeois urban intellectual?

The problem was not primarily the film, but very bad timing: the intellectual-bashing so characteristic of the Mao era had already begun. The main focus of attention was not Zheng's film but *The Life of Wu Xun*, the movie Kunlun had released just before *Husband and Wife*. Indeed, in the context of the Cold War, the Korean War, and the new movement to suppress counterrevolutionaries launched in early 1951, Mao Zedong personally intervened by writing a militant critique of *The Life of Wu Xun*. The result was the "first major campaign of criticism in literature and art after 1949."[14] Both *Husband and Wife* and Shi Hui's *Platoon Commander Guan* were ensnared in Mao's initial assault on bourgeois intellectuals. In case anyone failed to get the message, the May 5, 1951, *Wen hui bao* attack on *Husband and Wife* was published right beside an article titled "*The Life of Wu Xun*: A Film That Should Never Have Been Made." Zheng Junli and Republican-era cultural activists had to be wondering what the connection was between counterrevolutionaries who deserved to be shot and well-connected, loyal intellectuals who exhibited some bourgeois tendencies in the early transition to the new society.

Zheng scrambled to save himself. First, despite his initial unhappiness, he quickly surrendered unconditionally to the Party by writing a ritualistic and humiliating confession titled "With Deep Remorse I Must Reform Myself" (*Wo bixu tongqie gaizao ziji*).[15] Without such self-flagellating confessions, he and many others quickly learned, there was no hope of salvation. After writing his self-criticism, Zheng disappeared from sight for quite a while. In part, this was punishment for him and the others targeted. The Party used the 1951 campaign to frighten and terrorize friendly people like Zheng and to gain much tighter control of the cultural world.

In the post-Mao period sympathetic biographers continued to assert that Zheng had bourgeois tendencies, and that the "censure and criticism" he received in 1951 was appropriate.[16] Zheng was idle for the rest of 1951 and 1952, and then in 1953 he was allowed to remold his thinking by immersing himself in the lives of the "workers, peasants, and soldiers." He is credited with making two propaganda documentaries during this time of study and reflection: *The People's New Hangzhou* and a work about a factory in Shanghai titled *Glorious Creativity*.

Despite his sincere efforts to reform himself, Zheng was not allowed to direct another feature until 1954 when he made *The Rebels* (*Song Jingshi*), a story about an early-nineteenth-century peasant rebel at the state-run Shanghai Film Studio. The project was a test for Zheng and others recently suspected of bourgeois maladies. Zheng codirected the picture with Sun Yu, the director of the disastrous film about Wu Xun. Released in 1955, *The Rebels* was quite forgettable, but Zheng Junli clearly passed the test by mastering the Party's official position on the actual peasant rebellion led by Song Jingshi.[17]

Zheng kept a low profile, professionally speaking, for the next three years. He had learned his lesson, or so he thought, with the *Husband and Wife* debacle of 1951. He would keep his mouth shut. By contrast, the famous actor and director Shi Hui, who was criticized before and after the Wu Xun campaign, became active in the Hundred Flowers free speech movement of spring 1957. Shi Hui and other cultural workers criticized the Party (see chapter 6). Zheng's strategy of maintaining silence seemed at the time to pay big dividends. His outspoken colleagues were denounced, jailed, and driven to suicide during the brutal Anti-Rightist Campaign of mid-1957. Zheng and many like him did nothing to support these old friends from Republican days. Indeed, Zheng wanted more than ever to find a way into the Party. He was thrilled when he was included in a small group of Shanghai filmmakers visited by Mao Zedong on July 7, 1957.[18] Though it is not mentioned by his post-Mao biographers, Zheng's political life declined to a shameful low point in August 1957, at the height of the anti-rightist witch hunt, when he published an article that not only referred to the pernicious influence of rightists and the brilliance of Mao's ideas about literature and art, but also discredited the contributions of Republican-era filmmakers like himself. "We are opposed to going backward," he asserted, "we want to advance and then advance again" under the leadership of the Party.[19] Many respected non-Party cultural luminaries, including the famous writer Ba Jin, supported the Anti-Rightist Campaign. They no doubt felt they had no choice.

In 1958 Zheng Junli was rewarded for his loyalty. In fact, he was presented with the greatest opportunity of his life. He was told he might be able to direct the film that was going to be the visual centerpiece of the tenth anniversary celebration of the People's Republic scheduled for October 1959.

Mao Zedong's Great Leap Forward, a spectacular utopian effort to initiate a transition from socialism to communism, was now under way. With both Sino-Western and Sino-Soviet relations in serious disarray, and with China quite isolated in the international arena, the movement took on an extremely nationalistic, almost chauvinistic, tone. Mass mobilization was on an unprecedented scale and, by almost all accounts, a mood of euphoria swept through Chinese society in mid-1958. It appeared to those who were swept up by the Leap that China could shortly surpass the industrial West in virtually every field of endeavor. Zheng Junli was among those energized by all this.

The Chinese film industry, entirely state-owned by 1958, participated enthusiastically. In keeping with the fantastic production mania of the Leap, the industry was expected to produce "more, better, faster, and less costly" films. Output "leaped" from less than 50 titles in 1957 to more than 130 in 1958.[20] In spring and summer 1958, at the apogee of Leap zeal, ambitious plans were being made for film production in 1959, the eagerly awaited tenth anniversary of the People's Republic. Party leaders responsible for cultural affairs decided that the most important film project of 1959 was to be a lavish color movie on the Opium War titled *Lin Zexu* (*Lin Zexu*).

In some respects it was a strange choice. During the first decade of Party rule, filmmakers had generally avoided sensitive imperial-era historical topics. Indeed, the 1951 campaign against *The Life of Wu Xun*, a so-called "reactionary" film about Qing history, had sent chills through the film world.[21] Still, there was a strong sense that it was crucial to turn out a glossy film version of the story of Lin Zexu, a film consistent with Mao's view that anti-imperialist and anti-feudal activities associated with the Opium War marked the beginning of "modern Chinese history." Moreover, the old guard that dominated the film establishment, many of them based in Shanghai, was opposed to the idea that all film projects had to deal with life under socialism.[22]

The gala film was based on a draft titled *The Opium War* (*Yapian zhanzheng*), first published by Ye Yuan and others in late spring 1956. It was revised following the Anti-Rightist Campaign and republished in late 1957.[23] The movie was to be made at the Haiyan Film Studio in Shanghai, and director Zheng Junli, still very much a favorite of such major cultural bureaucrats as Xia Yan and Chen Baichen, was chosen to lead the project.[24] In fact, ever since the 1954–1955 *Song Jingshi* project that brought Zheng into the world of imperial-era peasant rebellions, he had expressed a strong desire to make historical films. In October 1956 Zheng had organized a small work group that explored ways to convert Ye Yuan's text into a usable screenplay.[25] After Zheng was chosen as director, Ye Yuan completed yet another revision of the screenplay in January 1958, renaming it *Lin Zexu*.[26] Caught up in the euphoria of the Leap, a jubilant Zheng Junli was finally offered membership in the Communist Party, one year after his dear friend Zhao Dan had been admitted.[27] Zheng's political problems of 1951 could now be forgotten, or so he thought.

Members of the cast recall that expectations were unusually high. Huang Shaofen, the famous cinematographer whose artistry dominated the Republican-era film world, was put in charge of filming. Zheng Junli's old friend Zhao Dan, who had starred in two ill-fated films (*The Life of Wu Xun* and *Husband and Wife*) was recruited to play the role of Lin Zexu.[28] Foreign actors virtually never appeared in Chinese films, but on this grand occasion Gerald Tannebaum, a leftist American expatriate residing in China, agreed to play the distasteful part of Lancelot Dent, a notorious British opium merchant, on the condition that he be allowed in the future to play the revolutionary role of Dr. Norman Bethune. A Czech resident of China played the part of Captain Charles Elliot, the British superintendent of trade.

Qin Yi, the actress assigned to the role of A Kuan sao, a fictionalized peasant activist, recalled that everyone associated with the production behaved in an ultra-leftist (*ji zuo*) manner. Tannebaum, "unusually obedient" during the shooting, rode about on a bicycle and cheerfully ate the ordinary Chinese food served in the staff canteen. Director Zheng constantly reminded the team of the political import of the film. He would not allow filming, much of it scheduled for autumn 1958 on location in Guangdong, Zheng's ancestral home, to get bogged down.[29]

The main political problem facing Zheng was the absolute need to find a way to make not merely a Marxist film about the Opium War, but a distinctively Maoist film. Despite his work on the Song Jingshi story, Zheng was not well suited to the task. Like many other privileged artists, Zheng wanted to prove his loyalty to Chairman Mao and the Leap to communism. But, even more than the Li Ke character in *Husband and Wife*, Zheng was a stereotypical urban intellectual with no practical revolutionary experience and no political links to Mao's rural-based revolution or to the Red Army. He had far more in common with the bourgeois cultural stars of Republican Shanghai than he had with the peasants and soldiers who had swept the Communist Party to power. Although elite cultural workers like Zheng were most comfortable in cosmopolitan cities like Shanghai, the politics of the Leap were profoundly anti-urban and anti-intellectual.

To qualify as a Maoist film, *Lin Zexu* would have to be militantly anti-imperialist and stridently nationalistic. Those who resisted British imperialism would have to be shown as not merely antiforeign, but motivated by modern ideas about devotion to nation. The Chinese people would have to be portrayed as broadly united in defiant struggle. But resistance to imperialism and defense of nation could not be described as rooted in a popular attachment to traditional Chinese culture. Class conflict would have to be accounted for, but it would be important to show that it was in the interest of all classes to rid China of imperialist aggressors. It would not be appropriate to suggest that the upper classes as a whole were the mortal enemies of the sacred national struggle. Instead, the film would have to say that only a small percentage of elites had betrayed the nation. Perhaps most important, a proper Maoist treatment of the Opium War would have to end on an optimistic note. It would have to show that China did not really lose the war. A politically acceptable ending would have to focus attention on the spontaneous uprisings of indignant Chinese masses. The unmistakable message of the Leap was that the broad masses, imbued with an unshakable will, could overcome even the most formidable obstacles and race ahead in the quest for revolutionary transformation.

Zheng Junli understood that the cultural politics of Maoism and the Leap imposed aesthetic standards as well. Although no one associated with the *Lin Zexu* project dared to mention the existence of *Eternity* (*Wan shi liu fang*, d. Bu Wancang, 1943), a politically tainted film about the Opium War made with Japanese approval during the Japanese occupation of Shanghai, artists like Zheng Junli, Huang Shaofen, and Zhao Dan had certainly seen the hopelessly discredited film and were keenly aware that among other things it had been criticized for blindly following the unsavory Hollywood "entertainment" model. But given the tensions in Sino-Soviet relations, it would not be advisable to make the sort of Soviet-type film that had been turned out in such large numbers in China in the mid-1950s. The new project was expected to have "national" aesthetic integrity, which meant that it would have to resonate with *respectable* Chinese cultural standards.[30]

The political stakes were extremely high, but Zheng and the others sincerely believed that they had fashioned a Maoist version of the Opium War. In sharp contrast to the discredited *Eternity*, *Lin Zexu* never loses its almost exclusive focus on the heroic activities of a saintly Commissioner Lin, and never explores Lin's personal life. The film makes extensive use of various conventions associated with traditional Chinese stagecraft to paint a picture of a Chinese universe inhabited by two types of people: proud patriots and detestable traitors. The first type will risk anything to defend the Chinese nation, while the second shamelessly sells out China to foreign aggressors for private gain. Furthermore, the heroes are all Hans (Lin Zexu; Guan Tianpei, who is the commander in chief of naval forces; and Deng Tingzhen, who is the governor-general of Guangdong and Guangxi), while the villains are all Manchus or Mongols (Muzhanga, who is an influential grand councilor and imperial favorite; Qishan, who is the governor-general of Zhili; and Yukun, who is the superintendent of customs in Guangzhou). When the heroes appear on screen, they stand upright and are flooded in bright light, while the villains, including the foreigners, are usually seen stooped over as they conspire in the shadows.

In structural terms, the film treats three specific episodes rather than the complex entirety of the conflict with the British. The first episode begins with the triumphant arrival of Lin Zexu in Guangzhou in March 1839 and ends with the seizure and destruction of foreign opium in June. This portion of the film treats the economic and moral dimensions of the opium trade, but the overriding focus is on the imposing personage of Commissioner Lin. In quick succession, Lin establishes his authority, gathers reliable intelligence, forges unshakable alliances with such Han patriots as Admiral Guan and Governor-General Deng, and discovers that a small group of corrupt and traitorous officials led by Superintendent Yukun is acting in concert with the odious foreign aggressors. Even more important, during an undercover tour, Lin comes into contact with honest and highly nationalistic local working people with whom he establishes warm relations. The masses are encouraged by the news that the emperor has sent a high commissioner to the region. Lin learns that the father of one of his new allies was shot by a "foreign devil" because he refused to unload opium. Arrogant opium merchants, by contrast, take delight in insulting China. "If this fellow Lin is Chinese," they laugh, "then he can be bribed!"

During this first portion of the film, Lin deals confidently with the foreign menace. Arrangements are made to improve coastal fortifications,

200   Chapter 7

The Emperor amuses himself with gadgets as war clouds gather in the south in *Lin Zexu* (1959, d. Zheng Junli). China Film Archive

isolate the foreign community, and confiscate all opium supplies. At one point, the British merchant Dent tries to escape to Macau with the help of corrupt local officials, but A Kuan sao, the militant young working woman, and others intercept his flight. Terrified of ordinary Chinese, Dent tries at first to intimidate them by saying: "I am a foreigner!" To the delight of the film audience, A Kuan sao, a woman, responds by slapping Dent across the face. The subsequent destruction of the confiscated opium in June 1839 is portrayed as a magnificent victory for the coalition of upright officials and patriotic masses led by Commissioner Lin.

The second part of the film covers the period from summer 1840, when British forces initiate the Opium War by attacking China, to September 1840, when the emperor removes Lin from his position. The political message of the film is quite clear at this juncture: despite the failure of traitorous local officials to lend their support, Chinese forces are able to defend Guangzhou. The credit is given to Lin, to the honest officials who surround him, and above all, to the popular masses who are led by a sagely charismatic fisherman named Kuang Dongshan. Lin is shown consulting Kuang and the others on a regular basis. An organic relationship of mutual respect guides their collective actions. Kuang tells Lin: "If you want to settle accounts with the foreign devils, rely on us!"

But when the British navy heads north in mid-summer 1840 to capture Dinghai in Zhejiang province, attack Tianjin, and threaten Beijing itself, the emperor panics. He blames Lin for causing all the problems, and replaces him with his rival, Qishan, who is sent to Guangzhou to do whatever is necessary to appease the British. The masses, now distraught about this sudden turn of events, come to pay their respects to Lin. Bowing before a disgraced Lin, they cry out "Tell us what to do!" Lin responds emotionally: "Never allow the foreign devils to fight their way into Guangzhou!"

The final segment of the film treats the period from autumn/winter 1840, when Lin is still on hand in Guangzhou trying in vain to assist Qishan, to spring 1841, when he leaves Guangzhou and the peasants stage an anti-British uprising at Sanyuanli. The emphasis is on how the Manchus, from the emperor in Beijing to Qishan in Guangzhou, betray Lin and the Han masses, who are prepared to sacrifice anything to defend China. Qishan asserts that the peace can be won if Elliot's various demands are met. These include dismantling coastal fortifications, disbanding local militia units, and reining in the patriotic masses. The film makes it clear, however, that by taking such actions the duplicitous Manchus are also defending against Han threats to Qing rule. Unfortunately for Qishan, however, the British continue to attack.

With the transfer of Lin Zexu to Zhejiang in April 1841, the patriotic masses are on their own. Led by Kuang Dongshan, local people gather in Sanyuanli village in May 1841. The assembled masses swear an oath to bring "death to the invaders," and rush out with primitive weapons in hand to take on a unit of British regulars. When driving rain makes it impossible for the British to use their rifles, the masses go on the offensive and force the frightened invaders to run away like cowards. The film ends with a shot of the proud and victorious throng massed on a lush hillside with weapons and battle standards held aloft.

In sharp contrast to the reception of Zheng Junli's *Husband and Wife* in 1951, *Lin Zexu* generated a veritable avalanche of enthusiasm in state-controlled news dailies in the weeks before and after its release on National Day 1959. Beginning with "Comments on a Splendid Movie," a glowing article by veteran cultural revolutionary Yang Hansheng, the popular press lavished praise on Zheng's epic film.[31] The fast-rising Maoist literary critic Li Xifan contributed a piece titled "An Heroic Historical Image That Is Authentic and Profound."[32] The old proletarian cultural romantic Zheng Boqi produced an open letter to director Zheng under the heading, "*Lin Zexu*: An Artistic Image That Excites the Heart."[33] Across the land, the headlines repeated the same triumphant message: "A grand and heroic historical poem,"[34] "An image of a resolute and steadfast patriot,"[35] "The first time we took up arms,"[36] "The outstanding film *Lin Zexu* is highly recommended,"[37] "A splendid poem that resists aggression,"[38] "The fury of the race,"[39] and

"The heroism of the race is not in decay."[40] *Lin Zexu* was portrayed as the most important film made in the short history of the People's Republic.

These glowing press accounts left the strong but highly misleading impression that Zheng Junli had succeeded in making a Maoist film at the peak of Leap euphoria in 1958. The problem was that by the time the film was released in late 1959 the political situation in China had shifted rather significantly. Mao and the Leap were now under attack at the highest levels of power. At the famous Lushan Conference in July 1959, Mao was the target of a stunning criticism by defense minister Peng Dehuai. The Leap had caused the worst famine in history. Tens of millions died in a holocaust that began unfolding in spring 1959. News of the disaster and of the political battles being waged at the summit of power was not carried in the media. But urban intellectuals heard rumors about starvation in the countryside, and mid-level Party members, including those like Zheng Junli who were engaged in cultural work, had access to information about high-level criticisms of Mao and the ultracommunist winds that had blown so hard in the first year of the Leap. Before 1959 ended, veteran cultural bureaucrats like Xia Yan were already mobilizing against the Maoist approach to art and culture.

The popular audience clearly enjoyed the movie. After all, it was beautifully filmed on location in an exotic coastal region, Zhao Dan's performance as Lin Zexu was unforgettable, it featured nonstop action that pitted valiant heroes against cruel villains, and it definitely aroused patriotic passions. But, in the transformed political environment of late 1959, influential senior intellectuals were starting to position themselves to the right of Mao, and pointing to problems with the film. For example, Professor Zhang Kaiyuan, a famous scholar of Qing history, published a commentary on the movie that conflicted with the universally upbeat tone of earlier popular reviews.[41]

Zhang stated that the film properly emphasized the main tendency of historical development, that is, the anti-imperialism of the Chinese people. But, he noted, the leading representatives of the masses, namely Kuang Dongshan, the young woman A Kuan sao, and others, were purely fictional. The invention of these characters posed problems about "the question of historical truth." Zhang conceded that it is permissible to invent characters who represent the "spirit of the times." But then he pointed to aspects of the film that he believed were simply inaccurate. The portrait of Yukun was excessively negative and betrayed the film's anti-Manchu bias. Furthermore, the film failed to show that Lin Zexu was open-minded about learning from advanced aspects of Western knowledge.

Even more interesting than Zhang's article was the seminar on *Lin Zexu* convened on September 2, 1959, by the Chinese Filmworkers Association.[42] The participants included such cultural notables as Yang Hansheng, the

Manchu novelist Lao She, leading playwrights Tian Han and Li Jianwu, film director Jin Shan, veteran actor Lan Ma, and film administrator Chen Huangmei. Here too, praise was heaped on Zheng Junli's film, but a number of intriguing questions were raised about the exaggerated quality of the production and its tendency to omit certain information and to take liberties with certain basic facts.

Lao She, an expert on Manchu culture, pointed to errors in the film's depiction of Qing rituals, official attire, modes of transportation, and greeting etiquette. He complained that the film should have been more explicit about the harmful effects of opium consumption. Historian Ding Mingnan expressed the view that the film seriously distorted the historical role of Yukun, the Manchu superintendent of customs. The historic Yukun was not so reactionary and had a good working relationship with Lin Zexu. Ding also pointed out that the dramatic meeting between Lin and Captain Elliot that is portrayed in the film never took place. According to Qing rituals, an official of Lin's rank would not have met face to face with the foreigner.

Qian Hong, another seminar participant, agreed that the characterization of Yukun "did not conform to the historical facts." Unfortunately, for the sake of simplicity, he noted, Yukun had been thrown into the broad, but stereotypical, category of corrupt officials. It is one thing to suggest that these people were ineffective in dealing with the British, but quite another to say that people like Yukun were actually colluding with foreigners. Since characters like Kuang Dongshan and A Kuan sao were invented, Qian quipped, it would have been better to invent some officials who were acting in concert with the British.

The famous playwright Tian Han (Zheng Junli's old mentor in the late 1920s) made perhaps the boldest statement about the Yukun issue. The filmmakers had sacrificed Yukun in order to bolster the image of Lin Zexu. Nevertheless, he observed, "Yukun stood on the side of the Chinese people at that time. We should give him a positive appraisal."

The most authoritative voice heard at the seminar was that of Yang Hansheng, who summed up the general feeling. The film was successful and moving, Yang said, not because all the historical facts were accurate, but because it made the powerful point that during the Opium War a broad spectrum of Chinese people took up arms for the first time to resist foreign imperialism. That theme was more important than the issue of class tensions in China, he seemed to say. It was important to see China united rather than divided in the face of a hostile external world. Thus, instead of offering a nuanced class analysis of Chinese society, the movie focused on the overwhelming mass of patriots and a small group of traitors. Yang regretted that Yukun was described as a negative figure. "The main problem in this movie," he concluded, "is that all the Manchu officials are described as corrupt and tending to compromise."

Furthermore, Yang argued, the need to represent a broad united front in the struggle with foreign enemies required that the masses be shown working in concert with others, rather than acting alone. "Though the struggle of the militia was spontaneous," Yang observed, "we can't say that it had no connection to the activities of Lin Zexu. Lin's policies were popular." Yang then made a comment that would haunt him in later years: "It was correct to describe the confluence of landlord and mass resistance."

Despite these reservations expressed in late 1959, the film continued to be shown throughout China as the massive famine deepened. But press coverage of *Lin Zexu* declined significantly in early 1960. The most interesting articles that appeared in 1960 were written by celebrities associated with the production. Ye Yuan, the author of the original screenplay, wrote several articles,[43] Zhao Dan contributed a couple of essays,[44] and Zheng Junli himself wrote two pieces, including one for *People's Daily* titled "Mao Zedong Thought Illuminates the Creative Path of Filmmaking."[45] Zheng was still trying hard to present himself as a loyal Maoist. All these works were written to defend the artistic choices made by the production team. Maoism and the Leap were in retreat by late 1959, but even anti-Maoists saw no reason why *Lin Zexu* should not continue to be promoted. Indeed, on September 22, 1959, the Film Bureau selected Zheng Junli to lead a film delegation to North Vietnam to participate in a ten-day Chinese film festival. *Lin Zexu* was the centerpiece of the Chinese titles screened in Hanoi.[46]

After *Lin Zexu* was finished, Zheng Junli immediately threw himself into yet another directorial effort associated with the tenth anniversary of the People's Republic. But this film, titled *Nie Er* (*Nie Er*), was a disappointment to both Maoists and anti-Maoists and received far less attention than the visually spectacular and highly emotional *Lin Zexu*. *Nie Er* was made because Xia Yan and other anti-Maoists at the top of the cultural bureaucracy saw Mao as a narrow nativist, while viewing themselves as cosmopolitans whose cultural activities in Shanghai in the 1930s were linked to sophisticated global currents. Consequently, they advocated the production of films that were based on important works of Republican-era fiction by Lu Xun, Mao Dun, Rou Shi, and others. By glorifying the 1930s, these cultural officials reinforced their own non-Mao lineage, legitimacy, and power in the rough-and-tumble cultural politics of China. Celebrating the 1930s also meant making biographical films that paid tribute to cultural heroes of the era, people like Lu Xun and Nie Er.

Born in 1912, Nie Er was a young composer who wrote popular Western-style songs for motion pictures.[47] In 1933 he joined the Communist Party and began work at the Lianhua studio where Zheng Junli was employed as an actor. Nie was connected to many well-known people, including Cai Chusheng and Tian Han. Among the tunes written by Nie was "March of the Volunteers," a revised version of which became the national anthem of

Commissioner Lin Zexu stands up to British opium dealers in *Lin Zexu* (1959, d. Zheng Junli). China Film Archive

the People's Republic. He drowned in 1935 at the age of twenty-three during a beach outing in Japan. Dead in youth and venerated by the Party, Nie was a perfect candidate for film biography.

But the movie was a flop. Jay Leyda, who was living and working in China at the time, wrote in his diary that *Lin Zexu* "had alerted me to some of the dilemmas of Chinese biographical films, but I was quite unprepared for the nonsense and uselessness" of *Nie Er*. People who knew Nie Er, Leyda wrote, "told me that the figure on screen was wholly fictional." The scenarists, the cinematographer, and Zheng Junli (who Leyda noted was "leaping from one anniversary film to another") knew Nie but had decided to "make a 'stronger' film story than could be made" from Nie's real life.[48] It must have been extremely painful for Zheng to produce a dishonest film about an old friend from Republican days, unless he had convinced himself that the real Nie Er and the one he had created on screen were one and the same. Zheng's embarrassment was lessened a bit when he learned that *Nie Er* had won a prize in 1959 for biographical films at the Karlovy Vary Film Festival in socialist Czechoslovakia.[49] The Czechs, no doubt, recognized and appreciated the Europeanized quality of Nie's life and work at a time when much of the Soviet bloc was disturbed by the chauvinism of Mao's Great Leap.

What Zheng Junli really wanted, though, was the chance to make the long-awaited film about culture icon Lu Xun. The eightieth anniversary of Lu Xun's birth created the perfect opportunity. What Zheng did not fully grasp, however, was that the towering figure of Lu Xun was not at all like the inconsequential Nie Er. Indeed, a film about Lu Xun would be even more difficult to make than a film about Lin Zexu. Various factions in the post-Leap Party were struggling for proprietary rights to Lu Xun's legacy. Maoists did not want a film that depicted Lu Xun as a member of the 1930s cosmopolitan camp. Anti-Maoists did not want to see a patently distorted, unrecognizable, Nie Er–like representation of Lu Xun.

While Zheng Junli waited patiently for a decision, his career began a long downward spiral. At first glance, it appears that Zheng was trying in 1961 to replicate, in political terms, what he did in 1951 after the *Husband and Wife* debacle. That is, he left Shanghai and his dangerously bourgeois cultural contacts and went out once again humbly to learn from the masses. This had become a standard strategy for cultural personalities with Zheng's sort of background. It amounted to a preemptive initiative, especially because Mao was in substantial retreat in 1961 and the cultural field was now more open and diverse than at any time since 1949–1950 and spring 1957.

On this occasion, Zheng's merge with the masses took the form of a dreadful film titled *Spring Comes to a Withered Tree* (*Kumu feng chun*, 1961). In this utterly predictable socialist realist tale, a poor peasant woman, Meizi, is afflicted with schistosomiasis. A young man named Dong, Meizi's childhood friend and now a tractor driver in socialist China, loves the rural woman and is determined to take care of her. Two bourgeois urban physicians arrive from Shanghai to work on the epidemic that haunts the region. But they have ideological problems. Progress is made only when the village head returns from a meeting with Mao (!) and reports that the Chairman wants people to work as a collective. Then, as if by magic, a cure is found, Meizi returns to full health, she marries the tractor driver, and she gives birth to twins. Dong is so excited he resolves to teach Meizi how to drive a tractor. No one, not even the Czechs, liked this movie. It is hard to imagine that Zheng was proud of the film. But years earlier he had learned that it was impossible to err in a direction too far to the left. The Party seemed to forgive leftist errors, but it never forgave rightist errors.

This time, however, Zheng's effort to learn from the masses did him little good. In spring 1962, after multiple stops and starts, the decision was made to kill the Lu Xun film. At a time when the new Socialist Education Movement was under way, there was simply no way to tell the Lu Xun story without deeply offending one power faction or another. Zheng must have been bitterly disappointed. This would have been the most important Chinese film since *Lin Zexu*. But at another level he was probably relieved. It would have been an impossible task, closely scrutinized and dissected by both sympathizers and political opportunists. Naturally, Zhao Dan was scheduled to play the lead role. Cultural insiders knew the project was dead when Zhao appeared for dinner at the Peace Hotel in Shanghai without the bushy Lu Xun–type moustache he had been sporting for several months.[50]

For more than two years after the filming of *Spring Comes to a Withered Tree*, Zheng Junli was denied filmmaking opportunities. He was only forty-nine years old in mid-1961, hardly a candidate for retirement. Life in socialist China had taught Zheng not to fall into a passive mode in times of change. Thus he made yet another desperate attempt, his final one, to prove his loyalty to Mao and the Party, and to secure his position on the "inside."

At a dance party in Shanghai in summer 1963, Zhou Enlai told Zheng and screenwriter Wang Lian that he wanted them to make a film based on a North Korean play titled *Red Propagandist* (*Hongse xuanchuan yuan*). The team dropped everything and rushed to Beijing, where it met Zhou twice more before traveling to North Korea for two months in September 1963. The screenplay was hurried to completion in early 1964, whereupon Zheng returned to North Korea to film exterior scenes. The picture was ready for release at the end of 1964.[51]

The movie, titled *Li Shanzi* (*Li Shanzi*), is set in North Korea and involves the never-ending activities of a woman propaganda activist named Li Shanzi to spread the word of Kim Il Song in her rural community. Initially, no one in the village is enthusiastic about collective work, and everyone, including the local leaders, is ideologically backward. Morale is low and people are suspicious. But Li's determined propaganda work is highly effective, and the whole community unites and happily sprints ahead under the banner of socialism. Kim Il Song is so pleased he grants Li a personal audience.

In late 1964 word came down that the film had problems. Screenwriter Wang Lian was urged to revise his work. Wang was puzzled, since the film had already been completed. A document titled "Criticisms by Leading Comrades at the State Center and Relevant Units Concerning the Film *Li Shanzi*" was circulated, and Zheng and the others were summoned to a series of meetings convened in Beijing starting in December 1964. Bombarded by criticisms, Zheng was advised by Zhou Enlai to "reform his world view" and pay a call on Mao's wife Jiang Qing (now active in a movement to "reform" the theater world) to seek her advice. The meeting with Jiang Qing did not go well. She told Zheng that he "was not standing alongside the proletariat" and that his film gave her "the shivers."

In July 1965 Zhou Enlai presided over one final gathering devoted to *Li Shanzi*. The film was not going to be released. Zhou asked Zheng how he was sleeping. Zheng responded that he was taking sleeping pills. According to a witness, Zhou laughed and said, "You should think hard about these questions."[52] Screenwriter Wang Lian wondered why Zheng had been singled out time and again over the years. Zheng was abandoned by Zhou Enlai, and his film career was finished, though the worst was yet to come.

Unfortunately for Zheng Junli and many like him, their agitprop work of the mid-1960s was unappreciated. Worse still, new and even deadlier political winds were beginning to swirl. One suspects, however, that Zheng still had hopes. Given that the thrust of rebel politics during the early stages of the Cultural Revolution was decidedly Maoist and that Zheng had distorted the historical record in 1958 in order to fashion a Maoist interpretation of the Opium War, Zheng might have thought that he and his greatest post-1949 film achievement were beyond criticism from the left, that he would escape the onslaught of the Red Guards just as he had avoided the cruelties of the Anti-Rightist Campaign in 1957. After all, it was only with the 1951 film *Husband and Wife* that he had erred to the right. In every other case he had been careful to stand to the left. He still loved the Party and continued to hope that the Party would at long last express its unconditional love for him. He was totally unprepared for the inhumanities that followed.

Red Guard publications attacked every film Zheng Junli made before and after 1949, including the unbearably propagandistic *Li Shanzi*. *Husband and Wife* was no good. *Nie Er* was no good. *Spring Comes to a Withered Tree* was no good. Indeed, Zheng was said to be part of a bourgeois plot led by Xia Yan, Tian Han, Yang Hansheng, and others who had sneaked into the Party to "oppose the formation of a film industry that served the workers, peasants and soldiers."[53] Not surprisingly, much was made suddenly of Zheng's extensive contacts in the 1930s with film personalities connected to the Nationalist Party and of his work for the Nationalist government in Chongqing during World War II.

But the harshest attacks on Zheng were reserved for his most celebrated film, *Lin Zexu*. The 1959 seminar on *Lin Zexu* had revealed that some leading intellectuals thought the movie was excessively leftist. But the Red Guards who waged war on Chinese culture concluded that it was a shameless right-wing project. It was labeled a "poisonous weed" (*du cao*) and a "black model" (*hei yangban*), and banned.[54] The problem was that the movie glorified not just one but a number of "feudal" officials. Even the Daoguang emperor was given credit at the outset of the film for pursuing an aggressive anti-British policy. From the Red Guard point of view (a perspective that focused almost entirely on domestic political battles, not the conflicts that pitted China against foreign enemies), the class struggle that raged in the 1840s was totally ignored in the film. Even its treatment of the popular uprising against the British was unacceptable. The masses not only take orders from Lin Zexu, a feudal official, but they express an almost slavish admiration for him. After Lin is removed from his post, the masses bow before him and beg him to issue directives. To make matters worse, before the masses attack the British at Sanyuanli, they are viewed in a Buddhist temple praying: "Lord Buddha, help us destroy the enemy!" Zheng Junli was guilty of defaming the patriotic masses.

Red Guard publications shrilly denounced Zheng and his film as reactionary to the core. A broadside prepared by Cultural Revolution insurgents in the Shanghai film world stated that it was a disgrace that Zheng and his "poisonous weed" *Lin Zexu* had been sent to North Vietnam in 1959.[55] Vicious biographical sketches of Zheng highlighted his appearances as an actor in many "right-wing" films of the mid-1930s and his cultural work for the Nationalist Party and government in the interior during the resistance war.[56] Zheng was destroyed by Chairman Mao's rebels. He was arrested in 1967 and died in prison on April 23, 1969, at the age of fifty-eight.[57]

In the late 1970s, a decade after Zheng's death, Chinese cultural production began to head in new directions. But if we focus on 1949 to 1976, and take note of the Party-state's nearly monopolistic control of the cultural sphere, the problem of the relationship between artists and the state remains the key issue. Denied research access to China until the late 1970s, scholars of Chinese culture working outside China tended to emphasize trends in policy formation, state-directed campaigns, and culture struggles at the center of state and Party power. More recently, scholars have used newly available biographical sources to approach the relationship between artists and the state in different ways. By looking in detail at a rank-and-file artist like Zheng Junli, we are able to learn how socialist cultural production was experienced by artists themselves. This type of research is by definition artist-centered and thus helps put a human face on an important aspect of state-society relations after 1949.

But highly personalized narratives of this sort inevitably move into sensitive areas. The Communist Party is still in power in China, and despite leaks, information about former state employees is still closely guarded. Scholars are thus hampered in their ability to address questions about the Party's relationship with the thousands of art and culture workers in its employ during the Mao era. One tries to imagine what sort of research on interactions between artists and the Party from 1949 to 1976 would emerge if the Communist Party lost power. Investigations of this sort were launched in places like East Germany, Hungary, and Czechoslovakia following the demise of the ruling Communist Party. It is possible that a new generation of scholars working in a postcommunist political environment and making research use of classified materials and oral histories would compare China after 1949 to China during Nationalist Party rule or to China under the Japanese occupation of 1937–1945. If one thinks of China as having been under the control of an unaccountable Communist Party after 1949, then the issue of "creative accommodation" arises. Who made accommodations with the Party? Who did not? To what extent were there degrees of accommodation? Why did artists choose to accommodate themselves to Party-state rule? Are accommodation and complicity the same thing? Is it going too far to speak of collaboration? Was resistance an option? Who resisted? Who stood by or benefited when colleagues were scapegoated? Who informed on colleagues or assisted in persecutions? How did artists maneuver to make themselves, their families and their friends in the arts less vulnerable politically? How did survival strategies evolve? What privileges and protections were afforded artists who were successful in joining the Communist Party? How did artists prove their loyalty? Did the Party love people like Zheng Junli who engaged in creative accommodation? Did such artists really love the Communist Party? Did they have any choice?

NOTES

An earlier version of this chapter appeared as "Zheng Junli, Complicity, and the Cultural History of Socialist China, 1949–1976," *China Quarterly* 188 (2006), 1048–69.

1. Italics added. For a discussion of power relations in Zhang's film, see Paul G. Pickowicz, "Filme und die Legitimation des Staates im Heutigen China," in *Peking, Shanghai, Shenzhen: Stadte des 21. Jahrhunderts*, ed. Kai Vockler and Dirk Luckows (Frankfurt: Campus Verlag GmbH, 2000), 402–11.
2. "Zheng Junli shengping yu nianbiao" (hereafter cited as ZJLSP), *Dangdai dianying*, no. 125 (2005): 63.
3. Zheng's visibility in the 1930s is captured in articles that appeared in the popular film press: Zheng Junli, "Ying mi yu 'mingxing' zhidu," *Ying mi zhoubao* 1, no. 1 (1934): 12; and Liu Baoxing, "Mingxing beiwanglu," *Dianying hua bao*, no. 39 (March 1, 1937).
4. Zhongguo dianyingjia xiehui dianying shi yanjiubu, eds., *Zhongguo dianyingjia lie zhuan* (hereafter cited as ZDLZ) (Beijing: Zhongguo dianying chubanshe, 1982), 2:287–90.
5. ZJLSP, 63.
6. *ZDLZ*, 2:290–91.
7. See ZJLSP, 63, and *Dianying xiju sishi nian liang tiao luxian douzheng jishi* (hereafter cited as *DYXJ*) (Shanghai: Shanghai hongqi dianying zhipianchang hongqi geming zaofan bingtuan, Shanghai tushuguan hongse geming zaofan pai, 1967), 82.
8. *Qingqing dianying* 17, no. 15 (August 1, 1949).
9. Shanghai shi dang'anguan (hereafter cited as SMA), B-172, 1–35.
10. See SMA, B-172, 35 for the screening statistics.
11. "*Fu fu zhi jian* de xiao fengbao," *Dazhong dianying*, no. 20 (April 10, 1951): 10–14; "Ping *Women fu fu zhi jian*," *Xin min bao*, April 21, 1951; Wang Qian, "*Fu fu zhi jian* guan hou," *Xin min bao*, April 24, 1951; Ying Wei, *Women fu fu zhi jian* jiao ren ruhe gao hao fu fu guanxi," *Xin min bao*, April 25, 1951.
12. Zhao Han, "Ping *Women fu fu zhi jian*," *Dazhong dianying*, no. 21 (April 25, 1951), reprinted with minor changes in *Wen hui bao*, May 15, 1951.

13. Fang Renshou, "Fandui waiqu geming ganbu," *Dazhong dianying*, no. 24 (July 5, 1951): 26-27.
14. Paul Clark, *Chinese Cinema: Culture and Politics since 1949* (Cambridge, UK: Cambridge University Press, 1987), 45-50.
15. *ZDLZ*, vol. 2.
16. *ZDLZ*, 2:293.
17. See Yingjin Zhang and Zhiwei Xiao, *Encyclopedia of Chinese Film* (London: Routledge, 1998), 393.
18. Chen Jinliang and Zou Jianwen, eds., *Bai nian Zhongguo dianying jing xuan* (Beijing: Zhongguo shehui kexue chubanshe, 2005), vol. 2, part 1, 357.
19. Zheng Junli, "Tan Zhongguo dianying de chuantong," *Zhongguo dianying*, no. 8 (1957): 13-15.
20. *Zhongguo yishu yingpian bianmu* (Beijing: Wenhua yishu chubanshe, 1981), 1:253-447.
21. Zhiwei Xiao, "Chinese Cinema," in Zhang and Xiao, *Encyclopedia of Chinese Film*, 23-24.
22. *DYXJ*, 82.
23. *Lin Zexu: cong juben dao yingpian* (Beijing: Zhongguo dianying chubanshe, 1979), 407.
24. *ZDLZ*, 2:293-94.
25. Zheng Junli, *Hua waiyin* (Beijing: Zhongguo dianying chubanshe, 1979), 64.
26. Ye Yuan's revised text is in *Lin Zexu*, 1-59. Zheng Junli's shooting script is in *Lin Zexu*, 61-204.
27. Shu Xiaoming, *Zhongguo dianying yishu shi jiaocheng* (Beijing: Zhongguo dianying chubanshe, 1996), 73.
28. See Zhao Dan, *Yinmu xingxiang chuangzao* (Beijing: Zhongguo dianying chubanshe, 1980), 67-104, for one of Zhao's 1960 commentaries on the project.
29. Qin Yi, "Pao long tao," *Bi hui wen cong*, no. 4, 121-26.
30. Lin Niantong, *Zhongguo dianying meixue* (Taibei: Yunchen wenhua, 1991), 67-112.
31. Yang Hansheng, "Tan youxiu yingpian *Lin Zexu*," *Renmin ribao*, September 17, 1959.
32. Li Xifan, "Zhenshi shenke de lishi yingxiong xingxiang," *Dazhong dianying*, no. 18 (1959).
33. Zheng Boqi, "*Lin Zexu*: jidong renxin de yishu xingxiang," *Shaanxi ribao*, October 14, 1959.
34. *Fujian ribao*, September 25, 1959.
35. *Shanxi ribao*, September 24, 1959.
36. *Gongren ribao*, September 24, 1959.
37. *Liaoning ribao*, September 27, 1959.
38. *Xinwen ribao*, September 23, 1959.
39. *Nanchang ribao*, September 27, 1959.
40. *Guangzhou ribao*, September 27, 1959.
41. Zhang Kaiyuan, "Ao shuanghua yan Lingnan zhi," *Renmin ribao*, November 15, 1959.
42. "*Lin Zexu* zuotan hui," *Dianying yishu*, no. 10 (1959), reprinted in *Lin Zexu*, 332-56.

43. Ye Yuan, "Lue tan ruhe biaoxian lishi renwu de juxian xing," *Shanghai dianying*, no. 4; Ye Yuan, "Lin Zexu yu Ping ying tuan de guanxi," *Wen hui bao*, April 29, 1961.

44. Zhao Dan, "Yanzhe kangzhuang dadao yongwang zhi qian," *Beijing ribao*, January 24, 1960; Zhao Dan, "Lin Zexu xingxiang de chuangzao," *Dianying yishu*, no. 5 (1961).

45. Zheng Junli, "Mao Zedong sixiang zhaoliangle chuangzuo de daolu," *Renmin ribao*, March 22, 1960.

46. *DYXJ*, 84.

47. See Richard Kraus, *Pianos and Politics in China: Middle-Class Ambitions and the Struggle over Western Music* (Oxford, UK: Oxford University Press, 1989) for a discussion of Nie Er and Xian Xinghai, another popular leftist musician.

48. Jay Leyda, *Dianying: An Account of Films and the Film Audience in China* (Cambridge, Mass.: MIT Press, 1972), 308.

49. ZJLSP, 63.

50. Leyda, *Dianying*, 309.

51. See Wang Lian, "Zheng Junli de yi zuo: *Li Shanzi*," *Dazhong dianying*, no. 9 (1996): 40.

52. Wang, "Zheng Junli de yi zuo: *Li Shanzi*," 40.

53. *DYXJ*, 130–31.

54. *DYXJ*, 131.

55. *DYXJ*, 84.

56. *DYXJ*, 130–31.

57. ZDLZ, 2:297.

8

The Limits of Cultural Thaw: Chinese Cinema in the Early 1960s

Chinese society was on the verge of complete physical and emotional exhaustion in the early 1960s.[1] The political honeymoon of the early 1950s was followed in rapid succession by the forced collectivization of agriculture, the terror of a vindictive Anti-Rightist Campaign against intellectuals, and the human catastrophe of the Great Leap Forward. The "communist winds" that had swept the land in the late 1950s led to the collapse of the economy, widespread starvation in the rural areas, and hunger and malnutrition in the cities. Reports of cannibalism surfaced, as they had during the great famine of 1943. To make matters worse, the Sino-Soviet split left China without allies for the first time in its postrevolutionary history. Not only was Soviet aid and advice withheld, but China's relations with India, Japan, and the West were exceedingly cool.

Although the economic and political situation remained grim throughout the early 1960s, an unusually important series of policy debates had been concluded by 1961, debates that resulted in both a rejection of the developmental strategy that guided the Great Leap Forward and a temporary political defeat for Mao Zedong. Among many other things, Maoist mass mobilization and ideological campaigns were terminated, and greater respect was shown for professional expertise. This desperate recovery program was short-lived. By 1966 Mao and his supporters launched the Cultural Revolution, and the Chinese people became the victims of political terror and economic stagnation for another decade.

The rejection of the Great Leap Forward was reflected in the motion picture industry in a variety of interesting ways during the 1960–1965 thaw. First, political control over the industry was loosened, and production was no longer discussed in military terms. Film workers were no longer required to experience "real life" by participating in farm or factory labor, unrealistic production quotas were no longer assigned to film studios, and pictures no longer had to be produced at a breakneck pace. In effect, filmmakers were given more artistic freedom by a government and Party that were anxious to regain the support of intellectuals. Economic hardship required the slashing of studio budgets, and production of motion pictures plummeted from a record high of 132 in 1958 at the height of the Great Leap to a mere 29 in the dismal months of 1961.[2] Yet, despite the drastic cutback, many of the most memorable films of the entire postrevolutionary Mao era were made in the six years following the Great Leap debacle. These works have not received the critical attention they deserve for the simple reason that they were condemned as "poisonous weeds" and withdrawn from circulation in 1966 by the architects of the Cultural Revolution. Not until the late 1970s were the films of the early 1960s reassessed and made available for viewing once again.[3]

The theoretical foundation of early 1960s filmmaking was set forth by Vice Minister of Culture Xia Yan in a remarkable article titled "Raise Our Country's Film Art to a New Level," which appeared in the 1961 National Day issue of *Hongqi*.[4] In the early 1930s Xia Yan was one of the first Communists to become active in the glittering film world of Shanghai. After the revolution he emerged as one of the most powerful leaders of the new state-owned film industry. His October 1961 article was a carefully worded but unmistakable attack on Great Leap Forward film policy. He complained that the artistic quality of most films was unacceptably low, the range of topics treated in motion pictures was woefully inadequate, and the cinematic forms employed were insufficiently diverse. The Great Leap Forward was nowhere mentioned, but he pointed out that films should not be produced in a hasty, assembly-line fashion; that it is unnecessary for every film to treat "grave topics" of immediate economic and political concern; and that deeply rooted artistic traditions should not be indiscriminately abandoned in the rush to carry out the transition to socialism in the arts. Furthermore, he noted that sudden and sporadic bursts of energy and sheer "enthusiasm" cannot make up for the absence of professional expertise and a detailed knowledge of the complexities of social life in the development of a viable film industry. The characters portrayed in films should not be one-dimensional abstractions whose only function is to convey the "spirit of the times."

Xia's discussion of Marxist aesthetic theory stressed the complexity of the relationship between the economic base and cultural superstructure of society and the special characteristics of the "laws of art." Because artistic work is a "product of the spirit," he observed, it cannot be regarded in the same way as other political work carried on by the Party. The transformation of the cultural superstructure of society, he added, is necessarily more gradual than the transformation of the economic base. Even more startling was Xia's implicit demand for less Party control and leadership in the film world. Quoting Lenin, not Mao, he asserted, "Indisputably, literary work has the least room for evenness, uniformity, and submission of the minority to the majority." "The likings and interests of the individual," he explained, "cannot be forced or regulated by authoritative orders."

It would be wrong to assume that Xia Yan's ideas were a departure from Marxist theory. On the contrary, he was acutely aware that the Western tradition of Marxist literary thought is highly ambiguous, and thus it can be interpreted in a variety of ways. Although he cited such non-Marxist figures as Aristotle, Hegel, Tolstoy, and the Song dynasty critic Yan Yu, he based his argument squarely upon writings by Marx, Engels, and Lenin that tend, in fact, to support his position. Mao was quoted, but only when he appeared to agree with Xia. What was being rejected was the Maoist or Great Leap interpretation of Marxist aesthetic theory.

It is significant that Xia called for more independence and artistic freedom for filmmakers, but by no means was he advocating an end to Party control or questioning the general assumption that filmmaking should be integrated into the machine of state. Neither did he retreat from the position that the function of art in socialist society is to assist in the shaping of popular consciousness. He simply asserted that such socialization work should not be done crudely.

Xia's article was received with interest because he stressed aesthetics. He agreed that when Mao delivered his "Yan'an Talks" in 1942, the central problems were the content of art and the political outlook of artists. But by 1961, he boldly proclaimed, Chinese intellectuals had been "completely" transformed, ideologically speaking. Thus, he implied, it was no longer necessary to be suspicious of them. The central issue facing artists of the early 1960s was the problem of enhancing the "quality of art," a task that demanded a high degree of professional competence. It is necessary for a film to be subtle and even "delicate," if its ideological message is to take root.

Xia's essay was provocative because it sought to liberate Chinese filmmaking from the rigidities of the Maoist approach by alluding to the rather ambiguous manner in which Marxist theorists of the pre-Stalin era treated the relationship between art and politics. But Xia himself made no attempt to speak with greater clarity on the subject. Filmmakers welcomed the retreat from Maoism signaled by Xia's authoritative article, but they were frustrated by his unwillingness to define in detail the limits of Party control.

Although Xia Yan spent more than eight years in prison during the Cultural Revolution for his ideological indiscretions, he was no liberal.[5] In no sense did he advocate an independent or critical cinema of the sort that flourished in prerevolutionary times. But in the early 1960s he received the enthusiastic support of many in the film world whose notions of artistic freedom were significantly broader than his own. Like Xia, they were disenchanted with Maoism and wanted to see Chinese filmmaking begin to move in a new direction. Their endorsement of Xia's views did not mean they had illusions about what was possible. All filmmakers were painfully aware of the hunger and despair that stalked the land. They also knew there was no chance they would be allowed by Xia Yan to treat these subjects in a candid fashion in their screenplays and films. Still, there was a sense of hope.

Two generations of artists dominated the major film studios in Shanghai, Beijing, and Changchun in the early 1960s. One was composed of veteran directors and screenwriters like Sun Yu (a graduate of the University of Wisconsin), Zhang Junxiang (who studied under George Pierce Baker at Yale), Xia Yan, and others who had contributed to the emergence of a powerful tradition of critical Chinese cinema during the 1930s and 1940s. Another group was made up of newcomers like Xie Jin, Ling Zifeng, and Xie Tieli, who were the brightest directors to rise to the fore in postrevolutionary days.

These artists responded to the thaw in a number of interesting and somewhat unanticipated ways. Some were exceedingly cautious, perhaps because they could not quite believe the door had been opened. Others used the opportunity to explore forgotten episodes in the dynastic history of China. The most daring directors decided to risk their careers by seeking to locate the outer limits of Xia Yan's vague formulations on the nature of Party control. Their works do not question the notion that motion pictures should serve as vehicles for socializing the masses, but they do reveal a surprising diversity of views on the question of precisely what sort of messages ought to be communicated.

The films of the early 1960s disclose more about the political and social thought of leading screenwriters and directors than they do about the life and thought of the vast film audience for whom they were intended. Yet, it is important to ask what the film audience thought about these works. Many of these movies were quite popular. Today most of these works seem hopelessly formulaic, structurally immature, and artistically weak. But when they are analyzed in the dreadful context of the years following the tragic Great Leap Forward, the warm response of the film audience becomes considerably more comprehensible. Almost none of these films is a great work of art, but together they served to ease the pain of living in China in the hungry days of the early 1960s.

IMPERIAL CHINA PROJECTED ON SOCIALIST SCREENS

Since the formation of the People's Republic in 1949, one of the most curious barometers of political change has been the willingness of the Communist Party to permit the production of films on prerevolutionary history and culture. Enormously popular films like *The Romance of Liang Shanbo and Zhu Yingtai* (*Liang Shanbo yu Zhu Yingtai*, d. Sang Hu and Huang Sha, 1954) and *Fifteen Strings of Cash* (*Shiwu guan*, d. Tao Jin, 1956) were tolerated in the mid-1950s. But imperial-era history and culture were considered to be politically subversive by leaders who were anxious to hasten the birth of a new socialist culture. Consequently, less than 10 percent of the motion pictures made in 1958, at the height of Great Leap frenzy, treated events that occurred during the more than two thousand years from the birth of Confucius to the demise of the imperial system in 1911. By contrast, more than 75 percent of the films made in 1958 focused on the eight-year-old socialist era, and most of these were docudramas (*yishuxing jilupian*) that heralded the Great Leap itself.[6]

The decision to produce more movies about the history and culture of imperial China was one of the most popular made by Chinese filmmakers in the bleak post-Leap era. The new trend gained momentum slowly, but it constituted a major concession to the tastes of a spiritually fatigued film audience. By 1962 more than 30 percent of the films produced, including a few that qualify as minor classics, were set in imperial times.[7]

The uniqueness of these works is suggested by the fierce ideological campaign launched against them during the Cultural Revolution. For nearly a decade following the thaw of the early 1960s, motion pictures on imperial-era themes were entirely eliminated from production schedules. Mao Zedong's Red Guards charged that the films glorified emperors, princes, generals, ministers, scholars, and beauties. Only six years after it had published Xia Yan's provocative article on problems in the film industry, *Hongqi* carried a bellicose editorial that accused Xia Yan of using traditional tales to "serve a counter-revolutionary restoration of capitalism."[8]

These constantly shifting political winds of the 1960s explain both the spectacular popularity and subsequent vilification of *Third Sister Liu* (*Liu Sanjie*, d. Su Li, 1962). An exceedingly light-hearted and cleverly written musical comedy, *Third Sister Liu* won three awards at the second annual "Hundred Flowers" film gala held in Shanghai in 1963. Political celebrities like Zhou Enlai, Guo Moruo, and Chen Yi mingled with the film stars at the ceremony.[9] Three years later, *Third Sister Liu* was taken out of circulation and condemned as a "poisonous weed."

The film is based on the legend of Third Sister Liu, the popular "Goddess of Song" who, according to countless folktales told by storytellers of the Zhuang ethnic minority, lived in the area of present-day Guilin during the Tang dynasty (618–907). Pixie-like in appearance, Third Sister Liu is a high-spirited and fearless singer of improvised mountain folk tunes that expose the immoral practices of the local ruling elite in a highly humorous fashion. Driven from place to place by local despots, she is taken in by peasants who inhabit a village in the breathtakingly beautiful environs of the Li

River. Before long she becomes the spiritual leader of a group of peasants that is resisting the attempt of Mou Huairen, a local gentry figure, to seize control of a once barren hill that has been converted by the local people into a bountiful tea-producing area. When addressed by her adversaries, Liu prefers to respond by spinning out hilarious but devastatingly critical songs. Concerned that Liu will unite local people as she has elsewhere, Mou devises a scheme that he hopes will rid him of this angelic menace. A singing competition is organized which pits Liu against three leading scholars who plan to make use of their vast learning to bombard her with impossibly difficult musical riddles. If she loses, she agrees to stop singing, but if she wins, the people get to keep the mountain. Needless to say, she humiliates the scholars, whereupon Mou decides he must put an end to Liu's infernal singing by abducting her. The peasants conspire to liberate her and manage to decoy the inept Mou long enough to permit Liu and her lover to flee downriver to a place where they presumably live (and sing) happily ever after.

The extraordinary popularity of this film is explained, in part, by its simplicity and innocence. The ugly realities of the present day are momentarily forgotten when the audience is allowed to escape to a fantasy world that existed a thousand years ago. Good and evil clash, as they must in almost all time-honored legends, but the audience is pleased by the unambiguous way in which these categories are defined.

Third Sister Liu, originally a modern folk opera performed on stage, works extremely well as a motion picture because the idea of filming on location is embraced by the director to an extent rarely seen in Chinese filmmaking. Furthermore, the film is memorable because the screenplay, and particularly the lyrics of the songs featured in the unforgettable contest between Third Sister Liu and the scholars, is written with great care.

Another dimension of the film's popularity is the attractiveness of the vivacious nineteen-year-old starlet Huang Wanqiu. One viewing of the film is enough to convince even the most skeptical observer that sex appeal was an important ingredient in Chinese films of the early 1960s. Liu's love affair with A Niu, the fisherman's son, is much more than a subtheme; it is present throughout and wins a permanent place in the memory of a film audience that was denied love stories during the Great Leap Forward. Every effort was made by the cameraman to highlight features of Liu's physical makeup, such as the shape of her nose, the distance between her eyes, the length and width of her neck, and the sound of her voice, that conformed to popular conceptions of female beauty articulated by interviewees. Liu acts as though she has "eaten the heart of a leopard" when she confronts local scoundrels, but her behavior does not threaten the masculinity of the male audience because she is always bashful and gentle as a lamb in the presence of the noble A Niu and his kindly father.

Liu Sanjie, the dazzling rural lass who fearlessly stands on the side of ordinary folks in *Third Sister Liu* (1962, d. Su Li). China Film Archive

In the first two years of the post-Leap thaw, many filmmakers exercised caution by making careful use of political themes that were certain to please Party censors. The clash between *Third Sister Liu* and Mou Huairen, for example, could be characterized as an episode of "class struggle" that pitted the peasant masses against tyrannical landlords. But upon closer inspection, the militant "politics" of this and many other films made in the early 1960s amounts to little more than superficial window dressing. The filmmaker merely superimposes categories of class on bipolar conceptions of absolute good and evil that are already deeply imbedded in the consciousness of viewers who love traditional stage conventions. The result is that the censor is satisfied, while many in the audience believe they are viewing something old and familiar.[10] The political message is thus overwhelmed and finally submerged in a sea of breathtaking landscapes and traditional artistry.

The sharp contrast between *Third Sister Liu* and *Women Generals of the Yang Family* (*Yang men nü jiang*, d. Cui Wei, Chen Huaikai, 1960) points to the thematic and artistic diversity of early 1960s films about imperial China. *Third Sister Liu* is charming folk entertainment that stresses the moral decency of the common people and assails the traditional elite. *Women Generals of the Yang Family* is a deadly serious drama that extols the patriotic virtues of certain members of the traditional ruling class.[11] The masses are hardly mentioned. *Third Sister Liu* is folk art derived from a rich oral tradition. *Women Generals* is filmed as an elaborate and highly refined Beijing opera. Unlike *Third Sister Liu*, it contains almost no humor. Instead, it speaks indirectly of the sudden rupture in Sino-Soviet relations.

Women Generals, a time-honored Beijing opera that was performed before patriotic audiences in the 1930s, is set in the Song dynasty during the reign of the emperor Renzong (1022–1064). The film version treats exclusively the constant threat to the Chinese nation posed by the Tanguts, a "barbarian" people of Tibetan stock who in the eleventh century ruled the kingdom of Xi Xia in northwest China along the former Sino-Soviet border. The Xi Xia are portrayed as unscrupulous and uncultured aggressors, while the defenders of the realm are viewed as heroic patriots.

As the film opens, the one-hundred-year-old matriarch of a prominent military family hears the tragic news that her grandson, General Yang Zongbao, the last of the adult males to survive the onslaught of the barbarians, has been killed. The household is now comprised of three generations of widows, and one teenage male, Yang Zongbao's son Wenchan. Despite the staggering sacrifices made by the Yangs, the tough old matriarch is shocked by the suggestion of some leaders that the only way to appease the cunning enemy is to abandon a portion of the sacred motherland to the aggressors. She insists that the women of the Yang family can continue in the glorious tradition of the men and, ultimately, repulse the invaders.

Yang Zongbao's young son wants to participate, but his grandmother objects on the grounds that his death would end the Yang line and disgrace the ancestors. The matriarch, who listens carefully to her daughter's powerful argument, suggests that the lad demonstrate his martial skills in a competition with his mother, the legendary Mu Guiying, a formidable military strategist in her own right. The mother allows her son to win the contest to guarantee his participation in the patriotic campaign. In the end, the ruthless enemy is pushed back by a guerilla-like coalition comprised of women, children, and old people.

Women Generals was vigorously attacked during the Cultural Revolution as a film that glorified the traditional elites by presenting them as natural leaders and genuine patriots prepared to make any sacrifice to defend the nation. The common people have no meaningful role in the story, and no attempt is made to blend in notions of class and class struggle. These accusations stand up when the political standards of the Cultural Revolution are used to analyze the film.

But in 1960 there was every reason for the Communist Party to welcome the production of this motion picture. Many people were disillusioned with the ideology of the Party following the class struggle and mass mobilization campaigns of the late 1950s. Consequently, efforts were made in the early 1960s to legitimate Party rule by stressing the purely nationalist component of Party ideology. It was enough for the people to believe that, regardless of its other failings, the Communist Party was, after all, the only authentic guardian of the nation. The Party welcomed the expression of nationalist sentiments because in the hungry years of the early 1960s it wanted to be perceived as the legitimate bearer of a tradition of nationalistic zeal. If citizens accepted the idea that expressions of patriotic fervor are at the same time expressions of loyalty to the Party, they might also accept the notion that opposition to the Communist Party and socialism is unpatriotic.

It is impossible to know how many people were influenced by this simplistic formulation, but the new emphasis on patriotism does explain how a film like *Women Generals* could be made during the thaw. It was the product of a confluence of interests. It gave intellectuals who were disgusted with the Great Leap and sought to escape to the world of early history a rare chance to make a film that was entirely safe politically, even though it said nothing of class struggle. All the directors had to do in the credits at the beginning of the film was to thank the Communist Party for supporting and encouraging the work of the opera troupe and film studio. The Party was satisfied because the film states indirectly that the Party, like the women of the Yang family, will defend the nation against the Soviets or any other foreign aggressor. In reality, however, the film could have been made and enjoyed as nothing more than good opera in either Taiwan or Hong Kong.

The political caution that surrounded the making of *Women Generals* becomes more apparent when it is compared to another Beijing opera film, *Wild Boar Forest* (*Ye zhu lin*, d. Cui Wei, Chen Huaikai, 1962), made by the same directors two years later. *Wild Boar Forest*, based on an episode in the beloved classic Ming dynasty novel *Water Margin* (*Shui hu zhuan*), offers a far more subtle and complex look at the traditional elite than the rather one-dimensional picture presented in *Women Generals*. *Wild Boar Forest*, a story of seduction, corruption, and betrayal during the reign of Huizong, a Song dynasty emperor who ruled from 1101 to 1126, is a fascinating treatment of the intersection of state power and social life.[12]

Lin Chong, a respected military instructor in the Imperial Guard in the Song capital of Kaifeng, learns that Gao Shide, better known as the "King of the Lechers," has made crude but unsuccessful advances on Lin's beautiful wife on the steps of the Temple of the Sacred Mountain. The situation is complicated by the fact that young Gao is the adopted son of Gao Qiu, Lin's superior officer, who is the powerful and corrupt commander of the Imperial Guard. Determined to have Lin's wife, Gao Qiu and his son maneuver to get Lin to bring his new sword to the high-security White Tiger Inner Sanctum, a government office where all weapons are prohibited. Lin is immediately arrested, accused of attempted assassination, tried, and sentenced to a life of exile. He prepares for his journey by signing a divorce proclamation that permits his devoted wife to remarry, but, of course, she refuses. Gao Qiu then arranges to have Lin Chong murdered on the road to his place of exile. With Lin Chong out of the way, Gao Qiu and his son prepare for their final move on Lin's wife by reporting that her husband has died in exile. Rather than submit to their advances, she commits suicide. But, in fact, the plot to murder Lin Chong had failed. Assuming that Lin will return to kill them when he learns of his wife's fate, Gao Qiu enlists Lin's best friend in yet another scheme to murder the wretched exile. Lin escapes and flees to the Liangshan Marsh in Shandong province where he joins a band of armed outcasts.

Neither *Wild Boar Forest* nor *Women Generals* is as adventuresome cinematically as *Third Sister Liu*. The directors of Beijing opera films must confront the challenge of filming what is, in reality, a stage production. The cameras remain fixed most of the time, although frequent close-ups are used to bring out the details of facial expressions and thus to heighten the effect of especially dramatic moments. Despite these constraints, opera movies have long been an important genre of Chinese filmmaking. *Wild Boar Forest* is considerably better than other Beijing opera films because the script, adapted for the screen by Li Shaochun (who also plays the role of Lin Chong), is written with grace and economy, and the cast includes exceptionally good players like Du Jinfang (the protégé of Mei Lanfang) in the role of Lin Chong's wife, and Yuan Shihai in the wonderfully comic role of the tattooed monk Lu Zhishen. The cultural thaw of the early 1960s also permitted limited contacts with filmmakers outside the People's Republic. The technical quality of *Wild Boar Forest* was enhanced by the fact that it was coproduced by the Beijing Film Studio and Dapeng Motion Pictures in colonial Hong Kong.

The political significance of *Wild Boar Forest*, which sets it apart from more cautious works like *Third Sister Liu* and *Women Generals*, resides in its remarkable fidelity to the original Ming narrative. *Wild Boar Forest* reveals that the cultural thaw had deepened by 1962. Unlike *Third Sister Liu*, it dispenses with Marxist window dressing altogether. The masses play no role in the story. Among the ruling elite, the viewer finds honorable people like Lin Chong. Yet the virtues of these elites are not explained by patriotism, as they are in *Women Generals*. Stripped of this cumbersome ideological baggage, *Wild Boar Forest* appears as a complex human drama of universal relevance.

Needless to say, the directors make no explicit attempt to draw parallels between the tragic plight of Lin Chong in the twelfth century and the predicaments of the powerless in the middle of the twentieth century—but it did not take much imagination for modern victims of injustice to identify with the pitiful Lin Chong. The tale of corruption, special privilege, and injustice had a familiar ring. Having lived through the infamous Anti-Rightist Campaign of 1957, ordinary citizens, and even those who enjoyed a certain measure of privilege, knew only too well that good people can be framed, exiled, and even killed at the whim of those with power. Legal checks were all but nonexistent. Suspects were expected to plead guilty to alleged crimes. Evil people, like Gao Shide, consumed by lust and greed, were easily protected by powerful relatives who held official positions. And it was common knowledge that the rules of self-survival often required friends to engage in cruel acts of betrayal.

Viewed in this context, *Wild Boar Forest* is an exceedingly depressing film. Yet it was undoubtedly comforting for the film audience to see these age-old vices exposed in ways that later infuriated the leaders of the Cultural Revolution.

Despite the distinctiveness of *Wild Boar Forest*, it was overshadowed from the beginning by the production of *Dream of the Red Chamber* (*Hong lou meng*, d. Chen Fan, 1962), perhaps the most renowned opera film ever made in China.[13] Based on a portion of the classic mid-eighteenth-century novel of the same title, *Dream of the Red Chamber* tells of family conflict in the Qing dynasty, during the reign of the emperor Qianlong (1736–1796). A popular item in the programs of Zhejiang opera troupes for many years, *Dream of the Red Chamber* was filmed as a lavish, three-hour coproduction of the Shanghai Haiyan Film Studio and the Hong Kong Golden Sound Motion Picture Corporation. Zhu Shilin, an eminent

Hong Kong director who made a number of important films in Shanghai in the 1930s, was recruited to serve as art director of the project.

In the film version Jia Baoyu loves his beautiful but painfully sensitive cousin Lin Daiyu, but his authoritarian parents are determined he will marry their personal favorite, Xue Baozhai, whose "golden lock necklace," it is said, is a perfect match for the "precious jade" worn by Baoyu. Baoyu detests Baozhai because she, like the family elders, wants him to pursue a career in high office. When the two are seen together by Daiyu, she fears that Baoyu has shifted his affections. But in the splendid "Burial of Flowers" scene Baoyu clears up the confusion by expressing his love for Daiyu. His parents are incensed when they learn of his intention to marry Daiyu, and they plot to alter the outcome of the ceremony by replacing Daiyu with Baozhai, whose face is concealed by the bridal veil. On the wedding day Daiyu believes that she has been betrayed and dies of a broken heart. When Baoyu discovers the ruse, he bitterly denounces his deceitful parents, abandons Baozhai, and breaks all ties with his family.

Dream of the Red Chamber is a spellbinding and absolutely magnificent work of art. The transition from classic novel to Zhejiang opera film is made without sacrificing the delicacy and fragility of the original. The exotic, one might even say erotic, quality of the film is related, in part, to the fact that in Zhejiang opera (*Yue ju*) all parts, including male roles, are played by women. Non-Chinese viewers in particular are quite likely to be transfixed by this unusual convention. The performances of Xu Yulan in the role of Jia Baoyu and Wang Wenjuan as Lin Daiyu are genuinely sensational.

Despite the commercial and critical success of *Dream of the Red Chamber*, it is far less enterprising politically than *Wild Boar Forest*. The universal significance of *Wild Boar Forest* can be appreciated because almost no effort is made to manipulate the original story in order to serve present-day ideological needs. The story can be enjoyed in an unadulterated form. The film version of *Dream of the Red Chamber*, on the other hand, consistently accentuates the iconoclastic and "antifeudal' tendencies of the original novel. The story is thus locked into a narrow analytical framework that is being used to shed light on a particular moment in Chinese history. Baoyu, for example, stands out more distinctively as a rebellious figure in the film than he does in the original novel. Baoyu and Baozhai marry and live happily together in the novel, but the film account ends with a defiant and unfilial Baoyu breaking ties with the family and leaving home.

The distortions in the film are clearly related to an ideological campaign against bourgeois ideology that began in 1954 as a Chinese Communist reevaluation of the novel *Dream of the Red Chamber*.[14] Mao Zedong himself wrote a letter to the politburo of the Communist Party to endorse the view that *Dream of the Red Chamber* should be interpreted as a contemporary protest against the decadence of "feudal" society.[15] Mao's Great Leap strategy had been thoroughly rejected by 1962, when the film version of *Dream of the Red Chamber* appeared. But to tamper with the Party's official interpretation of *Dream of the Red Chamber* would be to thumb one's nose at the Chairman. There were definite limits to the artistic freedom Chinese filmmakers enjoyed during the thaw. Ironically, the great caution exercised by the filmmakers afforded them little protection when the Cultural Revolution began. Red Guard publications charged that the film was a "poisonous weed" nurtured by Xia Yan for the purpose of propagating feudalism.[16]

Naval Battle of 1894 (*Jiawu fengyun*, d. Lin Nong, 1961) is different from the films on imperial China discussed above in that it treats modern history, a period in which the tottering traditional order struggled to survive in the face of economic, political, cultural, and military challenges from Japan and the West.[17] And unlike the other works, this picture is filmed as a "realistic" narrative (*gushi pian*). It contains no opera or folk music, other than the brilliant and highly dramatic *pipa* stringed instrument solo played by Li Moran, who stars in the role of naval hero Deng Shichang.

The film unfolds in late summer 1894 at a time when Japan and China are struggling for influence in Korea and on the brink of war. Hostilities begin when the Japanese sink the *Gaosheng*, a Chinese transport ship, and cause the death of 950 Chinese soldiers. During the ensuing debate on strategy held at the Qing court, two factions emerge. One party, led by Li Hongzhang, maps out a moderate course that is based on the hope that the Western powers will intervene and prevent warfare. A second faction, led by Admiral Ding Ruchang (and his subordinate, Commander Deng Shichang of the warship *Zhiyuan*) is eager to counterattack. Following a series of complex court debates and political caucuses, the moderate course is taken. Deng wants Li Hongzhang to forward his protest petition to the emperor, but Li refuses and Deng, a highly competent naval officer, is dismissed. Further acts of Japanese aggression lead to war, and Deng is reinstated. On September 17, 1894, the two fleets meet. Deng's commanding officer, Admiral Ding, orders eleven Chinese vessels into a wedge formation with two iron-clad ships at the point. But when the battle commences and Ding is incapacitated, the cowardly Captain Liu Buzhan orders a formation reverse into an inverted wedge to protect the iron-clads and his own ship. The Japanese proceed to annihilate the Beiyang fleet, but Ding Shichang orders the *Zhiyuan* to attack the Japanese flagship *Yoshino*. Deng's crew does well but runs out of ammunition. Deng decides to ram the *Yoshino*, but his ship is sunk by a torpedo and the crew perishes.

Naval Battle of 1894, like the other motion pictures mentioned here, was not born as a film idea.[18] It was originally produced as a stage play in 1960. Although the film version tells the story in a narrative form that bears a superficial resemblance to Hollywood film genres, the screenwriting and direction reflect an unwillingness to make a complete transition from stage play to film. For instance, many highly stylized acting conventions borrowed from the traditional theater are used to convert the story into the type of exaggerated moral drama that many Chinese viewers expect and enjoy. But like *Lin Zexu* (*Lin Zexu*, d. Zheng Junli, 1959), which tells the Chinese version of the Opium War, this interesting attempt to integrate Western and Chinese forms makes no room for "middle forces," heroes with tragic flaws, or villains with some redeeming characteristics. Consequently, a complex and rather sympathetic figure like Li Hongzhang emerges in the film as little more than a capitulationist.

Naval Battle goes well beyond *Women Generals* in its attempt to define the relationship between patriotism and class. Social classes are represented on screen, but the "class" struggle is defined in a strikingly un-Marxist fashion. The groups that contend are not classes in the Marxist sense but rather bipolar clusters of "patriots" and "traitors." The heroes are praiseworthy not because they are poor people who are oppressed by a particular social system, but because they are patriots. Similarly, the class enemy is detestable not because it exploits the people, but primarily because it betrays the nation. *Naval Battle* insists that the peasant masses and the rank-and-file sailors are united in their resolve to smash the alien aggressors, but the hero of the film, Deng Shichang, comes from the privileged class. Nevertheless, he is admired by the masses, who, in fact, depend upon him to champion their cause. Thus in the bipolar class scheme devised for the film, Deng and Admiral Ding stand squarely in the people's camp. Highly nationalistic in tone, *Naval Battle* suggests, by implication, that there was nothing inevitable about the various nineteenth-century imperialist victories. Modern Chinese history could have followed a different course. The defeat in the War of 1894 was the result of cowardice at the front and the policy of appeasement adopted by the Qing court.

Despite the superb performance by Li Moran, this film was subjected to strenuous criticism during the Cultural Revolution. The patriotic theme was acceptable, but the relationship between Deng and the masses was not. Although the film attributes to the masses a degree of consciousness and organization they clearly did not have, its critics would have been satisfied only if the masses were shown to be capable of resisting imperialism without the help of influential leaders among the traditional elite.

The filmmakers of the early 1960s encountered serious political difficulties during the Cultural Revolution because, among other things, their definition of patriotism was too broad. The sheer number of films that treated the imperial era reflected their deeply rooted emotional and nationalistic attachment to history and culture. The film artists' approach to the legacies of imperial China was not uncritical, but the pride they repeatedly expressed in this cultural heritage was meant to raise questions about the iconoclastic tenor of the Great Leap Forward. Where Mao was inclined to emphasize the cultural "blankness" of the masses, on the assumption that a people unfettered by a burdensome cultural tradition would be able to break from the past and leap into the future more easily, cultural leaders of the early 1960s like Xia Yan attempted to resurrect the basic Marxist notion that a measure of cultural continuity was not only desirable, but necessary for a smooth transition from one historical era to the next.

Using traditional cultural forms like Beijing opera, Zhejiang opera, and folk music to tell these tales of imperial China was also a manifestation of anti-Soviet sentiment. All the films discussed here represent an attempt to assert artistic independence from the Soviet Union. Chinese filmmakers were seeking to develop a cinema that was linked to Chinese cultural traditions rather than borrowed from the "socialist realism" models of the Stalin era. Filmmakers were convinced that the weary film audience would respond favorably to the renewed emphasis on customary Chinese forms, even if some artificial ideological gloss had to be applied to please the censors.

Finally, the nationalistic thrust of these works reveals the fractured condition of Chinese Marxist ideology in the post-Leap period. The Party was more than willing to fall back on nationalism and patriotism in a period of prolonged crisis. The class issue could be muted temporarily in order to create a sense of national unity. Intellectuals who associated with the Communist Party in the 1940s primarily because they were convinced that the Nationalist Party was not fulfilling its patriotic responsibilities were delighted to see the patriotic banner unfurled again. Indeed, films like *Women Generals* and *Wild Boar Forest* could just as easily have been made in Taiwan.

CINEMATIC INTERPRETATIONS OF THE REPUBLICAN ERA

One of the great ironies of postrevolution, Mao-era filmmaking is that cinema workers had difficulty making pictures that dealt directly with the history of the revolution. Films that treated the imperial era were often more successful precisely because filmmakers were working outside the exceedingly narrow framework of official Party history, and thus were able to go beyond the one-dimensional caricatures of Communist Party and Red Army heroes that cluttered films about the revolutionary struggle itself. During the 1960s thaw, however, considerable controversy was sparked by the production of several films that probed the Republican period in a variety of unorthodox ways.

One of the first careful steps taken in this direction was *Revolutionary Family* (*Geming jiating*, d. Shui Hua, 1960).[19] The screenplay, based on an autobiographical memoir by Tao Cheng that was later converted into a stage play, is important because it was written by Xia Yan himself, in collaboration with director Shui Hua. Although *Revolutionary Family* departs only slightly from the conventional ideological framework adopted in the 1950s for film scripts that treat the Republican era, it is an excellent example of a distinctively Chinese genre developed first in films like *Small Toys* (*Xiao wanyi*, d. Sun Yu, 1933; see chapter 3) and *Eight Thousand Miles of Clouds and Moon* (*Baqian lilu yun he yue*, d. Shi Dongshan, 1947; see chapter 5) produced in pre-revolutionary times. In this type of film the personal experiences and perceptions of a small group, usually a family unit, are used to interpret the significance of the major social and political upheavals of a ten- or twenty-year period.[20] *Revolutionary Family*, for example, covers the period from 1910 to 1937.

The film focuses on the life of Zhou Lian, a rural teenager who is forced into an arranged marriage with Jiang Meiqing, a schoolteacher who lives in Changsha. Fortunately for Zhou, her husband is kind and tender. He teaches her to read and write; she happily accepts her role as an obedient wife and devoted mother. But Jiang has said nothing about his enthusiasm for the revolutionary cause promoted by the Nationalist and Communist united front. In 1924 he simply disappears. In late 1926 he suddenly returns to Changsha as a member of the revolutionary Northern Expeditionary Army. He is also a member of the Communist Party. Jiang tells his wife she must change, and he forces her to cut her hair in the latest revolutionary style. But the euphoria of victory is dashed by the counterrevolution. Jiang promptly flees to Hankou. Zhou, who begins to understand the basics of her husband's political beliefs, soon follows.

The second and far less successful part of *Revolutionary Family* deals with Zhou Lian's response to family crisis. Her husband dies following a skirmish with Nationalist agents. But she is assured that she and her children will be cared for by their *new* family, the Communist Party. Zhou becomes a Party member and is sent with her children to Shanghai to do underground work. In 1931 Zhou and her eldest son are arrested. Her loyalty to her new "family" is tested in prison, where she is told her son will be executed if she does not agree to betray her comrades. She refuses to waver and her son marches heroically to his death. Finally, in 1937, she is released from prison following the formation of the second united front between the Nationalists and the Communists.

Although *Revolutionary Family* was later characterized in Red Guard periodicals as another of Xia Yan's "poisonous weeds," it was in reality a transitional film that points to Xia Yan's inability to break completely with the thematic conventions of the 1950s. The study of the young bride, played skillfully by Yu Lan, is refreshing, and Xia Yan's willingness to remind viewers of a time when the Nationalists and Communists were partners in revolution was certainly daring. But the interesting personalities who are introduced in the first portion of the film are suddenly transformed into stock revolutionary characters as soon as the story begins to discuss the rupture in relations between the two political parties.

The transitional nature of *Revolutionary Family* becomes even more evident when it is compared to *Early Spring* (*Zao chun eryue*, d. Xie Tieli, 1963), the critical yardstick by which all early 1960s films about the Republican period must be measured. Indeed, no film made in the early 1960s was castigated more in the Cultural Revolution than *Early Spring*.[21] This captivating film is based on the novel *February*, written in 1929 by Rou Shi, a Communist intellectual who was executed by the Nationalist authorities in early 1931. Although Rou Shi was heralded as a revolutionary martyr by the Communists, this particular novel was considered by some Party critics to be excessively sentimental and pessimistic, even by the political standards of the early 1960s. Questions were raised about the wisdom of making such a film, but the star-studded production was pushed ahead with great tenacity by the courageous young director Xie Tieli.

Unlike most films on the Republican era, which focus on the clash between the Communists and the Nationalists, this story, like the first part of *Revolutionary Family*, is set at a time when the two parties were united. A young intellectual, Xiao Qianqiu, who is uneasy about the direction of his life, becomes a teacher in a provincial town in eastern Zhejiang around 1926. Before long, Xiao becomes involved in the lives of two women. He loves Tao Lan, an obstinate and dejected young woman teaching at the same school, but he also does everything he can to help the pathetic young widow Wensao, whose husband, a former friend of Xiao's, was killed fighting for the Nationalist-Communist coalition. The pettiness and dispiriting viciousness of small-town life is revealed when one of Tao Lan's jealous suitors begins to malign Xiao by spreading groundless rumors about his innocent relationship with the widow. Soon parents begin to withdraw their children from the school. His humanitarian intentions misunderstood, Xiao offers to defend Wensao's honor by proposing marriage. But in a moment of helpless desperation, Wensao commits suicide. Emotionally distraught, Xiao decides to flee the small town. When Tao Lan discovers that Xiao is gone, she announces her determination to track him down in the great metropolis of Shanghai.

Early Spring is a remarkable film because, among other things, it refuses to preoccupy itself with praise for the Communist Party or condemnation of the Nationalists. It refers to a time when the two revolutionary parties cooperated, but the revolution is kept in the distant background. It does not intrude on the dismal account of life in a provincial outpost.

The characters are intriguing because they are neither heroic nor satanic. They belong to definite social classes, but their class identity does not automatically determine their moral character. Xiao and Tao are memorable precisely because they do not have full control of their emotions, are preoccupied with their personal lives, and have not yet become active in the revolutionary tide that is the focus of Xia Yan's screenplay *Revolutionary Family*. *Early Spring* is a sympathetic account of their wavering and ineffectiveness. In this respect the main protagonists are reminiscent of the complex characters who appeared on Chinese screens in the late 1940s, a high point of Chinese filmmaking.

The distance that separates the provincial town from the main currents of revolution serves to accentuate the universality of the themes explored in the film. *Early Spring* does shed light on a particular moment in Republican history, but it can also be interpreted as a comment on small-town life in general. The appeal of this unusual work is enhanced by the director's refusal to include an upbeat ending that provides clear-cut solutions to the various social and cultural problems. The film simply ends with the departure of Tao Lan. The source of the maladies that afflict the small town is never identified, and no vanguard political party arrives to promise salvation. In this respect *Early Spring*, like *Wild Boar Forest*, is a rare example of successful "slice of life" cinema in post-revolutionary China.

One of the finest early-1960s films on peasant life in the Republican era is *Red Flag Chronicle* (*Hong qi pu*, d. Ling Zifeng, 1960).[22] Based on a novel that Hebei writer Liang Bing began working on in 1953, *Red Flag Chronicle* uses the "historical narrative-family history" genre adopted by Xia Yan and Shui Hua for *Revolutionary Family*. The content of *Red Flag Chronicle* is, however, far more satisfying. In many respects, this underrated film anticipates the accomplishments of *Early Spring*. In fact, Xie Tieli, the director of *Early Spring*, worked as assistant director of *Red Flag Chronicle* three years earlier. Ling Zifeng, the director of *Red Flag Chronicle*, would resurface as one of the most admired film artists of the post-Mao era.

Red Flag Chronicle is set in Suojinzhen village, Lixian county in the plains of central Hebei province. The film opens in 1901, just after the Boxer uprising. Zhu Laofan, a respected local peasant, dies following an altercation with the village despot Feng Lanchi. Zhu's son, Laozhong, flees to Manchuria, but his distraught daughter commits suicide.

The story resumes in 1925 when Laozhong returns with his wife and children to seek revenge. The political climate is tense because the local warlords and "evil gentry" have heard rumors about the revolutionary alliance of the Nationalists and Communists. One of Laozhong's own sons is forcibly drafted into the local warlord's army. Laozhong feels helpless. But he and the others respond enthusiastically to a soft-spoken rural schoolteacher named Jia Xiangnong, a member of the Communist Party, who tells of the desire of the Nationalist-Communist alliance to crush the warlords and local tyrants who oppress the people. When the forces of the Northern Expedition arrive, landlord Feng Lanchi flees in terror. Laozhong's son returns with the revolutionary army. The peasants rejoice. Victory has been won.

The final portion of the film deals with the impact of the counterrevolution. Laozhong's son, a Communist, is arrested, and the tyrant Feng Lanchi returns. On the eve of the lunar New Year, 1928, Feng tries to enforce a new hog-slaughtering tax in the village. But Laozhong, now a member of the small Communist underground himself, leads a protest march to the county seat that threatens to become violent. The county magistrate quickly repeals the new tax, and the peasants win a limited victory.

The artistic success of *Red Flag Chronicle* has much to do with the painstaking efforts of the screenwriters and director to capture the rich details of peasant culture in central Hebei. Not only was the film shot on location in a dusty and unattractive village of the sort that dominate the central Hebei horizon to this day, but the chief screenwriter, Hu Su, a native of Zhejiang province in the south, had spent years observing peasant life in the region both before and after the founding of the People's Republic.[23] The rugged lead actor, Cui Wei, who plays the parts of both Zhu Laofan and Zhu Laozhong, was born into a peasant household in Shandong province in 1912. A student of North China culture, Cui codirected several Beijing opera films in the early 1960s, including *Wild Boar Forest* and *Women Generals of the Yang Family*. And, like Hu Su, he did resistance work in central Hebei during the Japanese occupation.[24]

One of the tasks assigned to the motion picture industry after the establishment of the People's Republic was to help create a "national" consciousness among the general population. It was hoped that urban and rural dwellers alike would gradually identify more with the nation-state than with their local region. But during the early 1960s, as the economy became more decentralized, there was a greater willingness to tolerate allegiances to local culture. *Red Flag Chronicle* can be understood as an unusually explicit example of regionalist cinema. The frequent use of the central Hebei dialect and local idioms plays an important role in creating a culturally specific environment. Short scenes that include the singing of Hebei *bangzi*, the most popular form of local opera; demonstrations of *wushu*, the type of martial art most favored in the region; and the displays of local mourning rituals all contribute to this celebration of central Hebei culture.

The ideological content of *Red Flag Chronicle* anticipates *Early Spring* in the sense that the main body of the film deals with the period in which the Communists and the Nationalists were united. The local despot is linked initially to a regional military force, not to the Nationalists. Indeed, the local warlord and his powerful supporters in the village are the targets of the joint Nationalist-Communist offensive. It is not until the end of *Red Flag Chronicle* that the landlord is tied to the Nationalist counterrevolution. Throughout the film the peasants want justice, but their sense of right and wrong is not shaped by a modern ideology. It is deeply rooted in the cultural traditions of the region. Their desire for revenge, for example, is related less to a sense of class consciousness than it is to family loyalty. When Zhu Laofan's son returns from Manchuria to settle accounts with Feng Lanchi, the first thing he does is bring his wife and children to his father's grave to bow and pay respects in the time-honored way. By central Hebei standards, the peasants live and dress rather well. They raise chickens and pigs, and the market town seems quite lively. Economic exploitation and class strife do not become major issues until the end of the movie.

Revolutionary Family, Early Spring, and *Red Flag Chronicle* deal with the period before the outbreak of World War II. But films about the war against Japan, another important genre of early 1960s films, are as important to the history of Chinese filmmaking as pictures about the antifascist struggle in Europe are to Hollywood. And Chinese war films are usually just as unimaginative as their Western counterparts. Indeed, most of the Chinese war films made during the post-Leap thaw fail to depart in any significant way from similar works produced in the 1950s. For example, Cui Wei, the actor who performed with such versatility in *Red Flag Chronicle*, codirected a low-budget, early-1960s film titled *Little Soldier Zhang Ga* (*Xiao bing Zhang Ga*, d. Cui Wei, Ouyang Hongying, 1963), which tells the story of Japanese marauders, Chinese traitors, and Eighth Route Army heroes through the eyes of a small boy who lives in a typical central Hebei village.[25] *Little Soldier Zhang Ga* does not even meet the artistic standard set in the early 1950s by *A Letter with Feathers* (*Jimao xin*, d. Shi Hui, 1954), a more natural and convincing look at a young boy caught in the middle of a war.

But the production of one war film, *Dr. Bethune* (*Baiqiuen daifu*, d. Zhang Junxiang, 1964), sent shock waves through the film world.[26] Based on a novel by Zhou Erfu, this work tells the true story of a flamboyant Canadian surgeon, Norman Bethune, who, supplied with medical equipment donated by American Communists, began working with the Eighth Route Army in Shaanxi and Hebei in early 1938 at the beginning of the resistance war. Bethune went personally to the front to perform surgical procedures, trained large numbers of Chinese medical workers, and designed medical equipment suitable for use in guerilla warfare. In late 1939 he cut his finger during an operation, suffered blood poisoning, and died. In December 1939 Mao Zedong wrote a short eulogy in which he described Bethune as a martyr from whom every Communist must learn.

The story of Norman Bethune is certainly very familiar to most educated Chinese, and there is little in the film that departs from the official, sanitized version of his time in China. Director Zhang Junxiang's idea was politically daring for the simple reason that *Dr. Bethune* was the first feature film made after 1949 that presented a Caucasian protagonist in a sympathetic light. Zhang Junxiang, who served in the 1980s as head of the Shanghai Film Bureau, had for a long time been among a relatively small group *within* the Communist Party that actively resisted the xenophobic and antiforeign elements that dominated Chinese political and intellectual life, especially during the Great Leap Forward and other episodes of zealous revolutionary fervor. Zhang devoured Western literature as a student at Qinghua University in the late 1920s, and he received a grant to study drama at Yale for three years in the late 1930s. Two of the films he directed in the late 1940s, *Diary of a Homecoming* (*Huanxiang riji*, 1947) and *Shortcut to Becoming a Son-in-Law* (*Chen long kuaishu*, 1947), established him as one of the most promising film artists of the postwar era.

Until the filming of *Dr. Bethune*, foreigners had appeared almost exclusively as crude caricatures of wicked and bloodthirsty imperialist aggressors. Gerald Tannebaum, the American expatriate who stars in the title role, had played the part of the evil foreigner several times in the 1950s before he got this rare chance to play a positive role. Zhang Junxiang had also waited years for this opportunity to make film history. Tannebaum is not an accomplished actor, and the script does not do justice to the complexity of Bethune's personality, but the film is of great importance because it was hoped that it would send a message to other filmmakers and the film audience: the appearance of works of art that treat non-Chinese subjects in a multidimensional way is not a sign of political weakness; it is a manifestation of genuine self-confidence and political maturity.

Production began in 1963, but even at the height of the cultural thaw the seeds of militant reaction were being scattered. *Early Spring*, the quintessential early-1960s film, was immediately and harshly attacked in the Party press for espousing "bourgeois humanitarianism" when it was released in 1964. The production of *Dr. Bethune* was simply stopped in 1965, on the eve of its completion. Currents of antiforeignism and concerns about alien spiritual pollution ran exceedingly deep. It was determined that the Chinese audience was not discriminating enough to consider an image of a friendly foreigner, even if it was the saintly Bethune.

The August First Film Studio, a cultural unit of the People's Liberation Army, specialized in military films after it was founded in 1955. Most of its early productions contributed rather little to the development of Chinese cinema. Experienced directors, actors, and actresses tended to be associated with the more prestigious studios, specifically the Beijing Film Studio, and the Haiyan and Tianma studios in Shanghai. But even the conservative August First Studio was affected by the cultural relaxation of the post-Leap era. For example, it coproduced the controversial *Dr. Bethune* with the Haiyan Studio.

Another August First project was *Serfs* (*Nongnu*, Li Jun, 1963).[27] Unlike most of the well-known films of the early 1960s, it was not based on a work of fiction, a memoir, a stage play, or an opera. Screenwriter Huang Zongjiang, a member of the Chinese military since 1949, studied Western literature at Yanjing University in the late 1930s and idolized the American playwright Eugene O'Neill. His first screenplay, *Family Reunion*

(*Da tuanyuan*, Ding Li, 1948), is linked to the rich legacy of Chinese films produced in the late 1940s.²⁸

The first half of *Serfs*, which traces the life of a Tibetan serf named Jampa through the 1930s and 1940s, ranks among the very best segments of film work done by the August First Studio. The black-and-white photography of Wei Linyue is unusually effective, and the acting of Wangdui, a Tibetan, in the male lead, is generally excellent. Rarely does a Chinese film of the postrevolutionary period look so closely at the psyche of a single person. Wangdui's assignment is especially difficult (and his achievements all the more remarkable) because he plays the part of a man who survives by pretending to be mute. Thus he is forced to develop the character of Jampa without relying upon dialogue. Unfortunately, the second portion of the film treats the period from the arrival of the People's Liberation Army in Tibet in 1950 to the suppression of the Tibetan revolt in 1959. Of course, relations between the Tibetan masses and the Han soldiers are always superb, and the behavior of the Chinese cadres is always exemplary, so there is very little in this segment that is new, interesting, or particularly realistic.

Jampa suffers horribly in mid-twentieth-century Tibet in *Serfs* (1963, d. Li Jun). China Film Archive

Serfs is important because it explores ethnicity in some detail. It discusses, among other things, the relationships between the landowning class and the serfs, the lamas and the masses, and the lamas and the traditional elite, and it takes a relatively detailed look at the role of Buddhism in daily life. The final portion examines the methods used by landowners to perpetuate the traditional socioeconomic system under new circumstances brought about by the arrival of the Hans, as well as the manner in which the Chinese relate to the various Tibetan groups, including traditional elites and religious leaders.

But why is the first portion of *Serfs* more effective than film treatments of the condition of the masses in the less exotic heartland of China? The use of an all-Tibetan cast, the decision to film on location, and the care given to photography certainly contribute to its success. More important, *Serfs* goes much further than other films in detailing the daily humiliations suffered and endured by the common people. The film is distinctive because the degradation it portrays is so utterly brutal. This graphic realism is convincing, in part, because the serfs have a low level of consciousness and adopt a fatalistic outlook on their plight. Those who suffer by no means enjoy their misery, but neither do they see the use of putting up much resistance. One gets the impression that this type of situation can be shown on screen only because the subjects are not Han Chinese. Chinese nationalism rarely permits the filming of Hans enduring such humiliation, even though it is well-known that they did. Films like *Naval Battle of 1894* and *Revolutionary Family* that depict Han behavior must find many ways to demonstrate that the masses are always ready to stand up to alien intruders or boldly defy the internal class enemy. Ironically, the absence of such requirements makes *Serfs* a more successful picture.

The relative passivity of the brutalized masses tends to serve the larger Chinese need to suggest that the Tibetan people were so downtrodden and manipulated that they were largely incapable of carrying out a successful antifeudal revolution themselves. When this theme is introduced in the second segment, the film collapses. Relations between the newly arrived Han forces and the local people are not merely smooth, they are patronizing. The unmistakable underlying message is that under such circumstances salvation can only be delivered from the outside.

Serfs also fails to address the controversial question of whether the overthrow of the old ruling class in Tibet and demolition of all links between feudal political power and the religious hierarchy will inevitably undermine customary Tibetan culture as well. But the filmmakers are clearly sensitive to the charge that Han presence in Tibet resulted in cultural genocide. *Serfs* carefully sets forth the official Chinese position that the distinctiveness of Tibetan "national" culture can be retained as the people travel along the road to socialism paved by the Hans. This is accomplished by contrasting the attitudes of two Living Buddhas, one of whom is profoundly anticommunist and in league with the reactionary element, and one called Chhoiphel who believes that Communism and Buddhism can be compatible. But Chhoiphel's understanding of Communism is rather shaky. The issue of ethnicity and socialist revolution is never raised because he seems to believe that Communism is synonymous with nationalism. The rebels of 1959 are detestable, in his view, and cannot be regarded as "true Buddhists," because they have "betrayed their country." Since *Serfs* was made in the aftermath of the Sino-Indian border war, it is hardly surprising that the Tibetan villains are shown to have been collaborating with the Indians all along. Consequently, the treatment of the 1959 rebellion contains few surprises. But, in order to show how the leaders of the rebellion were able to organize, it was necessary for the filmmakers indirectly to reveal how little had been done by the Hans in the 1950–1959 period to transform Tibetan society. But the main argument in the film is that the old elites were in a position to organize a rebellion only because they had not been divested of political and economic power in the 1950s because of the gradualistic united front approach to change adopted by the Chinese. Han chauvinism and economic stagnation had nothing to do with the rebellion.

Serfs was welcomed in the official press, but the difficulties encountered by *Early Spring* and *Dr. Bethune* signaled that the post-Leap cultural thaw was being questioned. New film production schedules were reminiscent of Great Leap priorities. Of the fifty-eight films made in 1965, the year before the eruption of the Cultural Revolution, only seven treated the history of the Republican era. Films on imperial history and culture were entirely eliminated.[29]

The last serious film made before the Cultural Revolution was *Stage Sisters*.[30] More than ten years passed before a film of similar quality was made. Like *Serfs*, *Stage Sisters* (*Wutai jiemei*, d. Xie Jin, 1965) is a rare example of an original screenplay developed exclusively for the cinema. Unlike *Serfs*, it was shown briefly, subjected to virulent criticism, and withdrawn from circulation. Red Guards later claimed that Chen Huangmei, head of the Film Bureau of the Ministry of Culture, sought to deemphasize the theme of class struggle in *Stage Sisters* in order to make the film marketable in Hong Kong, Europe, and America.[31]

Considering that many films made in 1965, such as *The East is Red* (*Dongfang hong*, d. collective, 1965), were beginning to promote the cult of Mao Zedong in preparation for the Chairman's startling political comeback, the content of *Stage Sisters* is most unusual. A throwback to films of the 1930s and 1940s that took delight in probing the seedy side of the glittering world of entertainment, *Stage Sisters* focuses on the complex personal lives of two actresses.

The story opens in 1935 in Zhejiang province. Abused by her in-laws, Zhu Chunhua, a child bride, takes flight. She is taken in by a small Shaoxing opera troupe as an unpaid performer. The dangers and hardships of life on the road draw her close to Yuehong, the troupe's leading actress. In winter 1941, during the Japanese occupation, the troupe encounters numerous financial difficulties and is eventually sold by its owner to a man named Deng who manages a Shaoxing opera troupe in metropolitan Shanghai.

The relationship between the two newcomers and the resident female star, Shang Shuihua, is one of constant friction. Before long, however, Yuehong and Chunhua emerge as popular stars in their own right. Corrupted by life in the big city, Yuehong is eventually seduced by Tang, the manager, and retires from the stage following their marriage. The aging opera queen, Shang Shuihua, commits suicide.

The moral decline of Yuehong is set in sharp contrast to the enlightened path followed by her sworn sister Chunhua, who has come under the influence of a progressive female reporter named Jiang Po. By the end of the war the two old friends live in separate worlds: Yuehong is sinking in the quicksand of a degenerate Shanghai culture, while Chunhua and her friends seek to perform works that are critical of the Nationalist government.

It is not until 1950, after the Communist victory, that the paths of the two "sisters" cross once again. Chunhua is the leader of a traveling company that performs revolutionary works. She discovers Yuehong living in seclusion in Hangzhou, abandoned by the unscrupulous Tang. Chunhua invites Yuehong to join the troupe, and the two women are finally reunited.

Stage Sisters, like *Early Spring* and many of the films of the early 1960s that treat the Republican era, failed by the official standards of the mid- and late-1950s to pay sufficient attention to the theme of class struggle. Director Xie Jin knew very well what standard treatments of the Republican era were like. One of his first works of the post–Great Leap period, *Red Detachment of Women* (*Hongse niangzi jun*, 1961) conforms almost perfectly to the textbook conception of class conflict between poor peasants and rich landlords in south China in the early 1930s.[32] Issues related to the emancipation of women are introduced in *Red Detachment of Women*, but they are immediately resolved by the simplistic application of Marxist theory. The oppression of women, it is assumed, is rooted in the class structure of society, and thus when the prevailing class system is toppled, women, like all other laborers, will be liberated. Women join the revolution not as feminists who have their own political goals, but as peasants who seek to end landlord rule.

Films like *Stage Sisters* and *Early Spring* acknowledge the existence of social classes but offer a decidedly humanistic perspective on the personal tragedies under review. The characterization of Yuehong, the "bad" sister who goes astray in the sinful city of Shanghai, is strikingly sympathetic. Like the classic humanistic "social concern" films of the 1930s, such as *The Goddess* (*Shennü*, d. Wu Yonggang, 1934), *Stage Sisters* seeks to understand rather than censure the behavior of those who have been degraded by evil forces. The compassion of the "good" sister, Chunhua, for the pathetic opera queen who commits suicide is another example of director Xie Jin's willingness to question the extent to which class identity explains human behavior.

Xie Jin was attacked and persecuted during the Cultural Revolution, but he reemerged as perhaps the most daring filmmaker of the early post-Mao period. Fate was less kind to other artists of the early 1960s who sought to highlight some of the human complexities of revolution in Republican China. The brilliant actress Shangguan Yunzhu, who played the widow who committed suicide in *Early Spring* and the declining opera queen who committed suicide in *Stage Sisters*, escaped the terror of the Cultural Revolution by leaping to her death from the roof of a building in Shanghai in 1969.

"CONTRADICTIONS AMONG THE PEOPLE": FILM IMAGES OF THE TRANSITION TO SOCIALISM

Making films about the imperial and Republican eras posed serious problems for filmmakers of the early 1960s, but nothing was more difficult than producing interesting movies about the postrevolutionary period itself. Disillusioned with the failures of the Great Leap Forward and supported by powerful politicians in the Ministry of Culture, filmmakers were eager to identify problems that plagued socialist society. Xia Yan's pronouncements of 1961 made it clear that filmmakers would be encouraged to supplement stories of heroic self-sacrifice in the name of the Party and state with films that addressed the issue of low morale and other nagging questions. Introducing a critical element into films about the socialist era was not new. During the brief Hundred Flowers episode of 1956–1957, films like *Before the New Director Arrives* (*Xin juzhang daolai zhi qian*, d. Lu Ban, 1956) poked fun at inefficient petty officials. But during the vicious Anti-Rightist Campaign that followed, film artists learned that the personal and professional price of making even mildly critical films could be staggeringly high. In the early 1960s Xia Yan urged screenwriters and directors to step forward once again, but his appeal failed to spell out the limits within which filmmakers had to work.

The film world moved with extreme prudence at first. Since Chairman Mao himself had acknowledged in February 1957 the existence of "contradictions among the people" during the transition to socialism, filmmakers adopted the framework of "contradictions among the people" to analyze social problems of the post-Leap period. To be sure, the contradictions discussed in these films are conveniently resolved in the end, and few hints are given about the likelihood of ongoing social conflict. But these works are interesting, nevertheless, because they reject the notion that social conflict inevitably pits absolute evil against absolute good. Moreover, many of these films question the idea that all social strife is a manifestation of class struggle. Instead, these films are filled with a host of intriguing "middle characters," that is, individuals who appear to be from "good" class backgrounds, but whose social behavior is seriously flawed. Three excellent examples of this early-1960s genre are *Li Shuangshuang* (*Li Shuangshuang*, d. Lu Ren, 1962), a light comedy starring the talented actress Zhang Ruifang, voted best actress of 1962; an urban melodrama titled *The Youth Generation* (*Nianqing de yidai*, d. Zhao Ming, 1965); and *Satisfied or Not?* (*Manyi bu manyi?* d. Yan Gong, 1963), a mildly satirical comedy.

The setting of *Li Shuangshuang*, selected as best film in 1962, is a village in a Henan people's commune in the immediate aftermath of the disastrous Great Leap.[33] It examines the problem of the tension between individual interest and collective interest in a period when the Party and state were seeking to restore a measure of public confidence in the socialist system. This issue is explored by means of focusing on the relationship between an outgoing young peasant woman named Shuangshuang, who seems always to be at the center of controversy in the village, and her husband Xiwang, a classic middle character, who prefers to mind his own business and remain inconspicuous.[34] Whenever Shuangshuang steps forward to speak out on cases involving the conflict between individual and community interest, Xiwang accuses her of meddling. The theme of gender equality is assigned a subordinate role, but it is significant, nevertheless, because at one point in the narrative Xiwang leaves Shuangshuang.

If the inevitable happy ending is ignored, the film leaves a lasting impression, particularly if one assumes that some of the issues that arise continued to plague the Chinese countryside. Indeed, this film has a critical, almost satirical, flare that is rare among Chinese films that treat the postrevolutionary period. For example, the film shows that people like Shuangshuang (who is both young and female) are perceived by many as disrespectful troublemakers when they step forward to speak in the public interest. The abuses she alludes to are, of course, rectified in the film, but the fact that they have been brought to light in the first place leaves the viewer with the impression that they are common throughout China. Among other things, Shuangshuang accuses an elderly woman of misappropriating public property, criticizes cadres who spend little time doing field work, exposes serious corruption in the work point system, and raises embarrassing questions about a speculation scheme that is operating in the local market. In fact this film raises a more general problem that afflicted all quarters of Chinese society before and after the Great Leap: the tendency of people to avoid taking political initiatives lest they expose themselves to attack later. At one point, Shuangshuang plots to foil an attempt by a local couple to arrange a marriage between their daughter (who is in love with a village lad) and an urban youth. Such marriages are normally arranged to enhance the family's financial position by getting an offspring in the city where higher-paying factory positions might be obtained. Needless to say, Shuangshuang's husband, played beautifully by the comic actor Zhong Xinghuo (selected as best supporting actor in 1962), is mortified by her behavior and constantly heckled by his friends, who charge that he cannot control his wife.

This film also has its defects. The unwavering support given Shuangshuang by the village Party branch is problematic, there is a marked contrast between scenes shot in the studio and the livelier and more convincing scenes shot on location, and the village has been excessively beautified by the filmmakers. Furthermore, the women's rights theme is allowed to evaporate during the compulsory reconciliation scene. *Li Shuangshuang* has very little of the ongoing dialectical force of the third portion of the magnificent Cuban film *Lucia* (d. Humberto Solas, 1968), which like its Chinese coun-

A politically backward rural husband feels threatened by the activism of his vivacious wife in *Li Shuangshuang* (1962, d. Lu Ren). China Film Archive

terpart ends with the socialist couple ruling out the option of dissolving the union—but in *Lucia* it is acknowledged that the contradictions confronting the marriage will be a permanent feature of the relationship. In fact, in the final scene of *Lucia*, the couple is engaged in a strange but convincing episode of physical confrontation that seems paradoxically to be uniting them.

But *Li Shuangshuang* is successful nevertheless. As a comedy it minimizes the sort of political tensions that would inevitably arise in a more serious narrative, and the acting is unusually good. The movie is also filmed in black and white, a format that is often aesthetically superior to color production in Chinese films.

The Youth Generation, produced by Shanghai's Haiyan Studio in 1964, is not nearly as entertaining as *Li Shuangshuang*, but it amply demonstrates the extent to which the lives and concerns of China's urbanites are removed from the world of peasants.[35] It raises the question of how young urban intellectuals can be motivated to serve in remote border regions where their skills are badly needed, but in doing so it brings to light many of the reasons why young people opposed the various "youth to the countryside" or "rustification" programs. Later, during the Cultural Revolution, the *xiaxiang* conception became highly controversial and remained so throughout the 1970s. It became so universally unpopular, especially in south China, that the program was no longer regarded as a suitable topic for scenarios, but *The Youth Generation*, a low-budget production that middle-school students were taken to see in organized groups, was released when the program was being introduced in a moderate way.

The film discusses, among other things, the ingenious techniques used by a young graduate of the Shanghai Geological Institute, named Lin Yusheng, to avoid returning to remote Qinghai province, where he had been working with an exploratory team. Another classic middle character with a good class background, Lin wants a comfortable life in Shanghai where he can advance his career by engaging in path-breaking research activity and cement the relationship he enjoys with his girlfriend, who is on the verge of graduating from the Institute. Lin's best friend and workmate, Xiao Zhiye, a one-dimensional "positive" character, expresses diametrically opposed views. He is happy to serve in Qinghai, adopts a selfless attitude in every scene, and understands the relationship between his work and the development of the nation's economy. In certain respects the central theme is the problem of how generations of "revolutionary successors" are to be produced in a society where low morale is widespread among urban youth. Lin, it is said, has been spoiled by permissive parents, while Xiao has been raised in a strict family environment.

The networking tactics employed by Lin were used both during and after the Mao era. For example, he forges a medical certificate to indicate that a rheumatic condition is aggravated by the climate in Qinghai. He is offered a moderately attractive bureaucratic position at the Institute, which he plans to take if the Institute's leadership agrees to a deal that involves assigning his girlfriend to work in Shanghai, even though her skills are needed elsewhere. Lin also discourages his younger sister from applying for admission to the Agriculture Institute, suggesting instead that she ought to seek entry to the Film Institute and relegate the Agriculture Institute to the status of "alternate course" (*hou lu*). Finally, as a last resort, Lin decides it will be necessary to speed up his marriage plans so as to guarantee his plan for a future life of urban bliss. The girlfriend, Jingru, another interesting middle character, is torn between her affection for Lin and her feeling that his many plots and schemes are somehow misguided.

The Youth Generation is interesting, not because there is any doubt about the outcome, but because Lin remains steadfast throughout. Indeed, his views change only when he learns that a genuine work-related injury will require the amputation of the leg of Xiao Zhiye, his ideological rival, and that his parents are, after all, merely his guardians, his natural parents having been martyred during the revolution. The conclusion is, of course, ludicrously contrived, but it is highly significant that such overkill was necessary for the final conversion.

Satisfied or Not? is another semi-satirical comedy that hints at social problems in the aftermath of the Great Leap; it tells the story of Yang Yousheng, a disgruntled young waiter in a Suzhou restaurant. Unhappy with what he believes to be his low status, the sullen Yang is often careless in his work and rude to his customers. Some of his coworkers try in vain to convince the lad that every job is of equal importance in the new socialist society. But Yang continues to express unhappiness in the self-criticism sessions he is required to attend.

Troubled by her son's problems at work, Yousheng's mother is convinced that a clever and attractive bride will improve his outlook on life. She arranges for Yousheng to meet a neighbor's niece in a local park. But the meeting proves to be a disaster when the young woman discovers that Yousheng is the insolent waiter who recently insulted her in the restaurant.

The hapless Yousheng tries to solve his problems by getting a more prestigious job in a factory. He becomes angry, however, when he learns that the best the manager can offer is an assignment in the factory's dining hall. On his way home, Yousheng has an accident on his bicycle. Among those who rush to help him are a bus driver and a physician he abused at the restaurant. The selfless nurse at the hospital is none other than the young woman he met in the park. Deeply moved by their kindness and by recollections about how bitterly his father had suffered in the "old society," Yang criticizes his poor attitude and resolves to become a model worker.

Li Shuangshuang, The Youth Generation, and *Satisfied or Not?* have several things in common. First, the relationship between ideology and class is defined in strikingly voluntaristic terms. The ideological problems of the middle characters have virtually nothing to do with their objective class backgrounds. Such films make a few feeble attempts to identify a couple of minor characters whose offensive social thought is related to undesirable class origins, but the leading characters do not fall into this category. The middle characters are mired in bourgeois individualism despite the fact that they come from "good" class backgrounds. Furthermore, they are able to rescue themselves even though they are not Party members. In the films of the 1960s, good class origins do not necessarily produce people with revolutionary consciousness, and "bad" class backgrounds (of the sort shared by the heroes of films that treat imperial China) do not automatically beget individuals with reactionary consciousness.

Second, these "social problem" films reflect the extent to which policies of the Great Leap had been rejected in the early 1960s. Indeed, it is implied that the disasters of the Leap are responsible for low morale. But the clear abandonment of the Great Leap should not be interpreted as contempt for socialism. Xia Yan and the film establishment sought to legitimize their criticisms of Mao by calling attention to their underlying commitment to basic socialist ideas. Some of the utopian themes of the Great Leap that were present in the original story by screenwriter Li Jun were dropped in the screen version of *Li Shuangshuang*, but it is significant that considerable emphasis continues to be placed on the superiority of socialist modes of organizing and rewarding agricultural labor, and on the need to subordinate individual interest to community welfare. Similarly, the policy toward "youth to the countryside" reflected in *The Youth Generation* is not the same as the radical Cultural Revolution outlook on "rustification" in that young intellectuals are allowed to complete their higher education, sojourns to the remote areas are for fixed periods of time, and the students continue to enjoy the elite status (and presumably salary) of technological "experts." But it is significant nevertheless that important questions are raised about the process of postrevolutionary deradicalization and the ongoing need to bridge the gap between city and countryside.

Third, although the film audience is vividly aware that many young people are dissatisfied with their boring jobs, that many women are bullied by their husbands, and that most young intellectuals look down upon peasants, every effort is made by the filmmakers to indicate that these problems are best understood as blemishes on the consciousness of specific *individuals*.[36] Dissatisfied *groups* are never mentioned directly. Each film begins with middle characters who already possess a "poor attitude." No attempt is made to explain precisely how the consciousness of the protagonist became perverted. No effort is made to explain the relationship between antisocial behavior and contemporary political, economic, and social conditions. Although the audience knows better, the implication is that the "system" is not responsible. These works merely identify individual cases of ideological impurity and point out the methods that should be used to gain redemption for those who have lost their way.

The failings of these "social problem" films become even more apparent when they are measured against the standard set by Xie Jin (the director of *Stage Sisters*) in a highly controversial work titled *Fat Li, Young Li, and Old Li* (*Da Li, Xiao Li he Lao Li*, d. Xie Jin, 1962). Like *Li Shuangshuang* and *Satisfied or Not?* this film uses the "light comedy" genre in order to soften its political implications. But in sharp contrast to the more cautious works that portray the Communist Party as the organization that plays the key role in the salvation of wayward individuals, *Fat Li, Young Li, and Old Li* points to the Party itself as the source of many problems.

Set in a meatpacking plant in Shanghai, the film involves the relationship among three men, all named Li. Old Li, who represents the Party, is the department head in charge of production. His son, Young Li, is an ordinary worker in the plant, as well as a sports enthusiast. Fat Li, no relation to the father and son, is head of the labor union in the plant.

The apparent tranquility of factory life is interrupted when the workers express a desire for a more active physical fitness and recreation program. Fat Li, the union head, is elected to chair the plant's sports committee. He balks at first and then accepts his new assignment with enthusiasm.

Old Li, the production boss, is disturbed by the new development. He believes that his son, Young Li, enjoys participating in sporting activities more than he likes to work. He tells the lad that the physical fitness craze is a waste of time. In fact, his main concern is that sporting activities will have an adverse effect on production. Old Li cannot understand why a responsible labor leader like Fat Li would participate in such a movement. Fat Li vows to promote the movement with even greater zeal when he learns that Old Li made a visit to Fat Li's apartment in an effort to convince Fat Li's wife that the physical fitness program should be abandoned.

The struggle continues. Old Li becomes increasingly isolated and sullen, until one day he is accidentally locked into a meat cooler by his son. In order to survive the low temperature, he must do calisthenics! After he is rescued, Old Li concedes that physical fitness is important and decides to support the local movement.

The difference between Old Li and the middle characters in *Li Shuangshuang* and *The Youth Generation* is that Old Li represents the Communist Party. He also represents Mao, authority in general, and the production mania of the Great Leap Forward. Fat Li, on the other hand, as the amiable head of the union local, represents the masses who are actively defying the authority of the Party. In contrast to the harmony that characterizes relations between Party and union in conventional Chinese films, the two are seen in an almost unheard of adversarial relationship. Old Li, the Party man, is explicitly criticized for interfering in the family life of Fat Li. Moreover, the audience is permitted a rare opportunity to laugh at the expense of an authority figure as the foolish Party leader hops about, half frozen, in the meat locker. The conflict is, of course, resolved in the end, as it is in the other social problem films of the early 1960s, but in this case it is the Party leader who transforms himself in the end, not a member of the rank and file.

Needless to say, few films made in the early 1960s tested the limits of Xia Yan's new policies as boldly as *Fat Li, Young Li, and Old Li* did. Indeed, in the year or two preceding the eruption of the Cultural Revolution, the mildly critical films on life in the new socialist society disappeared from the screen. They were replaced by disappointing productions like *Heroic Sons and Daughters* (*Yingxiong er nü*, d. Wu Zhaodi, 1964) that heralded the rebirth of Maoism.[37]

Based on *Delegation Member*, surely one of the worst novels ever crafted by the eminent writer Ba Jin, *Heroic Sons and Daughters* is set during the Korean War. Like other films of the early 1960s that discuss the socialist period, it says almost nothing about the theme of class struggle. But in contrast to the others, it seeks to rekindle patriotic pride among the people at large by recalling the personal sacrifices that common people made during the Korean conflict.

Heroic Sons and Daughters focuses on the story of a young woman named Wang Fang, who, together with her elder brother, Wang Cheng, is assigned to a Chinese military unit in Korea. One day their unit is visited by Wang Wenqing, a powerful political commissar. Wang Cheng quickly realizes that the dedicated commissar is his younger sister's real father. When the commissar was doing underground Party work in the early 1930s, he was forced to flee Shanghai suddenly. He left his daughter, Wang Fang, in the care of a revolutionary worker, who raised the girl as a member of his own family. Wang Fang grew up thinking that the worker was her natural father, and that Wang Cheng was her natural brother. Just before he dies a heroic death at the front, the young Wang Cheng writes a note to the commissar to inform him of the identity of his long-lost daughter.

The commissar tells Wang Fang of the death of her "brother," but he refrains from telling her the complete story of her own early years. A movement to "learn from Wang Cheng" is launched to inspire still greater patriotic self-sacrifice among the troops. The emulation campaign is a big success. At the end of the film the revolutionary worker shows up in Korea as a member of a Chinese delegation, meets the commissar, and breaks the news to Wang Fang that the commissar is her real father. Overcome by emotion, she rushes off to battle in high spirits.

There is very little that distinguishes *Heroic Sons and Daughters* from *Shangganling* (*Shangganling*, d. Shao Meng, Lin Sha, 1956), *Sentinels of the*

High Sky (*Changkong biyi*, d. Wang Bing, Li Shutian, 1958), and other simplistic Korean War films made in the 1950s. The purpose of such works is to remind the audience that no matter how difficult the domestic situation may be, the Communist Party is the rightful guardian of the nation against foreign aggression. Needless to say, there are no middle characters or anyone who has the slightest misgiving about risking his or her life in a remote Korean outpost. On the contrary, the soldiers vie with one another for the most difficult and dangerous assignments, and even the wounded strenuously resist transfer to the rear. Films like *Heroic Sons and Daughters* are little more than showcases for Chinese nationalism. The basic message is that the most difficult material obstacles can be surmounted provided that one has a high level of political consciousness and patriotic devotion. Not only does *Heroic Sons and Daughters* fail to shed light on what life on the battlefield is really like, but the enemy's incredible ineptitude makes the scenes of victory seem hollow. If *Fat Li, Young Li, and Old Li* and *Li Shuangshuang* represent the best pre–Cultural Revolution films about the problems of the new socialist era, this dimensionless military tearjerker represents the worst.

REFLECTIONS ON THE EARLY 1960s

By the time *Heroic Sons and Daughters* was released in early 1965, it was obvious that the post–Great Leap thaw was over. In the spring, cultural authorities announced plans to send approximately a thousand film artists, including Xie Jin, Shui Hua, Zhang Ruifang, and Shangguan Yunzhu, into the countryside for reeducation.

In terms of diversity of subject matter and artistic quality, the motion pictures these people made represent a high point in postrevolutionary filmmaking. With the exception of outstanding works like *Dream of the Red Chamber* and *Early Spring*, these films do not reach the standards set in the late 1940s, but as a whole they are more distinctive than the other works produced in the years between the formation of the People's Republic in 1949 and the death of Mao in 1976. Moreover, when the Chinese film industry began to recover in the early 1980s from the devastation of the Cultural Revolution, directors like Xie Jin and Ling Zifeng, who had made outstanding contributions in the early 1960s, led the way.

The willingness of major cultural leaders like Xia Yan and Chen Huangmei to resist the Great Leap approach to artistic culture was largely responsible for the relative success of film artists in the early 1960s. Xia's views were able to take root because Mao Zedong's political position was tenuous, the Great Leap developmental strategy was under attack, and Chinese cultural nationalism was allowed to resurface in the wake of the Sino-Soviet split. The result was rather startling. Films that explored the history of imperial

China were made in larger numbers than any time since 1949, and many made use of neglected traditional forms of art such as opera and folk music. Films on the Republican period deemphasized the theme of class struggle, while pictures about the socialist era alluded to festering social problems and legitimized the portrayal of sympathetic "middle characters."

The films of the early 1960s were superior to most works produced during the Great Leap Forward, but Xia Yan had by no means abandoned Marxism or the fundamental idea that the film industry should serve politics and be guided by the Party. He simply opposed Great Leap notions about how directly filmmakers should serve and how closely they should be supervised. Yet there is no question that he accepted the idea that the function of cinema is to shape and transform popular consciousness by offering carefully considered interpretations of Chinese history and by presenting clear examples of exemplary moral behavior. It was Xia Yan's flexible and sometimes imaginative approach to this basic task that was responsible for the film successes of the early 1960s. At the same time, however, his fundamental commitment to the principle of the integration of state power and artistic culture prevented the Chinese film industry from developing beyond the standards set in the late 1940s and realizing its true potential. The films of the early 1960s are filled with caricatures. Foreigners are almost never portrayed realistically, and the internal enemy, however defined, is almost always represented in a one-dimensional way. Individuals are usually introduced as representatives of particular types of moral beings, whose function is not development but struggle with their moral opposites.

These problems are related, in part, to the use of traditional theatrical conventions in the films of the early 1960s. The dependency on Chinese stagecraft conventions was responsible for both the strengths and the weaknesses of these works. By making widespread use of traditional techniques borrowed from the stage, films of the early 1960s (including those based on works of modern fiction) satisfied a national emotional need, broke away from the Soviet socialist realism model, and won greater acceptance by an audience that enjoyed traditional forms. But by relying on traditional stage conventions, filmmakers were unable to solve the problem of the stock character. Traditional stylization usually requires that the full dimensions of moral conflict be defined with great clarity at the outset. This is what makes the exaggerated characterizations in *Third Sister Liu* so necessary. Unfortunately, this reliance on the traditional theater served to perpetuate at least one tradition of the school of socialist realism from which many Chinese artists were trying to break: that is, the tendency to produce caricatures of real people.

Films like *Early Spring* and *Stage Sisters* represent attempts to strike out in a new and more independent direction. Even though they fail to suggest the full range of complexities of Chinese life, they introduce the audience to human beings whose behavior is not always predictable. The Cultural Revolution put an end to these experiments undertaken in the early 1960s. But the experiments would continue. When the directors and screenwriters of the early 1960s reappeared in the 1980s, they would make films that recounted the horrors of the Cultural Revolution. Films like *The Legend of Tianyun Mountain* (*Tianyun shan chuanqi*, d. Xie Jin, 1980) would not only introduce characters far more complex and human than the memorable protagonists in *Early Spring* and *Stage Sisters*, but would adopt a refreshingly critical approach to the entire political history of the People's Republic.

NOTES

An earlier version of this chapter appeared as "The Limits of Cultural Thaw: Chinese Cinema in the Early 1960s," in *Perspectives on Chinese Cinema*, ed. Chris Berry (Ithaca, N.Y.: Cornell University East Asia Papers, no. 39, 1985), 97–148.

1. I should like to thank Leo Ou-fan Lee, Charles A. Peterson, Harold Shadick, William Tay, and David Yu for their thoughtful comments and help on earlier drafts of this chapter.
2. *Zhongguo yishu yingpian bianmu* (hereafter cited as ZGYS) (Beijing: Wenhua yishu chubanshe, 1981), 1:5–10.
3. *Wen hui bao* (Xianggang), December 6, 1977; *Dagong bao* (Xianggang), December 6, 1977.
4. Xia Yan, "Ba wo guo diangying yishu tigao dao yi ge geng xin de shuiping," *Hongqi*, no. 19 (October 1, 1961): 5–17. This article is the text of a speech given by Xia Yan at a national conference of film artists convened in June 1961.
5. *Zhongguo dianyingjia liezhuan* (Beijing: Zhongguo diangying chubanshe, 1982), 1:274.
6. ZGYS, 309–447.
7. ZGYS, 689–741.
8. The *Hongqi* editorial of June 1967 appears in Chiang Ching, *On the Revolution in Peking Opera* (Peking: Foreign Languages Press, 1968), 9–10.
9. For discussions of *Third Sister Liu*, see *Guangming ribao*, August 1, 1960; and *Zhongguo qingnian bao*, December 27, 1961.
10. Another film of the early 1960s that makes use of similar window dressing is *Qin Niangmei* (*Qin Niangmei*, d. Sun Yu, 1960).
11. For critical discussions of *Women Generals*, see *Cui Wei de yishu shijie* (Beijing: Zhongguo dianying chubanshe, 1982), 80–84, 296–301.
12. See *Guangming ribao*, December 7, 1963; and *Cui Wei de yishu shijie*, 302–10.
13. For comments on *Dream of the Red Chamber*, see *Wen hui bao* (Xianggang), November 14, 1962; *Dagong bao* (Xianggang), November 14, 1962; and *Dagong bao* (Beijing), June 28, 1963.
14. Jerome B. Greider, *Hu Shih and the Chinese Renaissance: Liberalism in the Chinese Revolution, 1917–1937* (Cambridge, Mass.: Harvard University Press, 1970), 363.
15. Mao Zedong, *Mao Zedong xuanji* (Beijing: Renmin chubanshe, 1977), 5:363.

16. *Dianying xiju sishi nian liang tiao luxian douzheng jitou* (hereafter cited as *DYXJ*) (Shanghai: Shanghai hong qi dianying zhipian chang hong qi geming zaofan bingtuan, 1967), 93.

17. *Zhongguo dianying juben xuanji* (hereafter cited as *ZGDYJB*) (Beijing: Zhongguo diangying chubanshe, 1979), 8:207-82.

18. For comments on *Naval Battle of 1894*, see *Renmin ribao*, November 17, 1963; *Guangming ribao*, July 13, 1963; and *Wen hui bao* (Shanghai), August 23, 1963.

19. *ZGDYJB*, 7:147-98.

20. Tony Rayns and Scott Meek, *Electric Shadows: Forty-Five Years of Chinese Cinema* (London: British Film Institute, 1980), 52-53.

21. *ZGDYJB*, 9:65-120. See S. A. Toroptsev, *Ocherk istorii Kitaiskgo kino* (Moskva: Izdel'stvo nauka, 1979), chapter 4, for a discussion of Cultural Revolution criticism of *Early Spring*.

22. *ZGDYJB*, 7:199-258.

23. *Zhongguo wenxuejia cidian* (Beijing: Yuyan xueyuan, 1979), 348-49.

24. *Cui Wei de yishu shijie*, 314-17, 419-52.

25. *ZGDYJB*, 9:707-96.

26. *ZGDYJB*, 9:409-508.

27. *ZGDYJB*, 9:581-635.

28. For the screenwriter's remarks on the production, see *Nongnu* (Beijing: Zhongguo dianying chubanshe, 1979), 117-32.

29. *ZGYS*, 859-926.

30. *ZGDYJB*, 9:245-320.

31. *DYXJ*, 102.

32. *ZGDYJB*, 7:73-146.

33. *ZGDYJB*, 8:147-206.

34. For critical reviews see *Guangming ribao*, April 29, 1963; *Renmin ribao*, December 16, 1962; and *Beijing wanbao*, February 20, 1963.

35. *Wen hui bao* (Shanghai), September 20, 1965; and *Guangming ribao*, August 28, 1965.

36. Another good example of an early-1960s film that treats problems of the socialist era as manifestations of individual antisocial behavior is *Woman High Diver* (*Nü tiaoshui duiyuan*, d. Liu Guoquan, 1964).

37. *ZGDYJB*, 9:707-96.

9

Popular Cinema and Political Thought in Early Post-Mao China: Reflections on Official Pronouncements, Film, and the Film Audience

Students of popular thought pay relatively little attention to the proclamations of governing elites. The views found in official pronouncements, we assume, do not necessarily reflect the thinking of ordinary people. We like studies that contribute to our understanding of Chinese society by exploring the many realms of popular thought that have little to do with official politics or are generally ignored in official accounts of social life.

But our relative lack of interest in official statements does not mean that we seek to avoid discussions of politics or that we ignore the dynamic relationship that exists between elite and popular culture. The mental world of ordinary people, such as the educated young urbanites discussed in this chapter, obviously includes ideas and attitudes about high politics and state affairs. One of the challenges for scholars of popular thought is to throw light on the relationship between official political testimonies and popular political thought. We assume that the official and the popular are not identical, but does it follow that they are entirely different and do not interact with each other? In sorting out the relationship between what is official and what is popular it is crucial, first, to recognize that in the realm of elite culture there is tension between the official and the unofficial and, second, to consider the ways in which the unofficial political thought of elites interacts with the popular political thought of non-elites.

The purpose of this chapter is not to examine the entire spectrum of popular political views, but to focus specifically on popular attitudes toward the Party and state. These topics were important in the early post-Mao years because the Party and state wanted to be perceived as morally legitimate in order to win public support for the economic reform programs associated with Deng Xiaoping. Leaders did not want their ambitious plans to be sabotaged by a citizenry that harbored serious reservations about the moral rectitude of the state and Party.

The post-Mao leadership, like its forerunners, spent considerable time and energy fostering the view that ordinary citizens revered and supported the authorities. It is extremely difficult, therefore, for scholars (either Chinese or foreign) to do systematic research on something as controversial and complex as the ways in which popular political thought criticized the state and Party. Sources of information are scarce and, when available, pose many knotty methodological problems.

During my year of residence in Beijing in the early 1980s it occurred to me that feature films might be a useful, though hardly comprehensive, source of information on the elusive topic of popular political thought. The films produced in the 1950s, 1960s, and 1970s had an official feel and, with some exceptions, glorified the state and Party. But many of the most popular films of the early 1980s seemed different. I was especially interested in movies referred to by the audience as serious films (*yansu pian*). Produced by elite filmmakers in state production units, these melodramas were unusually popular and invariably included rare and frank criticisms of the Party and state. I wanted to know why these serious films were so popular and whether they revealed anything about popular political thought. I wondered whether motion pictures made in the People's Republic at long last could be studied as illuminating expressions of popular political thought, rather than as manifestations of the official worldview or reflections of political sparring among the elites.[1]

The advantages of using popular films to understand popular thought are obvious. First, the size of the sample group is staggering. In 1982 the Chinese film audience was estimated to be 10 billion people, a number that is larger, I suspect, than the audience for fiction. In the early 1980s, *Popular Cinema* (*Dazhong dianying*) was the most widely read magazine in China, with a monthly readership of 10 million.[2] Furthermore, it seems logical to assume that the behavior of the film audience was not random, that it is possible to know why the most popular films were more appealing than the least popular films. Scholars of popular political thought have good reason to be intrigued by an audience that consistently demonstrated a strong preference for serious films, especially when those films repeat similar criticisms of the Party and state.

But those who attempt to use popular film sources as a window on popular political thought must move with caution. For example, it is impossible to generalize about the entire Chinese film audience, which consists of many important subgroups such as children, young people, the elderly, ethnic minorities, urbanites, rural dwellers, men, women, factory workers, military personnel, educated people, and many others. This study of popular political thought focuses on urbanites between the ages of 18 and

35 (especially students, teachers, professionals, and other educated people) because there are strong indications that they were the primary, although by no means the only, audience for popular political films.[3] But generalizations about the political thought of educated young urbanites are not necessarily valid for other groups.

Furthermore, by stressing the interest of young urbanites in the burst of serious political films that appeared in the early 1980s, I do not mean to suggest that they thought only of politics, that they were not inclined to watch anything else, or that their political thought can be entirely understood by examining the serious films they watched. We know that in the early 1980s educated urban youth thought about many subjects and that their film viewing included love stories, martial-arts adventures, and foreign thrillers. This chapter dwells on the *yansu* (serious) films because they were especially well liked by educated young city dwellers and because, compared to the other popular film genres, they afford us the most direct access to the political thought of this influential group. But the access gained through popular political films is by no means total. A full study of the thought of educated young urbanites (an undertaking far beyond the scope of this exploratory chapter) would have to account, among many other things, for the popularity of other film genres with these people. Similarly, a comprehensive analysis of their political thought would require an evaluation of many sources, not just the film materials discussed here.

The films of the late 1970s, the immediate post–Cultural Revolution period, are not very useful for our purposes because the Chinese film industry recovered very slowly from the political and artistic ravages of the ten-year Cultural Revolution. Large numbers of films were produced after Mao's death (129 features were made from 1977 to 1979, compared to only 109 features turned out in the Cultural Revolution decade) and box-office receipts soared to unprecedented heights, but the new films broke very little fresh political ground. One critic observed that the film audience was starved: "They flocked to the cinema to watch any film that was showing."[4] While significant numbers of literary intellectuals and reform activists were participating in the political protest movements of 1978 and 1979, filmmakers, according to Ding Qiao, deputy director of the Film Bureau in the early 1980s, were still making movies that "bore traces of the stereotypes" associated with filmmaking in the Cultural Revolution.[5]

This is not to suggest that the film industry was totally unaffected by the political protests of the late 1970s. But the impact became widely apparent only after the crackdown on Democracy Wall in late 1979, as films echoing and popularizing the concerns of the protesters finally began to surface. Many of these motion pictures were based on works of fiction published before the demise of Democracy Wall. The new political thrust of Chinese cinema became evident around 1980. True, filmmakers constituted a privileged elite, the film industry was still monopolized by the state and monitored by Party censors, and the great majority of new works still contributed little to popular political discourse or to the development of film art in China—but beginning in 1980 a small but potent cinema of social criticism, linked both in terms of form and content to the rich traditions of the 1930s and 1940s, began to emerge as the most popular genre of new films, especially among educated urban youth. Unprecedented numbers of works that clearly expressed unofficial political views slipped through state censorship organs.

In my estimation, the most interesting group of popular political films was completed in the period from 1980 to early 1983, that is, the years between the fall of Democracy Wall and the launching of the campaign against spiritual pollution in 1983. Three of the most representative works that circulated in this unusual period are *The Legend of Tianyun Mountain* (*Tianyun shan chuanqi*, 1980), directed by Xie Jin; *A Corner Forgotten by Love* (*Bei aiqing yiwang de jiaoluo*, 1981), directed by Li Yalin and Zhang Ji; and *At Middle Age* (*Ren dao zhongnian*, 1982), directed by Wang Qimin and Sun Yu.[6] At the time, these films came closer than almost anything else produced after 1949 to an openly critical popular cinema. They were widely acclaimed by the film establishment, highly critical of the Communist Party, extraordinarily popular among the film audience at a moment when the film industry was beginning to get stiff competition from the television world, and subjected to tough criticism in the official press.

The Legend of Tianyun Mountain, based on a short novel by Lu Yanzhou published in 1979, is the tragic story of a young intellectual, Luo Chun, who was attacked in the 1957 Anti-Rightist Campaign and then cruelly victimized for more than twenty years.[7] The two women in Luo's life are a study in contrast. One woman, Song Wei, was engaged to Luo Chun in 1957, but in order to avoid trouble and advance her political career, she broke off the marriage plan and denounced her lover once he was identified as a rightist. The other woman, Feng Qinglan, who was Song Wei's best friend in 1957, fell in love with the pitiful Luo after he was denounced and then sacrificed her career and health to defend and comfort Luo during his long ordeal. More than twenty years later, in winter 1978, Song Wei, now a high-ranking local Party official, is in charge of the department in the prefectural Party office that decides who among those accused of rightism in 1957 will be rehabilitated. She wants justice to be done after so many years, but this would involve revealing the key role played by her present husband, the powerful secretary of the prefectural Party committee, in the persecution of Luo in 1957.

Despite the fact that the novel had been criticized by Party conservatives, the film version of *The Legend of Tianyun Mountain*, produced at the Shanghai Film Studio, was received with great enthusiasm by the film au-

Party bosses argue about whether it is wise to acknowledge their cruel and long-term persecution of a patriotic intellectual in *The Legend of Tianyun Mountain* (1980, d. Xie Jin). China Film Archive

dience and many film professionals. In early 1981 it was praised in *Wenyi bao*.[8] Then in June 1981, film periodicals announced that it had simply overwhelmed the competition (eighty-three feature films were produced in 1980) by taking first place in five categories, including best feature, best director, and best screenplay, at the first annual Jinji Film Award ceremony, a high-profile event presided over by the film establishment. Even more startling, *The Legend of Tianyun Mountain*, the first feature film made in China that focused on the Anti-Rightist Campaign of 1957, shared first-place honors in the fourth annual Hundred Flowers film competition sponsored by *Popular Cinema* magazine. It was named best picture on 861,831 of the 2,018,418 ballots cast by ordinary film fans.[9]

In spring 1981 and again in fall 1981, however, concerned film professionals were badly shaken by the assault launched by Party conservatives on another critical film, *Bitter Love* (*Ku lian*, 1980), written by Bai Hua and directed by Peng Ning at the Changchun Film Studio. Characterized in the official press as a manifestation of bourgeois liberalization, *Bitter Love* was never released nationwide, even though the screenplay had been published already, film previews had been held in late 1980, and advertisements were on display outside theaters and in popular film journals.[10] In a December 1981 address to 250 film artists, Party General Secretary Hu Yaobang, himself a victim of a subsequent campaign against bourgeois liberalization in 1987, tacitly acknowledged the existence of political factions among the privileged elite when he warned filmmakers about "attributing errors in Party work" to the nature of the "socialist system" itself. Films that reach such a conclusion were said to convey "unhealthy political sentiments and bad taste."[11] In a matter of weeks the official press began to carry articles that assaulted the much-heralded *The Legend of Tianyun Mountain*, now characterized as a film that "runs counter to reality" (*weifan zhenshi*).[12] Movie theaters and television stations were discouraged from screening it.

As a result of the controversy surrounding *Bitter Love* in 1981, a second important film, *A Corner Forgotten by Love*, was in serious political trouble even before it was released. A production of the small Emei Film Studio in Sichuan, this movie was based on an award-winning short story published in early 1980 by Zhang Xian, a victim of the Anti-Rightist Campaign in 1957.[13] Completed in late 1981, *A Corner Forgotten by Love* came extremely close to being "executed," that is, killed by cultural censors.[14] The film was finally released in early 1982, after the political dust of the first campaign against bourgeois liberalization had settled, but it was denied the usual publicity given to new productions.

Set in 1979, well after the death of Mao and the arrest of his leading proponents, the story is about an utterly destitute peasant household in a depressing and forgotten corner of a remote county. The head of the household, Shen Shanwang, had been a deputy co-op leader in the mid-1950s, prior to the collectivization of agriculture. During the Great Leap Forward in 1958, however, he was dismissed from his post and branded a rightist because he opposed the cutting down of valuable fruit trees to fuel backyard steel furnaces. Like the protagonist of *The Legend of Tianyun Mountain*, Shen was treated as a social outcast for the next twenty years. In 1974, during the Cultural Revolution, his eldest daughter, Cunni, committed suicide after the local militia discovered that she was having a sexual relationship with a hardworking local lad.

A Corner Forgotten by Love focuses on Shen's second daughter, Huangmei, who was born during the post–Great Leap famine. Haunted by the memory of her sister's awful fate, Huangmei must come to terms with the rumblings of her own sexual awakening in 1979. She is at once attracted to and frightened by a poor, but forward-looking, young cadre named Xu Rongshu, who insists that the grinding poverty the village has known since collectivization can be broken if the households are allowed to develop private cottage industries, sow cash crops, and sell their goods at the free market. Huangmei's mother suspects that the young man is about to make the sort of rightist errors that ruined her husband twenty years before and is terrified that another sexual scandal is on the horizon. Arrangements are

Innocent and tender sexual awakenings can have catastrophic political consequences in *A Corner Forgotten by Love* (1981, d. Li Yalin, Zhang Ji). China Film Archive

soon made for Huangmei to marry a man in another village for 500 yuan, a sum that will get her family out of debt.

In mid-1982, within weeks of its release, *A Corner Forgotten by Love* was attacked by hostile critics who disliked its graphic depiction of rural misery.[15] Still, *A Corner Forgotten by Love*, like *The Legend of Tianyun Mountain*, had many supporters in the press and film worlds. Zhang Xian's screenplay took first place at the second annual Jinji Film Award ceremony and He Xiaoshu, who portrayed the mother, Linghua, won the trophy for best supporting actress. Although this film was not among the top three vote-getters in the popular Hundred Flowers competition, it was on a very short list of works described at the award ceremony as the best-liked films of 1981. The Ministry of Culture also certified this film as one of the nine best features made in 1981.[16] Still, *A Corner Forgotten by Love* was not permitted to be screened publicly outside China.

The last film I want to discuss, *At Middle Age*, a product of the Changchun Film Studio, was based on a novella published by Chen Rong in January 1980.[17] Like the other movies mentioned here, the filming of *At Middle Age* was interrupted time and again by the ongoing controversy surrounding the original work of fiction. Released in early 1983, the film took more than two years to shoot.[18]

Set in 1979, this film tells the sad story of a forty-two-year-old woman, Lu Wenting, whose physical and emotional health breaks down as she unsuccessfully attempts to play the conflicting roles of eye surgeon, wife, and mother of two. A promising medical graduate in 1961, Lu is completing her *eighteenth* year of residency at a Beijing hospital as the film opens. Despite her dedication and high level of skill, Lu, a non-Party intellectual, earns only 56 yuan a month (that is, less than a barber) in 1979, and her family of four lives in a 130-square-foot room. Her workload is oppressive, she feels guilty about neglecting her children, and her marriage is passionless. As she is recovering from a debilitating heart attack that weakens her still further, a major question is posed. Should she try once again to carry on with her work in hopes that the Party's outrageous treatment of intellectuals will improve or, like her best friend and colleague Yafen, who has decided to emigrate to Canada, should she give up hope that life in China will someday change?

By the time *At Middle Age* appeared in early 1983, the political storm directed at the original work of fiction had subsided. It still had some

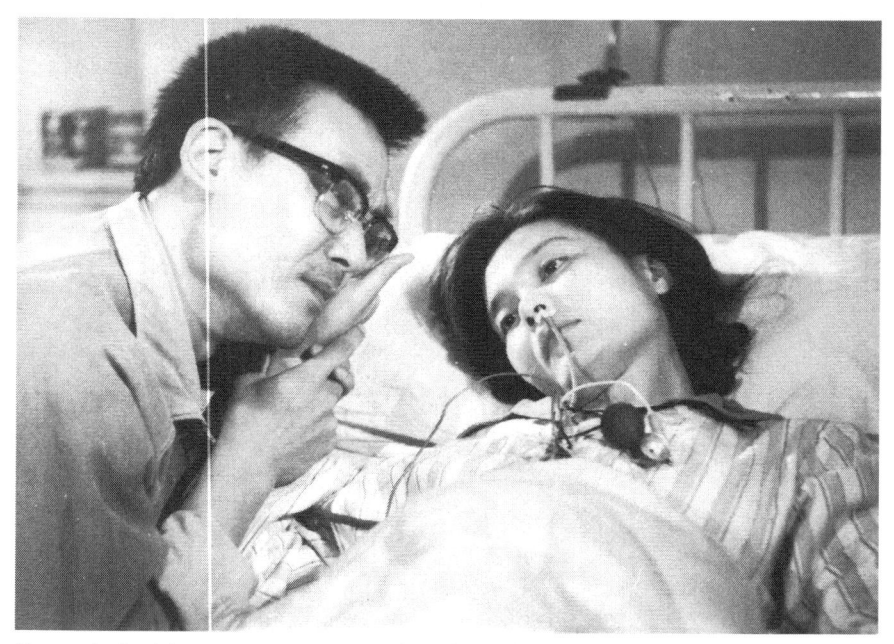

Devoted physician Lu Wenting is working herself to death, but her contributions are totally unappreciated by the Party in *At Middle Age* (1982, d. Wang Qimin, Sun Yu). China Film Archive

powerful detractors, but like *The Legend of Tianyun Mountain* and *A Corner Forgotten by Love, At Middle Age* did extremely well at the box office and was praised by many film professionals. Film viewers chose it as the best film of 1982 in the sixth annual Hundred Flowers competition, and actress Pan Hong took top honors in the best actress category at the third annual Jinji Film Award ceremony sponsored by the film establishment.[19]

One way to begin to understand the popularity of political melodramas like these among many film professionals and among educated young city dwellers is to contrast the social views contained in such works to important, even path-breaking, official pronouncements published at about the same time. Democracy Wall was gone by late 1979, but Party ideologists were still under considerable pressure to explain the "mistakes" made by the Party in the years after 1949. There was also a persistent call for a fundamental reevaluation of Maoism and the personal role of Mao Zedong following the establishment of the People's Republic. Reform-minded people inside and outside the Party were demanding that the Party send a clear signal that the nightmares of the past would not be repeated and that there was hope for political and economic reform. The spectacular trial of the Gang of Four, which opened in late November 1980, was welcomed by most urbanites, but even before the trial ended a flood of letters to *People's Daily* and other publications, repeating the concerns of films like *The Legend of Tianyun Mountain*, pointed out that the jailing of the defendants was only a partial solution to the political problems that plagued China.[20]

After much delay, the long-awaited official statement on the weighty issues mentioned above—a thirty-thousand-character document titled "Resolution on Certain Questions in the History of Our Party since the Founding of the People's Republic of China"—was issued on July 1, 1981.[21] Those who hoped this Central Committee document would be as forceful as Nikita Khrushchev's famous denunciation of Stalin and Stalinism in February 1956 were undoubtedly disappointed. This unprecedented public statement received enormous attention in the domestic and foreign press, but on balance, it amounted to a cautious and rather self-serving evaluation of the post-1949 period. Indeed, the resolution was considerably less critical than the highly popular films discussed here.

The 1981 resolution, published after the release of *The Legend of Tianyun Mountain* and before the completion of *A Corner Forgotten by Love* and *At Middle Age*, made headlines by admitting publicly what informed Chinese already knew: first, Mao Zedong "made mistakes in his later years," and second, the Cultural Revolution was "initiated and led" by Mao. Though the resolution was the first major public attempt by the ruling elite to repudiate the cult of Mao and to reject the myth of his infallibility, it hardly constituted a denunciation of Mao and Maoism or raised fundamental questions about Party rule. On the contrary, the tone was remarkably upbeat. There was virtually no criticism of Mao's role in the long period from the founding of the Communist Party in 1921 to the establishment of the People's Republic in 1949; high marks were given to Mao and the Party for their work in the 1949–1956 transitional period; and even more astonishingly, the tumultuous years from 1956 to 1965 were characterized as a time when "the material and technical basis for modernizing our country was largely established." The resolution briefly acknowledged that there were "shortcomings" in the agricultural collectivization drive after 1955, that the "scope" of the 1957 Anti-Rightist Campaign was "too broad," and that "left" errors had been committed during the Great Leap Forward, but no mention was made of the tens of millions of people who perished in the massive famine that followed the Great Leap.

The 1981 resolution treated in detail only the disastrous decade of the Cultural Revolution and left the clear impression that the social, political, and economic problems of the present day were attributable, in the main, to the upheavals of the Cultural Revolution, the diabolical machinations of Lin Biao and the Gang of Four, and the mistakes made by Mao in his later years. The resolution confidently asserted that the corner had been turned on the abuses and injustices associated with the Cultural Revolution once the Central Committee declared in December 1978 that socialist modernization was the main task of the Party and people.

Finally, in case anyone had misunderstood the significance of the assault on bourgeois liberalization waged in spring 1981, the July resolution stated in no uncertain terms that the Central Committee's criticisms of Mao and the Cultural Revolution reaffirmed, rather than questioned, the "four cardinal principles": the correctness of the socialist road, the proletarian dictatorship, the leadership of the Communist Party, and the ideological hegemony of Marxism-Leninism and Mao Zedong Thought. In no case, the resolution warned, should the Party's mistakes be used as a "pretext for weakening, breaking away from or even sabotaging its leadership." "It is imperative," the Central Committee added, "to maintain a high level of vigilance and conduct effective struggle against all those who are hostile to socialism and try to sabotage it in the political, economic, ideological, and cultural fields."

The basic social views expressed in the three films under review, it seems safe to say, were significantly more critical than the ones contained in this extraordinary benchmark resolution. The fact that these same films were highly acclaimed by many film professionals and young urban film fans tells us something about the gap between the official pronouncements of the Party and popular political thought in the early 1980s. Of course, I do not mean to suggest that the interests and thought of elite filmmakers were identical to the thought of the ordinary people who frequented movie houses, or to deny that, in structural terms, films and filmmakers belonged to the official realm. It seems to me, however, that the popularity of these films can be explained, in part, by the audience's obvious approval of the basic social views espoused. The making of serious political melodramas in the early 1980s was not simply a matter of a few elite filmmakers suddenly and inexplicably embracing the unofficial and popular political views of urban youth. Nor was it a matter of renegade cultural elites agitating among an apolitical and inarticulate urban mass. The process of political fertilization, I strongly suspect, was from both the top down and the bottom up. A central paradox of early 1980s Chinese filmmaking is that the serious political films were popular cultural artifacts produced by privileged state-employed filmmakers who were able to work outside the mainstream of official ideology. Their state-funded work was unofficial in the sense that it represented minority or dissenting political positions held by influential elites, including Party members. More importantly, at least for our purposes, their work was unofficial and popular in the sense that it actively sought to represent the political views of ordinary people who felt that Party reform policies were inadequate. The fact that educated elites produced this work and that the state, in a sense, allowed this activity to take place does not mean that these films cannot be considered as expressions of popular political thought.

At the level of raw political analysis, *The Legend of Tianyun Mountain* was considerably more provocative than the July 1981 resolution, going far beyond the scope of the well-received "scar literature" (*shangheng wenxue*) produced immediately following the Cultural Revolution. Whereas most scar literature dwelled on the abuses people suffered during the Cultural Revolution and heaped blame on the Gang of Four for the sorry condition of China in the late 1970s, *The Legend of Tianyun Mountain* said almost nothing about the Cultural Revolution. The underlying assumption of the film is that the difficulties that continued to plague China in the 1980s had their origins in the 1950s, especially during the time of the Anti-Rightist Campaign of 1957, an enormously destructive period that was essentially whitewashed in the 1981 resolution. It was implied that not all the problems confronting the Chinese people in the 1980s could be attributed to the odious Cultural Revolution leadership.

The film complained that those who stressed the destructiveness of the Gang of Four were missing the point. If there was moral justification for condemning the Cultural Revolution leadership after its fall from power (when such criticism was welcomed by the new leadership), should not the authorities acknowledge the contributions of those who had the courage to speak out during the Cultural Revolution (when such criticism was not welcomed) and those who protested obvious abuses before the Cultural Revolution?

The Legend of Tianyun Mountain pointed out that many of the Party faithful who were persecuted during the Cultural Revolution, cadres like Song

Wei and her husband, Wu Yao, were precisely the ones responsible for victimizing Party critics during the Anti-Rightist Campaign in 1957. Party veterans like Wu Yao were eager to have their names cleared and to be restored to positions of power after the Cultural Revolution, but they were extremely reluctant, once restored to power, to approve the rehabilitation of people like Luo Chun, who continued to suffer into the 1980s for speaking out in 1957. To rehabilitate such people would require admitting one's own complicity and conceding that the Anti-Rightist Campaign was extremely unjust. That is why Wu Yao, even at the very end of the film, continued to regard Luo Chun as a rightist who deserved to be punished for life.

By refusing to review Luo Chun's case, Wu Yao demonstrated that he had learned the most elementary political lessons taught by the Party in the 1950s. Never take the initiative; never question Party policy; wait for directives to come down from above before acting. If one is required to exercise judgment, it is better to lean to the left (for example, refusing to hear the case of a victim of the Anti-Rightist Campaign) than to lean to the right (being excessively lenient with those once accused of rightism). The Party forgives leftist mistakes; it does not forgive rightist errors.

Perhaps the most astonishing feature of *The Legend of Tianyun Mountain* is that it turned upside down many of the Party's sacred moral categories. In the films produced in the 1950s and 1960s, mainstream Party people, even those who wavered momentarily, were ordinarily characterized as honest and virtuous, while rightists were characterized as morally deficient and evil. In *The Legend of Tianyun Mountain*, these stock roles were reversed. The film audience was told that rightists like Luo Chun were pure of heart, selfless, and respected by the people, while many Party operatives who assumed power after the Cultural Revolution were vindictive and corrupt.

A Corner Forgotten by Love, like *The Legend of Tianyun Mountain*, looked well beyond the Cultural Revolution when it sought to identify the sources of problems that plagued China in the early 1980s. This work stated explicitly that grinding poverty became a characteristic of village life not in the Cultural Revolution, but with the advent of collectivization in 1956. The protagonist's father, Shen Shanwang, had been stripped of his leading position and ostracized because, like Luo Chun in *The Legend of Tianyun Mountain*, he spoke out against the Great Leap Forward in 1958. And, like Luo Chun, he was not among those whose reputations were cleared in the years immediately following the Cultural Revolution. Three years had passed since the death of Mao, but this village was still dirt poor. Shen's family did not have enough to eat or enough to wear, and they lived in a depressing hovel.

A Corner Forgotten by Love, even more than *The Legend of Tianyun Mountain*, argued that the Party's failure to address political problems that predated the Cultural Revolution made it extremely difficult for the rural economic reform policies adopted by the Party center in 1978 to be implemented and for economic progress to take place. Xu Rongshu, the young cadre who returned from the navy in 1979, has heard that popular economic reforms, such as private household sidelines and private commerce, have been implemented elsewhere, but the veteran leaders of the village, like the cadre Wu Yao in *The Legend of Tianyun Mountain*, are afraid of making rightist errors and refuse to consider reforms that will improve standards of living. They will wait until they receive the appropriate instructions from higher authorities.

The notion that China's economic development, especially in the rural sector, had stagnated for more than twenty years after 1956 was advanced in both films through the assertion that prosperity could be possible only by turning the clock back and adopting the plans set forth by those categorized as rightists and counterrevolutionaries in 1957. In the first film, rightist Luo Chun's elaborate plan for the development and modernization of the Tianyun Mountain region was dropped in 1957 and replaced by characteristically Maoist schemes, all of which failed miserably. Only in 1979 was Luo's plan rediscovered and adopted. In the second film, Shen Shanwang was victimized in 1958 for advocating the cultivation of cash crops. But in 1979 it was precisely the subject of cash crops that so excited young Xu Rongshu, who turned to the old rightist, Shen Shanwang, for advice.

Once again, the Party regulars were the negative characters, while the rightists who had suffered for twenty years were presented as martyrs of the people. This tendency was especially apparent in the titillating and controversial scenes of youthful sexual awakening that led to the suicide of Shen's elder daughter. Official moral doctrine taught that premarital sexual activity is degenerate. Yet the audience could see that the two young lovers were not only sympathetic characters, but also that their union seemed to be the only source of joy and spontaneity in an otherwise loveless, colorless, and oppressive environment. Like the rightists, the sexual partners were presented as heroes and martyrs. She was driven to suicide, and he began serving a long prison sentence. Critics of the movie, not surprisingly, accused the filmmakers of propagating bourgeois humanism. That is, instead of discussing the character of the young people within the framework of the various social classes, the film treated their behavior as a manifestation of universal human nature.

At Middle Age did not discuss the period before the Cultural Revolution in any detail. Instead, it focused on the sensitive topic of the Party's poor treatment of non-Party intellectuals, especially middle-aged intellectuals, during and after the Cultural Revolution, an issue scarcely mentioned in the 1981 resolution. The film reached two sobering conclusions. First, the Maoist approach to intellectuals was an almost unqualified disaster, and second, very little was done in the immediate post-Mao era to correct the problem. Consequently, intellectuals like Lu Wenting, who believed they had sacrificed their youth for the noble cause of reconstructing China, were now full of self-pity, burned out professionally, and ambivalent about the Party's latest modernization strategy. Lu Wenting was lonely, depressed, and indifferent toward life. Indeed, the ending of the film failed to resolve the issue of her willingness and ability to carry on in her work.

As in the other films, the sharpest contrast was between the alienated hero and Party bureaucrats who reassumed leading positions following a period of intense persecution during the Cultural Revolution. Vice Minister Jiao Chengsi, upon whom Lu Wenting performed successful cataract surgery, and his obnoxious wife, Qin Bo (openly ridiculed in the film as a typical "Marxist-Leninist old lady"), lived a life of extraordinary privilege and influence. Lu Wenting, on the other hand, did not even have the time to care for her children.

Qin Bo, a figure whose negative traits can in no way be traced to the Cultural Revolution or the Gang of Four, is the most interesting villain in the film. Lu Wenting's work was made much more difficult by this abusive Party veteran who constantly expressed distrust of the middle-aged surgeon and questioned her professional competence because Lu was not a Party member and because her official status was still that of a resident. The film suggested that even if people like Lu Wenting were able to summon up the energy to serve the Party and state, it was by no means clear that power holders like Qin Bo were prepared to give them a free hand to do their jobs. Lu Wenting made great sacrifices for the Party, but the Party did not appreciate or trust her.

The constant repetition of important political themes in these and other popular works produced in the early 1980s strongly suggests that the opinions of these privileged filmmakers resonated with the political thought of young and educated urban viewers. One of their most basic themes was the notion that the problems of the present were related to serious political failings of the Party and state that were apparent before the onset of the Cultural Revolution and persisted after it ended. On this crucial point, the political concerns of the audience and the filmmakers discussed here contrasted quite sharply with the views contained in official ideological statements such as the July 1981 resolution.

It seems to me, however, that these films were appealing at other, less explicit, levels as well. Their popularity also had something to do with *how* the stories were told. In early 1984 a group of students from eight universities in Beijing was asked: What film subjects move you most? By a wide margin (51 percent) respondents stated a preference for films that treated "life's hardships and difficulties," a topic that is inextricably linked to political issues, but one that does not necessarily have to be treated, artistically speaking, in an explicit, heavy-handed fashion.[22] The films reviewed here were clearly full of political content, but unlike the passionless treatment of Chinese life contained in official pronouncements like the 1981 resolution, the films humanized accounts of life's hardships and difficulties by converting them into melodramas that permitted, indeed encouraged, mass catharsis. North American and European viewers often find these works overly sentimental and unrealistic. But the Chinese audience, fond of such sentimentality, probably found it easy to identify with the victims of arbitrary force and injustice.[23] Skillful use and even manipulation of the weepy, melodramatic genre is precisely what links the popular political films produced in the 1980s by directors like Xie Jin to the rich tradition of Chinese cinema in the 1930s and 1940s.

The filmmakers' efforts to get the attention of the film audience and win its approval were facilitated by careful use of an important and time-honored Chinese storytelling device. The major characters are confronted by agonizing moral dilemmas that are familiar to the audience, especially dilemmas that involve complex love relationships, a subject that was virtually banned from Chinese screens during the Cultural Revolution. The films were appealing, in part, because the audience was not offered easy solutions to complex social problems. On the contrary, the audience was forced to witness and, in a sense, actually feel the intense suffering of the protagonists.

The dilemma that confronted Song Wei, the woman who abandoned Luo Chun in *The Legend of Tianyun Mountain*, is related to the important issue of life strategies. In 1957, during the Anti-Rightist Campaign, she had to make a difficult choice. She could remain loyal to Luo Chun, her true love; the film made it clear that this was the morally responsible thing to do. But to do so would have meant the destruction of her career, social isolation, scorn (young children are shown throwing rocks at rightists), and material deprivation. Or she could do the politically expedient thing by closely following the advice of Party insiders, but only at the cost of denouncing the man she loved and entering into an essentially loveless union with the doctrinaire Wu Yao, whose political star was rising. The audience undoubtedly knew that, in moral terms, the choice was clear, but they were probably not surprised when Song Wei reluctantly followed the practical path.

Shen Huangmei, the central protagonist in *A Corner Forgotten by Love*, faced a similar choice that also involved a triangular love relationship. She could demonstrate filial respect for her poor mother, erase the family debt, and have a more comfortable future in a prosperous village elsewhere by agreeing to a customary arranged marriage (to a man she had never met). The other option was to take her chances with the local lad, Rongshu, the first person to make her conscious of her sexuality. The problem with this choice was that she had not yet completely abandoned the notion, shaped by the tragedy of her sister's premarital love affair, that her emotions could not be trusted and that her natural instincts were somehow immoral.

Furthermore, it was by no means clear that the young man had a promising political future. The ideas he espoused were ones that had been identified with rightism time and again since the 1950s.

Once again, the choice was not as obvious as it might appear, especially if the audience dismissed the artificial happy ending tacked on to satisfy the censors. The popularity of *A Corner Forgotten by Love* among young people who wanted more freedom of choice in marriage does not mean that viewers, faced with the same problem in their own lives, would automatically defy their parents. Many young viewers who would not run the risk of choosing someone like Rongshu in real life were perfectly sincere when they applauded Huangmei's daring decision to do so on screen.

Lu Wenting, the heroine of *At Middle Age*, had no way to leave China. But the youthful urban film audience was undoubtedly interested in her reaction to the dramatic news that her alter ego, Yafen, had decided to emigrate to Canada, a rich capitalist country. The most poignant sequence in the film is a sad farewell dinner which Wenting and her husband share with Yafen and her bitter husband. A guilt-ridden Yafen confesses that she agonized over the decision to give up on China. Her husband, Xueyao, says that he is an "unworthy son of the Chinese people." He agrees that the bad times are behind the Chinese people, but he can no longer wait for the good times to come to his house.

Lu Wenting, like the film audience, was forced to choose. She could approve of Yafen's decision to leave the motherland and undergo a spiritual rebirth in another land, but to do so would be tantamount to conceding that the logic employed by the parting couple was correct. She could disapprove of Yafen's decision, but this would imply that she accepted the upbeat official view that the future is bright and would require her once again to muster the energy to serve the noble cause of nation building. If Yafen was wrong, there was every reason to continue to work hard and sacrifice; if Yafen, a good person, was right, then it would be enough to go through the motions at work. Again, the choice was not obvious. It is likely that many in the audience had high hopes for the future, while many others were skeptical of the Party's latest promises.

After *At Middle Age* was released in early 1983, many filmmakers and ordinary film fans were eager to see more serious films produced, films that dealt with life's hardships and difficulties. But the architects of the official campaign against spiritual pollution, initiated in autumn 1983, disapproved of films like *The Legend of Tianyun Mountain*, *A Corner Forgotten by Love*, and *At Middle Age* because these works challenged the notion that the primary purpose of the film industry is to communicate the official word of the Party to the audience. But Xie Jin and the other defiant directors of serious political melodramas who worked in the official sector continued to promote a cinema that gave greater expression to the unofficial political views of both privileged elites and ordinary people, even though the unofficial often clashed with the official.

The tension between these two tendencies was reflected in public remarks made by Shao Mujun, a senior researcher affiliated with the China Filmworkers Association, in October 1984, after the storm of the campaign against spiritual pollution had subsided. "Some people here," Shao insisted, "are quite loath to admit that there is a problem of freedom of expression in filmmaking. To talk about it is even considered a reactionary tendency of bourgeois liberalization." Shao boldly asserted, "A main target of the Chinese film industry on its road to reform is to fight for full freedom of creative expression, stand against 'crude interference,' and break away from the agitprop task of illustrating current policies."[24]

Despite the brutal suppression of alienated students and disaffected young workers that commenced in June 1989 and the subsequent launching of a nationwide cultural crackdown, none of the issues raised in this chapter have been settled. The struggle between directors who want to give expression to unofficial and popular political criticisms of the state and Party and cultural bureaucrats who demand that filmmakers engage in political agitprop work will continue for some time. Furthermore, the popular political complaints conveyed in the serious films of the early 1980s are still heard in urban China. The street demonstrations of disgruntled students in late 1986 and the massive peaceful protests in Tiananmen Square and elsewhere in spring 1989 were, in some respects, foreshadowed in the sometimes bitter speeches and remarks of characters in the films discussed here. Economic reforms were welcomed, these film voices seemed to be saying, but a political renovation of the system should be undertaken as well. It is hard to evaluate with precision the long-term impact of the crushing political and cultural repression carried out in summer 1989. But we do know that the short-lived official campaign against bourgeois liberalization launched in early 1987 did little to discourage filmmakers like Xie Jin or to dampen popular enthusiasm for political reform. Indeed, the spectacular success of Xie Jin's *Hibiscus Town* (*Furongzhen*) in 1987, when international film critics were focusing their attention on the imaginative but relatively low impact work done by the "new wave" of Fifth Generation filmmakers in China, underscores the profound popular appeal of political melodramas.[25]

But how should the political thought of young and educated urbanites be characterized? The evidence provided by the popular film material highlighted here is far from conclusive, but it suggests answers that would have been doubted by both the most uncritical supporters and the most vehement detractors of the Communist Party in the early 1980s. If these amazingly popular works offer any hints about the political thought of young urbanites in the early post-Mao years, it is that despite their self-pity and alienation they basically accepted the system and recognized, however grudgingly, the authority of the Party and state. The main audience for Xie Jin's films of the early 1980s was people like himself who thought primarily in terms of the reform of the Party and state rather than their elimination. The films reflect both a widespread popular disillusionment with the Party and a sincere hope that the Party will be able to reform itself. These works identified retrogressive forces that had to be eliminated from the Party and state, but had little in common with the views advanced by daring anti-Marxist dissident intellectuals who fundamentally opposed the Party (and who, before June 1989, enjoyed relatively little support among ordinary urbanites). Films like *The Legend of Tianyun Mountain* were depressing, but they usually included depictions of honest and loyal cadres who were dedicated to the reform of the system.

This tentative conclusion supports the notion that, while the official and the unofficial are not identical, they should not be thought of as being opposite. On the one hand, elements of popular political thought, filtered through films and many other media, helped fuel the political reform movement at the elite level by exerting a measure of political pressure. On the other hand, it seems clear that the contours of mainstream popular political discourse in the years immediately following the death of Mao were still being shaped to a significant degree by the political categories and even the language set forward by the Party in the early 1950s. Ordinary urbanites (who had very few options in the realm of politics) in all likelihood did not think much about alternatives to the socialist system when they demanded justice and accountability in the early 1980s. The enormously popular serious films of this period reveal the glaring gap between official political thought and the political thought of educated young urbanites, but they also suggest that the bitter complaints of many such urbanites had little in common with outright dissident behavior or the barely audible calls for organized opposition to the single-party state.

NOTES

An earlier version of this chapter appeared as "Popular Cinema and Political Thought in Post-Mao China: Reflections on Official Pronouncements, Film, and the Film Audience," in *Unofficial China: Popular Culture and Thought in the People's Republic*, ed. Perry Link, Richard Madsen, and Paul G. Pickowicz (Boulder, Colo.: Westview Press, 1989), 37–53.

1. For a solid study of cinema and elite politics after 1949, see Paul Clark, *Chinese Cinema* (Cambridge, UK: Cambridge University Press, 1988).
2. Margaret Pearson, "Film in China: The Domestic System and Foreign Imports," U.S. Department of State Cultural Background Series (Beijing: U.S. Embassy, January 21, 1982), 1–2.

3. In a 1983 survey of young Shanghainese, "serious films that reflect social issues" were preferred by more respondents than any other type of film, including foreign films. Among those surveyed, it was university students (93%), Youth League cadres (94.3%), and young industrial workers (83.2%) who showed the greatest degree of interest in serious films. Percentages of respondents who acknowledged liking certain types of film were as follows:

Serious	77%
Foreign	75.8%
Adventure	41.5%
Light comedy	33.8%
Revolutionary history	32.6%
Adaptations of great fiction	30.4%
Hong Kong films	27.7%
Ancient history costume dramas	13.1%
Military stories	8.1%
Operas	5.9%

See Xu Miaoting, "Shanghai shiqu qingnian dianying quwei qianxi," *Qingnian yanjiu*, no. 1, (1983): 40–46. There is also evidence that working-class youth had a strong interest in political melodramas in the early 1980s. See *Dangdai Zhongguo qingnian gongren de xianzhuang* (Beijing: Gongren chubanshe, 1984), 37–39. I want to thank Stanley Rosen for bringing these publications to my attention.

4. Shao Mujun, "Chinese Film amidst the Tide of Reform," *East-West Film Journal* 1, no. 1 (December 1986): 63.

5. Ding Qiao, "Chinese Cinema Today," *China Reconstructs*, August 1982, 62.

6. *Tianyun shan chuanqi* (1980, d. Xie Jin, Shanghai Film Studio); *Bei aiqing yiwang de jiaoluo* (1981, d. Li Yalin and Zhang Ji, Emei Film Studio); *Ren dao zhongnian* (1982, d. Wang Qimin and Sun Yu, Changchun Film Studio).

7. Lu Yanzhou's *Tianyun shan chuanqi* was published in the inaugural issue of *Qingming* (no. 1, July 1979).

8. "Tan yingpian *Tianyun shan chuanqi*," *Wenyi bao*, no. 2 (1981). Also see Cai Chuan and Lin Guang, "Dui yi bu hao yingpian de piping," *Zuopin yu zhengming*, May 1981, 49–51, for a friendly view.

9. *Dazhong dianying*, June 1981, 2–5.

10. See *Dazhong dianying*, September 1980, for an example of prerelease publicity.

11. Pearson, "Film in China," 1, 4.

12. Yuan Kang and Xiao Chuanwen, "Yi bu weifan zhenshi de yingpian: ping *Tianyun shan chuanqi*," *Wenyi bao*, no. 4 (1982).

13. Zhang Xian, "*Bei aiqing yiwang de jiaoluo*," *Shanghai wenxue*, January 1980.

14. Paul Fonoroff, "Perhaps the Beginning of a Vital Film Culture," *Far Eastern Economic Review*, May 3, 1984, 54.

15. See Liu Nan, "Yingpian *Bei aiqing yiwang de jiaoluo* de zheng lun," *Zuopin yu zhengming*, June 1982, 60–61, for a summary of the March 1982 debate.

16. *Zhongguo dianying nianjian, 1983* (Beijing: Zhongguo dianying chubanshe, 1984), 159–66.

17. Chen Rong, "Ren dao zhongnian," *Shouhou*, no. 1 (1980).

18. Qi Ming, "Intellectuals' Problems Spotlighted by New Film," *China Daily*, March 9, 1983.

19. *Dazhong dianying*, June 1983, 2, 8.

20. *Asia Week*, January 16, 1981, 32.

21. "Resolution on Certain Questions in the History of Our Party since the Founding of the People's Republic of China," *Beijing Review*, no. 27 (July 6, 1981).

22. Zhou Yongping, "Daxuesheng yu dianying," *Dangdai wenyi sichao*, no. 3 (1984): 22–32.

23. Commenting on the ability of films like *A Corner Forgotten by Love* to "arouse emotions of sorrow and joy" (*bei xi qinggan ciji*), a young respondent surveyed in Shanghai in 1983 said, "I felt as though my heart had been dealt a heavy blow and I too opened the gates and let my tears flow freely, feeling grief and indignation about the way feudalism, backwardness and poverty doomed these characters to a tragic fate." See Xu, "Shanghai shiqu qingnian dianying quwei qianxi," 44.

24. See Shao, "Chinese Film amidst the Tide of Reform," 65, 67.

25. *Furongzhen* (1987, d. Xie Jin, Shanghai Film Studio). *Hibiscus Town* was voted best picture of 1987 in both the Hundred Flowers and Jinji Film Award competitions.

10

On the Eve of Tiananmen: Huang Jianxin and the Notion of Postsocialism

It is easy merely to assert that Huang Jianxin was perhaps the most politically daring young director to appear in China in the troubled 1980s. The difficulty in assessing his work arises when one tries to locate Huang's highly innovative trilogy of films, *The Black Cannon Incident* (*Hei pao shijian*, 1986), *Dislocation* (*Cuowei*, 1987; also known as *The Stand-In*), and *Transmigration* (*Lunhui*, 1989; also known as *Samsara*), in any conventional conceptual framework. In a general sense, Huang's work belongs to the vaguely defined category of Fifth Generation films made between 1983 and 1989. However, he was really the only important director in the elite group consisting of Chen Kaige, Tian Zhuangzhuang, Zhang Yimou, Wu Ziniu, and a few others who dealt exclusively and explicitly with the complicated problems of the contemporary socialist city. One hardly needs to be reminded that it was precisely in this sector of Chinese society that the massive popular protests of spring and summer 1989 originated. Thus, more than the works of any other Chinese filmmaker, Huang Jianxin's films anticipated that extraordinary turmoil.

In December 1988, a time of considerable cultural openness in socialist China, I attended a prerelease screening of a rough cut of *Transmigration* at the China Film Archive. This screening was attended primarily by film specialists and critics in Beijing, including Li Tuo and Zheng Dongtian, who were eager to get their first look at a work that was rumored to be highly controversial. Huang Jianxin flew in from his base at the pace-setting Xian Film Studio to take part in the lively discussion that followed the screening. A sense of excitement pervaded the room because *Guangming ribao*, an official news daily aimed at intellectuals, had just reported that censors in the Ministry of Radio, Film, and Television had discussed *Transmigration* in a two-hour session that, for the first time since the establishment of the People's Republic in 1949, was open to journalists. The censors, it was said, had decided that the movie could be released uncut to Chinese theaters.[1] By contrast, *The Black Cannon Incident*, Huang's first film, had been cut in about thirteen places before release was approved in 1986.

After viewing the rough cut of *Transmigration*, it was easy to understand what the furor was all about. It, like Huang Jianxin's earlier films, left me with the same sense of astonishment that I had experienced at underground screenings in Beijing in 1983 of Andrzej Wajda's stunning films, *Man of Marble* (1977) and *Man of Steel* (1980). The films of both Huang and Wajda were produced in socialist societies, and yet they are not traditional socialist works of art. Indeed, their unmistakable subject is the *failure* of socialism in places like China and Poland. Their purpose is not to salvage socialism by advocating reform, but rather to demonstrate that traditional socialist societies are afflicted with various and deeply rooted terminal infirmities. Thus, well before the popular uprisings and gory massacres of spring 1989 in Beijing, Chengdu, and elsewhere that testified in blood to the failures of the Chinese Communist Party, I had begun to struggle with the issue of how to characterize the films of Huang Jianxin. They did not seem to fit into any of the most obvious analytical categories. I was forced to ask, what conceptual framework does one use to understand works of art that are made in socialist societies, yet document a popular and massive loss of faith in socialism?

It is virtually impossible to regard Huang Jianxin's films as socialist or proletarian in the sense that these concepts have been used by official ideologists in China since 1949. From 1949 to the early 1980s, socialist or proletarian culture has always meant culture that anticipates and contributes in an explicit way to the development of a socialist society. It is, above all, a *positive* culture, a culture that expresses faith in socialism. In its crudest, Stalinist form, such culture limits itself to singing the praises of the Party and state and attacking domestic and international class enemies who seek to block the socialist transformation. But socialist art in China, especially in the mid-1950s, early 1960s, and 1980s, has also included a reformist wing. This latter type of art also expresses faith in socialism, but it acknowledges that there are problems with the traditional socialist system itself (see chapters 8 and 9). The purpose of exposing such problems is to solve them and thus to perfect the socialist system. Xie Jin's films are perhaps the best examples of reformist works that fall squarely within this tradition of socialist artistic practice (see chapter 3). Ironically, even though these reformist films seek to save the socialist system, they are consistently singled out for harsh criticism by intolerant old-school cultural Stalinists like Deng Liqun and Hu Qiaomu, who regard them as a threat.[2]

If Huang Jianxin's films do not belong to any official tradition of socialist or proletarian culture in China, then perhaps they might be discussed productively within the framework of modernism. (I am using the term *modernism* in two senses here. In a general way it refers to the "modern," or post-feudal, bourgeois culture that developed in capitalist societies in eighteenth- and nineteenth-century Europe. In a second and more specific sense it refers to avant-garde "modernist" culture that arose in the West in the late nineteenth and early twentieth centuries.) My view, however, is that while modernism is more suggestive than the stale traditional socialist or proletarian categories, it does not provide a very useful conceptual framework for discussing what I regard as the dominant tendencies in mainland Chinese culture in the 1980s. As Fredric Jameson and others have shown,[3] the modernist framework helps us understand the development of urban culture and consciousness in such industrializing societies as Taiwan and Hong Kong in the 1970s and 1980s, but I think it is incapable of accounting for what is most distinctive about post-Mao cultural and political conditions in the decidedly socialist People's Republic.

For one thing, "modern" and "modernist" cultures are both associated with the sort of capitalist socioeconomic context that developed first in Western Europe and North America and later in places like Japan, Taiwan, and Hong Kong. As Leo Ou-fan Lee has pointed out, not only was modern culture developing rapidly in urban China in the late nineteenth century, but the embryo of a distinctively "modernist" culture was emerging in the late 1920s and early 1930s, when China was in the early throes of a modern or capitalist industrial transformation and when avant-garde Chinese intellectuals like Shi Zhecun were in touch with modernist cultural currents in Western Europe.[4] However, it is crucial to underscore that this phase was abruptly terminated (with far-reaching consequences), in culture as well as in industry, in 1949 and was followed by forty years of traditional socialist development, which included the full implementation of the Stalinist cultural model. Thus, while it is true that a few writers, poets, and visual artists, such as Li Tuo, Feng Jicai, and Bei Dao, exhibited a modernist consciousness and actively promoted the emergence of a modernist culture in the early years of the post-Mao period, it would be quite misleading to suggest that modernism was the primary cultural tendency of the 1980s.[5] In my view, we misuse the modernist framework and confuse the real issues when we try to employ it to explain recent cultural phenomena in a society that is perceived to be socialist by its citizens and has undergone half a century of traditional socialist development.

The problem of using a modernist framework is compounded when we recall that, borrowing directly from the Stalinist cultural tradition, the Chinese Communist Party has always used the term *modernism* in a pejorative sense.[6] When the Party introduced the idea of socialist "modernization" in the late 1970s, culture and politics were deliberately left off the list of the four sectors that needed "modernizing." The old-school wing of the Party, represented by both Deng Xiaoping and Li Peng, may have been hostile to many aspects of Maoism, but it was perfectly satisfied with the familiar socialist cultural and political models of the 1950s. Thus, theorists and critics in the 1980s who wanted to refer to "modern" or "modernist" culture in non-pejorative ways had difficulty because this terminology had been so thoroughly delegitimized in the past. The term "modern culture" conjured up images of bourgeois, capitalist culture. "Modernist culture" brought to mind images of a degenerate, self-indulgent culture, the sort of development attacked so vociferously by such Eastern European Marxists as Plekhanov and Lukács.[7] In a place where modernism has been presented for so long in the form of a crude caricature that portrays the cultures of the West as decadent and declining, what chance does the modernist framework have of addressing the contemporary cultural problems of socialism (or the late-1980s films of someone like Huang Jianxin) in a productive way?

What, then, about a postmodern framework? It is certainly sensible to argue that China should not be regarded as a totally isolated or unique cultural environment. Even though China is a socialist society, it now functions in a global context dominated by the economies and cultures of postindustrial giants. In this sense, China is part of the postmodern cultural world. As Masao Miyoshi has observed, contemporary international technology and global management permit the seemingly instant lateral transfer of countless fragments of contemporary global culture, including postmodern culture, to China and other preindustrial or industrializing nations.[8] It comes as no surprise, therefore, that young Chinese intellectuals know much about postmodernism and, on occasion, seek to introduce it into their work. This is especially apparent in the efforts of Chinese artists to "deconstruct" Maoist mythology. But these fragments do not add up to the emergence of an overarching postmodern cultural mode in places like China. It seems to me that the postmodern cultural condition, however one defines it, prevails in places like the United States and Japan that long ago underwent industrialization. The postmodern framework refers primarily to postindustrial contexts.[9] Postmodernism, that is, presupposes advanced capitalism.

Chinese culture in the late 1980s contained the vestiges of late imperial culture, the remnants of the modern or bourgeois culture of the Republican era, the residue of traditional socialist culture, and elements of both modernism and postmodernism. But in my view, the main tendencies of contemporary Chinese cultural development (and the films of Huang Jianxin) cannot be characterized as late imperial, bourgeois, traditional socialist, modernist, or postmodern. Each of these models fails to capture the distinctiveness and complexity of Chinese urban life in the 1980s and early 1990s. To call the early films of Huang Jianxin traditional socialist works is to confuse them with what they reject; to call them bourgeois (or anticommunist, as Party elders are inclined to do), modernist, or postmodern is to confuse them with something they are not. What is required is a new way of thinking about the art of people like Huang Jianxin, a fresh way of approaching the type of cultural identity and consciousness that prevails in urban China today.

I would like to suggest that we consider using a framework that might be called *postsocialist*. Arif Dirlik and others have already begun to use the notion of postsocialism to characterize the thought of post-Mao Party elites.[10] I use the concept in a very different way. In this chapter, postsocialism refers neither to the abstract realms of theory and ideology nor to the world of Party elites and official culture.[11] That is, I seek not to evaluate the contemporary Chinese world as it looks from the top down, but to understand the way it looks from the bottom up. My definition of postsocialism deals with the domain of popular perception.[12] Indeed, it seems to me that the idea of a distinctively postsocialist condition is best used to refer to the type of popular cultural diversity, cultural ambiguity, and cultural confusion that became so pronounced in China in the 1980s. Those who live in a postsocialist environment are inclined to look upon socialism not as a theory (relatively few people in China know or care much about socialist theory), but as an actual social system that has established a particular economic, political, and cultural record over the past fifty years and has affected daily life in various concrete ways.[13] The postsocialist condition, as former Party members Liu Binyan and Fang Lizhi no doubt understood, is not one in which the theory of socialism has been considered and rejected by ordinary people; rather, in postsocialist societies, it is the conduct of the Communist Party that has alienated people of all social classes, including the industrial proletariat, and given socialism a bad name. Dirlik implies that in the realm of theory there is much that is appealing about socialism, but this facile observation is irrelevant to the questions posed by Huang Jianxin's films. The powerful popular perception in postsocialist China is that the socialist system is bankrupt.

An advantage of acknowledging that ordinary urbanites in China have a distinctively postsocialist identity (an identity that strongly influences their ways of thinking and behaving) is that in doing so we are not treating China as an isolated cultural entity with an entirely unique set of problems. A postsocialist cultural identity is precisely what links China to such societies as Poland, the former Soviet Union, Hungary, eastern Germany, and the former Czechoslovakia, all of which underwent long periods of difficult Marxist-Leninist rule. Eastern Europeans, for example, would have no difficulty understanding *The Black Cannon Incident*. Indeed, these experiential links between Eastern Europe and China were acknowledged in late 1989 when demonstrators in socialist Prague carried candles to show support for their counterparts who were ruthlessly cut down in Beijing in June 1989 and when Lech Wałesa appeared at the Robert F. Kennedy Human Rights Award ceremony to honor Fang Lizhi, the 1989 award winner. Needless to say, the postsocialist condition will assume different forms in each country, but what is shared is the broad context of public awareness of the failure of the traditional socialist system and the absence of a socialist identity among ordinary people who live in or have lived in traditional socialist societies. It is characteristic of the postsocialist mode that most Party members do not possess a socialist cultural identity. In late summer 1989, before the sudden collapse of the unpopular socialist regime, a Hungarian film director made the following remark about how Party functionaries who formerly espoused puritanical values now lusted after Armani suits and Gucci loafers: "Party members now have a son involved in a joint business venture with a foreign firm, a daughter with a boutique, and Daddy can still be the Communist factory boss. This is the new leadership of the country."[14]

Postsocialism, it seems to me, refers in large part to a negative, dystopian cultural condition that prevails in late socialist societies. People may not know exactly what kind of society they want, but they know what they do not want. They do not want what life has taught them to regard as socialism. The postsocialist condition exists in societies that have been organized for decades according to what the ruling Communist parties and ordinary citizens alike view as socialist principles. But early popular faith in socialism, if it ever existed, has long since vanished. It has vanished because the Party's performance in the economic, political, and cultural fields has discredited the socialist vision. It is not that ordinary people (following the lead of Dirlik) view the system that oppresses them as false socialism and therefore that they long for "real" socialism: in an experiential sense, people regard the socialist system under which they live as the real thing. In some postsocialist societies, the Communist Party still wields almost monopolistic power in the government, military, and public security sectors and may continue to do so for some time to come. I include China, Cuba, Vietnam, and North Korea in this category. But paradoxically, in such places there is an almost universal belief, shared by many, if not most, Party members, that what is known as socialism has failed and has no prospect of solving fundamental problems. In such societies socialist economic, political, social, and cultural forms remain deeply entrenched. Even loyal reform elements in the Party cannot root them out. In these postsocialist settings, discredited and failed socialist forms have a life of their own. As I have suggested, the postsocialist condition also prevails in places like Poland, Hungary, eastern Germany, the former Czechoslovakia, the former Soviet Union, Bulgaria, Romania, and Mongolia, where Communist Party power has been entirely eliminated. It does not matter who is in power; one will find a distinctively postsocialist condition and postsocialist behavior in any place where popular faith in socialism has vanished, but the economic, political, and cultural legacies of the traditional socialist era continue to have a profound influence on daily social life.

It is hard to say exactly when the postsocialist period began in China. It would be wrong, however, to suggest that the phenomenon of postsocialism appeared only after the death of Mao or that it is simply a cultural by-product of the reform decade. If the popular disillusionment with a system that has been experienced as socialist is a reform-decade phenomenon, then it is possible to hold the reform leadership fully responsible for the popular loss of faith in socialism. Such an analysis might constitute a vindication of Maoism.[15] In reality, however, the massive disillusionment with socialism among true believers and ideological agnostics and the onset of an alienated postsocialist mode of thought and behavior began midway through the Cultural Revolution (and perhaps earlier in the countryside). It found expression in the huge Tiananmen demonstrations of April 1976 (before the death of Mao) and is linked to the Democracy Wall movement of 1978 and 1979, as well as to the various popular protests of the 1980s. The shocking massacre of citizens in June 1989 did not initiate the age of postsocialist China; the massacre was a brutal response to a current that had been forming at least since the publication of the famous Li Yizhe poster in 1973 and the release of Chen Ruoxi's short stories in 1974 and after.

Although this chapter (and Huang Jianxin's trilogy) focuses exclusively on the metropolis, the postsocialist mode is not simply an urban phenomenon. There may be substantial gaps between urban and rural culture (and these gaps also existed in the Maoist era), but a postsocialist mode of thought and behavior is one thing that urbanites share with rural dwellers. The international press missed the point on this issue when it stated that the Deng Xiaoping regime survived the summer 1989 crisis because it seemed to enjoy the support of "contented" peasants. I do not mean to deny the existence of deeply rooted antidemocratic traditions in rural China, but one needs to question the assumption that peasants are satisfied. As Perry Link has pointed out, the distance between peasants and intellectuals does not imply peasant support for the state.[16] If the peasantry seemed happy in the early 1980s, it was precisely because so much of what constituted the socialist system in the countryside had been dismantled by the state. The rich popular folklore and oral culture that flourish in the Chinese countryside contain much that is postsocialist in thrust.[17]

THE BLACK CANNON INCIDENT: POSTSOCIALISM AS INDICTMENT

The postsocialist sense of profound disillusionment with the traditional socialist system pervades Huang Jianxin's first film, *The Black Cannon Incident*, completed in late 1985 and discussed with enthusiasm in leading film circles in early 1986. Unlike the reform films of Xie Jin, which encourage a cathartic and therapeutic purging of pent-up frustrations and which always identify righteous and heroic figures within the Party who will save the socialist system, *The Black Cannon Incident* conveys an overwhelming feeling of hopelessness and alienation from beginning to end. The citizens of postsocialist Czechoslovakia were generous to the discredited socialist state when, in late 1989, they began to set all public clocks at five minutes to twelve, suggesting thereby that the old regime still had a few moments left to do something constructive. At the end of *The Black Cannon Incident*, the public clock is set at twelve. The pessimism conveyed by this film is heightened because its subject is not China at some point in its troubled Stalinist or Maoist past; rather it is China in the midst of the much-publicized era of reform and openness, a time when everyone was supposed to be confident and hopeful. Huang's unwillingness to suggest how the socialist system might be saved gives rise to the feeling that it cannot be saved. If there are sources of hope, Huang gives us no information about where they might reside.

The focal point of Huang's analysis of China in the mid-1980s is the pathetic intellectual Zhao Shuxin, a late-twentieth-century version of Lu Xun's infamous Ah Q, a socialist Ah Q, for whom Huang Jianxin seems to have almost no compassion or respect. Zhao's mind has been circumscribed, but as the critic Li Zhongyue has stated, like many other Chinese intellectuals, he also engages in self-constricting (*ziwo yasuo*) behavior.[18] Even Zhao's name, "Shuxin," is revealing. At one level it suggests a scholarly man who is highly moral, but at a more ironic level it suggests that his morality is related to his loyal submission to ethical norms dictated by others. He is moral only in the sense that he behaves in accord with codes set down by those who wield power. Zhao would be a more sympathetic victim of the system if his persecution stemmed from defiance of socialist norms, but in *The Black Cannon Incident* his persecution has nothing to do with defiance. His behavior is consistently conformist. Indeed, *The Black Cannon Incident* is painful to watch, far more painful than the sentimental melodramas of Xie Jin, because Zhao Shuxin is stripped time and again of his human dignity before our very eyes, and each time he submits without protest. He has long since been reduced to the "docile slave" referred to in the writings of the prominent Marxist theoretician Su Shaozhi.[19]

The post-Mao world of China in reform is exposed in Huang Jianxin's postsocialist work as an Orwellian realm of dictatorship and arbitrary jus-

On the Eve of Tiananmen: Huang Jianxin and the Notion of Postsocialism   279

Humiliated time and again by the Party, docile antihero Zhao Shuxin (*right*) accepts his fate without protest in *The Black Cannon Incident* (1986, d. Huang Jianxin). China Film Archive

tice. Zhao is never accused of criminal activity, is never informed that he is being investigated, and is never allowed to defend himself. And when the investigation leads to nothing, he receives no apology. A Party secretary simply states that there would have been no trouble at all if Zhao had just bought a new chess piece instead of sending a cable in order to retrieve his missing "black cannon." In other words, the nightmare is Zhao's fault, and Zhao ought to thank the Party for finally clearing his name. The most powerful line in the film is the last one, in which the spineless Zhao declares that he has learned an important lesson: "I'm not going to play chess any more." This socialist Ah Q always assumes that if he is being punished, he must have done something wrong to deserve it, and he should be grateful to those who are in charge of maintaining discipline and national security.

The postsocialist critique of contemporary Chinese society conveyed in *The Black Cannon Incident* involves more than political issues; it also touches on critical economic problems. Throughout the 1980s the regime of Deng Xiaoping made it abundantly clear that its quarrel with Maoism was related to economic rather than political matters. Deng Xiaoping never gave any indication that he had lost faith in the single-party Leninist dictatorship established by Mao Zedong, Liu Shaoqi, Zhou Enlai, and himself in the 1950s. Thus, he wanted modern economic development to occur without the Party having to revise the Leninist-Stalinist social and political system in a fundamental way. What *The Black Cannon Incident* suggests is that the Leninist political system is so deeply entrenched that it is not capable of making even the cosmetic changes that would allow a significant degree of modern progress to occur. Compared with conditions that prevailed during the Cultural Revolution, China seemed "open" to the outside world in the 1980s. But, Huang shows, China is still essentially closed. "Openness" is a cruel public relations hoax. This film suggests that the state simply wants to expropriate the advanced industrial technology required to complete a major industrial project. It is only under these circumstances that the presence of Hans, the German engineer, is tolerated. Although there is a veneer of "friendship," Hans is never accepted in China. Indeed, he is regarded by those who wield power as a representative of the international bourgeoisie and, thus, as a latent class enemy. The old-style Leninist investigation of Zhao Shuxin and the suspicious nature of his relationship with the German engineer are far more important to the life of the entrenched power system than is the successful completion of the modern industrial project. In fact, it is better to put the whole multimillion-dollar project at risk than to suspend the investigation of Zhao. The Party leaders are not solely concerned about economic modernization; toward the end of the film they are shown to be preoccupied with the problem of assigning blame. Everything will be fine if, somehow, the destruction of the priceless modern equipment can be blamed on the German. It does not occur to anyone, including Zhao, to question the priorities of the Leninist political system, a system that, to borrow the words of Xie Fei, requires that nonspecialists exercise leadership over specialists (*waihang lingdao neihang*).[20]

Film critics in China expressed great admiration for *The Black Cannon Incident*, but even in the relatively "open" political atmosphere of early 1986, they were obviously not at liberty to elaborate at length on exactly why they liked it. In January 1986 two conferences were convened in Beijing on *The Black Cannon Incident*, one organized by the editors of *Film Art* (*Dianying yishu*) and the other held at the China Film Art Research Center. Huang Jianxin told one of the gatherings that only in the most superficial sense was the film about "leftist thought," a well-known euphemism for Maoist excesses. Far more important was the treatment of the "many things" that lurked below the surface of post-Mao society.[21] Nevertheless, many commentators couched their praise of the film in the familiar and harmless political rhetoric of the post-1978 reform movement. Li Zhongyue and Chen Xihe, for example, anticipating the critique of socialist China contained in the 1988 television documentary titled *River Elegy* (*Heshang*),[22] asserted that Huang was exposing evils that were two thousand years old, the vestiges of "feudalism" and the "small peasant" mentality, evils that had resurfaced in the Cultural Revolution.[23] Zhong Chenxiang, commenting in a similar vein, said that Huang was making a contribution by calling for the "modernization of self" (*zishen de xiandaihua*) and the "modernization of concepts" (*guannian de xiandaihua*).[24] This vague and inoffensive language does not do justice to Huang Jianxin, because it fails to accept his challenge to look below the surface of the film.

Other critics did everything they could under the circumstances to demonstrate that *The Black Cannon Incident* was something strikingly new. Huang's purpose, they implied, was not to show support for the Four Modernizations or to heap additional abuse on the convenient Cultural Revolution scapegoat. As a film that did nothing to reassure people that economic and political reforms would be implemented, *The Black Cannon Incident* functioned more as an indictment of the traditional Leninist political system than as an endorsement of Deng Xiaoping's economic reform program. According to the insightful critic Li Tuo, *The Black Cannon Incident* can be seen as a film that deals with "the attitude taken in socialist countries or socialist systems toward the issue of individual personality."[25] That is to say, the film deals with the rights of the individual in socialist societies. Kong Du, a scholar at the Beijing Film Institute, argued in a similar way.[26] *The Black Cannon Incident*, he said, does not really deal with the surface problems of the "modernization" drive. At a "deeper structural level" (*jiegou shenceng*) it addresses the more fundamental issues of "human dignity" (*ren de zunyan*) and the "value of human beings" (*ren de jiazhi*). In matters related to human dignity (a concept that Kong Du implies transcends national boundaries), the humiliation heaped on helpless and innocent people like Zhao Shuxin ought to be regarded as abnormal. But the tragedy of life in present-day China is that such humiliation has been imposed for so long it is regarded as normal and rational (*heli*). By submerging his analysis of inhuman conditions below the surface of the conventional narrative (*zhengju*), Kong stated, Huang Jianxin was one of the first people to challenge the "ultrastable structure" of Chinese filmmaking since 1949 (*chao wending jiegou*). However, even those critics who saw clearly that *The Black Cannon Incident* was in a class by itself failed to comment on the far-reaching implications of Huang's analysis. Like Kong Du, veteran critic Shao Mujun, a victim of anti-rightist campaigns of the 1950s, simply noted that the film deals with "the problem of the value of human life" in a way that reveals "long-term weaknesses" in the socialist legal system.[27] Xie Fei hinted that this "small" story permits one to see the "big" picture (*xiao zhong jian da*) and asked rhetorically whether China would ever be able to modernize as long as its intellectuals were like Zhao Shuxin, but he did not elaborate on these points.[28]

None of these writers dealt at length with the grim significance of Huang Jianxin's concept of circularity. Huang himself has pointed out that the wooden chess piece leaves Zhao Shuxin's hands at the beginning of the film as a meaningless object.[29] However, by the time it comes full circle and is returned to him at the end of the narrative, it has become enormously significant. But its significance has to do with the fact that nothing of importance has been learned from this absurd case. The entrenched system, exposed as sterile and incapable of reforming itself, continues to function at the end of the film in the same way it functioned at the outset. This point is reinforced in the closing scene when the pitiful Zhao Shuxin, mockingly described by He Yanming as a "model" (*yangban*) socialist intellectual, encounters small boys (i.e., China's hope for the future) playing in a park with bricks lined up like dominoes. These Zhao Shuxins of the future giggle with delight as the upright dominoes fall, like programmed robots, without resistance, once the first one is pushed. After all the bricks have fallen, the boys hasten to set them up again. The traditional socialist system thus reproduces itself and the familiar game can be started again as if nothing were wrong.

DISLOCATION: POSTSOCIALISM AS THEATER OF THE ABSURD

Like *The Black Cannon Incident*, the second installment of Huang Jianxin's postsocialist trilogy, *Dislocation*, was made at the Xian Film Studio, an institution that, under the bold leadership of Wu Tianming, seems to have specialized in the production of postsocialist artworks. And like *The Black Cannon Incident*, *Dislocation* uses a bitter "black humor" (*heise youmo*), which Huang says is inspired by such Western films as *Catch-22* (d. Mike Nichols, 1970) to deal with conditions that are inherently "absurd" (*huangdan*).[30] Actually, Chen Xihe is closer to the truth when he insists that Huang Jianxin's humor is "red humor" (*hongse youmo*).[31] The concept of "red humor" resonates more fully with the idea of a uniquely postsocialist art that comments specifically, and often viciously, on what James Watson calls the "rigors of life under socialism."[32]

One of the important characteristics of socialist theory is that it includes a built-in utopian vision of the future. That is to say, the point of socialist revolution is to hasten the inevitable arrival of a promised land of freedom, justice, and abundance. In socialist states, citizens are taught that, compared with capitalist society, the fully developed socialist realm of the future will be a "good" society. The communist realm that eventually replaces socialist society will be even better. Yet in spite of this visionary quality of socialist theory, since 1949 artists in China have produced very few works of science fiction that try to imagine what this promised land will be like. Thus, as a work of "science fiction," Huang Jianxin's *Dislocation* was the first film of the post–Cultural Revolution era to explore this unfamiliar genre. There is nothing utopian, however, about Huang's postsocialist vision. Indeed, he seems to be saying that the socialist utopia will never arrive. The Chinese future that one sees on screen is a decidedly dystopian nightmare that has nothing in common with the socialist promise of an ideal society.[33] Needless to say, it was not Huang's intention to take a serious look at the future. By mocking the future, he mocks (and subverts) the present order of things. Nonetheless, it is significant that he is the first Chinese filmmaker to suggest that China's socialist future will, in all likelihood, be a technologically dazzling version of the oppressive "present-day" China depicted in *The Black Cannon Incident*. In this sense, *Dislocation* elaborates in a consistent and logical way on themes that are introduced in the first film of the trilogy. There is a clear chronological progression of thematic development in Huang's work. *The Black Cannon Incident* indicts the traditional socialist system; *Dislocation* deals with the abortive attempt of one individual to rebel against conformity and slavish obedience.

The socialist antihero of *The Black Cannon Incident*, Zhao Shuxin, is reintroduced in *Dislocation*, this time as the main actor in a series of dream (or rather, nightmare) sequences. The time is the distant future, and the place is China. At first glance, the setting bears little resemblance to the China we know so well. Miraculously, it is a land of great modernity and abundance. The city in which the action takes place is full of futuristic buildings; homes and offices are equipped with a glittering array of futuristic machines and appliances. But, alas, things are too good to be true. The incredible technological revolution that has taken place has done nothing to improve the human condition. The dust and grime may be gone in this faceless and sterile world of the future, but so too are the people. The streets and shopping centers are practically deserted. China now consists almost entirely of bureaucrats and Party functionaries, whose meeting tables are adorned with black bunting, a grim decor of death. There are myriad towering glass structures, but one never sees the people who presumably inhabit them. Zhao Shuxin, the quintessential socialist team player, has been rewarded for his unquestioning loyalty to the system. He is now a department chief (*juzhang*) in an unspecified engineering ministry. Despite the dazzling "modernity" of this China of the future, the political system seems to function precisely as it did in the old socialist China of *The Black Cannon Incident*. It is abundantly clear that no political reforms were ever carried out in the past. Directives (*zhongyang wenjian*) issued by the Party center literally rain down on faceless and uncaring bureaucrats who attend endless rounds of meaningless meetings. Frustrated by the mind-bending bureaucracy of the system, Zhao decides to rebel by building a robot that looks and acts as he does and by programming the machine to attend meetings in his place. For reasons that are left unexplained, China has the dubious distinction of being unusually advanced in the field of robotics. Foreign scientists rush to China to learn how to make mechanical men who obey every order they are given.

A problem emerges, however, when Zhao's robot twin has rebellious ideas of its own and, consequently, cannot be totally controlled by its master. In an effort to reform the system, Zhao has unwittingly created a monster. The robot becomes addicted to meetings and gets corrupted by bureaucratic life. Not only does the robot enjoy Soviet movies; it also drinks, smokes, and eats to excess. Before long it even tries to seduce Zhao's girlfriend. In the end, the robot attempts to take over Zhao's position. Realizing that his plan is doomed to failure, Zhao tells the robot, "You think too much. That's dangerous. I didn't design you to have your own ideas. You're meant to obey my will. If you don't I'll have to destroy you." Zhao's attempt to liberate his own distinctively human creative powers (by allowing a robot to do a robot's work) fails miserably. Furthermore, the robot's rebelliousness is reactionary rather than revolutionary; its actions will lead not to a humanization of the system, but to more dehumanization. Zhao is left with only two options, both of which are depressing: he can allow the corrupt monster to run wild, thus worsening an already intolerable situation, or return to the lifeless but predictable ways of the traditional socialist order.

In a superficial sense, *Dislocation* condemns the evil of bureaucratism that plagues all traditional socialist societies. Its defenders (and the censors who approved its release) could reasonably argue that bureaucratism is actually alien to the idea of socialism. If bureaucratism is regarded as a manifestation of "leftist thinking" (false socialism) or as a vestige of China's presocialist past (something external to socialism that is corrupting the socialist system), then *Dislocation*, especially when it is viewed in isolation from the first film of the trilogy, can be interpreted as a reform work that is consistent with Party ideology and supports the Four Modernizations drive. I would argue, however, that *Dislocation* cannot be viewed apart from

Zhao Shuxin's robot look-alike (*right*), hopelessly corrupted by the system, soon learns to enjoy political meetings, liquor, cigarettes, and women in *Dislocation* (1987, d. Huang Jianxin). China Film Archive

The Black Cannon Incident. It is not a reform film at all, but a work that expresses a profound disillusionment with what ordinary people in China (and throughout the former Soviet Union and Eastern Europe) perceive as the socialist system. The problem of bureaucratism is not treated here as a remnant of "leftist thinking." Nor is it criticized as something external or foreign to the traditional socialist system; it is treated as a phenomenon that is fundamental to twentieth-century socialist systems. If oppressive bureaucratism is an elemental and inescapable ingredient of the traditional socialist system, then the issue of genuine reform does not really arise. In both *The Black Cannon Incident* and *Dislocation*, bureaucratism is associated with the basic day-to-day workings of the Leninist single-party state. The idea of Party-sponsored political reform is a contradiction in terms, and isolated acts of individual protest accomplish nothing. Real reform, *Dislocation* implies, would require dismantling the Leninist Party and denouncing the way it has functioned in China since 1949. In *The Black Cannon Incident*, Huang Jianxin already established that the perpetuation of the Leninist system (i.e., the power of the Party) is more important to the leadership than anything else.

The discussion of *Dislocation* among film critics was seriously compromised by a sudden, unforeseen shift in the political climate in China in January 1987. Throughout December 1986, a large number of students marched through the streets of Beijing and elsewhere, making demands that amounted to a rejection of the Leninist single-party dictatorship. For several months, intellectuals had been expressing the view that "the relationship between Marxism and non-Marxism should not be one between the ruler and the ruled."[34] The authorities reacted swiftly by suppressing the student movement, forcing Party General Secretary Hu Yaobang (now held responsible for the relatively open political climate that prevailed in 1986) from office, and launching an old-fashioned political campaign to stamp out manifestations of "bourgeois liberalization."[35] The campaign expired by early summer because it had almost no support. Indeed, intellectuals in the film world with whom I spoke in Beijing in February 1987 were determined to subvert it. Still, the chill lasted long enough to have a negative effect on the public discussion of *Dislocation*.

In mid-January, during the most discouraging phase of the crackdown, the editors of *Dianying yishu* held a lifeless symposium in Beijing on *Dislocation*. Some of the discussants, including Huang Jianxin himself, opted to focus almost entirely on the admittedly novel and interesting formalistic and stylistic aspects of the film.[36] One gets the feeling, however, that they did so in part to avoid any discussion of its far-reaching political implications. Mid-January 1987 was not an opportune time to raise fundamental questions about the hopelessly rigid structure of the Leninist Party-state. Although *Dislocation* dealt with many of the same large political issues treated in *The Black Cannon Incident*, the *Dianying yishu* symposium packed no political punch. Some speakers, like Jia Leilei of the Academy of Social Sciences (a stronghold of the postsocialist outlook), tried, I suspect, to protect Huang Jianxin by denying that *Dislocation* meant to suggest that Chinese society was "absurd" (*huangdan*).[37] Twelve months before, during the discussions on *The Black Cannon Incident*, many commentators, such as Huang Shixian, had agreed that it was appropriate to use a term like "absurdity" to characterize Chinese social life. In China, he asserted, reality was quite often absurd.[38] But suddenly, in January 1987, it was dangerous to suggest that Chinese society was absurd or that a cinematic theater of the absurd was an appropriate way to approach the problems of socialist society. Jia Leilei denied, therefore, that Huang Jianxin meant to say that Chinese society was absurd. If society is absurd, then life is absurd. If life is absurd, it is meaningless, and there is no reason to have any hope for the future. *Dislocation*, therefore, should not be regarded as a modernist work. Here, of course, Jia was using the term "modernist" in the pejorative sense, modernism understood as an ideology of despair.

Actually, Jia explained, *Dislocation* does not deal exclusively with China. The problems it considers are of "global significance" (*shijie yiyi*), ones that all people confront in a postmodern (*houxiandai*) or postindustrial (*hougongye*) society. Jia's friendly interpretation stripped *Dislocation*, a film that is perhaps even more subversive than *The Black Cannon Incident*, of its contemporary political significance—but in doing so it served, in part, to remove Huang Jianxin from the glaring spotlight of the campaign against bourgeois liberalization, a campaign with clear anti-Western overtones. The remarks of veteran film critic Luo Yijun, in contrast, were more in tune with the thrust of the Anti-Bourgeois Liberalization Campaign.[39] Luo was more inclined to identify *Dislocation* with unhealthy "surrealist" (*chaoxianshi*) and modernist currents found in the bourgeois West. In the West, Luo proclaimed, modernist art was the product of the alienation and "solitude" (*gudu*) of intellectuals in postindustrial capitalist society. In China, however, the situation was quite different, Luo insisted. Everyone, including intellectuals, he proclaimed, had a "common ideal" (*gongtong lixiang*) and the problem of spiritual "confusion" (*kunhuo*) scarcely existed. Thus, Luo confidently concluded, "there is no fertile ground in our country for the art of the absurd and other Western modernist schools."

TRANSMIGRATION: POSTSOCIALISM AS ANOMIE

The 1987 campaign against bourgeois liberalization collapsed in the middle of the year, as the new Party general secretary, Zhao Ziyang, pressed for a fresh round of economic and political reforms. In some respects 1988, the year in which Huang Jianxin completed *Transmigration* (also known as *Samsara*), was more "open" in a cultural and intellectual sense than any other year in the history of the People's Republic. And in some respects, *Transmigration* was Huang Jianxin's most provocative treatment of the phenomenon of postsocialist disillusionment and alienation. Adapted from a novel by the remarkably popular "new wave" writer Wang Shuo titled *Emerging from the Sea* (*Fuqu haimian*), *Transmigration* shifted the focus of Huang Jianxin's attention away from intellectuals and bureaucrats and toward the controversial subject of directionless urban youth. Huang's new antihero, a smooth young hustler named Shi Ba, lives an empty, meaningless life. His parents are dead, and he has no job.

Indeed, *Transmigration* was one of the first Chinese films to deal with the widespread problem of alienation and disaffection among urbanites who were too young to have experienced the Cultural Revolution. But Huang Jianxin's decision to explore the case of Shi Ba is of special interest because the cynical Shi Ba is no ordinary young man. He is the son of a high-ranking official (*gaogan zidi*). As such, he has benefited far more from the socialist revolution than ordinary young people. He lives a life of exceptional comfort and privilege in Beijing. His enormous apartment, for instance, is filled with state-of-the-art consumer goods and appliances. Although raised by people committed to the socialist revolution, Shi Ba has no faith in socialism or the Communist Party. His friends have similar backgrounds and hold similar views. Indeed, they openly mock the socialist state and the Party at every opportunity. In one rather amazing (and chillingly ominous) scene left unaltered by the censors at the Film Bureau, Shi Ba and two fashionable female companions stand in Tiananmen Square (the large portrait of Mao Zedong looming in the background) and ridicule the stone-faced soldiers of the People's Liberation Army who are guarding Mao's remains. (In a matter of months, the same spot would become a bloody battleground that pitted armed soldiers against young demonstrators.) Huang's film discussion of the corrupt sons and daughters of the ruling elite seems to conclude that it is those who know the socialist system best who are the least committed to its preservation.

One of the most interesting aspects of *Transmigration* is that it raises the question of why "the best and the brightest" among the ruling elite are so corrupt and spiritually shallow. The official answer, of course, is that the alienation of the sons and daughters of the ruling class is a new phenomenon associated with China's opening to the outside world in general and to the "spiritually polluting" decadent West in particular. The unstated and therefore untested assumption is that such problems did not exist in the past. The correct response to the problem of spiritual pollution is to heighten class struggle by launching periodic assaults on bourgeois liberalization. As film critic Xia Hong pointed out some time ago, this classic approach, which in itself alienates people, amounts to "shining the flashlight of Marxism-Leninism on others, but never shining it on oneself" (*Maliezhuyi de diantong guangzhao bieren, buzhao ziji*).[40]

Even in the atmosphere of political openness that prevailed throughout 1988, Huang Jianxin was in no position to state explicitly that the single-party Leninist dictatorship had only itself to blame for the alienation of Chinese youth and that Shi Ba and his kind were literally and figuratively children of socialism. But it is highly significant that the film explicitly rejects the suggestion that alienation and corruption in China are linked to foreign influences. Indeed, Huang turns the spiritual-pollution argument on its head by illustrating two cases in which Chinese defraud unsuspecting foreigners. In the first instance we encounter the brassy Liu Hualing, a former classmate of Shi Ba, who openly admits that she married a foreigner she did not love in order to get out of China and establish a legal residence abroad. Soon after, she divorced the man in order to be free of him and to receive regular alimony payments. In the second instance, Shi Ba, who engages regularly in quasi-legal activities, gets involved with a slick young woman who operates a vicious extortion ring. She employs pretty young women to seduce naive foreign men. Once the couple gets into bed, a male accomplice, pretending to be a public security officer, enters the room to make an "arrest." To avoid arrest, the foreigner agrees to pay a "fine" on the spot and the matter is resolved. Not only is the stereotype of wholesome, dedicated Chinese youth exploded in this film (in one especially gory scene, members of a violent street gang use a power drill to mutilate Shi Ba's knee), but Huang Jianxin also refrains, as he does in *The Black Cannon Incident*, from placing the blame for China's sorry condition on foreigners.

As in the case of Huang Jianxin's first two films, it is possible to argue that *Transmigration* is compatible with the priorities of the Four Modernizations reform drive. One might say that people like Shi Ba comprise only a small segment of Chinese youth and that the purpose of the film is to raise the issue of youth alienation so that it can be resolved. The problem with this approach is that it ignores the fact that Huang Jianxin does nothing in

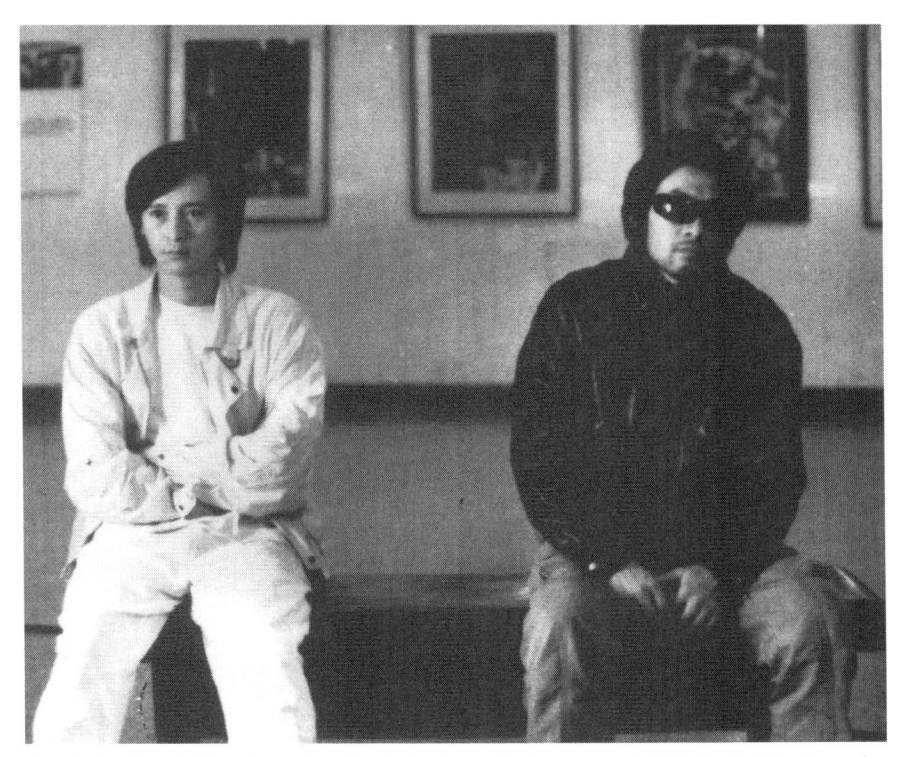

Caught in the middle of another shady business deal, a paranoid Shi Ba (*left*) believes he is being watched by an unsavory gang member (*right*) in *Transmigration* (1989, d. Huang Jianxin). China Film Archive

this or any of his films to suggest precisely how such problems might be solved. On the contrary, his films increasingly convey a profound sense of hopelessness. If *The Black Cannon Incident*, like Lu Xun's *The True Story of Ah Q*, is about the need for Chinese people to awaken, and *Dislocation* is about a failed protest, then *Transmigration*, the last element of Huang's analytical progression, is, logically, about individual resignation and anomie in postsocialist society.

Transmigration (*lunhui*) is a Buddhist term for the cyclical process in which one's soul takes on a new body after death. Shi Ba's deep depression culminates in a shocking ritual suicide, the ultimate act of despair. His troubled and alienated soul presumably passes to his yet unborn son, who is named Shi Xiaoba (Little Ba), after his father. The son, we are told in a clinically cold postscript, is born several months later in a small black room. The message is that nothing has changed. This depressing sense that the system simply reproduces itself over and over is strikingly similar to the feeling one gets at the end of *The Black Cannon Incident* when Zhao Shuxin watches the small boys set up the brick dominoes time after time. A mechanical house ornament known as a *yongdongji*, or "perpetual motion device," is used throughout *Dislocation* to convey this same sense. It moves back and forth, lurching to the left and then to the right without ever really going anywhere; it just repeats the same pattern of movement forever. Even the music in *Transmigration* indicates that the traditional socialist system is capable only of reproducing itself. The film begins and ends with what all Chinese will recognize as "The Song of the Young Pioneers," a song that each generation must learn in school even though it is widely regarded as a meaningless relic of socialist culture in China.

It seems almost incredible now that some early Western commentary on *Transmigration* interpreted the film as a work that indirectly attacked the reform policies of the 1980s by showing the "underside" of the reform tide.[41] In this view, Shi Ba is a young man who cannot cope with the new competitive system, a person unable to obtain jobs or promotions based on merit. *Guangming ribao*, in a similar vein, said that *Transmigration* was an attempt to "portray the reactions of young people to the reform era."[42] It seems to me, however, that only in the most superficial sense does the film comment on the social consequences of recent economic reforms. When one views *Transmigration* as the third in the trilogy of films, all of which deal with life in the reform period, it becomes obvious that Huang Jianxin is not an opponent of the reform. He clearly supports the rejection of Maoism. But the underlying message is that the reforms are inadequate; they are not going to work. The problem with contemporary Chinese society is not that reforms have been introduced to save socialism, but rather that the reforms of Deng Xiaoping, Hu Yaobang, and Zhao Ziyang have not gone far enough. Indeed, each reform that is introduced is an admission that the traditional socialist system set up in Eastern Europe and in China after World War II is not working and cannot meet the political, economic, social, and cultural needs of the people. The reforms do not work because they are artificially superimposed on the deeply rooted Leninist system. The more that piecemeal reforms are introduced, the more it becomes evident that no one has any faith in the traditional socialist system and the more it becomes obvious that the only way reforms can make a significant impact is if the traditional system and the single-party dictatorship are dismantled as they have been in the former Soviet Union, Poland, Hungary, the former Czechoslovakia, and eastern Germany. Even then there is no guarantee of success, given that decades of socialism have left behind a mind-boggling legacy of waste, inefficiency, corruption, environmental devastation, and moral resignation. Ordinary people are ill prepared to make a new beginning.

Thus, Huang Jianxin does not expect us to feel sorry for Shi Ba (or Zhao Shuxin). Shi Ba and his friends are not the offspring of the reform era; they are the children of the Communist Party and a socialist system that have been abusive and dictatorial for decades. Like their corrupt parents, they have no real faith in the socialist future of China. Unlike their parents, however, they are not hypocrites. They do not pay lip service to the alleged superiority of the socialist system. They do not join the Party to advance their careers and to gain more perks. They have been taught by the system to ignore the childish platitudes contained in "The Song of the Young Pioneers." They think only of themselves and how best to maximize short-term gains. Their greed and obsession with collecting material objects has little to do with flaws in the reform policies; their selfish irresponsibility derives from a process that conditions people to grab whatever they can after forty years of socialist scarcity. It is the socialist system, not the well-intentioned reform measures, that produces people who are the antithesis of Lei Feng, the plastic socialist hero who happily wasted his life for the Party and the people.

The early critical responses to *Transmigration* were quite positive. Dai Jinhua, a young faculty member at the Beijing Film Institute, praised the film's "exquisite artistry and quality production." In no sense, she argued, could Huang Jianxin be accused of celebrating the alienated and self-indulgent ways of people like the antihero Shi Ba. According to Dai, the "grimness and gruesomeness of urban life" is a reality of contemporary Chinese life that needs to be documented.[43] Even the cautious Shao Mujun, who thinks that all the films based on works of fiction by Wang Shuo contributed to an emerging "culture of vulgarity" (*pizi wenhua*) in the late 1980s, conceded that *Transmigration* "transcended" this unflattering category.[44] Predictably, critical discussion of *Transmigration*, one of the most important films made in post-Mao China, was cut short by the tragic events of June 1989. The film was no longer shown, and the bits and pieces of commentary that appeared in the press were generally negative. For example, Su Bing, writing more than a year after the initial release of *Transmigration*, severely criticized Huang Jianxin for allegedly glorifying and romanticizing Shi Ba's ritual suicide.[45] Ironically, Dai Jinhua, writing before the Beijing massacres, had characterized the same scene as "brilliant."[46]

THE POSTSOCIALIST CONDITION: SOME FINAL REFLECTIONS

Huang Jianxin's impressive postsocialist filmmaking activities came to a sudden halt after the brutal massacres of June 1989 and the onset of the massive repression that temporarily strengthened the hand of those committed to the Leninist dictatorship. It has been suggested by some dissident Chinese intellectuals, who now reside outside China, that the strange lull in Huang's creative life had nothing to do with his political activities in April and May 1989. He was in Australia during those tumultuous weeks, and thus cannot be accused of having participated directly in antigovernment protests or street demonstrations. Some observers suggest that Huang was under a cloud for nearly five years because of the political activities of his mentor, Wu Tianming, who chose to live in exile in the United States. This much is clear: Huang was not among those directors invited to attend a tightly controlled national film festival held in Beijing in late September 1989. And apparently *The Black Cannon Incident*, *Dislocation*, and *Transmigration* were not among the twenty feature films of the 1980s selected for screening at that time. Instead, titles like Tian Zhuangzhuang's *Rock 'n' Roll Youth* (*Yaogun qingnian*, 1988) were offered as films reflecting "present-day life."[47] It was not until 1993 that Huang was back at work in Xian on a new film, *Straighten Up* (*Zhan zhi luo, bie paxia*).

There is no guarantee that Huang's future work will continue his exploration of China's postsocialist condition. Paul Clark went so far as to suggest that the bloodletting of June 1989 may well "spell the death of domestic cinema" in China.[48] In the immediate aftermath of the massacres (during which four Beijing Film Institute students were arrested), I received frightening letters from friends who had graduated from the Beijing Film Institute in the early 1980s. One letter, dated June 16, from a well-known person who was desperate to get out of socialist China, said, "I'm certain you know all about the situation here, so there is no need for me to say a lot. There's not much time, so I'll just jot down a few things quickly. Please, whatever you do, stay in touch with me. There is no way to convey to you the sense of total hopelessness that I feel (*juewang xinqing*) under these circumstances." In a letter dated July 11, another Beijing Film Institute graduate wrote, "I often have the feeling now that I've reached a dead-end in life. My self-confidence has practically disappeared. None of the things I have wanted to do, none of my hopes, have been realized. I've tried very hard, but nothing has turned out the way I imagined. Sometimes I feel terribly discouraged and have no sense of hope (*shiwang huixin*)."

In mid-1990 Teng Jinxian, the new head of the Film Bureau under the Ministry of Radio, Film, and Television who replaced the capable Shi Fangyu in 1988, publicly announced that the party-state would now insist that the film world function once again within the traditional Stalinist framework. Teng called for a dramatic increase in the number of political propaganda films. Among other things, he said, this would require more films about "advanced workers, peasants, soldiers, and intellectuals," the sort of thing that abounded in the 1950s. Teng charged that filmmakers were guilty of "national nihilism" and "blindly worship Western film theory and artistic genres." This, of course, was a charge made time and again by Red Guards during the Cultural Revolution. Echoing remarks made by Mao Zedong in the 1940s, Teng condemned filmmakers who are interested in the subject of human nature. Such works, he intimated, dilute the class consciousness of the people and strengthen the hand of the class enemy.[49]

Huang Jianxin was perhaps the only important young director to come out of the Beijing Film Institute's direction program in the early 1980s who set all of his first three films in the present and, in doing so, dealt directly with many of the overriding issues taken up by the street demonstrators cut down in June 1989. This took considerable courage. Many other directors carefully avoided commenting critically on the present day. The films made in the 1980s by Huang's well-known contemporaries (Chen Kaige, Tian Zhuangzhuang, and Zhang Yimou) that have received the most critical attention are set in the presocialist Republican era or in exotic non-Han border areas. When *The Black Cannon Incident* was released in early 1986, Huang Jianxin was noticeably defensive about the charge, leveled by some film critics in China, that the filmmaking of his generation was "far removed from present reality" (*yuanli xianshi*) and "failed to bravely confront the problems of present-day reality" (*meiyou yongqi zhengshi xianshi wenti*).[50] Huang denied the charge (by pointing to *The Black Cannon Incident*), but in fact the critics were right. In 1989 it became clear just how dangerous it is to raise questions about the fundamental nature of Leninist, single-party socialist systems and the social malaise and disaffection they engender. Thus, one wonders how in mid-1987 the *Economist* reached the odd conclusion that Huang Jianxin is "staunchly committed" to the "basic structure" of the socialist system in China.[51] Huang Jianxin's films simply do not amount to a vote of confidence in the Leninist system or the reform strategy. It is not that Huang does not want change; it is that he expresses serious doubts about the structure of the system and the likelihood that it can actually reform itself. To be a reformer one has to believe that the "errors" committed by the Party in the past are alien to the Leninist system, and that the

Party can weed out these "leftist" perversions and adopt, in a creative way, new modes of operation to deal with the realities of the present. To put it simply, a reformer must believe that necessary changes can be made within the framework of the Four Cardinal Principles of the Leninist dictatorship. One strongly suspects that Huang's views are closer to those articulated by Solidarity in Poland, Civic Forum in Czechoslovakia, and New Forum in eastern Germany on the eve of the collapse of traditional socialism in Eastern Europe. His films show that the problems of Party dictatorship (*The Black Cannon Incident*), mindless bureaucratic stagnation (*Dislocation*), and anomie (*Transmigration*) are, in essence, unrelated to the "leftist" excesses of the Cultural Revolution and other episodes of ideological extremism, as well as to the piecemeal reforms of the 1980s. These overarching problems are perceived as endemic to socialist states set up after 1917. Solidarity, Civic Forum, and New Forum were not reform movements; they were popular movements that recognized the need to demolish the traditional socialist system before life-enhancing changes could take place.

By using the framework of postsocialism, then, I am rejecting the notion that the devastatingly critical and artistically innovative works of people like Andrzej Wajda and Huang Jianxin must inevitably be categorized as either socialist or capitalist. Huang clearly rejects traditional socialism, but there is no evidence that he possesses a bourgeois consciousness or looks forward to a capitalist future for China. Postsocialism, the ideological counterpart of postmodernism, refers to a cultural crisis that is unique to societies that have undergone decades of Leninist-Stalinist (i.e., what I call traditional socialist) development. I realize, of course, that others may choose to place Huang's films in more conventional frameworks. One could argue, for example, that Huang's perspective is nothing more than old-fashioned Cold War anticommunism, an ideology inspired by a profound confidence in the superiority of capitalism. But in my view, such an argument would be patently untenable. There is no evidence to support it.

A more interesting view (and one that is not necessarily incompatible with the concept of postsocialism) is one suggested to me by Krzysztof Wodiczko, the brilliant and highly controversial visual artist whose works had a major impact on the New York art world in the 1980s. Wodiczko, it is crucial to point out, is a nonsectarian socialist or social democratic thinker who is a strident critic of both capitalism and the sort of traditional socialist society he experienced firsthand in his native Poland. Wodiczko, who now resides in the United States, has experienced both capitalism and traditional socialism from the inside. He does not want Poland to head in a capitalist direction, but neither does he want it to revert to the inhumanity and oppressiveness of traditional socialism. Wodiczko argues that critics of socialist societies, that is, people like Huang Jianxin, can still be regarded as socialists. When they are criticizing what I call traditional socialism, he insists, they are criticizing "false" socialism, not "real" socialism. Poland, Wodiczko fervently believes, was never really socialist. Thus, it is possible for an artist or critical thinker to reject traditional or "false" socialism while looking forward to the arrival of a genuinely humane and liberating socialist era. Such an artist (and Huang Jianxin might be an example) would thus place himself or herself in the socialist category.

Wodiczko's argument, however, does not deal with the fact that traditional socialist regimes have, by their many failures, discredited all forms of socialism in the public mind. Thus, it is exceedingly difficult (if not impossible) for "real" socialists in such postsocialist settings to build a social base of support for a "real" socialist revolution. Nonetheless, Wodiczko's argument is correct at a theoretical level and is largely consistent with Herbert Marcuse's notion that the role of authentic art is to subvert the "dominant consciousness" and "break the monopoly of established reality" in order to define what is real.[52] Here Marcuse was referring to what he regarded as outstanding art in industrial and postindustrial societies, but he was also aware of the crushing inhumanity of life in socialist China. While it is true that Huang Jianxin's work (and especially *Transmigration*) is pessimistic, Marcuse reminds us that the pessimism of genuine art "is not counterrevolutionary."[53] "In the transforming mimesis," he argued, "the image of liberation is fractured by reality. If art were to promise that at the end good would triumph over evil, such a promise would be refuted by the historical truth. In reality it is evil which triumphs. . . . Authentic works of art are aware of this; they reject the promise made too easily; they refuse the unburdened happy end."[54] Marcuse's dynamic conception of art as a "dissenting force" can very easily be applied to art in traditional socialist societies. Indeed, this is precisely what Wodiczko has in mind. The result is socialist art that rejects Marxism-Leninism-Stalinism. It may well be that Huang Jianxin's work is socialist in this sense.

By arguing that Huang's contemporary and urban films are best understood through the analytical lens of postsocialism, I do not mean to suggest that the only films we can regard as postsocialist are those that are set in the present day and that deal directly with the contemporary predicaments of Chinese socialism. Many of the works of Chen Kaige, Tian Zhuangzhuang, and Zhang Yimou that are set in presocialist times or in non-Han border regions are also illuminated by the concept of postsocialism. They "subvert" (in the sense that Marcuse used the term) the oppressive traditional socialist system by deconstructing the mythology of Chinese socialism (demolishing, for instance, the romantic and heroic image of the Chinese peasantry that has been so central to Chinese socialism since the late 1930s) and rejecting the wooden class-struggle paradigm that served as the structural foundation for almost all works of art in the 1949–1979 period. It is important to point out, however, that Huang's work (and the work of the deconstructionists just mentioned) has little in common with the remarkably popular films of Xie Jin. It is extremely difficult to locate Xie Jin's work in the postsocialist paradigm. Xie Jin believes in the Leninist Party, has faith in the basic structure of the traditional socialist system, and, judging by films like *The Legend of Tianyun Mountain* (*Tianyun shan chuanqi*, 1980), discussed in chapter 9, and *Hibiscus Town* (*Furongzhen*, 1986), discussed in chapter 3, is confident that the Leninist Party is capable of reforming itself and rooting out leftist influences. Xie Jin complains vociferously about injustices under socialism, but he believes that such injustices are foreign to the socialist system, rather than fundamental to its nature.

Although this chapter has focused on the political significance of filmmaking, the glaring difference between Xie Jin, the reformer, and Huang Jianxin, the postsocialist artist, is also readily apparent in the stylistic realm. In many ways Xie Jin's films are melodramatic caricatures of real life, filled as they are with righteous socialist heroes and true believers who suffer unspeakably and are persecuted by leftist zealots or Party hacks who fail to realize that their arbitrary and undemocratic style of work is influenced by discredited leftist modes. In the end, however, socialist justice always prevails, and wrongs are righted. There is plenty of human agony in Xie Jin's films, but those who have been wronged never give up the hope that an appropriate socialist solution to China's problems will be found. It is to his credit that Xie Jin's films get attacked in China, but those who attack him are frightened antireformists who believe that the reform path will undermine the thing that is most important to them—absolute Party rule.

As a number of scholars have argued, melodrama is a major genre of Chinese filmmaking. Among other things, it was a genre that was particularly well suited to the task of establishing a disturbingly one-dimensional socialist culture in China after 1949. It should not surprise us, then, that one of the most important characteristics of Huang Jianxin's approach to filmmaking is his total rejection of the emotional, melodramatic format. He analyzes the Chinese world with an icy detachment that allows little room for sentiment. His antiheroes are victims of socialism, but not heroes or martyrs; they are alienated from the socialist system, but they participate in the process that results in their own victimization. Xie Jin's films are meant to elicit tears (and stimulate a cathartic healing), whereas Huang Jianxin's devastating postsocialist "red humor" mocks what is most fundamental to the socialist system and produces the kind of bitter laughter that only those who have spent their lives in traditional socialist societies can fully appreciate.

In sum, the postsocialist condition that is revealed in Huang Jianxin's films is neither socialist nor capitalist. The postsocialist condition exists only in cultures that have functioned for significant periods of time as traditional socialist societies. That is, postsocialism presupposes socialism. In some postsocialist settings the Leninist Party still exercises a virtual monopoly on power, while in others it has been forced to share power or has been pushed entirely from the political arena. But it is not the political situation at elite levels alone that defines the postsocialist condition. Postsocialism involves a perception among ordinary people at the bottom that socialism has failed, that it is not the solution to what ails society, but rather the very cause. The general sense is that Leninist parties that have been in power for decades are inherently incapable of reforming society. Postsocialism, in brief, involves a massive loss of faith. Some of the alienation, frustration, and anger it engenders leads to a politically healthy search for alternatives to traditional socialism, but some of that disaffection (such as the sort one sees in *Transmigration*) produces self-destructive social and psychological behavior. In postsocialist society, failed institutions remain deeply rooted and continue to have a damaging impact on social, political, economic, and cultural life even though popular alienation is widespread and nonsocialist political forces have emerged. Indeed, socialist institutions and habits are even more deeply entrenched than the ruling Leninist Party.

Thus, when we try to evaluate Chinese cinema in the 1980s and the works of artists like Huang Jianxin, it might not make much sense to compare them with Chinese films made in capitalist Taiwan and Hong Kong. Over the years I have noticed that ordinary people in mainland China have little interest in and experience difficulty understanding the themes of most films made in Taiwan and Hong Kong. If there is interest in this cinema, it is because these films are perceived to be utterly exotic and otherworldly. That is to say, they have little to do with the postsocialist realities of mainland life. Similarly, ordinary people who grew up in Taiwan have difficulty relating to problems that get thrashed out in films made in mainland China. There may be a temporary interest in seeing what was once taboo, but curiosity quickly evaporates when it becomes clear that mainland films treat issues that are far removed from the problems that Taiwan residents face. In brief, multiple decades have created a huge cultural gap between the people of mainland China and those of Taiwan and Hong Kong. Indeed, it seems to me much more fruitful to compare films made in China in the 1980s with films produced in Eastern Europe both before and after the disintegration of the old socialist regimes. One is tempted to say that, after many decades of socialism, the people of mainland China have more in common with the people of the former Soviet Union, Bulgaria, and Hungary than they have with the people of Taiwan. Similarly, the people of Poland, eastern Germany, and the former Czechoslovakia would have no difficulty recognizing and understanding the issues raised by Huang Jianxin, because, like the Chinese people, they have experienced socialism and now find themselves struggling in the uncharted waters of postsocialist reality.

NOTES

An earlier version of this chapter appeared as "Huang Jianxin and the Notion of Postsocialism," in *New Chinese Cinemas: Forms, Identities, Politics*, ed. Nick Browne, Paul G. Pickowicz, Vivian Sobchack, and Esther Yau (Cambridge, UK: Cambridge University Press, 1994), 57–87.

1. *Guangming ribao*, December 15, 1988; *South China Morning Post*, December 16, 1988.
2. For a discussion of the reform films of Xie Jin and others, see chapter 9.
3. See Fredric Jameson, "Remapping Taipei," in *New Chinese Cinemas: Forms, Identities, Politics*, ed. Nick Browne, Paul G. Pickowicz, Vivian Sobchack, and Esther Yau (Cambridge, UK: Cambridge University Press, 1994), 117–50.
4. Leo Ou-fan Lee, "In Search of Modernity: Some Reflections on a New Mode of Consciousness in Twentieth-Century Chinese History and Literature," in *Ideas across Cultures: Essays on Chinese Thought in Honor of Benjamin I. Schwartz*, ed. Paul A. Cohen and Merle Goldman (Cambridge, Mass.: Harvard University Press, 1990).
5. See *Shanghai wenxue*, August 1982, for the views of Li Tuo, Feng Jicai, and Liu Xinwu, and see *Wenyi bao*, September 1982, for a criticism of their "modernist" views.
6. For a discussion of early Chinese Marxist encounters with Stalinist literary thought, see Paul G. Pickowicz, *Marxist Literary Thought in China: The Influence of Ch'ü Ch'iu-pai* (Berkeley: University of California Press, 1981), 179–86.
7. Fredric Jameson, *Marxism and Form* (Princeton, N.J.: Princeton University Press, 1974), 160–205.
8. Masao Miyoshi, "Against the Native Grain: The Japanese Novel and the 'Postmodern' West," in *Postmodernism and Japan*, ed. Masao Miyoshi and H. D. Harootunian (Durham, N.C.: Duke University Press, 1989), 143.
9. This is the sense I get from reading Brian Wallis, ed., *Art after Modernism: Rethinking Representation* (New York: New Museum of Contemporary Art, 1988).
10. Arif Dirlik, "Post-socialism? Reflections on 'Socialism with Chinese Characteristics,'" in *Marxism and the Chinese Experience*, ed. Arif Dirlik and Maurice Meisner (Armonk, N.Y.: M. E. Sharpe, 1989), 362–84. For other theoretical discussions, see Ernesto Laclau and Chantal Mouffe, *Hegemony and Socialist Strategy* (London: Verso, 1985); Norman Geras, "Post-Marxism?" *New Left Review* 163 (May–June 1987); Nicos Mouzelis, "Marxism or Post-Marxism?" *New Left Review* 167 (January–February 1988).

Dirlik uses the concept of postsocialism to characterize official Chinese Communist Party ideology in the post-Mao era—that is, the notion of "socialism with Chinese characteristics." He thinks of postsocialism as a coherent and elite ideology with specific traits. The ideology of Deng Xiaoping, in this interpretation, is postsocialist in the sense that it acknowledges serious deficiencies in the traditional socialist system, especially in the economic realm, and resorts to capitalist methods of economic development and management to overcome these deficiencies. At the same time, however, Deng regards capitalist society as inherently defective. Thus, postsocialism seeks to avoid a capitalist future for China. Dirlik likes the concept of postsocialism because, in matters related to theory and ideology, it gets analysts out of the intellectual quicksand of the simple socialist-capitalist dichotomy, a discourse that requires critics to identify an ideological development as essentially capitalist or essentially socialist.

At one level, Dirlik's formulation is highly subversive and would be most unwelcome to Deng Xiaoping. In effect, Dirlik, an independent and nonsectarian socialist critic of traditional Marxist-Leninist states, is saying that Deng Xiaoping's new socialism with Chinese characteristics is not genuine socialism. But perhaps more important, he is also saying something that would be welcomed by Deng, namely that post-Mao Communist Party ideology is not capitalist either. Dirlik's conception of a distinctively postsocialist ideological mode was mapped out before the violent crisis of spring 1989 exploded in China and well before the authority of the Communist regimes suddenly evaporated in Poland, eastern Germany, the former Czechoslovakia, Hungary, and Romania in late 1989—that is, at a time when it was still possible for sympathetic critics to hope that "real," humane socialism (as opposed to traditional Stalinist socialism or Deng Xiaoping's socialism with Chinese characteristics) might have a future in what was known as the socialist world. Dirlik's work is, in this strict sense, a rigorous effort to salvage what he regards as important, life-enhancing aspects of nineteenth- and twentieth-century socialist theory by denying that Deng's program or ideology is really socialist.

11. For a longer discussion of Dirlik's work, see Paul G. Pickowicz, "The Chinese Anarchist Critique of Marxism-Leninism," *Modern China* 16, no. 4 (October 1990): 450-67.

12. The subject of popular thought in contemporary China is treated in various ways in Perry Link, Richard Madsen, and Paul G. Pickowicz, eds., *Unofficial China: Popular Culture and Thought in the People's Republic* (Boulder, Colo.: Westview Press, 1989).

13. Paul G. Pickowicz, "Postsocialism and Chinese Cultural Identity in the 1980s: A Comment on James Watson's 'The Renegotiation of Chinese Cultural Identity in the Post-Mao Era: An Anthropological Perspective,'" unpublished manuscript, University of California, San Diego.

14. *Los Angeles Times*, September 8, 1989.

15. This is essentially the position adopted by William Hinton in *The Great Reversal* (New York: Monthly Review Press, 1990).

16. Perry Link, *Evening Chats in Beijing: Probing China's Predicament* (New York: Norton, 1992), 27-28. For a discussion of decollectivization and the mood of the peasantry, see Paul G. Pickowicz, "*Long Bow*: The Movie," *American Anthropological Association Society for Visual Anthropology Newsletter* 3, no. 3 (Fall 1987): 1-5; and Edward Friedman, "Deng versus the Peasantry: Recollectivization in the Chinese Countryside," *Problems of Communism*, September-October 1990, 30-43.

17. Popular culture in rural North China in the 1950s and early 1960s is discussed at length in Edward Friedman, Paul G. Pickowicz, and Mark Selden, *Chinese Village, Socialist State* (New Haven, Conn.: Yale University Press, 1991).

18. "*Heipao shijian* zongheng tan," *Dangdai dianying*, no. 3 (1986): 58.

19. Su Shaozhi, "The Crisis of Marxism in China," *The World and I*, no. 10 (October 1989): 74.

20. "Cu ren shen si de *Heipao shijian*," *Dianying yishu*, no. 4 (1986): 16.

21. "Cu ren shen si de *Heipao shijian*," 9.

22. Su Shaokang and Wang Luxiang, *Heshang* (Xianggang: Sanlian shudian, 1989).

23. "*Heipao shijian* zongheng tan," 57-59; "Cu ren shen si de *Heipao shijan*," 12-13.

24. "*Heipao shijian* zongheng tan," 62.

25. "*Heipao shijian* zongheng tan," 54.
26. "*Heipao shijian* zongheng tan," 50-54.
27. "Cu ren shen si de *Heipao shijian*," 17.
28. "Cu ren shen si de *Heipao shijian*," 16.
29. "Cu ren shen si de *Heipao shijian*," 10.
30. "Cu ren shen si de *Heipao shijian*," 10.
31. "*Heipao shijian* zongheng tan," 57-58.
32. James Watson, "The Renegotiation of Chinese Cultural Identity in the Post-Mao Era: An Anthropological Perspective," in *Popular Protest and Political Culture in Modern China: Learning from 1989*, ed. Jeffrey N. Wasserstrom and Elizabeth J. Perry (Boulder, Colo.: Westview Press, 1992), 78.
33. For a discussion of utopian and dystopian visions of the Chinese future, see Maurice Meisner, *Marxism, Maoism, and Utopianism: Eight Essays* (Madison: University of Wisconsin Press, 1982), 184-211.
34. See Jim Mann, *Beijing Jeep* (New York: Simon and Schuster, 1989), 260.
35. For a discussion of the historical background of recent campaigns against bourgeois liberalization, see chapter 2.
36. "*Cuowei* cuowei?" *Dianying yishu*, no. 6 (1987): 46. Instead of publishing the comments of scholars and critics, *Dangdai dianying* published remarks made by the production crew of *Dislocation*. See "Ningyuan zai tansuozhong shibai, buyuan zai baoshouzhong gouan," *Dangdai dianying*, no. 3 (1987): 111-23.
37. "*Cuowei* cuowei?" 40-41.
38. "Cu ren shen si de *Heipao shijian*," 12.
39. "*Cuowei* cuowei?" 44. For an example of Luo Yijun's cautious approach to film criticism, see his *Fengyu yinmu* (Beijing: Zhongguo dianying chubanshe, 1983).
40. "*Cuowei* cuowei?" 45.
41. *South China Morning Post* (Associated Press wire story), December 16, 1988.
42. *Guangming ribao*, December 15, 1988.
43. Dai Jinhua, "Ideology, Wang Shuo, 1988," *China Screen*, no. 4 (1989): 28.
44. Shao Mujun, "Why Did a Wang Shuo Cinema Craze Occur?" *China Screen*, no. 4 (1989): 29.
45. Su Bing, "Zisha milian de goucheng," *Dangdai dianying*, no. 2 (1990): 95-99.
46. Dai, "Ideology, Wang Shuo, 1988," 28.
47. *Beijing Review* 32, no. 44 (1989): 44.
48. Paul Clark, "June 4, 1989, and Chinese Cinema," *Asian Cinema* 4, nos. 1-2 (1988-1989): 14-15.
49. Teng Jinxian, "Harmful Trends in Film Creation," *China Screen*, no. 3 (1990): 2.
50. "Cu ren shen si de *Heipao shijian*," 9. I do not mean to suggest that there were no veteran directors who approached contemporary society in a direct and critical way. Wu Tianming and Huang Jianzhong are two obvious examples of artists who did so quite successfully.
51. "The Three Screen Faces of China," *Economist*, July 4, 1987, 87-90.
52. Herbert Marcuse, *The Aesthetic Dimension: Toward a Critique of Marxist Aesthetics* (Boston: Beacon Press, 1978), 9.
53. Marcuse, *The Aesthetic Dimension*, 14.
54. Marcuse, *The Aesthetic Dimension*, 47.

11

Velvet Prisons and the Political Economy of Chinese Filmmaking in the Late 1980s and Early 1990s

In the 1980s and earlier, late state socialist regimes in Eastern Europe loosened their Stalinist grip on society in order to address serious economic problems. The retreat of the state was especially apparent in the concessions that were made to market forces in the economy and in the sprouting (or resprouting) of relatively autonomous social groups both inside and outside the state sector. At the same time, the state also largely abandoned Stalinist strategies of cultural and ideological control. Although the reforms were designed to breathe new life into the state socialist project, the outcome was exactly the opposite. By the late 1980s, these regimes simply collapsed without much warning. The new market, social, and cultural forces let loose by the state indubitably played a part in undermining its long-term stability. But important questions remain. How extensive was the role of these forces? Do reform initiatives inevitably lead to the demise of such states?[1]

The Soviet bloc is gone, but it still makes sense for China specialists to continue to ask questions about the experiences of those regimes in the late state socialist phase of their development (see chapter 10). It would be a mistake to assume that, just because the Communist Party survived the Tiananmen crisis and is still in power, no meaningful historical connections link China to the failed regimes of the former Soviet bloc, China is somehow a unique case, or China need only be studied with reference to itself. Not only do such Chinese thinkers as Liu Binyan tell us to comprehend the things that connect China to Eastern Europe and the Soviet Union, so too do the writings of Eastern Europeans. Hence, when we explore a complex subject like the crisis of Chinese filmmaking in the post–Cultural Revolution reform era, analysis in terms of the cultural criticisms formulated by someone like Miklos Haraszti in Hungary can be useful.

Haraszti's brilliant discussion titled *The Velvet Prison: Artists under State Socialism*, a work that mentions China several times, was first published in France in 1983 under the title *L'Artiste d'état* and then clandestinely in Hungary in 1986 as *A cenzura esztetikaja*.[2] An extraordinarily pessimistic work written well before the unexpected collapse of state socialism throughout Europe, the book solemnly concluded that, despite all appearances, a totalizing and hegemonic culture of state socialism was even more deeply rooted in post-Stalinist regimes than it was in the Stalin era.

Haraszti acknowledged that state cultural planners overhauled the socialist cultural arena in the post-Stalin era. Their reforms were discussed in the West under the headings of "thaw," "liberalization," and "openness," all of which were supposed to contribute to the articulation of private rather than public expressions, and humanistic rather than class interests. After these regimes had achieved consolidation by using time-honored Stalinist tactics, cultural bureaucrats at the state center no longer needed to resort to arrests, show trials, and strong-arm methods.

The cultural strategy of the more mature and self-confident state socialist regime (plagued with economic problems) amounted to gently placing artists in a comfortable "velvet prison." It was more efficient for the state to flatter and bribe artists by offering them perquisites and a chance to wield a bit of power than to continue to bludgeon them with the familiar instruments of crude censorship. Artists were no longer restricted to doing agitprop work; they could travel abroad and could even obtain approval to recycle the outmoded cultural refuse of contemporary capitalist societies. All that was required was their loyalty (passive or active) to the state. Expressions of a non-Marxist mentality were acceptable; anti-Marxism was not. An advantage of the system was that the state had the option to revert, however briefly, to Stalinist modes of control and assimilation.

Heraszti argued passionately that the new plan worked. Artists sold out to the state in droves and deceived themselves by calling it progress. Some even convinced themselves that they had achieved independence or autonomy. In reality, they enjoyed the power and the comforts and were unlikely to do anything to jeopardize their new status. Although few admitted it, the vast majority of artists collaborated with the socialist state in the post-Stalin era. Their art was an art of complicity that legitimized and perpetuated the hegemony of the state. All artists were on the state payroll. If they were not on the state payroll, by definition they were not artists. As loyal professionals, artists benefited from generous state funding for the arts. Indeed, they became addicted to state funding and privately shuddered at the plight of artists in nonsocialist states who, unable to count on a regular state paycheck, were required to navigate the treacherous waters of the capitalist marketplace. Socialism was not so bad after all.

Observers outside the Soviet bloc invariably interpreted this thaw or retreat as a manifestation of the weakening of state power. The wider scope of artistic creativity seemed to suggest greater independence and autonomy for the artist. Apparent criticisms of the state, especially those that Haraszti said were being communicated "between the lines," could easily be interpreted as examples of an emerging civil or independent artistic culture. In reality, he insisted, the state was all too pleased to provide space for loyal critics. It was all part of the subtle cultural construction known as the velvet prison. In brief, Heraszti argued that cultural reforms that brought the apparent retreat of the state, liberalization, thaw, opening, individualism, market reform, and even criticism did not engender artistic autonomy or the emergence of civil society. Under the ingenious velvet prison arrangement of post-Stalinism, the state counted upon artists to engage in self-censorship and self-mutilation.

THE RETREAT OF THE STATE IN THE POST-MAO FILM INDUSTRY

By the standards of the Cultural Revolution, the Chinese state retreated substantially from the world of filmmaking after the death of Mao (see chapter 9).[3] Indeed, if one thinks of Haraszti's conceptualizations, it is clear that the post-Mao state sought to do what the post-Stalin regimes of the Soviet bloc attempted to do as early as the 1960s—that is, convert to the less heavy-handed, more nuanced velvet prison mode of cultural control.

The state apologized to film professionals, almost all of whom had been brutalized in one fashion or another by the profoundly anti-intellectual policies of the Cultural Revolution decade. Like the post-Stalinist leadership of the USSR, the post-Mao Chinese leadership had everything to gain in the short run by allowing film workers to denounce the "abuses of the past." The same thing happened throughout the Soviet bloc. It was cathartic and consistent with Party policy. The new leadership piously admitted that it should have been obvious all along that the state could not survive without intellectuals in its bureaucratic apparatus. (Haraszti argued that artists in the Soviet bloc actually liked the idea of being politely invited to work in the service of the state.) The Chinese, of course, had refined the idea of intellectual elites serving the state many centuries ago, so it was relatively easy to restore them to their "rightful" and "natural" position after 1976.

Along with the new power and prestige came better housing, higher incomes, access to slush funds and special stores, drivers, banquets, foreign travel, foreign friends, restricted publications, restricted foreign films, and special opportunities for children. The now famous 1978 entering class of the elite Beijing Film Institute (Beijing dianying xueyuan), the most prestigious art school in China at the time, was said to have been recruited entirely by competitive examination; in fact, its ranks included many of the offspring of well-known film professionals and cultural dignitaries (including Bai Yang's daughter, Chen Huaikai's son, Zhao Dan's son, Hua Junwu's son, Ai Qing's son, and Tian Fang's son). Like other intellectuals, filmmakers understood that benefits derived from institutionalized bureaucratic corruption had always been a dividend enjoyed by those who worked in the service of the state. It should come as no surprise that virtually all Chinese filmmakers were attracted to the velvet prison.

The retreat of the state also brought some welcome changes in the structure of the film industry, all analogous to changes made in the Soviet bloc much earlier. China's film studios, which grew in number from ten in 1979 to nearly thirty in 1983, were given almost complete authority to determine which films they wanted to make. Film professionals, after all, were tired of making militant class struggle sagas. The films of the early 1980s featured attacks on the Cultural Revolution and other Maoist campaigns, love stories, accounts of famous historical events and people, folk legends, tales of crime detection, and martial arts adventures.[4] From 1979 to 1989, an average of well over a hundred feature films were produced each year. Foreign and domestic observers (including myself), numbed by the narrowness of Cultural Revolution productions, were impressed by the diversity of the content of many post–Cultural Revolution films. Of particular interest was the new priority that filmmakers gave to exploring the complexities of private and individual life in the urban sphere.

The new diversity of content, including the attention given to private life, was closely related to elementary economic reforms carried out in the film industry. Studios had to balance their budgets as state subsidies were phased out. Forced to make profitable pictures, filmmakers had to worry for the first time since the late 1940s about audience tastes.[5] Thus, the idea of a single, integrated national audience was abandoned. Studies of market conditions revealed that there were many popular audiences, some of which had more to spend on entertainment than others. Under these circumstances, filmmaking took on a more distinctively urban orientation. Some filmmakers raided the rich treasure-house of late imperial and early Republican urban popular culture, while others dwelled on such time-tested genres as martial arts adventures and family melodramas (see chapter 3). Veteran directors sought to reestablish contact with the heritage of May Fourth literature by making films based on Republican-era fiction. Young directors were eager to incorporate foreign currents to reassure a weary post–Cultural Revolution urban audience that Chinese city life was "modernizing" in ways that were consistent with "modernity" in "advanced" foreign nations. Relatively few films were made about rural China, and those that were set in the countryside often involved more than a bit of peasant bashing. In brief, they were not really being made for peasants. The heavy hand of Cultural Revolution and pre–Cultural Revolution state censorship was also lifted. Some filmmakers even began working political criticism into their movies, especially implied criticism that was conveyed at subtextual levels.

The response of the starved film audience was extraordinary. Although it is difficult to be confident about statistical estimates, it appears that film attendance in China set a record of approximately 29 billion viewers in 1979. Urban film fans especially appreciated the revival of the "star" system. Such actresses as Siqin Gaowa, Chen Chong, Liu Shaoqing, Pan Hong, Zhang Yu, and Gong Li became household names. Glossy film magazines like *Popular Cinema* (*Dazhong dianying*), featuring images of young starlets in sexy poses and gossipy news about the private lives of film personalities, were snapped up by newly fashion-conscious urbanites. Filmmakers' new concerns about the tastes of the audience and the dynamics of the marketplace were intensified by the television revolution, which exploded on the scene in the late 1970s. The film studios regarded the television studios as powerful adversaries; the two competed for the same audience. Television was bound to rob the film industry of a share of its audience, and filmmakers were panicking in the mid-1980s. But according to the well-known director Wu Tianming, by 1988 the movie audience still numbered around 18 billion.

POST-MAO URBAN CINEMA: TWO CASE STUDIES

One of the most striking developments of the 1980s was the emergence of a new-style cinema that probed the contours of the emerging culture of urban individualism. Of special interest were the works of young filmmakers who dwelled on the mood of alienation and disaffection that prevailed in major cities. Space limitations prevent a comprehensive overview of the new urban cinema, but a brief discussion of a couple of representative titles provides some sense of its remarkable range.

For example, the striking cynicism of post-Mao urban youth is captured rather well in *The Trouble-Shooters* (*Wan zhu*, d. Mi Jiashan, 1988), a stylish black comedy released on the eve of the Tiananmen crisis. A postsocialist cross between *Ghostbusters* (d. Ivan Rietman, 1984) and *Easy Rider* (d. Dennis Hopper, 1969), this film tells the story of three enterprising young men in Beijing who launch a popular, new-age private firm called the Triple T Company. These likable con artists earn money by solving the problems of bewildered urban dwellers who are struggling with personal difficulties in the brave new world forged by Deng Xiaoping. One client is a frustrated and deservedly obscure young writer who desperately wants to win a literary prize.

The company stages a lavish award gala to make him feel important. Another customer is an angry and unhappily married housewife who wants to heap verbal abuse on her husband, but he is never home. For a price, Triple T is more than happy to assign someone to play the part of the missing husband and take all the tongue-lashings the woman can dish out. Another poor soul is having problems with unwanted seminal emissions. He is advised not to go to bed too early, not to wear tight underwear, and not to look at pictures of pinup models. An unattractive young man with a thick Shanghai accent is disgusted by his bedridden mother, a veteran revolutionary (hence, "the mother of us all") who now does little more than "shit in her bed" every day. He hires Triple T to clean up the mess.

The most remarkable segment of the film is a bizarre sequence about the "Triple T Award Ceremony" that has been staged for the benefit of the talentless young writer. To fund the event, tickets are sold to hundreds of people who feel lucky to be able to witness such a glamorous event. Not only does the audience get to hear high-sounding speeches about the stunning accomplishments of the various award winners (all of whom are fakes), they also get to see a group of sleek and beautifully dressed fashion models who parade around a brightly lit boardwalk. In a surprise development, however, the models are suddenly joined on stage by characters dressed in Beijing opera costumes, followed by female bodybuilders wearing skimpy bikinis, People's Liberation Army soldiers, Qing aristocrats, public security officers, Nationalist-era generals, warlords, Red Guards, rustic peasants, and muscular factory workers. The audience is familiar with all these stock characters but knows they are strangely out of place when they interact with good cheer on the same stage. At the end of the performance, all the characters begin dancing with one another to the thumping sound of contemporary popular music; the Red Guards cavort with the slinky Western-style models, and the Qing elites frolic with the brawny and oily-skinned female bodybuilders.

The Trouble-Shooters, cowritten by the immensely popular Wang Shuo, is about young urbanites who have no connection to the revolution and find themselves lost in the postsocialist city.[6] The film opens to the heavy metal music of rock star Cui Jian, who shouts:

> Dreamed 'bout livin' in modern city space;
> Now it's hard to explain what I face;
> Skyscrapers poppin' up one by one;
> But let me tell ya, life here's no fun.

The lives of the urban youth portrayed in this film are directionless and devoid of much meaning. Beijing is a vast stage occupied by masked players who are performing in a never-ending theater of the absurd.

Triple T partner Yu Guan (*right*) sleeps over at his girlfriend's apartment whenever he wants in *The Trouble-Shooters* (1988, d. Mi Jiashan). China Film Archive

A film that captured a very different thrust of the new-style urban cinema of the late 1980s was *Obsession* (*Fengkuang de daijia*, d. Zhou Xiaowen, 1988). Unlike *The Trouble-Shooters*, a cleverly written and genuinely humorous work that consciously seeks to document the phenomena of a generation gap and youth alienation, *Obsession* is an escapist adventure designed to make money by providing spectacular "modern-style" entertainment. In short, *Obsession* is an example of new urban exploitation films that pander to the curiosities of a restless and bored urban film audience.

For example, the title sequence is set in a women's public shower and contains extensive frontal nudity. The camera dwells voyeuristically on a group of young women who are helping each another wash. The youngest bather suddenly experiences menstruation for the first time. Several scenes later this innocent teenager is kidnapped, brutally raped, and beaten senseless by a muscle-bound thug who spends most of his time reading pornographic magazines imported from Hong Kong and Taiwan. His room is decorated with posters of Sylvester Stallone and Bruce Springsteen. When the police interview the victim, the camera gratuitously zooms in on her tattered and bloody underwear, which is displayed on a nearby table.

Obsession is a Chinese version of *The French Connection* (d. William Friedkin, 1971). The victim's elder sister, Qingqing, teams up with Zhao, a nonconformist, Gene Hackman–like retired policeman, to track down the rapist. In the end, a spectacular car chase is followed by a wild shoot-out and the arrest of the culprit. In a surprise ending, Qingqing avenges her sister's rape by suddenly pushing the suspect off a tall building.

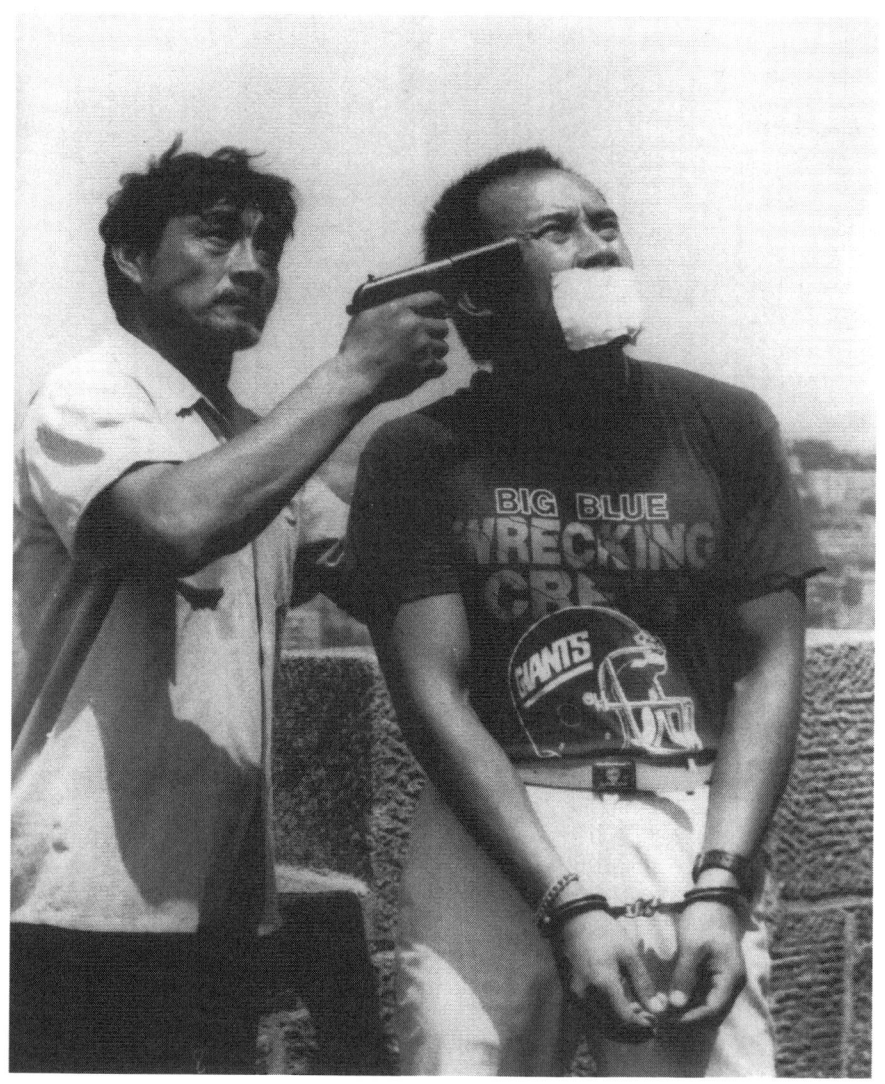

Zhao, a nonconformist police officer, uses a hostage to capture a rapist, in *Obsession* (1988, d. Zhou Xiaowen). China Film Archive

Obsession is an interesting example of the globalization of Chinese urban culture in the post-Mao period. The narrative, flattened and generic in quality, could have unfolded anywhere. In sharp contrast to *The Trouble-Shooters*, this film simply dispensed with meaningful references to Chinese history and culture. The film is unsettling in the sense that it delivers bad news: China is a mess. At the same time it is reassuring: China may be in bad shape, but in that respect it is no different from the rest of the world. Unlike *The Trouble-Shooters*, *Obsession* does not convey muted political criticisms, but like *The Trouble-Shooters* it left the strong impression that modernity is chaotic and unstable.

Compared to *Obsession*, films like *The Trouble-Shooters* are much more conscious of their Chineseness. Repeated references are made to China's socialist past and present. But the allusions are so scrambled and confused that the viewer cannot get a clear picture of the sources of contemporary problems. The purpose of the references is to mock the revolutionary legacy. *The Trouble-Shooters* reveals much more about the late state socialist context of China than a work like *Obsession*, but like almost all post-Mao urban movies, it gives no indication of how the alienation of urban youth will work itself out. Perhaps that is why films on the theme of urban restlessness and disaffection usually end on a depressing note.

THE STRUCTURE OF THE CHINESE VELVET PRISON

New urban films like *The Trouble-Shooters* and *Obsession* seemed path breaking when they first appeared, but later, especially in light of the Tiananmen crisis, it appears that their significance was exaggerated. In the 1980s many foreign and Chinese observers, impressed by the new developments brought by the reforms, failed to appreciate the importance of many underlying and partially hidden structural and psychological dimensions of the Chinese film world that blocked progress. It is here that Haraszti's gloomy conceptual framework can help explain aspects of cultural conditions in urban China that were ignored when the international spotlight focused almost exclusively on sparkling new films like *The Trouble-Shooters*.

Haraszti would readily concede that the post-Mao state retreated on many cultural and ideological fronts. But he would also argue that the result was nothing like an independent or autonomous film industry. Filmmakers were flattered, empowered, bribed, and co-opted just as their Soviet bloc counterparts had been ten or twenty years earlier. In exchange for comfort, privilege, greater freedom, and access to foreign culture and the storehouse of presocialist Chinese culture, artists had to agree to play by the rules. This meant policing their own industry, knowing the limits, and engaging in self-censorship—in brief, collaborating with the socialist project in ways that were designed to perpetuate and legitimize state control of society.

In the West many observers, including myself, got very excited about the startling rise of the vibrant Fifth Generation film directors in the 1984–1988 period. The remarkable works by Chen Kaige, Zhang Yimou, Tian Zhuangzhuang, Wu Ziniu, and others were exceptionally striking in visual terms. They seemed to be the Chinese equivalents to the late state socialist films of Milos Forman, Jan Kadar, Elmar Klos, and Jiri Menzel produced in Czechoslovakia before 1968. And like most of the Czech films, they could be interpreted as expressions of individual criticisms of the current regime.

While virtually all of us enjoyed wrestling with the multilayered meanings of these challenging and aesthetically pleasing films (works like *Yellow Earth* [*Huang tudi*, d. Chen Kaige, 1985], *Horse Thief* [*Dao ma zei*, d. Tian Zhuangzhuang, 1986], etc.), one of the great ironies of their production—an irony not lost on the directors themselves—is that these spellbinding experiments in "fine art cinema" could not have been made without massive state subsidies. Many of the most experimental films, especially those set in the Republican era, had small audiences and lost money for the studios that produced them. Filmmakers, including irreverent young upstarts, knew well that huge subsidies for experimental works were one of the prized fringe benefits for those who willingly worked in the velvet prison. Virtually no Fifth Generation artist turned down funds provided by the state. Indeed, they and all other filmmakers were almost totally dependent on the state for funding. All filmmakers remained on the state payroll.

Young filmmakers like Mi Jiashan, who insisted on making new-style films like *The Trouble-Shooters* set in a present-day socialist city, were no different from their colleagues who set their work in earlier times. Although they were alienated from the socialist state, they had to include material that gave official reviewers a way out—that is, a way to proclaim that the work was, after all, a loyal, patriotic, and constructive elucidation of social problems whose correction would serve to stabilize the drive for socialist modernization.

When the reform of the film industry deepened in the late 1980s and the state was openly encouraging the production of lightweight "entertainment films" (*yule pian*)—that is, films with higher profit margins—it was the young "pure art" directors (just as Haraszti's framework suggests) who protested the loudest. With profits in command as never before since 1949, the individual studios were no longer inclined to sustain the losses associated with experimental productions—unless, of course, the state was willing to provide special subsidies.

The content and artistic forms of both the new-style films and the films of older directors were certainly more varied than almost anything that had been produced in the 1949–1976 period. Many of the most interesting works (stamped with the seal of state approval) did indeed explore the heretofore ignored realm of individual and private life. Of special note were works like *The Trouble-Shooters* and *Obsession* that treated such problems as social fragmentation, alienation, and youth crime. But there is agreement now that none of these works, including all the new-style productions, amounted to a dissident, independent, or autonomous cinema. It is not even clear whether these films should be regarded as indications of the true state of mind of their creators. Private conversations with filmmakers invariably revealed that even the best of these works fell far short of what film artists really wanted to do. The works we see, however controversial they may seem, should not be regarded as examples of the best these artists can do. In reality, no one, including the filmmakers themselves, knows what their best work would look like if the motion picture industry were independent of the state. Few if any filmmakers saw themselves as collaborators, but almost all were conscious of the fact that they engaged in self-censorship virtually every day. In the late 1980s the alternative to self-censorship and voluntary participation in the velvet prison was silence and inactivity.

In a formal sense, none of the remarkable films of the 1980s era can be viewed as manifestations of unofficial or dissident culture. They are official in the sense that they were all produced in state-run film studios. The state retreated in some important ways from the film industry, but the retreat did not result in an autonomous or independent film world on the eve of the Tiananmen horrors.

THE POLITICAL ECONOMY OF FILMMAKING IN THE REFORM ERA

If the state center gave up direct control over what was produced by the film studios, if screenwriters and directors were encouraged to treat themes related to private space and the culture of individualism, and if filmmakers were permitted to take into account the tastes of ordinary consumers in the market, then why did the reforms of the 1980s fail to produce an independent or autonomous film culture?

The most obvious answer is that the state never really gave up control. A more complicated answer would detail the unique complexities of the organization of film production in the 1980s. The state never reformed the vast bureaucratic structure of the socialist film world. The state-controlled Chinese Filmworkers Association (Zhongguo dianyingjia xiehui) continued to function as the uncontested professional (Party-controlled) union for all film workers. The dominant publisher of books related to cinema continued to be the state-owned China Film Press (Zhongguo dianying chubanshe). The many film magazines and journals continued to be owned and published by the state. The powerful Film Bureau (Dianying ju), presided over by the broadminded but loyal Shi Fangyu in the mid-1980s and by the insufferably bureaucratic Teng Jinxian in the late 1980s, was a department in the Ministry of Culture until the late 1980s, when it was shifted to the new Ministry of Radio, Film, and Television. The individual film studios could decide what they wanted to make, but the final product had to be submitted to the Film Bureau for censorship review. Moreover, central state planners still dictated the number of films a single studio could produce in one year. State organs controlled the various high-profile award programs, such as the Hundred Flowers (Bai hua) and Golden Rooster (Jin ji) competitions. All film workers (a vast community estimated to include more than seventeen thousand people in the late 1980s) were on the state payroll, and all studios remained state-owned. The studios continued to be laid out and organized like small socialist walled cities: housing and dining facilities were provided by the studio, welfare and retirement benefits were administered by the studio, and permanent employment was virtually guaranteed.

The nature of film production itself facilitated ongoing state control in the early post-Mao era. Many intellectuals, including novelists, poets, essayists, and visual artists, worked alone at home, and the cost of their basic materials was often quite modest. Independence from the state was easier to achieve for solitary artists who worked beyond the scrutiny of the state. For a variety of practical and logistical reasons, their works were more likely to circulate outside China.

Film production was quite different and, thus, far easier to control. According to Wu Tianming, the average cost of making a film was 400,000–500,000 yuan in the mid-1980s and jumped to 800,000 yuan by 1988.[7] Under the reforms the studios themselves did not have the money to fund such projects and had to rely on bank loans that were not available to individuals to finance new work. Private investment in film production was virtually unheard of in the 1980s. Production equipment was expensive, and production staffs were enormous. Representatives of the state were aware of what was going on almost every step of the way. No private entrepreneurs (*geti hu*) were making commercial films.

But more than anything else, the Chinese film industry, even in its velvet prison configuration, was controlled by the almost totally unreformed iron-grip workings of a poorly understood distribution system. A tightly organized state monopoly, the China Film Distribution Corporation (Zhongguo dianying faxing gongsi), settled almost all matters related to film distribution from its headquarters in Beijing. In the late 1980s its general manager was Hu Jian. Nothing got screened aboveground in China without the corporation's approval. Because all films were the property of the state, they had to be handed over to this state monopoly after they were completed by the studios. Only the corporation had the distribution rights. This system was borrowed in its entirety from the Soviet Union, surviving both the apocalyptic surges of Maoism and the market reforms of Deng

Xiaoping.[8] Even if a film passed censorship screening in the Film Bureau, it could not be seen if the corporation did not order and distribute copies. The corporation could decide not to order copies or to order only a few copies if it found a new film politically offensive or (as was increasingly the case) lacking a popular market. If few or no copies were ordered, the film studio sustained staggering financial losses.

The corporation's various branch offices (more than fifty provincial and municipal offices, two thousand county-level companies, and 3,700 village stations) made direct and exclusive contact with the extraordinary number of 161,777 state-owned projection units.[9] No film projection units were privately owned (although in urban settings by the late 1980s thousands of privately run video parlors showed Hong Kong and Taiwan *gongfu* and romance tapes). Altogether approximately 500,000 workers were on the state payroll in the distribution and projection monopolies at that time, all of whom had to be housed, guaranteed permanent jobs, and provided with pensions.[10]

Wu Tianming, the former head of the Xian Film Studio, living in exile in Los Angeles in the early 1990s, complained that the distribution system denied the state studios and, thus, the individual filmmakers employed by the studios, any meaningful control of their destiny.[11] In brief, the studios took most of the risks and were deprived of most of the rewards.

The system worked in the following way. The corporation decided how many prints of a film it would need. It then sold the prints to its provincial and municipal branch agencies for the set price of 10,500 *yuan* each, regardless of the quality of the film or the studio's cost of production. For a fee the branch agencies then arranged distribution of the film to various projection units in their regions. The local projection units had no control over which titles were offered or when they were offered. If they refused to show the films offered to them by the branch agencies, they would not be able to show anything. Income from screenings was adversely affected by both the high cost of a single screening (from 51 *yuan* in Shanghai for a single screening in 1983 to 99 *yuan* in 1988) and the extremely low cost of tickets (between 20 and 25 *fen*). Throughout the 1980s, the state's Price Control Bureau refused to consider price increases even though the cost of production and distribution of films had increased. Thus, after expenses, very few projection units showed a profit, and theaters that were already uncomfortable and unattractive declined even further.

The funds collected by the regional agencies of the corporation were used to pay their costs, most of which involved salaries and benefits for their heavily bloated staffs. Because provincial and municipal governments controlled personnel appointments in the regional agencies of the corporation, the agencies were commonly used by local governments as dumping grounds for their own unwanted bureaucrats. One particularly notorious county-level agency had eleven vice managers.

The cycle was completed when the regional agencies turned over their after-expense profits to the main office in Beijing. The profits were then divided: approximately 29 percent went to the studios that actually made the films, and 71 percent to the corporation itself. If the individual studios showed any profit after meeting their expenses (including the repayment of bank loans), the state imposed a gargantuan 55 percent industrial tax. Not surprisingly, under such a system of distribution only two or three studios were able to turn a profit each year during the 1980s. Consequently, the technical infrastructures of the studios steadily declined.

The overall impact of state control over distribution is reflected in the statistics for 1987. The Film Distribution Corporation reported that the total income for all film screenings was 516 million *yuan*. Of this the provincial and municipal agencies got 250 million *yuan*, while the main office in Beijing got 158 million *yuan*. Presumably the projection units retained 108 million *yuan*. But the parent corporation claimed its expenses for the year were 183 million *yuan* (including the payment of distribution rights to the studios); thus it claimed a loss of 30 million *yuan*.

Some of the consequences of such a system are less apparent than others. The corporation did not really care if the studios made high-quality and experimental art films that have a small audience. It simply failed to buy many copies. *Yellow Earth, Horse Thief, Evening Bell* (*Wan zhong*, d. Wu Ziniu, 1988), and *King of the Children* (*Haizi wang*, d. Chen Kaige, 1987), all of which won international awards, were distributed in amounts of fifteen or fewer copies in China. If studios wanted to absorb the huge losses of making such films (while simultaneously trying to balance their own budgets), that was up to them.

But was it not possible in the late 1980s for studios to make money on art films in the foreign market? Filmmakers knew that foreigners loved such films and devoted large amounts of time to analyzing them. The problem was that export profits could not be reaped by the studios. The corporation also ran the China Film Import and Export Corporation (Zhongguo dianying jin chu kou youxian gongsi), which opened a branch office on Wilshire Boulevard in Los Angeles. The corporation alone could sell the rights (for sums sometimes amounting to hundreds of thousands of dollars) to foreign buyers. The studio got only 14 percent from the corporation.

On the eve of the Tiananmen political crisis, the studios really had no choice about what kind of films to make. Popular "entertainment" films that featured violence and romance were produced in large numbers because that is what the corporation believed urban consumers wanted to see and, therefore, that was what the corporation was willing to distribute. In Wu Tianming's words, the studios were thus cornered into working as prostitutes for the corporation. Films that lost money, namely, crude political propaganda films and experimental art house films, were out.

DEVELOPMENTS SINCE TIANANMEN: THE DEEPENING OF A CRISIS

The harsh political crackdown that followed the massacres of June 1989 revealed all the flaws in the velvet prison construct. The first instinct of the state was to revert to the crude Stalinist mode of control. It cracked down by mobilizing the conservative Filmworkers Association, the Film Bureau, and, of course, the Film Distribution Corporation.[12] Controversial films of the 1980s, including *The Trouble-Shooters*, *Obsession*, and most Fifth Generation works were effectively banned when the corporation simply stopped distributing them. (The corporation continued, nevertheless, to distribute many of these films abroad in order to earn hard currency.) At the same time, the Film Bureau ordered the studios to produce a small flood of films on contemporary and historical topics that praised the army, the Party, and the police, while condemning the polluted ways of foreign cultures. Given the nature of the distribution system, these films, and only these films, were guaranteed to be shown throughout the nation. Schools required students to attend free mass screenings of such works. Most filmmakers faced the difficult choice of making these "command" films or making nothing at all.

Interestingly, however, the freeze did not last long. Films of the 1980s began to be screened once again, the state quickly reassembled the Chinese velvet prison, and leading artists just as quickly returned to work. But not surprisingly, tensions related to issues of autonomy and control continued to mount. The post-Tiananmen film world was a jumble of contradictions.

At one level, the production of several visually stunning films in the early 1990s, including Zhang Yimou's *Judou* (*Judou*, 1990), *Raise the Red Lantern* (*Da hong denglong gaogao gua*, 1991), and *The Story of Qiu Ju* (*Qiu Ju da guan si*, 1992), and Chen Kaige's *Farewell My Concubine* (*Bawang bie ji*, 1993) appeared to indicate that the political crisis of 1989 did not have much of a lasting impact on the film world. *Judou* and *Raise the Red Lantern* were nominated for Oscars, *The Story of Qiu Ju* won the grand prize in Venice, and *Farewell My Concubine* took the Palme d'Or in Cannes and was nominated for an Oscar in 1994.

Foreign writers in particular heaped praise on these works for their considerable artistic merits and for what was often interpreted as their politically critical subtexts. Films like *Judou* and *Raise the Red Lantern*, set in the 1920s and 1930s, were read as indictments of the dark side of Chinese culture. The legacy of oppressiveness and brutality criticized by iconoclastic New Culture and May Fourth intellectuals in the 1910s, Zhang Yimou and the others seemed to be saying, never really gave way and remained deeply rooted in Chinese culture. The Communist Party is the heir to this dubious heritage. Its undemocratic, bureaucratic, and brutish ways are symptomatic of a long-term cultural infirmity. When Zhang and other young directors bashed the traditions of the Chinese patriarchy, it was said, they were bashing the decrepit male autocrats who controlled China and oppressed its people. Given the harshness of the post-Tiananmen crackdown, the appearance of these films was a pleasant surprise. They were so fresh that it was difficult at first to figure out their connection to the culture of the velvet prison.

Actually, the making of these works was closely related to issues that had surfaced well before Tiananmen, namely, the need to find sources of funding for serious art films. On the eve of Tiananmen, it was clear that the state was no longer willing to subsidize movies of this sort. But it was agreed that filmmakers could try to raise money outside China for coproductions or productions entirely financed by foreign capital. *Judou* was funded largely by Japanese interests, and *Raise the Red Lantern* was funded entirely by Taiwan investors who channeled their money through Hong Kong. The producer of *Raise the Red Lantern* was openly acknowledged in the film's credits as Hou Hsiao-hsien (Hou Xiaoxian), the famous Taiwan director. The astounding sound technology used in the film was the responsibility of a cutting-edge Japanese firm.

Because Zhang Yimou, Chen Kaige, and other young post-Mao directors sometimes got into trouble with state authorities in the early 1990s, they were often viewed by foreign critics as quasi-dissident filmmakers. Actually, these artists are highly privileged insiders who are closely connected to and enjoy good working relations with the cultural establishment. It is precisely because they are so well connected and so well funded by foreign sources that they could do what other filmmakers could not: make finely textured art movies for an international audience.

It is true that *Judou* and *Raise the Red Lantern* were banned in China until mid-1992 and received no awards in China at the time of their completion. The bans fueled the idea that Zhang Yimou was some sort of dissident. Zhang, Chen Kaige, and others actively cultivated the notion that they were political renegades, in part because this is what their foreign audience wanted to hear. Actually, the reason why *Judou* and *Raise the Red Lantern* were not released for a time, and why *Farewell My Concubine* was heavily edited before its release in mid-1993, has more to do with what might be called their "self-Orientalism." In a word, these trendy new works, funded by foreign sources and made primarily for foreign audiences, revealed the exotic and erotic Chinese world that foreigners like to see rather than a Chinese world that is recognizable to the Chinese people themselves. As one particularly unkind critic stated privately, "Zhang Yimou makes his living by pulling down his mother's pants so foreigners can get a good look at her ass." But by mid-1992, Zhang and the authorities had come to terms again. His banned films were finally screened publicly, and Zhang made a new Hong Kong–financed movie, *The Story of Qiu Ju*, that had fewer Orientalist implications and portrayed China's feared Public Security forces in a surprisingly favorable way. In late 1993 Zhang was even allowed to win a couple of highly coveted domestic film awards.

The banning of *Judou* and *Raise the Red Lantern* had more to do with the issues of bureaucratic control and money making than dissident politics. The post-Tiananmen state permitted directors to raise money abroad, but it reserved the right to determine which films could bear the "Made in China" label, and it insisted on getting its fair share of foreign earnings. Foreign interests could invest in Chinese filmmaking, but the state intended to stay in control. Thus the state claimed that Hollywood had no right to nominate *Judou* for an Oscar without its approval; the state protested again when *Raise the Red Lantern* was nominated for an Oscar as a Hong Kong film. Only the Chinese state had the right to decide whether it was a "Hong Kong" or a "China" title. The primary issues were not Zhang Yimou's politics or the content of these particular films; the problem was that the state did not want to see the realms of filmmaking, film distribution, and foreign marketing spin beyond its control. In short, the state wanted to find a way to make the velvet prison arrangement work in the newly emerging multinational global economy.

For this system to work, directors and screenwriters had to be willing to engage in velvet prison–type self-regulation. Minor indiscretions could be forgiven, but basic loyalty had to be maintained. Regardless of how a film was funded, the shooting script and the final product had to be approved by the state. Zhang Yimou and others who produced primarily for the foreign market often based their stories on works of fiction published in the People's Republic, works that had already been through the censorship process once. Directors sometimes tried to manipulate the censorship process and thereby win small concessions, by submitting one script for official approval and making up another when they actually shot the film. Needless to say, the state reserved the right to limit the screening of such works in China on the assumption that films designed for foreign market conditions may not be suitable for domestic audiences.

Foreign investors involved themselves in the process to make money. The case of *Raise the Red Lantern*, funded by Taiwan concerns, is particularly illustrative of the complex (postsocialist?) regional financial and marketing arrangements that were playing an increasingly important role in Chinese filmmaking in the 1990s. Investors suspected that the film would not be shown widely in China. It could not be screened in Taiwan because it features lead actors and actresses who reside on the mainland. But laser disks, the technology of choice of the large and growing Taiwan middle class at that time, could be marketed in Taiwan. Incredible as it seems, investors in Taiwan suspected even before the film was produced that they could make a profit by marketing laser disks in Taiwan and by selling the international screening rights and videotape rights in North America and Europe. When multinational financing and marketing became part of the picture, the behavior of consumers in the People's Republic was of secondary importance. In the new era, foreign investors who were willing to spend money promoting artists like Zhang Yimou and Chen Kaige could profit even when domestic distribution of their work was restricted.

Just as interesting is the case of the Zhang Yimou–like film *Five Girls and a Rope* (*Wuge nüren he yi gen shengzi*) made in 1991 by Taiwan director Yeh Hung-wei (Ye Hongwei). This powerful film about the collective ritual suicide of five rural women during the Republican era was funded, produced, and directed by the Taiwan side. The director shot on location entirely in the People's Republic, made almost exclusive use of (low-cost) mainland actors and actresses, and had virtually all postproduction work done on the mainland. The film was not screened widely in the People's Republic and, because of its use of mainland players, was not screened widely in Taiwan. (One consideration here is that Taiwan actors and actresses did not want to be driven out of their trade by the existence of cheap labor in the People's Republic.) Still, the film's investors, who put up the equivalent of nearly one million *yuan*, made money by selling laser disks and by marketing the film in Europe and North America. State leaders in socialist China went along with such arrangements because they provided employment for film workers, generated hard currency income, and appeared to pose no domestic political threats. In brief, China's landscapes, processing and editing labs, actors and actresses, film studios, and production crews were all available for rent. Chen Kaige's *Farewell My Concubine* was only the first of several films he contracted to do on this basis for the Taiwan-linked Tomson Film Company in Hong Kong.

The political economy of Chinese filmmaking underwent some fascinating shifts in the immediate post-Tiananmen period, but critics should not lose sight of the fact that the activities of Zhang Yimou and Chen Kaige were not perceived as posing any fundamental challenges to the velvet prison arrangement. In the mid-1990s the state continued to view these artists as loyal (if highly privileged) insiders.

IS HARASZTI RIGHT OR WRONG ABOUT ARTISTS UNDER STATE SOCIALISM?

The utility of the Haraszti conceptualization of artists under state socialism is hard to deny. I fully agree with such scholars as Gérémie Barmé who believe that it is important to try to understand the realities of state socialism in China within the larger context of state socialist regimes in general, and that the pre-1989 writings of Haraszti, Václav Havel, and other East Europeans shed a great deal of light on China.¹³ Two notions associated with the Eastern European and Soviet experiences are particularly important. One is the idea that state socialist regimes can jettison the heavy-handed Stalinist approach to cultural control without sacrificing control itself. This is precisely what the Chinese state sought to do to the film industry after 1976.

The other (and more unsettling) idea is that we should not feel too sorry for artists in late state socialist regimes, artists who work within the framework of the velvet prison. That is, we should be more critical than we are of their active and willing collaboration with the culturally "liberalizing" regime.¹⁴ Virtually all their activities legitimize and thus help perpetuate the regime. Of course, this is a very sensitive issue. No self-respecting artist in China is likely to admit to having played a collaborative role. On the contrary, in their private utterances, they protest the inhumanities of life under state socialism. The fact is, however, that post-Mao artists engaged in self-censorship and self-mutilation on a regular basis. Very few arrived at the position articulated so eloquently by Havel before 1989, that is, the idea that they should stop placing all the blame on the faceless bureaucratic state for everything that ails the nation and people.¹⁵ Artists should not be viewed simply as helpless victims of oppression; all along they have participated in their own oppression; they are partly responsible for constructing and maintaining the system that prevails.¹⁶

If we follow Haraszti's logic, we would have to conclude that in the realm of Chinese filmmaking nothing that happened in the wake of the state's retreat in the 1980s resulted in real independence or autonomy for this type of art creation. At best, what one finds is indirect and implicit criticism buried between the lines of what can only be regarded as "official" texts. But, as Haraszti pointed out, the velvet prison mode allows for such individual expressions, provided that they can be interpreted as loyal and constructive.

Still, one cannot help feeling that, for all the light Haraszti's work sheds on the situation in China, he was, in the end, wrong. He was wrong about his native Hungary, he was wrong about the Soviet Union, and he is probably wrong about China.

The problem with his gloomy and pessimistic account, written at a time of apparent hopelessness in 1983, is that it argued that the battle is over and state socialism has won. The culture of state socialism, he said, is entrenched in large part because intellectuals have been co-opted by the velvet prison framework. There is a profound finality to his work. Absolutely nothing in his writings anticipated or prepared us for the defeat of state socialism. At precisely the moment he was declaring its permanence, it suddenly collapsed. The reader is left wondering how that could have happened if his brilliant analysis was correct.

In a hastily written afterword prepared in 1987 for the English edition of *The Velvet Prison*, Haraszti acknowledged the apparent contradiction between his thesis and the enormous significance of the Solidarity movement in Poland.[17] Writing in an uncharacteristically defensive manner, he was willing to hold out the possibility (however remote) that at some point in the future places like Poland and Hungary that were on the "western coast" of the state socialist empire and whose communism was not sui generis might be able to support a truly independent resistance to state power. "Dissent, however feeble," he stated, "can at least draw upon a democratic past that is altogether absent in the Soviet Union and in China."[18] Still, he was totally unprepared for the sudden collapse of state socialism even in his own homeland, never mind in the Soviet Union.

> It might well be that my most pessimistic message is the seemingly good news of the spreading of the Hungarian model. . . . The Hungarian model might well represent a more rational, more normative, and more enduring version of directed culture. Mr. Gorbachev understands that in order to have a truly successful society with a modern economy he must boost the intelligentsia's sagging morale by giving it a stake in administering the future. But in Hungary we know very well the cost of such liberating collaboration.[19]

Thus, as late as March 1987, Haraszti clung stubbornly to a velvet prison paradigm that ruled out the emergence of critical and nondirected culture in places like the Soviet Union and China.

It is in this connection that I came to disagree with Gérémie Barmé in 1991. Barmé, to his credit, takes the velvet prison conceptualization very seriously. This, I suspect, is why he took strong exception to my suggestion that even a thoroughly establishment figure like Xie Jin, who was able to work comfortably in both Stalinist and velvet prison environments and whose amazingly popular films must be regarded as "official culture," gave highly dramatic expression to popular and unofficial discontent with the Communist Party-state.[20] Xie Jin was not a dissident; he was not operating in an independent or autonomous realm. Much of what he did legitimized and perpetuated the dominance of state socialism. However, the many ways in which his works chipped away at the foundation of state socialism should not be dismissed.

Barmé and I undoubtedly agree that, personally, we appreciate the works of the younger directors much more. Still, we must admit that many of the remarkable films of Chen Kaige, Huang Jianxin, Zhang Yimou, Tian Zhuangzhuang, and others were no less official than Xie Jin's, and that as individuals they enjoyed the benefits of the velvet prison arrangement. It is not untrue to say that they also collaborated with the state and that their work also legitimized and perpetuated the dominance of state socialism. They also engaged in self-censorship and self-mutilation. But, just as in the case of Xie Jin and other old school melodramatists, it would be a mistake to refuse to see the many ways in which their work, even that set in the presocialist era, undermined state socialism and exacerbated the problem of popular alienation, especially among urban youth.

It is important for us to understand how the works of Xie Jin and the works of the new-style artists subverted state socialism and eroded public confidence in the system. Of course, it would be wrong to exaggerate the ways in which their work subverted. This would cause us to underestimate the post-Mao regime's staying power. But so, too, would it be wrong to hold rigidly to the powerful Haraszti model and dismiss too quickly the surprisingly wide range of criticism that emanates from the velvet prison.[21] To do so would be to overestimate the state's staying power, which is exactly what Haraszti did.

If our definition of autonomy requires the existence of *communities* of artists who are independent of the state, then we can surely conclude that Chinese filmmakers in the late 1980s and early 1990s did not enjoy (in the way they did in the prewar 1930s and postwar 1940s) autonomy from the state. If, on the other hand, we take into account individual acts of subversion, even when they were carried out well within the framework of the velvet prison arrangement, we can safely speak of artistic activity that, despite the smug confidence of cultural bureaucrats, was beyond the control of the state. Haraszti and Barmé take the self-confidence of the state too seriously. In the 1980s and early 1990s, the interests of the state were being undermined in this way every day. The state believed that it had control of culture, especially in an industry like filmmaking that seems so easy to control. But in fact, with the deepening of the reform era, much was permanently out of control.

In 1993, for example, the film bureaucracy was enraged by the production of unauthorized "underground" films, including *Beijing Bastards* (*Beijing zazhong*, d. Zhang Yuan), *Red Beads* (*Xuan tian*, d. He Yi), and *The Days* (*Dong chun de rizi*, d. Wang Xiaoshuai) that sketched grim and depressing pictures of life in urban China. In fact, the films were not underground productions in a literal sense. They were shot quite openly on the streets of Beijing and elsewhere. They were attacked by officialdom because, unlike all the work produced by the Fifth Generation, these Sixth Generation films were independent and relatively low-budget productions funded by the filmmakers themselves with help from backers in places like Hong Kong. These defiant filmmakers were not working in conjunction with any state studio, and they consulted with neither the Film Bureau nor the Film Distribution Corporation. One of the films, *Beijing Bastards*, won the Critics Circle award at the 1993 Lucarno Film Festival. In fall 1993 the official Chinese delegation to the Tokyo Film Festival stormed out in protest when it learned that *Beijing Bastards* had been entered in the competition. Later the state tried to take legal action against Zhang Yuan for shooting the film and distributing it abroad without state approval. In a word, Zhang and the others were the first to pursue the idea of the privatization of film culture to its logical end.

And Fifth Generation insiders continued to get into trouble for violating velvet prison norms. Officials in the Ministry of Radio, Film, and Television alleged that Tian Zhuangzhuang's splendid 1993 movie *The Blue Kite* (*Lan fengzheng*), financed by the Hong Kong-based Longwick Production Company, was shot without state approval and then "smuggled" abroad, where it won top honors at the Tokyo Film Festival. An artist as well connected as Tian Zhuangzhuang was unlikely to experience difficulties for very long, but his problems with *The Blue Kite* highlighted the stresses and strains that constantly reconfigured the velvet prison. Skeptics might argue that films like *Beijing Bastards* and *The Blue Kite* will have no long-lasting impact so long as the state continues to monopolize film distribution. But in late 1993, film scholars in China predicted that another wave of change would hit the film world in the mid-1990s. The Film Distribution Corporation, it was said, would soon be broken down into many competing provincial and municipal organizations. Film studios and filmmakers would soon be doing business directly with the regions rather than with the center. Moreover, industry specialists also insisted that privately owned movie theaters were about to become a fact of cultural life.

Even now, in the early twenty-first century, it is too early to know precisely how the crisis of the post-Mao film industry will be resolved. Periodic efforts to reactivate the Stalinist mode of cultural control can only be temporary. Haraszti was wrong when he said that criticism expressed by those who are on the state payroll is hopelessly compromised. That is one of the reasons he failed to anticipate the collapse of state socialism in Hungary and the Soviet Union.

The socialist state in China knows what it is talking about when it rails against "peaceful evolution." The problem is that the state can now do surprisingly little about it. The cultural realm is out of control largely because no one, least of all those who are Party members, believes in socialism. One of the ironies of late state socialist China is that even a hard-core propaganda film like *Mao Zedong and His Son* (*Mao Zedong he tade erzi*, d. Zhang Jinbiao, 1991), ordered up by the state immediately after Tiananmen, is unable to play its proper reactionary role. The film was popular for the wrong reasons. Images of a perfect Mao, no matter how unconvincing, only served to remind the audience of the moral failings of the current leadership. In late state socialist China, even crude propaganda works subvert state power.

Perhaps, then, we are asking the wrong question about the future of the socialist state. Does it matter whether fully autonomous and independent social groups in China are chipping away at the state's hegemony when so many quasi-autonomous groups and individuals, all of them heirs to the cultural legacy of late state socialism in the former Soviet bloc, are already doing the job in a "peaceful and evolutionary" way?

NOTES

An earlier version of this chapter appeared as "Velvet Prisons and the Political Economy of Chinese Filmmaking," in *Urban Spaces: Autonomy and Community in Contemporary China*, ed. Deborah Davis, Richard Kraus, Barry Naughton, and Elizabeth Perry (Cambridge, UK: Cambridge University Press, 1995), 193–220.

1. By referring to the experiences of the former Soviet bloc, I do not mean to suggest that the retreat of the state was a one-way street. Retreats in one sector were sometimes followed by advances in another. Similarly, by mentioning the appearance of relatively autonomous groups, I do not mean to imply that such groups enjoyed total autonomy from the state. I am only asserting that certain sectors, especially the urban cultural sector, enjoyed more autonomy than they did during the heyday of state socialism. By raising questions about the role played by comparatively autonomous social groups and by quasi-autonomous individuals in the undermining of late state socialist regimes, I am not asking whether such people played the *leading* role in the demise of state socialism. I doubt that they did. Finally, I am not posing questions about whether quasi-autonomous cultural actors did anything in the late state socialist era that might contribute to the construction of democratic alternatives in the future. That is a separate issue.

2. Miklos Haraszti, *The Velvet Prison: Artists under State Socialism* (New York: Noonday Press, 1989).

3. On the post-Mao thaw in the film industry, see also Paul Clark, *Chinese Cinema: Culture and Politics since 1949* (Cambridge, UK: Cambridge University Press, 1987), 154–84.

4. On the various trends of the 1980s, see Nick Browne, Paul G. Pickowicz, Vivian Sobchack, and Esther Yau, eds., *New Chinese Cinemas: Forms, Identities, Politics* (Cambridge, UK: Cambridge University Press, 1994), 1–113.

5. See Chris Berry, "Market Forces: China's 'Fifth Generation' Faces the Bottom Line," in *Perspectives on Chinese Cinema*, ed. Chris Berry (London: British Film Institute, 1991), 114–25.

6. For an interesting discussion of Wang Shuo, see Gérémie Barmé, "Wang Shuo and *Liu-mang* ('Hooligan') Culture," *Australian Journal of Chinese Affairs*, no. 28 (July 1992): 23–64.

7. Most of the information on the film distribution system presented here is contained in an important unpublished manuscript by Wu Tianming, "Bing shu qiantou wan mu chun: lun Zhongguo dianying faxing tizhi gaige," 1990. Unless otherwise noted, the statistics given in this section are based on Wu's calculations.

8. For a brief account of the early distribution system, see Clark, *Chinese Cinema*, 34–38.

9. Hu Jian, "On the Long Road into the Future," *China Screen*, no. 3 (1991): 34.

10. For a brief history of the development of the distribution system, see Mei Chen, "1949–1989 China Film Distribution and Exhibition," *China Screen*, no. 3 (1990): 26–27.

11. Wu, "Bing shu qiantou wan mu chun."

12. Teng Jinxian, "Teng Jinxian Expounds China's Film Policy," *China Screen*, no. 3 (1989): 10.

13. Gérémie Barmé, "The Chinese Velvet Prison: Culture in the 'New Age,' 1976–89," *Issues and Studies* 25, no. 8 (August 1989): 54–79.

14. For a critique of Chinese intellectuals, see Timothy Cheek, "From Priests to Professionals: Intellectuals and the State under the CCP," in *Popular Protest and Political Culture in Modern China: Learning from 1989*, ed. Jeffrey Wasserstrom and Elizabeth J. Perry (Boulder, Colo.: Westview Press, 1992), 124–45.

15. See Václav Havel, *Living in Truth* (London: Faber and Faber, 1990).

16. The best Tiananmen-era discussion of the relationship between Chinese intellectuals and the state is Perry Link, *Evening Chats in Beijing: Probing China's Predicament* (New York: Norton, 1992).

17. Haraszti, *The Velvet Prison*, 160–62.

18. Haraszti, *The Velvet Prison*, 160.

19. Haraszti, *The Velvet Prison*, 162.

20. Gérémie Barmé, "Outsiders," *Far Eastern Economic Review*, February 21, 1991.

21. Barmé, "The Chinese Velvet Prison," 75.

12
Social and Political Dynamics of Underground Filmmaking in Early Twenty-First-Century China

In late fall 2004 a Hong Kong news daily breathlessly reported that "underground filmmaker" Jia Zhangke was "joining the mainstream, with official approval."[1] In the past, it was said, Jia had "secretly created" such outstanding works as *Artisan Pickpocket* (*Xiao Wu*, 1997), *Platform* (*Zhantai*, 2000), and *Unknown Pleasures* (*Ren xiaoyao*, 2002) in his "small two-room studio in a dark Beijing basement." These low-budget films were acclaimed internationally but rejected by officialdom and denied standard distribution in China.[2] By contrast, the report stated, his new, "legitimate," and very expensive movie, *The World* (*Shijie*, 2004), filmed at the socialist state-run Shanghai Film Studio as a coproduction with United Star (Hong Kong), Office Kitano (Japan), and Celluloid Dreams (France), failed to win the Golden Lion award at Venice, though it will be screened in China. "It's the work that I've spent most time and energy on," Jia observed, "but so far it hasn't landed a prize."

According to Jia Zhangke, it was an overture from the state film bureaucracy in late 2003 that resulted in his movement from underground to aboveground creative activity. He added that Wang Xiaoshuai (*Beijing Bicycle* [*Shiqi sui de dan che*], 2000) and other leading underground filmmakers were successfully wooed by the state at about the same time. Jia said he agreed to work aboveground because he wanted his films to be viewed beyond the confines of international art-house venues. He wanted the Chinese people to see his work. "If you want to reach a wider audience, you have to go through the system," he conceded. "It's just the way it is."

The pesky Hong Kong reporter asked Jia if he now had to engage in "self-censorship." A bit defensive, Jia claimed "I didn't change," the censorship system had changed in ways that supposedly allowed greater artistic freedom these days. When it was pointed out that Jia's earlier underground films are still banned, Jia actually came to the defense of the censors. "It's an issue involved with previous [state] opinions on underground films," he stated. If the authorities permitted his blacklisted films to be shown, "it would mean they'd have to overturn the verdict on underground films that they've had for ten years."

Jia Zhangke's posture seems riddled with contradictions. He was flattered to be courted by the state and given access to its vast resources, but he quickly recalled that not long ago "whenever I heard a police siren, I'd jump out of bed to check if the film rolls were hidden." Now he wants to make films for the vast Chinese audience, but he does not want to "cater to their commercial taste." Former underground filmmakers, he says, should guide the people "towards appreciating the sense of modernity in our movies." Underground artists who have not yet been seduced by state patrons are skeptical of Jia's sense of optimism. As one pointed out, "The government has appeased these directors in order to better control them. Now they can bring down the axe at any moment."[3]

With the appearance in the early 1990s of Zhang Yuan's *Beijing Bastards* (*Beijing zazhong*, 1993) and other feature and documentary works, underground filmmaking became an undeniable fact of Chinese cultural life. By 2003 there was a virtual explosion of underground filmmaking. Individual underground works have received some critical attention outside China, but there have been few attempts to evaluate the genre as it has taken shape over the entire ten-year period. Indeed, the Hong Kong article on Jia Zhangke's apparent transition to aboveground activity raises more questions than it answers. Conceptual problems abound. For example, what do we mean by "underground film" (*dixia dianying*)? Is it a useful term?

One advantage of the term *underground* is that many Chinese filmmakers (including Jia Zhangke) choose to use it themselves. It is part of their identity. People outside the underground camp, including both friends and foes of the movement, also use the term. "Underground film" seems better than "independent film" (*duli dianying*), a concept in the American art lexicon that suggests a small art-house movie privately financed by someone like Robert Redford. "Independent" in the American setting means independent from "Hollywood." This American distinction between *independent* and *Hollywood* has little to do with the role of the state, since almost all American filmmaking takes place in the private sector.

If scholars and critics decided to make exclusive use of the term *independent* to refer to the early films of Zhang Yuan, Wang Xiaoshuai, and Jia Zhangke, it would be necessary for them to point out that in the Chinese case the concept means independence from the Chinese state rather than independence from the sort of powerful private conglomerates that have dominated Hollywood. It is true that in the early decades of Chinese filmmaking (from the early twentieth century to 1937), Chinese filmmaking was in fact almost totally controlled by the private sector, including such legendary studios as Lianhua and Mingxing. Chinese government-controlled filmmaking began in fits and starts only in 1938 at the beginning of the Pacific War and picked up a measure of steam in the postwar period with the nationalization in 1945 of two studios in Shanghai and one in Beijing. But as late as 1949 the industry was dominated by the private sector, including such stellar enterprises as the Wenhua and Kunlun studios.[4]

The Communist Party moved aggressively to strengthen the state filmmaking sector after it came to power in 1949.[5] By 1953 private filmmaking was completely eliminated and played no role whatever in the nearly forty years of exclusively state-controlled socialist film production that followed. During that period, all filmmakers worked for the state, and all production, censorship, and distribution was controlled by the Communist Party or its state organizations, as was nearly all film-related critical and scholarly publishing.

In the early 1990s younger filmmakers began very quietly to challenge what remained of the system of state control of Chinese filmmaking. The term *underground*, though not without problems, does a better job of capturing the unofficial nature of the work and the clear intention of these young artists to resist state control.[6] To put it starkly, most of their work was (and still is) in violation of various laws. For reasons that will be explained later, the state was not inclined to enforce the law in a rigorous way, but the activity of almost all early underground filmmakers was illegal in one way or another.

What about the suitability of the term "private" filmmaking? It is true, of course, that all underground filmmaking since the early 1990s has been private in the sense that the state does not provide meaningful funding, including American-style National Endowment for the Arts–type production grants. As a rule, funding for underground projects must come from nongovernment sources, including both domestic and foreign. But in the Chinese case "private" is a misleading label because to many readers it might suggest "capitalist," "commercial," and "motivated by profit making." To those who have seen many of these works it seems highly unlikely that typical Chinese underground films are motivated by "capitalist goals." The people who make them are clearly entrepreneurial, but they are artistic, cultural, and political entrepreneurs more than they are economic entrepreneurs. The filmmakers want greater freedom of expression, including freedom from oppressive and restrictive political and bureaucratic controls, more than they want vast sums of money. Clearly they are not the least bit opposed to money making, but thinking realistically, they understand that there are unlikely to be many money-making opportunities for them in the near or even distant future. For every Jia Zhangke now courted by the state, there are a thousand underground filmmakers who will never be wooed. And even Jia, poised now to enter the mainstream, insists he is motivated by access to audience, not money.

In the end, it appears useful to acknowledge that unofficial, nonstate work is indeed "underground" in many respects. Most producers of this work submit neither their scripts nor their rough cuts to state film bureaucrats as required by the law. Others submit the scripts, but then complete production and even screen their films for private audiences, before getting an official response or legal approval from the state.

Still, the term *underground* poses difficulties, and some Chinese filmmakers and scholars prefer not to use it. One reason is that the films are not really made underground. *Underground* suggests politically illicit, secret production that stands in subversive opposition not only to state domination of the film industry, but more importantly to the state's and the Party's domination of political life. To some extent, underground filmmaking started out in a highly critical mode in China in the early and mid-1990s with fine works like Tian Zhuangzhuang's devastatingly oppositional *Blue Kite* (*Lan fengzheng*, 1993), which treated unwelcome state intrusions in family life in Beijing in the 1950s and 1960s. But explicitly political production was not a major characteristic of subsequent underground filmmaking. For instance, there were oblique references in some films to the ghastly events of spring and summer 1989, but no early independent works (prior to Lou Ye's 2007 *Summer Palace* [*Yiheyuan*]) dealt explicitly with the bloodletting and persecutions that followed the popular demonstrations staged in Beijing and elsewhere.

In truth, there is no term in either Chinese or English that perfectly captures the essence of nonstate Chinese filmmaking. The character of the movement seems to change each year with the latest flood of works. Many analysts will persist in using "underground," even though most of the films in that category are in view well aboveground during production, even though the state is fully aware of most of the activities of unofficial filmmakers, and even though very little of the work is explicitly oppositional in political terms. Indeed, much of it is surprisingly apolitical. To avoid conceptual problems, some writers in China prefer to use the politically neutral term *post–Sixth Generation* (*hou liudai*) when discussing this body of work. Others complain that the notion of a post–Sixth Generation is as conceptually sterile as the notions of a Fifth and Sixth Generation.

DANCING WITH THE STATE

If underground filmmakers have not been hiding out, toiling in secret, or trying to overthrow the state, what have they been doing? The answer is that they have been constantly negotiating with the state. They have been involved in an elaborate dance with the state, a state that is itself evolving politically in various ways.[7] Few deny that the state, controlling the means of repression and knowing when and in most cases where underground films are being made, is in a position to snuff out any particular underground project. At present, the state clearly prefers not to repress on a grand scale. Later, we will discuss why that is the case.

The main problem in the delicate dance involving underground filmmakers and the state is the issue of content, not form. This may surprise those who have not yet seen Chinese underground productions. Film buffs and critics in the West are in the habit of thinking of underground or independent films as being artistically experimental by their very nature. But, in the Chinese case, with very few exceptions, underground filmmaking has had surprisingly little to do with artistic innovation. Whether one speaks of underground documentaries or underground features, there is not much in China that departs in any meaningful way from the familiar conventions, including narrative conventions, of mainstream Chinese and international documentary and feature production. Indeed, when it comes to aesthetics, Chinese underground movies are quite disappointing. An exception that proves the rule is Ying Weiwei's fascinating film, *The Box* (*Hezi*, 2001), which employs both color as well as black-and-white cinematography. It "looks like" a documentary (and is usually classified as a documentary), but shows many signs of the involvement of people who are taking direction, that is, acting.[8]

In China, nuanced negotiations about content are both complicated and intriguing. The state clearly allows underground films to be made. But, with one important exception, the state refuses to spell out in any detail what is acceptable and unacceptable in terms of subject matter. The exception, of course, is that no direct criticism of the Party or state is allowed. Those who engage in such criticism will be isolated, detained, and even jailed. It is crystal clear that underground filmmakers generally accept this foundational ground rule. That is to say, despite Jia Zhangke's protestations to the contrary, they willingly engage in self-censorship as the price that must be paid to make underground, private, independent, unofficial films. Jia's denial of self-censorship is itself a transparent act of self-censorship.

In return, underground filmmakers get to explore subjects that are not treated in mainstream state productions. Needless to say, there is no guarantee that just because a topic is not taken up in the state sector, it automatically can be addressed in underground works. Each new probe is attempted on a shaky trial-and-error basis. Underground filmmakers, to their eternal credit, persistently try to push out the boundaries of what can be done. Sometimes they get slapped back, only to try again with success at a later date.

Gay sexuality is a subject that the monopolistic state sector has never been willing to treat seriously, even though gay sexuality is an important facet of Chinese life. Initial efforts by underground filmmakers to deal with this subject (for example, Zhang Yuan's *East Palace, West Palace* [*Dong gong xi gong*], 1996) were highly controversial.[9] Filmmakers moved ahead only at considerable risk. But, for reasons I will explain later, at a certain point the state no longer felt threatened by this topic, even though state studios still avoid it in their own work. Suffice it to say that the state now has little problem with underground filmmakers treating gay sexuality as a strictly personal matter that involves private behavior behind closed doors. As a consequence, a significant percentage of underground films that appeared just before and after 2000 explored gay and lesbian themes.

Filmmaking about gay sexuality sheds light on the issue of agency in contemporary Chinese cultural production. Where does the agency responsible for this notable change in the content of underground filmmaking reside? It clearly resides with society, but it also resides with the state. We must constantly remind ourselves that change in this and other cases could not have happened without the tacit approval and indirect participation of the state. The same forces are at play in underground films that take up the subjects of prostitution, incest, child abuse, drug addiction, decadent life styles, and extreme poverty—all of them themes that the state sector refuses to treat because it is believed that such phenomena reflect poorly on the Chinese nation and people and thus on the Chinese state and Party.

It is important to ask why the state allows underground filmmakers to make movies about these unsettling topics when the state itself will not touch them. The answer has something to do with the fact that there are cultural liberals in the Party and state who believe there are many advantages to allowing such artistic activity.[10] They are opposed by conservative Stalinist/Confucian-type state cultural bureaucrats who continue to insist on state control of all cultural production and who are highly suspicious of all individual, private, and entrepreneurial initiatives. These combatants are locked in an elite-level moral (and political) struggle. The conflict does have economic implications with respect to who would gain income and who would lose if the state's near monopoly on cultural production is broken. But it is the moral dimension that concerns us here.

The liberals see underground filmmaking as a useful pressure-release mechanism. They argue (mostly out of public view) that it is in the state's political interest to let these young people blow off steam in the unofficial sector. Moreover, since the liberals see themselves as more cosmopolitan and more global than the conservatives, they insist that allowing underground film production in China, along with turning a blind eye to the overseas screening of underground films made in China, makes China look good. As the 2008 Olympics approached, foreigners would be impressed, they thought, by China's apparent flexibility. The goal is to project a softer

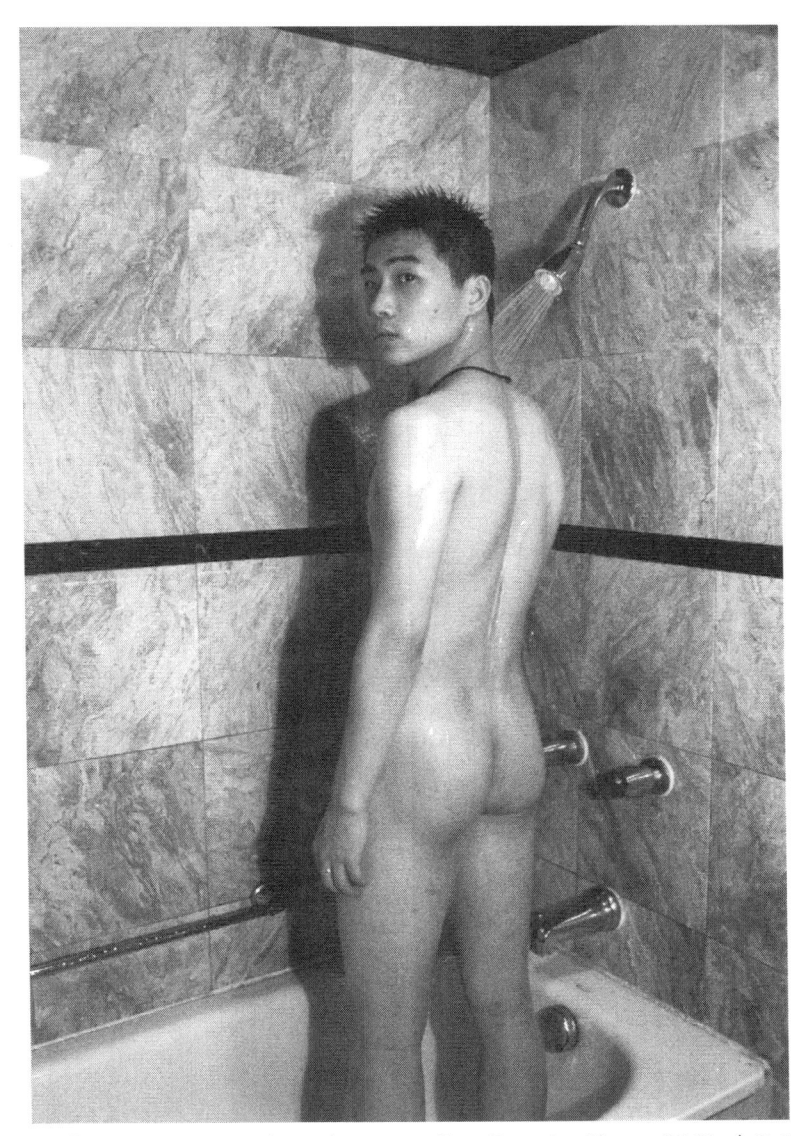

Challenging scene in independent queer film, *Enter the Clowns* (2001, d. Cui Zi'en). Photo courtesy of Cui Zi'en.

image of China (considerably friendlier than the image of tanks in Tiananmen Square). This approach is a variation of the "velvet prison" paradigm tested in some Eastern European late-socialist states during the late 1960s (see chapter 11). In such an arrangement, artists are granted special privileges and a degree of freedom of expression, so long as they police themselves in ways spelled out by the state.

Underground filmmakers, the liberal elites suggest, will accept the ground rules. They will refrain from criticizing the party-state and avoid making explicitly mobilizational films in exchange for the right to make films on many subjects the state usually ignores. Moreover, since there is an acute shortage of job opportunities in the state filmmaking sector (primarily because worn-out senior people with special access to state resources do not want to compete on a daily basis with the vast pool of young talent), the underground sector gives ambitious newcomers something to do. In fact, the state sector can recruit among the ranks of the best (and most willing to compromise) of the outsiders. Indeed, the underground film world, from this perspective, may be viewed as a training ground in which the cream of the crop will eventually rise to film in the state sector.

It is clear that this ongoing negotiation—this complex dance with the state—actually allows some underground filmmakers to move rather freely back and forth across underground and aboveground boundaries. Aboveground superstars like Tian Zhuangzhuang and Jiang Wen occasionally move underground to make certain works the state is unwilling to touch; then they move back aboveground for their next project. Tian's underground *Blue Kite* was followed by his disappointing aboveground *Springtime in a Small Town* (*Xiao cheng zhi chun*, 2000). Jiang Wen, one of the most interesting state-sector actors and directors, went underground to make *Devils on the Doorstep* (*Guizi lai le*, 2000), a stunning film that deals quite sympathetically with Shandong peasants who, from a doctrinaire Party perspective that is openly questioned by Jiang, collaborated with Japanese forces during World War II. The openly gay Cui Zi'en, a well-known producer of underground films on the theme of gay sexuality (e.g., *Old Testament* [*Jiuyue*], 2001), was also a faculty member at the prestigious Beijing Film Institute and, as such, an employee of the state.

Zhang Yuan, a noted pioneer of the underground movement, is another important figure who moves with ease back and forth between underground and aboveground. In late 2003 Zhang cancelled on short notice a scheduled appearance at a film festival in the United States. This led to concerns that he might be in political trouble. No, he reported from his mobile phone, he could not attend because he had just received delivery of his new Porsche and needed to break it in on the open road. Younger underground filmmakers take careful note of Zhang's career trajectory. Some frankly concede that their goal is to make a big splash at a foreign film festival by entering "controversial" underground works, thus forcing the state to pay attention to them and later provide them with opportunities to make expensive aboveground movies and earn substantial amounts of money (and buy a Porsche for themselves). In short, they need to make a large impact abroad, but without offending the Party. This can be a delicate balancing act.

It will be interesting to see what happens to underground director Li Yang. His excellent film *Blind Shaft (Mang jing,* 2002), a work that deals frankly with the rough-and-tumble coal-mining industry in northwest China and the hustlers who circulate in the floating population of migrant mine workers, won the Silver Bear award at the Berlin Film Festival in 2003.[11] Will Li remain underground for a few more pictures? Will he be recruited for work in the state sector? Will he move back and forth between the two worlds? Only time will tell, but the main point is that a simple binary interpretive approach that pits heroic political dissidents against a ruthless police state does not work very well in the complicated Chinese case.

THE QUESTION OF IMPACT: WHO CARES?

What sort of impact do underground films have on the film audience in China? The short answer is that initially they had very little impact. For the first ten years or so their influence outside China was far greater than their impact in China. In fact, this is a point that Party cultural liberals no doubt make when they battle with cultural conservatives. They ask the conservatives what they are so worried about. Let the young people make underground films; few in China will ever see them.

The liberals are right for the simple reason that while underground filmmaking is allowed, the state socialist system still controls virtually all the important film distribution and film exhibition networks. Young artists can make underground films, but if they want to exhibit them in conventional ways and in meaningful venues, they have to deal with the state. This sort of exhibition is, of course, not going to happen. It appears that even extremely high-quality and high-budget underground works like *Blue Kite* and *Devils on the Doorstep* were not allowed to be screened domestically in any significant way in state venues.

There are both political and economic forces at work here. It is true, of course, that the state has political reasons for blocking domestic screening of these films. It is also true that the directors (and their publicists at home and abroad) make much of "censorship" issues when these works are exhibited abroad. It is as if ambitious underground films actually require a "banned in Beijing" pedigree to get attention abroad. But in the cases of *Blue Kite* and *Devils on the Doorstep,* censorship issues were largely a smoke screen. The political problems were not that serious. It is possible to argue that economic issues were as important, if not more important. Just as the stuffy veteran directors in the state-run film studios do not want artistic competition from young upstarts, state distributors do not want to compete with underground filmmakers for domestic and foreign market share. It is for this reason (economic monopoly of cultural production) that the state-controlled television industry is not a viable option for underground works at this point. Television programming is expanding rapidly in China, but still very much under the control of the state broadcast system.

But is it really the case that underground films, including both documentaries and features, have no domestic impact at all? No, it is not. But the domestic impact is limited to videotape and especially VCD and DVD sales, which are brisk in some sections of some major cities. The Geisel Library at the University of California, San Diego, contains a collection of more than a thousand Chinese underground titles, with many more on the way. Determined people in China can acquire these films almost as easily as foreign institutions. It is apparent that small groups gather in homes to view these works. Underground film festivals are sometimes scheduled on university campuses. Some of these events have been successfully staged, while others have been shut down by the police or school officials. It is possible, though, for couples or small groups to rent private rooms for film viewing. Seating capacity is limited and enterprises of this sort open and close on an irregular basis. But they do exist, even in small towns, and are frequented by students and urban youth. Jia Zhangke's *Unknown Pleasures* includes several scenes in which young people gather to view videotapes. Increasing numbers of film clubs provide additional venues for viewing independent titles. The Internet revolution in China, a dynamic and ever-changing phenomenon, also offers various ways for film fans to download and view underground Chinese titles available at home and abroad. Finally, it is also interesting to note that there are lively discussions of and even debates in the Chinese media about underground filmmaking, especially in art-related and scholarly publications.[12] In short, there is in China a critical and scholarly literature on underground filmmaking that scholars outside China have not yet examined in sufficient detail.

Nevertheless, it is still the case that Chinese underground films often have a bigger impact abroad than at home. In most cases the state allows underground filmmakers to travel abroad to attend festivals and special events. It is no exaggeration to say that underground artists are deeply concerned about the foreign reception of their works. Many seem to adopt the following strategy: make a relatively low-budget underground film on a fresh and somewhat sensitive topic (prostitution, for example), call it a censored work, find an agent who will help place the film, try to enter the film in a foreign film festival, hope it gets attention, hope it gets picked up by art-house circuits abroad, if necessary bribe a critic to write about it as a "wonderful but controversial work banned in China," hope against all odds that it gets broadcast on foreign cable television, hope the attention it gets abroad permits funding for another (even more notable) underground work, hope the Chinese state finally takes notice, hope the state makes friendly overtures by offering aboveground (mainstream and moneymaking) opportunities, and hope it will be possible to move back and forth aboveground and underground in order to address the different consumer needs and interests of both foreign and domestic viewers. Naturally, an indispensable element in this new formula for success is an understanding of and entry into foreign funding, production, and distribution networks. Without foreigners, the sequence of events described above simply cannot unfold in the desired way.

FRACTURED IDENTITIES: THE NEW OCCIDENTALISM?

The determination of some underground artists to chase foreign funding, production, distribution, and discourse networks causes various difficulties, the most obvious of which is the need to make movies about China that one imagines foreign viewers, especially foreign art-house viewers and critics, would like to see. This phenomenon gets to the heart of the issue of "Occidentalism," that is, the domestic social, political, economic, and cultural considerations that shape the ways in which Chinese artists talk about the Occident and the Occidental viewer, meant here to include places like Japan, South Korea, and Taiwan that are part of the Occident in various economic, social, and cultural senses, but not part of the Occident in a strictly geographical sense. Just as "Orientalist" perspectives have been driven historically by domestic priorities in the Occident, Chinese Occidentalism has been shaped primarily by domestic agendas in China.[13] Indeed, Occidentalist and Orientalist views are said to be crude caricatures of the imagined "Other" that tell us more about the people who are doing the imagining than the people who are being imagined.

Underground filmmakers in China are probably close to the truth when they conclude that Western audiences would like to see politically dissident films (even politically suicidal films) that boldly confront the Party and directly challenge party-state domination of Chinese life, films that deal with the massacres of 1989, or films that expose official corruption at the highest levels. But this sort of filmmaking is precisely what is not going to happen very often under current circumstances. Such work would violate the unofficial contract underground filmmakers have with the Party.

But many underground filmmakers also imagine that films on another topic—films that scream out "Look at me!"—can attract foreign audiences and perhaps even foreign investment without violating the filmmakers' contract with the party-state. These are films that explore the "self" and rapidly evolving notions of self-identity. The state, for its part, is clearly indicating that it is no longer necessary, as it was in the Mao era, for citizens to think solely in terms of a single national identity that characterizes all decent people in China. It is fine to engage in identity explorations. Thus, it comes as no surprise that a very high percentage of underground work deals with the topic of "Who am I?" As a consequence, many underground films involve a marked, often irritating, self-centeredness. Many underground directors seem to think that people in the Occident like films about exploration of self because they resonate with ego-centered Western artistic agendas, and because the picture of China that emerges in them is a diverse one, the image of a society that looks more like a complicated human one and less like the artificial inhuman, lock-step society of Mao-era propaganda.

Preoccupation with self-exploration and the liberation of the ego is by no means new in modern Chinese cultural production. Priorities of this sort may not have been sanctioned in the Mao era, but they were an extremely important part of the New Culture and May Fourth era of the 1910s, 1920s, and 1930s, a time when urban young people sought to break away as individuals from the Confucian, family-centered group. Yu Dafu, Ding Ling, and many others produced a great deal of highly self-indulgent fiction of self-exploration early in this period.[14] Thanks to the path-breaking scholarship of Leo Ou-fan Lee, we have a wonderfully rich portrait of the fascinating and profoundly decadent modernists who flourished in Shanghai in the 1930s.[15] In the aftermath of the Mao-era interlude, a related pattern of cultural output is clearly reemerging in the realms of both offbeat fiction and underground filmmaking, output that so far has had relatively little impact on society at large, though its influence continues to grow. But while urban young people seem once again to be asserting "self" and breaking away from "society," this time it is Mao-era norms that are being abandoned, a direction that gives the new movement a decidedly postsocialist coloring.[16] In both cases, though, the direction is from "group, group, group" to "me, me, me."

Current preoccupation with self underscores yet again the explanatory power of Ci Jiwei's thesis about the highly disturbing but remarkably logical shift from utopianism to hedonism in the post-Mao period.[17] Ci argues quite convincingly that the ascetic, self-denying, collective-oriented excesses of Chinese utopianism laid the groundwork and then generated the hedonistic and narcissistic excesses of the postutopian or postsocialist era. The individualist excesses of the present, that is, presuppose the collectivist excesses of the past.

The picture of China that emerges in many early-stage underground films is thus not merely diverse; it is a view that reveals a China that is fractured into many parts and strikingly disconnected, a China in which people go about, without much guidance or knowledge, sorting out their own individual "identities." Earlier it was everyone as "patriot," "revolutionary," and "Chairman Mao's Little Red Soldier." Now it is specialized, individualized identities. I'm homeless. I'm a prostitute. I'm a club singer. I'm a homosexual. I'm confused. I'm a drug addict. I'm a lesbian. I'm a migrant.

Slick, new-age woman in slick, new-age car in *Lunar Eclipse* (1999, d. Wang Quan'an). Photo courtesy of Wang Quan'an.

I'm really confused. I'm a bohemian. I'm a con artist. I have AIDS. I'm a criminal. I'm crazy. I'm confused beyond imagination. Interestingly, the state seems to have no fundamental objection to these identity explorations and the various (sometimes outrageous, sometimes immature) expressions of individuality that are articulated along the way. The state seems to be saying (and underground filmmakers are always listening very closely) that it no longer cares very much about what people do in their private life, especially behind closed doors. The state, or at least the cultural liberals in the bureaucracy, have apparently given up on the Maoist (and Confucian) desire to order family and private life.

This explains why underground cinema seems so obsessed with the search for individual identities and why so much of what was produced in the early phase seems so self-centered (and self-indulgent). Many of the characters who appear in documentaries and feature films seem superficial precisely because they are so self-absorbed. The portraits, coming after so many decades of group-oriented socialist filmmaking, are fascinating at first, but with repeated viewing the people who appear on screen often seem quite shallow and unattractive—and remarkably humorless.

In various ways, the "contract" with the state ties the hands of underground filmmakers. That is, the problems faced by their protagonists are often interesting, but little or no effort is made to explain the origins or sources of their problems beyond the incredibly narrow confines of closed, private, residential spaces. The films often feel claustrophobic. Still less is there an inclination to assign blame for social problems or to hold the Party or state accountable. Moving beyond private spaces and locating the problems of the individual in a larger social or political context seldom occurs because it would violate the informal contract. There are plenty of problems to see (problems avoided by the state studios), but only rarely are explanations offered as to exactly why there are so many problems. Mainly we see individuals trying to give meaning to their fractured lives by latching on to some specialized identity. Underground films, to their credit, are long on ethnographic descriptions—but they are often frustratingly short on analysis.

In trying to resolve their personal problems, it never occurs to most protagonists to connect their problems to trends unfolding in the larger society. They seem utterly uninformed. They have few or no political or social ideas. Their lives are not embedded in any social context, and we learn little or nothing about the society in which they live. With important exceptions, they seem like characters in an endless, asocial, ahistorical soap opera that might be called *As the Chinese (Postsocialist) World Turns*. Detached in this way, the protagonists often seem rather hollow. And China seems to have no history. Today is center stage; there is no yesterday.

What factors are responsible for the shallowness and sadness we witness on screen? Are underground filmmakers, limited by self-censorship, unable to tell a more socially and historically grounded story? Or do the films reflect a postsocialist anomie that has in fact reduced people to such a state of shallowness? Perhaps is it an Occidentalist preoccupation with the imagined needs of foreign audiences that explains why the quest for individual identity has been represented in post-Mao China in this particular manner. In all likelihood, the fixation on self in underground Chinese films involves a convergence of all these forces. In any case, the phenomena described above necessarily give rise to characters like Coco, the central figure in Chen Miao's documentary titled *The Snake Boy* (*Shanghai nanhai*, 2001). These conditions produce floating characters who seem lost and without cultural bearings. Coco, a gay youth who sings in the trendy jazz clubs of Shanghai, obviously believes that he is a charming, hip, slick, cutting-edge, young, urban guy. But something very sad and melancholy comes through in the film. Coco seems superficial, shallow, incapable of self-reflection, and, worst, unable to see himself as a neocolonial invention and soulless plaything of the new and profoundly unattractive expatriate community in Shanghai, a group that wants to see more Chinese who look and act like "us." Coco's appeal to the expatriates is that he is a Chinese Billie Holiday or a Chinese Lena Horne. In their imagination Coco can never be better than Billie Holiday or Lena Horne. He is merely a Chinese Billie Holiday, that is, a patronized, amusing, lesser version of the original. Anyone familiar with the piano bar scene in Japan, Taiwan, and Hong Kong from the 1970s to the present recognizes at once that Coco is not that talented and will soon be replaced by someone just like him. An underground movie has been made about him only because he arose in the immediate aftermath of the wreckage of post-Mao China. His expatriate patrons like him because he is not like Mao. He is like a foreigner. Coco's friend Casper is even more pathetic. We are never even told the Chinese names of Coco and Casper.

The bohemian artists featured in Wu Wenguang's early underground documentary *Bumming in Beijing* (*Liulang Beijing*, 1990) are alienated, even lost, in postsocialist China. The viewer never gets any solid clues that explain why they are lost. They are just lost. At the outset, one is sympathetic with these "free spirits" but soon tires of their often incoherent whining. Each artist eventually leaves China, and Wu monitors their activities in places like Paris and Palo Alto in his sad, genuinely interesting, and ironically titled sequel, *At Home in the World* (*Sihai wei jia*, 1995). Abroad, the artists are lost (again). Like Coco, who is back in Shanghai, they want, but cannot win, genuine acceptance in Europe and America. They are amusing curiosities. Ignored or patronized, they are forced to deal with Orientalist expectations. But unfortunately for the viewer, the artists rarely reflect on exactly why they are abroad and how their lives are related to patterns that have been unfolding in China over a twenty-five-year period.

GLOBALIZATION, OR MAOISM WITH POST-MAO CHARACTERISTICS?

The problems of self-indulgence, shallowness, and excessive self-centeredness evident in underground filmmaking in China are hardly confined to this filmic realm of contemporary cultural production. It is also quite apparent in the world of popular fiction. Sensational and trashy novels such as Wei Hui's *Shanghai Baby* (*Shanghai baobei*, 2000), Chun Shu's *Beijing Doll* (*Beijing wawa*, 2002), and Mian Mian's *Candy* (*Tang*, 2000) are remarkably similar to many of the underground films discussed in this chapter.[18] One suspects that this is because they are shaped by many of the same cultural forces. Self-indulgent to an extreme, *Shanghai Baby* is described by its foreign publisher as an "everybody-look-at me" story that explores "the outer limits of a woman's sexuality." Its dust jacket trumpets the claim that the book has been "banned and burned in China." Likewise, *Candy* is marketed abroad as an "underground bestseller" that has been banned in China.

This sort of new fiction resembles underground films in several obvious ways: it deals with controversial subject matter that mainstream publishers are disinclined to touch, it is highly conventional in stylistic terms, and it is preoccupied with post-Mao identity explorations. Indeed, the last line of *Shanghai Baby* is "Who am I?" These works are also similar to many underground films in that they show a fractured China that seems to have no history. Somehow, China's history, politics, and society have been erased. Social and cultural phenomena (including disturbing problems) are almost never located in the context of China's own history; instead they are seen in a larger and decidedly global context. Wei Hui's tiresome protagonist in *Shanghai Baby* is constantly dropping in-the-know global cultural references (Joni Mitchell, Erica Jong, Allen Ginsberg, Quentin Tarantino, Mother Teresa, Van Morrison, Bob Dylan, Marilyn Monroe, and Salvador Dali) but is totally ignorant of China's own recent and distant history. No connections are made between the problems that plague troubled young people and China's own history or contemporary society. It is as if China does not have a history. There are virtually no references to socialism, the Party, Mao, the Cultural Revolution, and Tiananmen, nor is anything said about longer-term cultural legacies. The characters are certainly aware of being Chinese, but strangely, they know little or nothing about China. They do, however, know a great deal about the global scene and take great pride in their global identities.

What accounts for the preoccupation with self and world (especially the capitalist world) and disinterest in nation in recent Chinese underground artworks? One explanation is self-censorship. It is fine to talk about self, and it is fine to talk about the world. But is not fine to talk about power and politics in China itself, past or present.

Another explanation centers on the dynamics of globalization and commercialization. The protagonist of *Shanghai Baby* proudly announces, "Every morning when I open my eyes I wonder what I can do to make myself famous."[19] In short, some underground filmmakers and young writers are busy chasing global fame (and in some cases global money). The themes of hedonistic excess and self-indulgence are highlighted not only because post-Mao China produced postsocialist malaise and alienation (which it clearly did), but because young artists and writers have convinced themselves that this is what foreign audiences expect.

Critics of globalization lament the fact that young people in places like China twist, turn, and distort to adjust to the needs of the global market. If underground films or trashy novels reveal disturbing excesses in contemporary Chinese society, some insist, it is the fault of globalization in two respects: first, alien modes have indeed penetrated China and negatively influenced Chinese youth and, second, Chinese artists are all too eager to give the foreign market what it seems to want. There is some validity, of course, to the notion that the dynamics of the global market force marginalized Chinese artists to deliberately engage in self-Orientalization.

But a problem with the globalization explanation is that it is one-dimensional. It not only focuses all the attention on a single external factor, it ignores internal factors, fails to locate globalization in the context of recent domestic history, and in many ways denies agency to the Chinese people. Globalization is thus a convenient scapegoat for all that ails China, an excuse for neglecting research on the internal factors that have shaped the current cultural scene.

Following Ci Jiwei's lead, it is possible to argue that the hedonistic excesses of the present, detailed so graphically in underground films and trashy fiction, are best understood as the logical result of failed Maoist asceticism. After all, few would argue that the representations of global modernity and globally modern lifestyles contained in sensational underground films and literature have much in common with daily life in the global industrial world. They are more like Occidentalist caricatures of life and values in modern nations. But what is the source of the caricatures? It is hard to avoid the conclusion that images of the modern condition that dwell on gluttony, drug addiction, greed, social climbing, alcoholism, selfishness, and sexual excessiveness are derived in one way or another from the sort of Maoist propaganda stereotypes that dominated in China from the 1950s. Ironically, anti-Maoism in the 1990s and after sometimes embraced and celebrated precisely those excesses of modernity that Mao was believed to despise. Never mind that the representations of modernity were one-sided and distorted in the first place. Once the ascetic self-denial

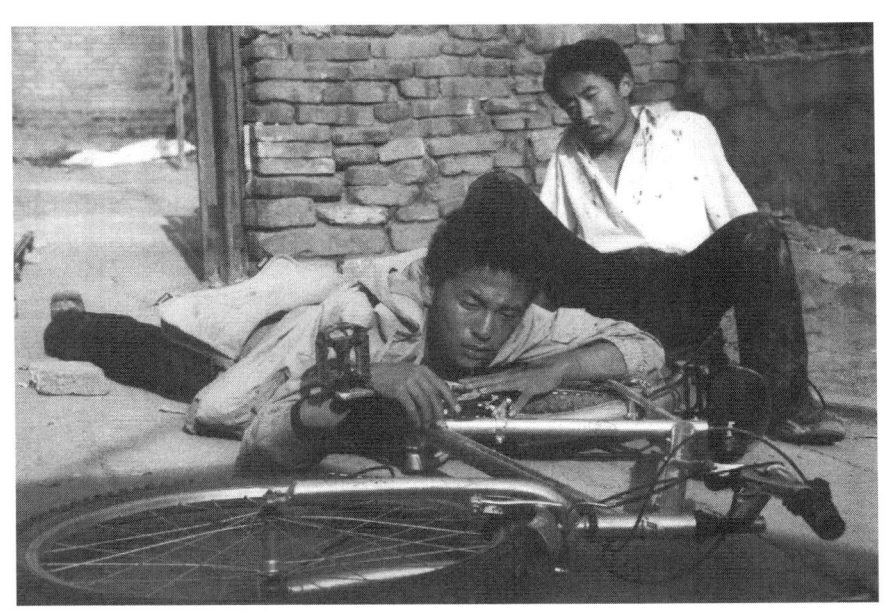

Nothing seems to go right in *Bejing Bicycle* (2001, d. Wang Xiaoshuai). Photo courtesy of Wang Xiaoshuai.

modes of the revolution were rejected, the hedonism of the modern global enemy imagined by Maoism was embraced with a passion. Thus, if anything is to blame for the soullessness, emptiness, and directionlessness of many of the urban youth on display in underground films, it is not globalization but the excesses of Maoism. In brief, one excess gives rise to another. In rejecting Maoism, many post-Mao youth consciously or unconsciously took Maoist caricatures of global modernity at face value and embraced the caricatures as their own modern values.

It is, of course, easy to be critical of underground filmmaking in China. But critics should not lose sight of the extremely difficult fiscal and political circumstances under which this new work has been produced in the last decade. As Yingjin Zhang reminds us, China is much better off for having such an active unofficial filmmaking sector. But, he insists, it would be wrong for sympathetic scholars to adopt a patronizing attitude toward these films. It is hard to avoid the conclusion that most of the work is quite rough and much of it is quite forgettable. A good deal of it is numbingly depressing. That is why we need constantly to remind ourselves that the best underground work is far more interesting and vastly superior to anything that is being produced in the sterile state socialist sector.

Whither underground filmmaking in China? A central goal of underground work, of course, is to liberate the bottled-up creative genius of the Chinese people from repressive state controls. It is hard to imagine this happening as the result of the activities of independent filmmakers working in isolation. It is also difficult to imagine it happening without an underground sector constantly pushing in new directions. But nonstate filmmakers will continue for the foreseeable future to need liberal allies in the state bureaucracy and even in the Party. Pressures from below (an increasingly sophisticated film audience) and beyond (the global community) will also play a role. Underground filmmakers surely fantasize about what life would be like if the state continued to relax political controls and provide no-strings-attached grants for independent productions instead of wasting vast resources on such disappointing state-sponsored embarrassments as Zhang Yimou's *Hero* (*Yingxiong*, 2002) and *House of the Flying Daggers* (*Shimian maifu*, 2004). But no matter what happens in the future, the underground film movement is here to stay, and scholars of contemporary Chinese culture need to understand it much better than we do at present.

NOTES

An earlier version of this chapter appeared as "Social and Political Dynamics of Underground Filmmaking in China," in *From Underground to Independent: Alternative Film Culture in Contemporary China*, ed. Paul G. Pickowicz and Yingjin Zhang (Lanham, Md.: Rowman & Littlefield, 2006), 1–21.

1. Joey Liu, "Welcome to the Reel World," *South China Morning Post*, November 2, 2004, C5.

2. *Artisan Pickpocket* won the Wolfgang Staudte Prize at the Berlin International Film Festival in 1998, among other prizes.

3. Liu, "Welcome to the Reel World."

4. For a recent study that discusses the prewar private-sector film industry, see Yingjin Zhang, *Chinese National Cinema* (London: Routledge, 2004), 58–83.

5. For general histories of state-sector filmmaking in post-1949 China, see Jay Leyda, *Dianying: An Account of Films and the Film Audience in China* (Cambridge, Mass.: MIT Press, 1972), 181–344; and Paul Clark, *Chinese Cinema: Culture and Politics since 1949* (Cambridge, UK: Cambridge University Press, 1987), 25–184.

6. For a discussion of the term *unofficial*, see Perry Link, Richard P. Madsen, and Paul G. Pickowicz, eds., *Unofficial China: Popular Culture and Thought in the People's Republic* (Boulder, Colo.: Westview Press, 1989), 1–12.

7. For a stimulating discussion of interactions between artists and the state, see Richard Kraus, *The Party and the Arty: How Money Relaxes Political Control over China's Arts* (Lanham, Md.: Rowman & Littlefield, 2003).

8. I want to thank Nick Browne for sharing this observation with me.

9. For a discussion of *East Palace, West Palace*, see Paul G. Pickowicz, "Filme und die Legitimation des Staates im Heutigen China," in *Peking, Shanghai, Shenzhen: Stadte des 21. Jahrhunderts*, ed. Kai Vockler and Dirk Luckow (Frankfurt: Campus Verlag GmbH, 2000), 402–11 (German), 566–70 (English).

10. For an example of how cultural liberals in the Party approach and cultivate young artists, see Zhao Shi, "He qingnian pengyou tanxin," *Dianying yishu* 2000, no. 1, 4–7.

11. For an analysis of *Blind Shaft*, see Ban Wang, "Documentary as Haunting of the Real: The Logic of Capital in *Blind Shaft*," *Asian Cinema* 16, no. 1 (2005): 4–15.

12. For an example of one such publication in 2003, see Cui Zi'en, *Diyi guanzhong* (Beijing: Xiandai chubanshe, 2003).

13. For a stimulating discussion, see Xiaomei Chen, *Occidentalism: A Theory of Counter-Discourse in Post-Mao China* (New York: Oxford University Press, 1995).

14. Celebrated works of this sort include Yu Dafu's famous short story titled "Sinking" (*Chenlun*, 1921) and Ding Ling's provocative work titled "The Diary of Miss Sophia" (*Shafei nüshi de riji*, 1927).

15. Leo Ou-fan Lee, *Shanghai Modern: The Flowering of a New Urban Culture in China, 1930–1945* (Cambridge, Mass.: Harvard University Press, 1999).

16. Chris Berry, *Postsocialist Cinema in Post-Mao China: The Cultural Revolution after the Cultural Revolution* (London: Routledge, 2004).

17. Ci Jiwei, *Dialectic of the Chinese Revolution: From Utopianism to Hedonism* (Stanford, Calif.: Stanford University Press, 1994).

18. See Chun Sue, *Beijing Doll: A Novel*, trans. Howard Goldblatt (New York: Riverhead Books, 2004), and Chun Shu, *Beijing wawa: shiqisui shaonü de canku qingchun zibai* (Hohhot: Yuanfang chubanshe, 2002); Mian Mian, *Candy*, trans. Andrea Lingenfelter (Boston: Back Bay Books, 2003) and *Tang* (Taipei: Shengzhi chubanshe, 2000); Wei Hui, *Shanghai Baby*, trans. Bruce Humes (London: Robinson, 2001) and *Shanghai baobei* (Taipei: Shengzhi chubanshe, 2000).

19. Wei, *Shanghai Baby*, 1.

Additional Work on Chinese Cinema by Paul G. Pickowicz

BOOKS

Exhibiting Chinese Cinemas, Reconstructing Reception. Special issue of *Journal of Chinese Cinemas* 3, no. 2 (2009). (Coedited with Matthew Johnson)

From Underground to Independent: Alternative Film Culture in Contemporary China. Lanham, Md.: Rowman & Littlefield, 2006. (Coedited with Yingjin Zhang)

New Chinese Cinemas: Forms, Identities, Politics. Cambridge, UK: Cambridge University Press, 1994. (Coedited with Nick Browne, Vivian Sobchack and Esther Yau)

ARTICLES

"Single Women and the Men in Their Lives: Zhang Ailing and Postwar Visual Images of the Modern Metropolis." In *Visualizing China: Life/Still Images in Historical Narratives*, edited by Christian Henriot and Wen-hsin Yeh. Leiden: Brill Publishers, forthcoming 2012. (Coauthored with Yap Soo Ei)

"Chinese Filmmaking on the Eve of the Communist Revolution." In *The Chinese Cinema Book*, edited by Song Hwee Lim and Julian Ward, 76–84. London: Palgrave Macmillan, 2011.

"Independent Chinese Film: Seeing the Not-Usually-Visible in Rural China." In *Radicalism, Revolution, and Reform in Modern China*, edited by Catherine Lynch, Robert C. Marks, and Paul G. Pickowicz, 161–84. New York: Lexington Books, 2011.

"Revisiting Cold War Propaganda: Close Readings of Chinese and American Film Representations of the Korean War." *Journal of American-East Asian Relations* 17, no. 4 (2010): 352–71.

"China's Soft Power: The Case for a Critical and Multidimensional Approach." *China Review International* 16, no. 4 (2009): 439–55.

"Exhibiting Chinese Cinemas, Reconstructing Reception." *Journal of Chinese Cinemas* 3, no. 2 (2009): 99–107. (Coauthored with Matthew Johnson)
"Three Readings of *Hong Kong Nocturne*." In *China Forever: The Shaw Brothers and Diasporic Cinema*, edited by Poshek Fu, 95–114. Urbana: University of Illinois Press, 2008.
"From Yao Wenyuan to Cui Zi'en: Film, History, Memory." *Journal of Chinese Cinemas* 1, no. 1 (2007): 41–53.
"Women and Wartime Shanghai: The Strange Case of Tian Han's *Li ren xing*." In *In the Shadow of the Rising Sun: Shanghai under Japanese Occupation, 1937–1945*, edited by Christian Henriot and Wen-hsin Yeh, 346–61. Cambridge, UK: Cambridge University Press, 2004.
"Filme und die Legitimation des Staates im Heutigen China" (Filmmaking and the State's Quest for Legitimacy in Contemporary China). In *Peking, Shanghai, Shenzhen: Stadte des 21. Jahrhunderts* (Beijing, Shanghai, Shenzhen: Cities of the 21st Century), edited by Kai Vockler and Dirk Luckow, 402–11, 566–70. Frankfurt: Campus Verlag GmbH, 2000.
"Sinifying and Popularizing Foreign Culture: From Maxim Gorky's *The Lower Depths* to Huang Zuolin's *Ye dian*." *Modern Chinese Literature* 7, no. 2 (Fall 1993): 7–31.
"Early Chinese Cinema: The Era of Exploration." *Modern Chinese Literature* 1, no. 1 (September 1984): 135–38.
"Cinema and Revolution in China: Some Interpretive Themes." *American Behavioral Scientist* 17, no. 3 (January–February 1974): 328–59.

DOCUMENTARY FILMMAKING

Academic adviser, *China: Born under the Red Flag, 1976–1992*. 2 hours. New York: Ambrica Productions; Boston: WGBH, 1997.
Associate producer, *The Mao Years, 1949–1976*. 2 hours. New York: Ambrica Productions; Boston: WGBH, 1994.
Academic adviser, *China in Revolution, 1911–1949*. 2 hours. New York: Ambrica Productions; Boston: WGBH, 1989.

Index

absurdity (*huangdan*), 286, 306
advertising: for films, 92, 148–49; in film, 181–83
aesthetics, experimental, 329; Marxist, 214
Ah Q, 278, 290
Ai Qing, 304
AIDS Victims (*Aisibing huanzhe*, d. Xu Tongjun), 60, 70
alcohol, in film, 29, 48, 49, 51, 61, 68, 70, 131, 284
alienation, 278, 287–89, 296–97, 305, 309, 339
anarchism, 39
Anhui, 45
anomie, 290, 294
anti-Americanism, 102, 107, 116, 160, 177, 181–83
Anti-Bourgeois Liberalization Campaign, 286-87
Anti-Rightist Campaign (1957), 116, 158, 185, 196–97, 208, 213, 238, 256, 260–62, 265, 282
Aristotle, 215
Artisan Pickpocket (*Xiao Wu*, d. Jia Zhangke), 325
At Home in the World (*Sihai wei jia*, d. Wu Wenguang), 339

At Middle Age (*Ren dao zhongnian*, d. Wang Qimin, Sun Yu), 14, 254, 257–58, 258, 263–64, 266
athletics, in film, 51
audience(s): addressed directly in film, 137; categories of, 41, 67; foreign, for Chinese films, 149, 236, 265, 314, 316–18, 325, 330, 332, 334–35, 340; gender of, 27–28, 151; for historical films, 129, 144–45, 150, 217; for melodrama, 78–79, 89; numbers (box office), 162, 166, 169, 171, 174, 176–78, 192–93, 252, 259, 305; for nuanced films, 95; political attitude or education of, 193–94, 251–70; for political films, 77; preferences and needs of, 47, 76, 122, 152, 216, 264–65, 269n3, 304, 311, 313; reaction to modern marriage, 22, 40; for theater (stage plays), 171; for underground film, 333–34, 342; urban, 251–70, 305; working-class, 269n3
August First Film Studio, 233–34
automobiles, in film, 35, 54, 68, 85
awards, 128; Human Rights award, 276; Hundred Flowers competition, 90, 255, 257, 259, 312; Jinji

(Golden Rooster) Film Award, 90, 255, 257, 312; Oscars, 315, 317; Palme d'Or, Cannes, 315; Silver Bear, Berlin, 333; Venice, 315; Zhongzheng jiang (Chiang Kai-shek) Culture Prize, 148, 163, 191

Ba Jin, 59, 196, 245
Bai Guang, 149
Bai Hua, 255
Bai Jingrui, 70
Bai Yang, 9, 115, 134, 139, 148, 163, 177, 185, 304
Baker, George Pierce, 216
ballets, in film, 13
Bando Tsumasaburo, 104, 112
Bao Qicheng, 56
Barmé, Gérémie, 318, 320
beds, in film, 28, 29
Before the New Director Arrives (*Xin juzhang daolai zhi qian*, d. Lu Ban), 89, 238
Begonia (*Qiu Haitang*, play), 159
Bei Dao, 273
Beijing: cinemas in, 158; in film, 164, 175, 305–6, 339; film industry in, 60, 123, 216, 222, 325, 327
Beijing Bastards (*Beijing zazhong*, d. Zhang Yuan), 325–26
Beijing Bicycle (*Shiqi sui de dan che*, d. Wang Xiaoshuai), 325, *341*
Beijing Doll (*Beijing wawa*, novel by Chun Shu), 339
Beijing Film Institute (Beijing dianying xueyuan), 2, 3, 89, 281, 291–93, 304, 332
Beijing Film Studio, 60, 222, 233
Bethune, Norman, 232–33
Bible for Daughers, A (*Nüer jing*, d. Xia Yan, 1934), 53–56, 58–59, 66
Bible for Daughters, A (*Nüer jing*, d. Bao Qicheng, 1987), 56
Big Circus, The (*Da maxituan*, play), 159
Big Road, The (*Da lu*, d. Sun Yu), 128, 190
biographical films, 204

Bitter Love (*Ku lian*, d. Peng Ning), 255–56
Black Cannon Incident, The (*Hei pao shijian*, d. Huang Jianxin), 14–15, 95, 271–72, 275, 278–82, *279*, 289–90, 293–94
black humor (*heise youmo*), 282. *See also* red humor
Blind Shaft (*Mang jing*, d. Li Yang), 333
Blue Kite (d. Tian Zhuangzhuang), 16, 328, 332–33
Blue Shirt movement, 54, 66
Boatman's Daughter, The (*Chuanjia nü*, d. Shen Xiling), 81
body, and nationalism, 51–53, 199
Bosanquet, Theodora, 99n17
bourgeois liberalization (*zichanjieji ziyouhua*), 43, 56
box office. *See* audience: numbers
Box, The (*Hezi*, d. Ying Weiwei), 329
Boxer uprising, in film, 230
Bright Sunny Days (*Yan yang tian*, d. Cao Yu), 159
Brooks, Peter, 48, 78–79, 87
Brown, Jeremy, 179
Bu Wancang, 45, 47–49, 67, 75, 82, 198
Buddhism, 290; in film, 208–9, 236
Bulgaria, 277
Bumming in Beijing (*Liulang Beijing*, d. Wu Wenguang), 339
bureaucracy, 284, 287, 294, 311, 313. *See also under* marriage
butterfly dramas, 39, 45, 53, 54, 55, 66–67, 79–80

Cai Chusheng, 4, 47, 57, 67, 75–77, 80, 85, 124–25, 127–28, *141*, 204
Candy (*Tang*, novel by Mian Mian), 339
cannibalism, 213
Cao Yu, 159
Catch-22 (d. Mike Nichols), 2, 282
Celluloid Dreams Studio (France), 325
censorship: of films, 9–14, 55, 93–95, 102, 122, 148, 154, 162, 170, 184–85, 195, 206–8, 227, 236, 247, 254–57, 266, 271–72, 286,

288, 291–93, 301–2, 315, 317, 327, 333–34 (*see also* filmmakers: persecution of); of other art forms, 192, 339–40; of research, 1–4, 8, 12, 80–81, 116, 188n56, 209, 252; self-, 15, 116, 129, 162, 170, 190, 195–96, 206, 225, 303, 309, 317, 325, 329, 331, 340; system for, 311–14, 325–26
Central Cinematography Studio (Zhongyang sheying chang), 126, 128
Changchun Film Studio, 255, 257
Changchun, film industry in, 216, 255, 257
Changsha, in film, 228
Changzhou, in film, 134
Chaplin, Charlie, 75, 122, 158
Chen Baichen, 126, 184, 190, 192, 197
Chen bao, 125
Chen Chong, 305
Chen Fan, 223
Chen Huaikai, 220, 222, 304
Chen Huangmei, 203, 236, 246
Chen Kaige, 16, 73, 79, 95, 271, 293, 295, 310, 314–15
Chen Liting, 87, 124–30, *132*, 134, 149, 152, 161
Chen Mian, 158
Chen Miao, 338
Chen Ruoxi, 277
Chen Xihe, 9, 175, 281–82
Chen Yanyan, 113–14
Chen Yi, 187n25
Chen Yunshang, 113
Cheng Jihua, 3–4, 8, 101, 116
Chiang Ching-kuo, 151
Chiang Kai-shek, 53, 55, 60, 63, 148, 190
child abuse, in film, 330
children. See *under* family
Children of Troubled Times (*Fengyun er nü*, d. Xu Xinzhi), 63–67, *65*
children's films, 184
Children's Theater Troupe (Haizi jutuan), 129, 191

China Art Theater Society (Zhongguo yishu ju she), 126
China Drama Film Company (Hua ju yingpian gongsi), 34
China Film and Theaters Workers' Association (Zhongguo dianying xiju gongzuozhe xiehui), 163
China Film Archive, 2, 101–2, 116–17, 271
China Film Art Research Center, 281
China Film Association, 267
China Film Distribution Corporation (Zhongguo dianying faxing gongsi), 312–14
China Film Import and Export Corporation (Zhongguo dianying jin chu kou youxian gongsi), 314
China Film No. 1 Studio, 123
China Film No. 2 Studio, 84, 123, 126
China Film No. 3 Studio, 123
China Film Press (Zhongguo dianying chubanshe), 311
China Film Studio (Zhongguo dianying zhipianchang, Chongqing), 126–27, 129, 155n1, 191
China Girl (*Hua guniang*), 114
Chinese Academy of Social Sciences, 286
Chinese Communist Party: criticism or mockery of, in film, 7, 90–96, 184, 238, 239, 244, 251–70, 283–88, 296, 303–5, 309, 316, 328–29; as family, 228; involvement in film industry, 39, 42n7, 47–48, 53, 54, 60, 62, 67, 76–77, 79–80, 84, 88, 90, 94–98, 114–15, 148, 160–63, 169, 170–71, 183–85, 195, 197, 201–2, 207, 213–15, 238, 254, 272, 293, 301–24; popular attitudes towards, 251–70; praise for, in film, 172–74, 176, 189–90, 193, 198, 228, 230–31, 315; self-criticism by, 259–60
Chinese Filmworkers Association (Zhongguo dianyingjia xiehui), 2, 202, 311, 315

Chinese Traveling Theater Troupe (Zhongguo lüxing jutuan), 158
Chongqing, 51; in film, 134, 140, 145, 174; film industry in, 87, 123, 125–29, 134, 139, 155n1, 191, 208
Christianity, 62–63; in film, 61–63, 107, 110
Chun Shu, 339
Ci Jiwei, 336, 341
cinemas, 313. *See also under* Beijing; Shanghai
cities. *See* urban areas
civil society, 301, 303
civil war, Chinese, 56, 102, 150, 191; in film, 9, 167
Clark, Paul, 292
class, social: in film, 22–26, 35, 40, 46–47, 51, 54, 63, 90–91, 93, 133–34, 146–47, 168–69, 172, 174, 190, 194, 226, 229, 232, 237, 243; and gender, 237; and marriage (*see under* marriage); struggle, 58, 61, 66, 90–91, 95–96, 177, 198, 208, 220–21, 226–27, 236–37, 245, 247, 280, 288, 293, 295, 304; in theatrical plays, 171
clothing and jewelry in film, 21–22, 29, 35, 37, 46, 48, 49, 54, 64, 68, 131–32, 135, 137, 172, 306
Cold War, 195, 294
collaborators and traitors, 112–13, 116–18, 123, 144–45, 150, 210; in film, 83–88, 136, 140, 145, 165, 167, 199, 203, 226, 232, 236, 332
"collective" as director of film, 172, 236
collectivization of agriculture, 213, 256, 260, 262
comedy films, 74, 89, 217, 239, 242, 244; black, 305–6
communes, in film, 239
concubines, in film, 35
conformity, in film, 278, 283
Confucian(ism), 25, 123; critique of, in fiction, 59; critique of, in film, 26, 33, 74, 76–77, 167, 169, 336–37; and marriage, 26; and Marxism, 96;

Nationalist support for, 76; support for, in film, 56–60, 63–64, 74, 109, 139, 143, 150-51, 190; virtues, 60
consumer goods, in film, 283, 288, 291
consumption, conspicuous, 41
Corner Forgotten by Love, A (*Bei aiqing yiwang de jiaoluo*, d. Li Yalin, Zhang Ji), 14, 254, 256–57, 257, 262–63, 265–66
Corner Forgotten by Love, A (*Bei aiqing yiwang de jiaoluo*, story by Zhang Xian), 256
Corruption (*Fushi*, film, d. Huang Zuolin), 174–77
Corruption (*Fushi*, novel, Mao Dun), 174-75
corruption: in film, 84, 135, 140, 145, 146, 149; nepotism, 304; political, 153, 288, 313
corruption, spiritual. *See* spiritual pollution
costume dramas. *See* historical subjects in film
Country Love (*Xiang qing*, d. Hu Bingliu and Wang Jin), 46
Crows and Sparrows (*Wuya yu maque*, d. Zheng Junli), 191–92
Cuba, 276; film industry in, 240–41
Cui Jian, 306
Cui Wei, 220, 222, 231–32
Cui Zi'en, *331*, 332
Cultural Revolution: effect on film industry, 12–13, 73, 80, 96, 116, 128–29, 167, 208–9, 213, 217, 220, 225–26, 220, 238, 241, 253, 293, 303; in film, 91, 94, 248, 256, 264–65, 304; and postsocialism, 277
cultural thaws, 12, 13, 213–49
culture: democratization of, 74; elite, 44, 67, 251; and industrialization, 274; late imperial, 274, 304; modernist, 273–74; popular, 44, 67, 251, 304; postsocialist, 275; socialist or proletarian, 272, 290; Western (*see* Western culture)
Czechoslovakia, 205, 275, 277–78, 294, 310

Dai Jinhua, 291-92
dance halls (*wu ting*), 49, 51, 54, 68
Dapeng Motion Pictures, 223
Darnton, Robert, 129, 154
Datong Film Company, 87
Daxia University, 125
Daybreak (*Tianming*, d. Sun Yu), 51, 81
deconstructionism, 89
defense, national, in film, 63
dehumanization. *See* humanity
Delegation Member (novel by Ba Jin), 245
democracy, 134
Democracy Wall (1978-79), 13-15, 253-54, 259, 277
Deng Liqun, 94, 272
Deng Xiaoping, 97, 251, 274, 277, 280-81, 290, 298n10, 305, 312-13
detective films, 74, 304
deus ex machina endings, 23-24, 31-32, 33-34, 36, 42
Devils on the Doorstep (*Guizi lai le*, d. Jiang Wen), 332-33
dialects. *See* language
Dianying (magazine), 149
Diary of a Homecoming (*Huan xiang riji*, d. Zhang Junxiang), 153, 233
Ding Li, 234
Ding Ling, 336
Ding Mingnan, 203
Ding Qiao, 253
Ding Wen, 177
Dirlik, Arif, 275-76, 298n10
Dislocation (*The Stand-in*; *Cuowei*, d. Huang Jianxin), 14-15, 282-87, 285
distribution system. *See under* film industry
divorce, 41; in film, 29, 32, 34, 48, 222, 240, 288-89
docudrama films (*yishuxing jilupian*), 217
documentary films, 191, 195, 281, 329, 338
Don't Change Your Husband. See Oceans of Passion, Heavy Kissing
Donnersmarck, Florian Henckel von, 10

Dr. Bethune (*Baiqiuen daifu*, d. Zhang Junxiang), 232-33, 236
Dream in Pink, A (*Fenhongse de meng*, d. Cai Chusheng), 47-50, 52, 55-57, 59, 66-67, 127-28
Dream of the Red Chamber (*Hong lou meng*, d. Chen Fan), 223-25, 246
Dream of the Red Chamber (*Hong lou meng*, novel), 224
drug addiction, in film, 330
Du Jinfang, 222
Dumas, Alexandre, 75
dystopia, 283

Early Spring (*Zao chun eryue*, d. Xie Tieli), 229-33, 236-38, 246-48
East China Normal University, 5
East China People's Revolutionary University, 172
East is Red, The (*Dongfang hong*, d. collective), 236-37
East Palace, West Palace (*Dong gong, xi gong*, d. Zhang Yuan), 189
Eastern Europe, 15, 43, 275-76, 291, 294, 297, 299n10, 318-20, 331. *See also* names of individual countries
Eastman, Lloyd, 54
Easy Rider (d. Dennis Hopper), 2, 305
economic development, 263, 280
Economist, 293
editing, 49
Eight Thousand Miles of Clouds and Moon (*Ba qian li lu yun he yue*, d. Shi Dongshan), 127, 133-37, *137*, 139, 143, 145-49, 151-54, 228
Elephant Man (d. David Lynch), 2
Emei Film Studio, 256
Emerging from the Sea (*Fuqu haimian*, novel by Wang Shuo), 287
emigration, in film, 258, 266
Endless Passion, Deep Friendship (*Qing chang yi shen*), 184
Enter the Clowns (d. Cui Zi'en), 331
entertainment, films as (*yule pian*), 16, 67, 117, 122-23, 199, 307, 310, 314; and propaganda, 102-3
epic films, 164

escapist films, 307
Esherick, Joseph, 97
Eternity (*Wan shi liu fang*), 113, 117, 198–99
ethnicity, in film, 199–200, 202, 220, 234–36, 293, 295. *See also* race; *and specific ethnicities*
Evening Bell (*Wan zhong*, d. Wu Ziniu), 314
expressionism, German, 8

Fake Bride, Phony Bridegroom (*Jia feng xu huang*, d. Huang Zuolin), 157, 159
Family (*Jia*, d. Yue Feng), 115
Family (*Jia*, play), 159
Family (novel by Ba Jin), 59
Family Reunion (*Da tuanyuan*, d. Ding Li), 233–34
family: childlessness, in film, 84, 90, 167, 221; children, in film, 84, 88, 143, 232; collective, in film, 151; Communist Party as, 228; extended, in film, 28; in film, 28–29, 31, 36, 45, 48, 61, 82–83, 89, 94, 110, 124, 132, 134–36, 139, 141–44, 147, 228, 245, 266, 328; traditional, in film, 28, 57, 150, 224, 232, 336. *See also* marriage
famine, 202, 204, 260
Fang Lizhi, 97, 275
Fang Peilin, 124
fanshen (term), 171, 187n32
fantasy, in film, 36
Far Away Love (*Yaoyuan de ai*, d. Chen Liting), 126, 129–33, *132*, 134, 135, 139, 143, 145–48, 151–54
farce, 154
Farewell My Concubine (*Bawang bie ji*, d. Chen Kaige), 315
fascism, 55, 59, 66
Fat Li, Young Li, and Old Li (*Da Li, Xiao Li, he Lao Li*, d. Xie Jin), 89, 244, 246
February (novel by Rou Shi), 229
Fei Mu, 57–60, *58*, 62, 67, 159
feminism, in film, 54, 56
Feng Jicai, 273

Feng Jie, 102
feudalism, in film, 93
Fifteen Strings of Cash (*Shiwu guan*, d. Tao Jin), 217
Fifth Generation filmmakers, 89, 95, 118, 267, 271, 310, 315, 328
Filial Piety (*Tian lun*, d. Fei Mu, Luo Mingyou), 57–60, *58*, 62–64, 66, 128, 190
Film Art (*Dianying yishu*), 281, 286
Film Bureau (Dianying ju), Ministry of Culture / Ministry of Radio, Film, and Television, 3, 127–28, 236, 238, 253, 288, 293, 311, 313, 315
film, uses and purposes of, 68, 123–24, 215, 247, 295, 327–28
film industry: distribution system, 312–15, 327, 333; funding and finances, 142, 183, 214, 304, 310–14, 316, 327, 335, 342; independence of, 309; independent sector (*duli dianying*), 16, 326; political economy of, 311–14; private sector, 10–11, 14, 16, 157–88, 192, 193, 312, 327; professionalism in, 214–14; state sector, 10–12, 14, 148, 154, 160–61, 183, 191, 195–96, 252, 312, 325, 327, 342; underground sector (*dixia dianying*), 16, 325–43. *See also under* Chinese Communist Party *and* Nationalist government; *see also* filmmakers; *and see also names of specific cities or countries*
filmmakers: accommodation with Communist Party, 191, 198, 207–10, 220, 229, 243, 246–47, 272, 301–24, 328–33; independent (*duli dianying*), 16, 326; persecution of, 11–13, 127–29, 167, 178, 183–85, 189, 196, 207–8, 215, 238, 246, 292, 303, 313, 329 (*see also* censorship: of films); political responsibilities of, 319; rehabilitation of, 188n56, 190; remuneration and privileges of, 303–4, 312–13, 332

Fisherman's Song (*Yu guang qu*, d. Cai Chusheng), 128
Five Flowers filmmakers (Wu hua she), 184
Five Girls and a Rope (*Wuge nüren he yi gen shengzi*, d. Yeh Hung-wei), 318
Fogel, Joshua, 104–5
folk music, 227, 247
folklore, 125, 277, 304
food, in film, 131, 140, 284
foreign actors, 197
Forman, Milos, 2, 310
Fortress Besieged (novel by Qian Zhongshu), 2
Four Modernizations, 281, 284, 289
France, 46
France, film industry, 325
Frankfurt school, 154
French Connection (d. William Friedkin), 308
French Revolution, 78–79
Fu, Poshek, 101, 117

gambling, in film, 54, 56
Gang of Four, 259–61
gangs, in film, 289
gangsters, 50
Gao Zheng, 134, 139
Garlands at the Foot of the Mountain (*Gaoshan xia de huahuan*, d. Xie Jin), 89
gay people, in film, 330, 338–39
gender: of actors in Zhejiang opera, 224; of audience, 27–28; and class, 237; equality, 5–6, 75, 130, 239–40; and nationalism, 46
gender roles in film, 22, 26–27, 33, 37–40, 51, 53, 54, 56, 146–47, 190, 228
German expressionism, 8
Germany, eastern, 275, 277, 294; film industry in, 10–11
Ghostbusters (d. Ivan Rietman), 305
globalization, 41, 118, 339–42
Glorious Creativity (d. Zheng Junli), 195
Goddess, The (*Shennü*, d. Wu Yonggang), 60, 81, 238

Gong Li, 305
Gorbachev, M.S., 320
gothic films, 36
Great China Film Company (Da Zhonghua baihe yingpian gongsi), 27
Great Dictator, The (d. Charlie Chaplin), 158
Great Japan Productions (Dai Nippon eiga kaisha), 103
Great Leap Forward, 11, 196, 198, 202, 204–5, 213–14, 217, 224–26, 233, 239, 243–44, 256, 260, 262
Great Wall Film Company (Changcheng huapian gongsi), 21
Gregory, Augusta, Lady, 125
Griffith, D.W., 75, 81
Gu Hua, 90
Guangdong, in film, 198
Guangming ribao, 271
Guangzhou, 47
Guilin, in film, 132, 217
Guo Moruo, 126, 129
Guotai film studio, 160

hairstyles in film, 21–22, 35, 54, 68
Haiyan Film Studio, 126, 197, 223, 233, 241
Han Fei, 9
Han Langen, 103
Hangzhou, in film, 195
Hankou, in film, 131, 139, 145, 228
Haraszti, Miklos, 15, 301–3, 309, 318–22
Havel, Václav, 318–19
He Feiguang, 155n1
He Xiaoshu, 257
Heavenly Match (*Tian xian pei*), 184
Heavenly Spring Dream (*Tiantang chun meng*, d. Tang Xiaodan), 7, 84–87, 85, 94, 149, 153–54
Hebei province, in film, 230, 232
hedonism, 336
Hegel, G.W.F., 215
Henan province, in film, 239
Herdsman, The (*Muma ren*, d. Xie Jin), 70, 89, 94, 116

Hero (*Yingxiong*, d. Zhang Yimou), 342
Heroic Sons and Daughters (*Yingxiong er nü*, d. Wu Zhaodi), 245
Hershatter, Gail, 175
Hibiscus Town (*Furongzhen*, d. Xie Jin), 89–93, *92*, 97, 267, 296
hierarchy, in film, 180
High, Peter, 103
historical subjects in film, 16, 39, 66, 102, 164, 177, 184, 195–206, 233–36, 246–47, 293, 295, 304, 315; distortion of, 107, 109, 113–14, 118, 129, 202–3, 208, 216–38
Hitchcock, Alfred, 154
holidays, in film, 36, 53, 61, 81–82, 138, 140, 144, 146, 164, 166, 231
Hollywood. *See* United States film industry
Home is in Taibei (*Jia zai Taibei*, d. Bai Jingrui), 70
Hong Kong Golden Sound Motion Picture Corporation, 223
Hong Kong, 273, 307; film industry in, 114–16, 128, 162, 223, 297, 313, 317–18, 325
Hong Shen, 53, 75–76, 87
Hongqi, 214, 217
Honig, Emily, 99n29
Hopper, Dennis, 2, 305
horror films, 34–38
Horse Thief (*Dao ma zei*, d. Tian Zhuangzhuang), 310, 314
Hou Yao, 21
House of the Flying Daggers (*Shimian maifu*, d. Zhang Yimou), 342
Hu Binglu, 46
Hu Jian, 312
Hu Qiaomu, 94, 272
Hu Su, 231
Hu Xinling, 103, 106, *108*, *109*
Hu Yan, 112–13
Hu Yaobang, 255–56, 286, 290
Hua bei ying hua (magazine), 111–12
Hua Junwu, 304
Huang Jianxin, 14–15, 89, 95, 271–300, *285*

Huang Sha, 217
Huang Shaofen, 103, 157, 167, 169, 173, 181, 197–98
Huang Wanqiu, 218
Huang Zongjiang, 2, 9, 157–58, 185, 233
Huang Zongying, 161–62, 192, 233–34
Huang Zuolin, 9, 157, 159, 161, 172, 174, 177, 178, 181, 183, 185
Huaying (Zhonghua dianying lianhe gongsi), 102–3, 114–15
Human Condition, The (*Ningen no joken*, d. Masaki Kobayashi), 142
human nature, 263. *See also* humanism
humanism, 62, 64, 167, 169, 171, 180, 237–38, 263, 293
humanity and dehumanization, 173, 176, 281–82
Hundred Flowers campaign (1956–57), 184, 196, 238
Hung, Chang-tai, 152
Hungary, 15, 275–76, 301
Husband and Wife (*Women fu fu zhi jian*, d. Zheng Junli), 129, 192–95, *194*, 197, 200, 206, 208
Husband and Wife (*Women fu fu zhi jian*, novel, Xiao Yemu), 192

Ibsen, Henrik, 34, 75
Ideological Problems (*Sixiang wenti*, film, d. collective), 171–74, 176, 178, 180
Ideological Problems (*Sixiang wenti*, play), 171
illiteracy, in film, 178, 193, 228
imperialism, in film, 74, 77, 93, 106–11, 113, 118, 151. *See also under* Japan
Inagaki Hiroshi, 103, 106
incest, in film, 330
India, in film, 109, 236
individualism, 283, 335–37; urban, 305. *See also under* rights
industrial(ization), 196, 274; in film, 23–24, 83, 195, 240, 242; post-, 287
intellectuals, 47, 57, 79, 178–79, 198, 213–15, 221, 268, 286, 303, 312,

319; in film, 130, 146, 172, 178, 193–94, 218, 229, 241, 243, 256, 258, 264, 278, 287, 305
Internet, 334
Ireland, 125

James, Henry, 99n17
Jameson, Fredric, 273
Japan: invasion and occupation of China by, 8, 38–39, 47, 76, 83–84, 101–20, 122, 128, 159, 190, 198; invasion and occupation, in film, 64, 81, 83–84, 88, 117, 121–56, 165, 167, 232, 237; investment in Chinese films (post-Mao), 316, 325; nineteenth century, in film, 105–11; *Japanese Spy* (*Riben jiandie*, d. Yuan Congmei), 151n1
Jia Leilei, 286
Jia Zhangke, 325–26, 329
Jiang Qing, 13, 97, 207
Jiang Wen, 332
Jiangsu province, 61, 178
Jin Shan, 203
Jin Yan, 45, 163
journalists, in film, 237
Judou (d. Zhang Yimou), 315, 317

Kadar, Jan, 310
Kaifeng, 62; in film, 222
Kawakita Nagamasa, 102, 106
Ke Ling, 9, 174
King of the Children (*Haizi wang*, d. Chen Kaige), 314
Klos, Elmar, 310
Kong Du, 281
Korea, North, 276; in film, 207
Korean War, 177, 179, 195, 245
Kugan Players (Kugan jutuan), 159
Kunlun Film Studio (Kunlun yingye gongsi), 125–29, 160, 191–92, 194

labor, 99n29; in film, 75, 93, 139, 146, 258, 306, 333; unions, in film, 182, 244–45
Lan Ma, 161, 203

landlords, in film, 88, 172, 204, 220, 235, 237
Lang, Robert, 86
language, 40–41, 49, 118, 176, 178, 231, 306
Lao She, 163, 203
Lay Down Your Whip (*Fan xia ni de bianzi*, play, d. Chen Liting), 125–26, 134
League of Left-Wing Dramatists, 125
Lee, Leo Ou-Fan, 42n9
"leftist thought," 281, 284
Legend of Tianyun Mountain, The (*Tianyun shan chuanqi*, d. Xie Jin), 14, 89, 94, 248, 254–56, *255*, 257, 259, 261–62, 265–66, 296
Legend of Tianyun Mountain, The (*Tianyun shan chuanqi*, novel by Lu Yanzhou), 254
legitimacy, 251
Lenin, 215
Letter with Feathers, A (*Jimao xin*, d. Shi Hui), 184, 232
Leyda, Jay, 66, 101, 205
Li Bai, 156n23
Li Jianwu, 203
Li Jun, 233
Li Lihua, 8, 9, 103, 106, 112–14, 116, 157–58
Li Lili (Lily Li), 2, 51
Li Moran, 225–26
Li Peng, 274
Li Shanzi (d. Zheng Junli), 207–8
Li Shaochun, 222
Li Shuangshuang (d. Lu Ren), 239–44, *240*, 246
Li Tuo, 271, 273, 281
Li Xifan, 201
Li Yalin, 254, *257*
Li Yang, 333
Li Zhongyue, 278, 281
Li Zeyuan, 21, 24, 74
Lianhua Film Studio, 57, 75, 125–29, 190, 327
Lianhua Symphony (*Lianhua jiaoxiangqu*), 57

Life of Wu Xun, The (*Wu Xun zhuan*, d. Sun Yu), 177–78, 193–95, 197
Light of East Asia (*Dong ya zhi guang*, d. He Feiguang), 155n1
Lin Biao, 97, 260
Lin Sha, 245
Lin Zexu (d. Zheng Junli), 11, 118, 124–25, 196–206, *200*, *205*, 208, 226
Ling Zifeng, 2, 216, 230, 246
Link, Perry, 45, 79, 277
Little Angel (*Xiao tianshi*, d. Wu Yonggang), 60–64, 66
Little Soldier Zhang Ga (*Xiao bing Zhang Ga*, d. Cui Wei, Ouyang Hongying), 232
Liu Binyan, 275, 301
Liu Guoquan, 249n36
Liu Qiong, 103, 114, 116
Liu Shaoqi, 97, 280
Liu Shaoqing, 305
Lives of Others, The (d. Florian Henckel von Donnersmarck), 10
local identity, 231, 306
Long Live the Missus (*Taitai wan sui*, d. Sang Hu), 159
Long Live the Nation (*Minzu wan sui*), 191
Lou Ye, 328
love-story films, 66, 218, 253, 304, 313–14
Loyal and Virtuous Family (*Zhong yi zhi jia*, d. Wu Yonggang), 124
Lu Ban, 89
Lu Ren, 239, *240*
Lu Xun, 57, 129, 204, 206–07, 278, 290
Lu Yanzhou, 254
Lucia (d. Humberto Solas), 240–41
Lukács, George, 274
Lunar Eclipse (d. Wang Quan'an), 337
Luo Mingyou, 57, *58*, 75, 190
Luo Yijun, 287
Lushan Conference (1959), 202
Lynch, David, 2

Macau, in film, 200
majiang, in film, 61, 135

Malaya, 41
Man of Marble (d. Andrzej Wajda), 272
Man of Steel (d. Andrezej Wajda), 272
Manchus, 203; in film, 199–200, 202
mandarin duck and butterfly dramas. *See* butterfly dramas
Mao Dun, 174, 204
Mao Zedong, 49, 178, 187n25, 195–98, 202, 204–5, 213, 215, 224, 226–27, 236, 238, 243, 246, 259–60, 276, 280, 293, 336, 341; China after death of, 251–70; in film, 206, 244, 288, 339
Maoist films, 198, 202, 204
"March of the Volunteers" (*Yiyongjun jinxing qu*), 63, 204
Marcuse, Herbert, 295
marriage: arranged, in film, 32, 34, 167, 224, 228, 240, 257, 265; and bureaucracy, in film, 91; and class, in film, 36, 45, 194; finances of, in film 21, 32, 38, 40; "free," 56; modern, 5–6, 19–42; by mutual choice, in film, 21, 224. *See also* divorce; family
martial arts, in non-martial-arts films, 231
martial-arts films, 37, 39, 66, 74, 127, 253, 304, 313
Masaki Kobayashi, 142
Masao Miyoshi, 274
masochism, in film, 86–87
Maupassant, Guy de, 25, 75
May Fourth Movement, 39, 55, 56, 336; critique of, 56–60; fiction of, 47, 164; in film, 164; and gender equality, 6; and marriage, 26; myths about, 80; tradition of, 7, 65–67, 73–100, 174, 304, 315
medicine, in film, 32, 60–62, 70, 206, 232, 258
Mei Duo, 169–70
Mei Xi, 8, 103, 107, 113
melodrama (*tongsu ju*), 7, 9, 13–14, 60, 73–100 (esp. 78, 99n15), 239, 252, 265, 296, 304

Menzel, Jiri, 310
methodology, 1–4, 19–20, 73, 80–81, 101, 209, 252
Mi Jiashan, 305, *307*, 310
Mian Mian, 339
"middle characters," 183, 226, 239, 244–45, 247; and class, 243. *See also* moral ambiguity
Military Affairs Commission (Junshi weiyuanhui zhengzhi bu, Nationalist government), 127
military, 7, 97, 126, 134, 162, 170–71; in film, 63, 107–10, 130–33, 166–67, 177–80, 222, 225–26, 230, 232, 245, 306, 315; involvement in film industry, 233
Ming bao, 125
Mingxing Film Company, 76, 327
mining, in film, 333
Ministry of Culture, 3, 13, 174, 238, 257, 311. *See also* Film Bureau
Ministry of National Security (Anchuan bu), 3
Ministry of Propaganda (Wang Jingwei government), 102, 114
Ministry of Radio, Film, and Television, 271, 293, 312
modernity and modernism, 39, 273–74, 286, 304, 341; and marriage (*see under* marriage); and nationalism, 5; and tradition, 28–35, 39–40, 48, 55, 59, 74, 147, 198
Molière, 75
Mongolia, 277
Mongols, in film, 199
monks, in film, 223
moral ambiguity, 95, 239, 243, 265. *See also* "middle characters"
moral polarity, 78–82, 85–87, 91, 93, 97, 173, 218, 220, 247. *See also* political polarity
morality-tale films, 74
Mother (*Muqin*, d. Shi Hui), 159
Mukerji, Chandra, 154
Mulan Joins the Army (*Mulan cong jun*), 113, 117

music, 158; in film, 35, 48, 49, 54, 61, 63, 68, 70, 106, 111, 131, 204, 217, 247, 290, 306
musical films, 74, 217

names, personal, in film, 27, 84, 91, 278
Nanchang, 139
Nanhui county, 125
nationalism, 41, 43, 76, 119, 178–79, 196, 227, 235, 246; and the body, 51–53, 199; films promoting, 57, 74, 198–99, 221, 226, 231, 246, 335; and gender, 46; and modernity, 5
Nationalist government: criticism of, in film, 9, 84, 88, 94, 96, 119, 153, 166, 168; involvement in film industry, 61, 63, 113–14, 122–23, 125–28, 148–49, 152–54, 160; support of, in film, 134, 151
native place identity, 99n29
Naval Battle of 1894 (*Jiawu fengyun*, d. Lin Nong), 225–26, 235
Naval Battle of 1894 (*Jiawu fengyun*, play), 225–26
New Culture Movement, 33, 39, 44, 55, 56, 66–67, 74, 79, 315, 336; and Confucianism, 57, 59, 336; and gender equality, 6; and marriage, 26
New Life Movement, 53, 55, 60, 62, 63, 66, 190
new wave literature, 287
newspapers, in film, 21–22
Nichols, Mike, 2, 282
Nie Er (d. Zheng Junli), 204–06
Nie Er, 63, 204–06, 208
Night Voyage on a Foggy Sea (*Wu hai ye hang*), 184–85
nightclubs, in film, 61, 131, 338
North China Revolutionary University, 88
nudity, 307

O'Neill, Eugene, 233
Obsession (*Fengkuang de daijia*, d. Zhou Xiaowen), 307–9, *308*, 315

Occidentalism, 6–7, 335–39, 341
Oceans of Passion, Heavy Kissing (*Qing hai zhong wen*, d. Xie Yunqing), 27–34, 29, 30, 39–42
Office Kitano Studio (Japan), 325
old people, in film, 88
Old Testament (*Jiuyue*, d. Cui Zi'en), 332
Olympic games (2008), 330
On Film Acting (book, V. Pudovkin), 125
One Flew Over the Cuckoo's Nest (d. Milos Forman), 2
openness: cultural, 303, 330; political, 280
opera, 224, 227; in film, 13, 74, 184, 220, 222–24, 231, 237, 247, 306; folk, 218
opium, in film, 108, 203
Opium War, in film, 11, 107–8, 113, 118, 196–206
Opium War, The (*Yapian zhanzheng*, draft of Lin Zexu), 197
Orientalism, self-, 316–17
Orphan in the Snow (*Xue zhong gu chu*, d. Zhang Huimin), 34–42
Orphan Island period, 103, 122
Ouyang Hongying, 232
Ouyang Yuqian, 75
overseas Chinese, 40

Pan Hong, 259, 305
patriarchy, 28, 33, 147, 151, 316
patriotism, 66, 79, 84, 127, 134, 145, 146, 177, 199, 203, 220–21, 223, 226–27, 336
Peaceful Spring (*Taiping chun*, d. Sang Hu), 167–71, 174, 177
Peach Blossom Weeps Tears of Blood (*Taohua qixue ji*, d. Tian Han), 45–48, 52, 55–57, 59, 66–67, 69, 70
peasants. See rural areas and villages
Peng Dehuai, 202
Peng Ning, 255
People's New Hangzhou, The (d. Zheng Junli), 195
Philippines, 41

Pioneers, The (*Zhuang zhi ling yun*, d. Wu Yonggang), 60
Platform (*Zhantai*, d. Jia Zhangke), 325
Platoon Commander Guan (*Guan lianzhang*, film, d. Shi Hui), 177–80, 193, 195
Platoon Commander Guan (*Guan lianzhang*, novel, Zhu Dingyuan), 177
Plekhanov, G.V., 274
Plunder of Peach and Pear (*Tao li jie*, d. Ying Yunwei), 81
Poland, 272, 275–76, 294, 320
police, in film, 163–66, 189, 306, 315, 317
political ambiguity, 243
political films, 77, 166
political polarity, 173. See also moral polarity
Popular Cinema (*Dazhong dianying*), 90, 170, 194, 252, 255, 305
postmodern (*houxiandai*), 274, 287, 294
post-Sixth Generation (*hou liudai*), 328
postsocialism, 14, 271–300, 305, 317, 336, 338–39; definition, 275, 294, 298n10
poverty, in film, 330
Price Control Bureau, 313
private firms, in film, 305
private life, in film, 304, 310–11, 328, 337
private sector, and film industry. See under film industry
propaganda, 13, 16, 68, 123–24, 152, 192, 195, 207, 293, 341; and entertainment, 102–3
prostitution, 175; in film, 60, 175–76, 330, 334
Pudovkin, Vsevolod, 125

Qian Hong, 203
Qian Xingcun, 53, 76, 80
Qian Zhongshu, 2, 17
Qin Yi, 126, 197
Qingdao, in film, 64

Qinghai province, in film, 241
Qinghua University, 233
Qingqing dianying, 162
Qiu Haitang (d. Maxu Weibang), 115
Qu Baiyin, 184
Qu Qiubai, 55, 68
Qu Yan (play, Guo Moruo), 126
Queen of Sports (*Tiyu huanghou*, d. Sun Yu), 50–53, *52*, 54, 57, 59, 65, 66

race, in film, 110. *See also* ethnicity
radio, 162
Raging Bull (d. Martin Scorsese), 2
Raise the Red Lantern (*Da hong denglong gaogao gua*, d. Zhang Yimou), 315, 317
realism, 7, 87, 89, 154. *See also* social realism; socialist realism
Rebels, The (*Song Jingshi*), 184, 195, 197–98
"rectification" campaign (1951), 178
Red Detachment of Women (*Hongse niangzi jun*, d. Xie Jin), 13, 237
Red Flag Chronicle (*Hong qi pu*, d. Ling Zifeng), 230–32
Red Flag Chronicle (*Hong qi pu*, novel, Liang Bing), 230
red humor (*hongse youmo*), 282–83, 296
Red Propagandist (*Hongse xuanchuan yuan*, play), 207
reeducation, in film, 176
reform: cultural, 302, 309; economic, 276, 280–81, 287, 290–91, 303, 312; political, 43, 74, 76, 267–68, 272, 276, 278, 284–85, 287, 289–91, 293–94, 320
refugees, in film, 133
Remorse in Shanghai (*Chun jiang yi hen*, d. Hu Xinling, Inagaki Hiroshi), 8–9, 101–20, *108*, *109*; audience reception of, 111–15; investigation of, 113–14; legacy of, 115–19
Renmin ribao (*People's Daily*), 178, 204, 259
Revolution of 1911, 79; in film, 164

Revolutionary Family (*Geming jiating*, d. Shui Hua), 227–30, 232, 235
Revolutionary Family (*Geming jiating*, memoir by Tao Cheng), 227
Rhapsody of Happiness, A (*Xingfu kuangxiangqu*, d. Chen Liting), 126
Rickett, Adele, 172
Rickett, Allyn, 172
Rietman, Ivan, 305
rights, individual, 281
Rising of the Moon, The (play, Lady Gregory), 125
River Elegy (*Heshang*), 281
robots, 284
Rock 'n' Roll Youth (*Yaogun qingnian*, d. Tian Zhuangzhuang), 292
Rogues, The (d. Xu Changlin), 3
Romance of Liang Shanbo and Zhu Yingtai (*Liang Shanbo yu Zhu Yingtai*, d. Sang Hu, Huang Sha), 217
Romance of the Fruit Peddler (*Laogong zhi aiqing*, d. Zhang Shichuan), 74
Romania, 277
Rou Shi, 204, 229
Ruan Lingyu, 45, 47, 82
rural areas and villages, 202, 213, 277, 305; in film, 81, 88, 93, 95, 146, 178, 193, 217–20, 237, 257, 263, 304, 332; romanticization of, 295. *See also* collectivization; urban-rural differences
rural-urban differences. *See* urban-rural differences
rustification program, 241, 243, 246

sadism, in film, 86–87
Salon Troupe (Shalong jutuan), 158
Sang Hu, 9, 115–16, 157, 159, 169, 173, 184–85, 217
satirical films, 154
Satisfied or Not? (*Manyi bu manyi?*, d. Yan Gong), 239, 242, 244
"scar literature" (*shangheng wenxue*), 261
Schmalzer, Sigrid, 173
Schudson, Michael, 154

science fiction, 283
Scorsese, Martin, 2
self, in film, 335-37
self-censorship. *See under* censorship
self-criticism sessions, in film, 242
self-Orientalism, 316-17, 340
Sentinels of the High Sky (*Changkong biyi*, d. Wang Bing, Li Shutian), 245-46
Senzaimaru, voyage of (1862), 103-5; in film, 105-11
Serfs (*Nongnu*, d. Li Jun), 233-36
serious films (*yansu pian*), 252
sexual relations, in film: coerced, 37, 165, 222; gay (*see* gay people, in film); outside marriage, 27-28, 41, 45, 48, 51, 61, 64, 68, 139, 256, 263
Shandong province, in film, 193, 222, 332
Shangganling (d. Shao Meng, Lin Sha), 245
Shangguan Yunzhu, 3, 140, 167, 177, 238, 246
Shanghai: cinemas in, 86, 122, 126-28, 162, 166, 169, 170, 173, 176, 178, 192-93; film industry in, 2, 5, 20, 38-39, 50-51, 74, 84, 87, 122-23, 125-29, 157-88, 192, 196-97, 204, 214, 216, 223, 233, 241, 327; in film, 19-42 (esp. 41), 48, 64, 81-82, 106-11, 118, 124, 131, 133-34, 136, 139, 145, 172, 192, 195, 229, 237, 242, 244, 306, 338; Japanese occupation of, 8, 47, 144
Shanghai Amateur Experimental Drama Troupe (Shanghai yeyu shiyan jutuan), 125, 128
Shanghai Baby (*Shanghai baobei*, novel by Wei Hui), 339
Shanghai Film Bureau, 232
Shanghai Film Studio (Shangying), 2, 161, 163, 183-84, 195, 254, 325
Shanghai Film Studio Pictorial, 92
Shanghai Literature and Art Office (Shanghai wenyi chu), 163
Shanghai People's Art and Theater Institute (Shanghai renmin yishu ju yuan), 172

Shanghai Professional Theater Troupe (Shanghai zhiye jutuan), 159
Shanghai Salvation Drama Troupe (Shanghai jiuwang yanju), 126, 128, 191
Shanghai Theater and Film Association (Shanghai xiju dianying xiehui), 161, 171, 192
Shanghai Theater Art Society (Shanghai ju yi she), 159
Shanghai Yingxi Film Company (Shanghai yingxi gongsi), 126
Shao Meng, 245
Shao Mujun, 89, 93, 95, 267, 282, 291
Shen bao, 148
Shen Fu, 192
Shen Ji, 184
Shen Xiling, 53, 77, 81, 84
Shi Dongshan (Shi Kuangshao), 75, 124-25, 126-28, *137*, 152, 154, 228
Shi Fangyu, 3, 293, 311
Shi Hui, 10-11, 157-88, *165*, 192, 195-96, 232
Shi Linghe, 80
Shi Yu, 2, *3*, 9, 192
Shi Zhecun, 273
Shortcut to Becoming a Son-in-Law (*Chen long kuaishu*, d. Zhang Junxiang), 233
Shu Xiuwen, 139
Shui Hua, 227-28, 230, 246
Sichuan, film industry in, 256. *See also under* Chongqing
Singapore, 40, 41
Sino-American relations, 2
Sino-Japanese War (1890s), in film, 225
Siqin Gaowa, 305
Sisters Stand Up (*Jiejie meimei zhanqilai*, d. Chen Xihe), 175, 177
Situ Huimin, 80, 84
Situ Zhaodun, 3-4
Sixth Generation filmmakers, 118, 328
Small Street, A (*Xiao jie*, d. Yang Yanjin), 70
Small Toys (*Xiao wanyi*, d. Sun Yu), 7, 51, 81-83, *82*, 86, 88, 90, 94, 228

Snake Boy (*Shanghai nanhai*, d. Chen Miao), 338
social democracy, 294-95
social mobility in film, 23
"social problem" films, 243-44
social realism, 87
socialism, 39: collapse of, 301-3; definitions of, 294-95; opposition to, 272, 276, 278, 285, 290, 293-94, 296, 309; "with Chinese characteristics," 290n10
Socialist Education Movement, 206
socialist realism, 206, 227, 247. *See also* realism
Solas, Humberto, 240
Song of the Red Flag (*Hongqi ge*, play), 171
"Song of the Young Pioneers, The," in film, 290, 291
Songbird on Earth (*Ying fei renjian*, d. Fang Peilin), 124
Sorrows and Joys of Middle Age (*Ai le zhongnian*, d. Sang Hu), 157, 169
Soul of the Sea (*Hai hun*, d. Xu Tao), 70
Southeast Asia, 40. *See also* names of specific countries
Southern Art Institute (Nanguo yishu xueyuan), 128
Soviet Union, 275, 277, 312, 320; and China, 69, 125, 174, 199, 213, 220, 227, 246, 284
Special Economic Zones, in film, 60
Spirit of the Nation (*Guo feng*, d. Luo Mingyou), 190
spiritual pollution (*jingshen wuran*), 6, 29, 43-71, 150, 233, 254, 266, 288
sports, in film, 51
Spring Comes to a Withered Tree (*Kumu feng chun*, d. Zheng Junli), 206-8
Spring River Flows East, A (*Yi jiang chun shui xiang dong liu*, d. Cai Chusheng, Zheng Junli), 4, 49, 128-29, 137-42, *141*, 145, 147-49, 151-54, 191-92
Springtime in a Small Town (*Xiao cheng zhi chun*, d. Tian Zhuangzhuang), 332

Stage Sisters (*Wutai jiemei*, d. Xie Jin), 236-38, 247-48
Star Film Company (Mingxing yingpian gongsi), 127
star system, 305
state-sector film studios. *See under* film industry
Storm on the Border (*Saishang fengyun*, d. Ying Yunwei), 155n1
Story of Qiu Ju (*Qiu Ju da guan si*, d. Zhang Yimou), 315-17
Straighten Up (*Zhan zhi lou, bie paxia*, d. Huang Jianxin), 292
Street Angel (*Malu tianshi*, d. Yuan Muzhi), 81
String of Pearls, A (*Yi chuan zhen zhu*, d. Li Zeyuan), 21-27, 24, 39-42, 74
struggle meetings, 185; in film, 172-74, 177
student demonstrations of 1986, 286
Su Li, 217
Su Shaozhi, 278
Su Yi, 155n1
Subei, in film, 176
suicide, 127, 167, 185, 188n56, 238; in film, 33, 35, 141, 181-83, 222, 229-30, 237-38, 263, 290, 292
Summer Palace (*Yiheyuan*, d. Lou Ye), 328
Sun Daolin, 9
Sun Society, 76
Sun Yu, 50-53, *52*, 57, 65, 67, 75-77, 79-84, 82, 85, 177, 195, 216, 228, 254, *258*
Sunrise (*Richu*, play by Cao Yu), 159
surrealism, 287
Suzhou, in film, 134, 242

Taiping Rebellion, 104-5; in film, 102, 118
Taiwan, 273, 307; film industry in, 70, 227, 297, 313, 318
Tang Xiaodan, 83-87, *85*
Tanguts, in film, 220
Tannebaum, Gerald, 197, 233
Tao Cheng, 227
Tao Jin, 134, 139, 217

Tao Qin, 103
taxes, 314; in film, 139, 231
teachers, in film, 51, 52, 136, 139, 229–30
technology, in film industry, 127, 283, 317–18; for viewers, 334
television, 254, 281, 305, 333
Teng Jinxian, 293, 312
theater (stage plays, *huaju*, etc.), 67, 125–26, 133–34, 158–60, 162, 170, 190–91, 218, 220, 222, 225–6, 247
theater, street (*jietou ju*), 125
Third Sister Liu (*Liu Sanjie*, d. Su Li), 217–20, *219*, 222–23, 247
This Life of Mine (*Wo zhei yi beizi*, film), 163–66, *165*, 171, 176
This Life of Mine (*Wo zhei yi beizi*, novella by Lao She), 163, 168–69, 177
thought reform, 170, 172
thriller films, 253
Thunderstorm (*Lei yu*, play by Cao Yu), 159
Tian Fang, 304
Tian Han, 45, 60, 63, 67, 75–76, 80, 84, 87, 126, 203–4, 208
Tian Zhuangzhuang, 16, 89, 271, 292–93, 295, 310, 328, 332
Tiananmen demonstrations (1976), 277
Tiananmen massacre (1989), 7, 60, 97, 267, 272, 291–92, 301, 315–18, 328
Tianma studio, 184, 233
Tibet, in film. 234–36
time, in film, 86, 93
tobacco in film, 21–22, 29, 35, 48, 49, 51, 61, 64, 68, 70, 131, 284
Tolstoy, L.N., 215
Tomson Film Company, 318
Tong Baoling, 184
Toroptsev, Sergei, 66
tradition and modernity. *See under* modernity
tragedy, 166, 226
tragicomdies (*bei xi ju*), 154

Transmigration (*Samsara; Lunhui*, d. Huang Jianxin), 14–15, 95, 271, 287–92, *289*, 294
Trouble-Shooters, The (*Wan zhu*, d. Mi Jiashan), 305–7, *307*, 309–10, 315
Twain, Mark, 69

underground film (*dixia dianying*), 16, 325–43
unemployment, in film, 27, 32, 287
United Front, 228, 230
United Kingdom film industry, 162
United Star Studio (Hong Kong), 325
United States: in film, 181–83; film industry, 50, 68, 75–77, 81, 99n15, 114, 122, 124, 149, 160, 162, 198, 225–26, 326–27
universities, in film, 172
University of California, San Diego, 334
University of Wisconsin, 51
Unknown Pleasures (*Ren xiaoyao*, d. Jia Zhangke), 325
urban areas, 251–70; in film, 41, 85, 239, 271, 287, 304. *See also* urban-rural differences
urban exploitation films, 307
urban-rural differences, 45, 46, 57, 81–83, 85, 134–35, 143, 146, 179, 192, 198, 240–41, 277
utopia, 283, 336

vaudeville (*gewutan*), 50
Velvet Prison, The: Artists under State Socialism (Miklos Haraszti), 302–3, 319
video parlors, 313
Vietnam, 276
violence: domestic, in film, 34, 37; in film, 289, 307–9, 314

Wajda, Andrzej, 272, 294
Wałesa, Lech, 276
Wang Chenwu, 80
Wang Danfeng, 2, 8, 103, 107, 112, 114, 116
Wang Jiadong, 3

Wang Jin, 46
Wang Jingwei, 102
Wang Lian, 207
Wang Qimin, 254, *258*
Wang Quan'an, *337*
Wang Renmei, 2
Wang Shuo, 287, 291, 306
Wang Xiaoshuai, 325–26, *341*
Wangdui, 234
War of Resistance, in film, 121–56
warlords, in film, 75, 77, 81, 164, 230–31, 306
Waste of the Best of Times, A (*Huanghua xudu*, d. Yue Feng), 113
Water Margin (*Shui hu zhuan*, novel), 222
Watson, James, 283
Wei Hui, 339
Wei Linyue, 234
Wei Wei, 9
Wen hui bao, 169, 195
Wenhua Studio, 157–88, 193, 327
Wenyi bao, 255
Western culture: appeal of, 69, 202, 336; critique of, 6, 29, 44, 54, 63–64, 66, 106, 151, 287, 293; in film, 35–36, 40, 48, 53, 61, 64, 68, 106, 130, 135, 150, 307
Wild Boar Forest (*Ye zhu lin*, d. Cui Wei, Chen Huaikai), 222–24, 227, 230
Wilde, Oscar, 75
Window on America (*Meiguo zhi chuang*, d. Huang Zuolin, Shi Hui, Ye Ming), 181–83a
Wodiczko, Krzysztof, 294
Woman Basketball Player No. 5 (*Nü lan wu hao*), 184
Woman High Diver (*Nü tiaoshui duiyuan*, d. Liu Guoquan), 249n36
Women Generals of the Yang Family (*Yang men nü jiang*, d. Cui Wei, Chen Huaikai), 220–23, 226–27
Women Side-by-Side (*Liren xing*, d. Chen Liting), 126
women: in male roles, 224; as symbolic of China in film, 82–83, 93; strong, in film, 108, 113, 147, 151, 200, 218; as victims, in film, 88
women's rights. *See* gender equality
workers. *See* labor
World, The (*Shijie*, d. Jia Zhangke), 325
Wu Guozhen, 113
Wu Renzhi, 87, 159
Wu Tianming, 282, 292, 305, 312–14
Wu Wenguang, 339
Wu Yin, 126, 185, 192
Wu Yonggang, 57, 60, 66–67, 76–77, 80–81, 124, 161, 184, 238
Wu Zhaodi, 245
Wu Ziniu, 271, 310, 314
Wu Zuguang, 2, 126
Wuer Kaixi, 97
Wuhan: in film, 134; film industry in, 123, 127

xenophobia, 60; in film, 232
Xi Xia kingdom, in film, 220
Xia Hong, 288
Xia Yan, 11–12, 45, 47, 51, 55, 58, 60, 62, 63, 68, 76–77, 79–81, 84, 126, 161–63, 190, 192, 197, 202, 204, 208, 214, 216–17, 225, 227–28, 230, 243, 245–47
Xian Film Studio, 271, 282, 292, 313
Xiao Yemu, 192
Xiao Zhiwei, 101
Xie Fei, 280
Xie Jin, 7, 8, 70, 73, 87–96, *92*, 184, 216, 236–38, 244, 246, 254, *255*, 265–68, 272, 278, 296, 320
Xie Tieli, 216, 229–30
Xie Yunqing, 27, *29*, *30*
Xin min bao, 194
Xu Changlin, *3*, 184
Xu Tao, 70
Xu Tongjun, 60
Xu Xinzhi, 63, *65*
Xu Yulan, 224

Yan Gong, 239
Yan Jiaqi, 97
Yan Jun, 103

Yan Yu, 215
Yan'an Talks, 215
Yang Hansheng, 76, 84, 201, 202–4, 208
Yang Liuqing, 177
Yang Yanjin, 70
Yanjing University, 233
Yao Wenyuan, 13
Ye Ming, 181
Ye Yuan, 197, 204
Yeh Hung-wei (Ye Hongwei), 318
Yellow Earth (*Huang tudi*, d. Chen Kaige), 95, 310, 314
Yi Lizhe, 277
Ying Ruocheng, 8
Ying Weiwei, 329
Ying Yunwei, 81, 155n1, 161
Young China (*Qingnian Zhongguo*, d. Su Yi), 155n1
Youth Generation, The (*Nianqing de yidai*, d. Zhao Ming), 239, 241–42
youth, in film, 287, 305–6
Yu Dafu, 336
Yu Huijun, 3
Yu Lan, 228
Yu Ling, 161, 163, 192
Yuan Congmen, 151n1
Yuan Muzhi, 63, 81
Yuan Shihai, 222
Yue Fei, 155n19
Yue Feng, 103, 106, *108*, *109*, 113, 115

Zhang Ailing, 159
Zhang Fa, 192
Zhang Huimin, 34, 37
Zhang Ji, 254
Zhang Junxiang, 9, 153, 163, 232–33
Zhang Kaiyuan, 202
Zhang Ruifang, 9, 246
Zhang Shankun, 102
Zhang Shichuan, 74, 106
Zhang Xian, 256–57, *257*
Zhang Yimou, 16, 271, 293, 295, 310, 315, 342
Zhang Yingjin, 101, 342
Zhang Yu, 305
Zhang Yuan, 325–26, 332
Zhao Dan, 115, 126, 129, 163, 178, 185, 192–93, 197–98, 202, 204, 207, 304
Zhao Han, 194
Zhao Ming, 239
Zhao Ziyang, 287, 290
Zhejiang province, in film, 229, 237
Zheng Boqi, 53, 76, 80, 201
Zheng Dongtian, 271
Zheng Junli, 4, 10–11, 63, 115, 118, 128–29, *141*, 161, 189–212, *194*, *200*, *205*, 226
Zheng Xiaoqiu, 87
Zheng Zhengqiu, 53, 127–28
Zhong Chenxiang, 281
Zhong Xinghuo, 240
Zhongguo yingtan, 113
Zhonglian (Zhongguo lianhe zhipian gufen gongsi), 102
Zhou Enlai, 127, 207, 280
Zhou Xiaowen, 307, *308*
Zhu Dingyuan, 177
Zhu Shilin, 75, 223

About the Author

Paul G. Pickowicz is Distinguished Professor of History and Chinese Studies at the University of California, San Diego, and inaugural holder of the UC San Diego Endowed Chair in Modern Chinese History. His books (authored, coauthored, and coedited) include *Marxist Literary Thought in China* (1981), *Unofficial China* (1989), *Chinese Village, Socialist State* (1991, winner of the Joseph R. Levenson Prize of the Association for Asian Studies), *New Chinese Cinemas* (1994), *Popular China* (2002), *Revolution, Resistance, and Reform in Village China* (2005), *From Underground to Independent* (2006), *The Chinese Cultural Revolution as History* (2006), *Dilemmas of Victory* (2007), *China on the Margins* (2010), and *Radicalism, Revolution, and Reform in Modern China* (2011). He has won three distinguished teaching awards: UC San Diego Alumni Association (1998), Chancellor's Associates (2003), and Academic Senate (2009), and he is associate producer of the documentary film *The Mao Years, 1949–1976* (1994).